PREVENTION FOR PETS.

THE
FIRST✚AID
COMPANION FOR
DOGS & CATS

Amy D. Shojai

With Advice from More Than **80** of America's **Top Veterinarians**
Advisor: Shane Bateman, D.V.M., D.V.Sc., Diplomate ACVECC

RODALE

© 2001 by Amy D. Shojai
Illustrations © by Randy Hamblin
Cover photographs © 2001 by The Stock Market

Cover designer: Joanna Williams
Interior designer: Richard Kershner
Illustrator: Randy Hamblin

Library of Congress Cataloging-in-Publication Data

Shojai, Amy, 1956–
    The first-aid companion for dogs and cats : what to do now, what to do later; over 150 everyday accidents and emergencies; essential medicine chest; at-a-glance symptom finder; how to prevent accidents; illustrated, clinically proven techniques / by Amy D. Shojai.
         p.   cm.
    Includes index.
    ISBN 1–57954–197–6 hardcover
    ISBN 1–57954–365–0 paperback
    1. Dogs—Wounds and injuries—Treatment—Handbooks, manuals, etc.   2. Cats—Wounds and injuries—Treatment—Handbooks, manuals, etc.   3. Dogs—Diseases—Treatment—Handbooks, manuals, etc.   4. Cats—Diseases—Treatment—Handbooks, manuals, etc.   5. Veterinary emergencies—Handbooks, manuals, etc.   6. First aid for animals—Handbooks, manuals, etc.   I. Title.
SF991.S55   2001
636.7'0896025—dc21   00–011856

Distributed to the book trade by St. Martin's Press

    6   8   10   9   7   hardcover

    6   8   10   9   7   5   paperback

Visit us on the Web at www.rodalebooks.com, or call us toll-free at (800) 848-4735.

WE **INSPIRE** AND **ENABLE** PEOPLE TO IMPROVE
THEIR LIVES AND THE WORLD AROUND THEM

For all the pets in our lives—

May this book help keep them safe from harm,
speed recovery from illness and injury,
and save the lives of those in peril.

And especially for Seren, my furry daredevil,
this one's for you—I pray you never need it!

Board of Advisors

C. A. Tony Buffington, D.V.M., Ph.D., professor of veterinary clinical sciences at Ohio State University College of Veterinary Medicine in Columbus

Karen L. Campbell, D.V.M., professor of veterinary dermatology and endocrinology at the University of Illinois College of Veterinary Medicine at Urbana-Champaign

Liz Palika, owner of the Dog Training with Liz obedience school in Oceanside, California; a columnist for *Dog Fancy* magazine; and author of *All Dogs Need Some Training*

Allen M. Schoen, D.V.M., affiliate faculty member in the department of clinical sciences at Colorado State University in Fort Collins; director of the Veterinary Institute for Therapeutic Alternatives in Sherman, Connecticut; and author of *Love, Miracles, and Animal Healing*

John C. Wright, Ph.D., a certified applied animal behaviorist; professor of psychology at Mercer University in Macon, Georgia; and coauthor of *The Dog Who Would Be King* and *Is Your Cat Crazy?*

Foreword

Many people, thankfully, will never have to cope with a serious pet injury or illness. For those who will, however, the lack of preparation or knowledge can be crippling. And the time you lose through fear and uncertainty can be critical to your pet's recovery. It can literally mean the difference between life and death.

I should know. As a professor specializing in emergency medicine, I see hundreds of cases pass through our veterinary emergency room every year. In many of those cases, prompt action on the owner's part could have saved a beloved pet from a long and costly hospital stay or painful emergency procedures. That is where this book comes in.

The First-Aid Companion for Dogs and Cats is a comprehensive and easy-to-follow resource to guide you to quick and decisive action when your pet needs it most. In this book, you will find simple remedies for common injuries and ailments, and you will also find advanced methods of dealing with life-threatening problems. Most important, *The First-Aid Companion for Dogs and Cats* will help you distinguish minor problems from major crises and assist you in deciding when to involve your veterinarian. The information has been thoroughly researched and contains up-to-the minute instructions. The numerous illustrations will help guide you as you follow the directions for your pet's first-aid procedures.

It was a great pleasure to be involved with this book, and I hope that it will not only help you keep your pet safe and well but also provide some peace of mind that you're now prepared for whatever you and your pet may encounter. I think that, for caring pet owners, *The First-Aid Companion for Dogs and Cats* is indispensable.

Shane Bateman, D.V.M., D.V.Sc., Diplomate ACVECC and assistant professor of emergency and critical care medicine in the department of veterinary clinical sciences at Ohio State University College of Veterinary Medicine, Columbus

Contents

PART ONE

First Steps in First Aid

PART TWO

Common Injuries and Conditions

Acknowledgments

This book would not have been possible without the help of many people—and pets—who offered their expertise, help, and inspiration along the way. Most especially my parents, Phil and Mary Monteith, who have always been my cheerleaders; my husband, Mahmoud, who supports my every dream; Seren, who is the best assistant a writer could have; and my furry muse, Fafnir, who remains always in my heart. I am blessed with my family, and can never thank them enough.

My colleagues, of the pet persuasion and otherwise, continually inspire me with their professionalism, friendship, and untiring support. I'd especially like to thank the members of the Cat Writers Association and Dog Writers Association of America—you make me proud to be a pet writer!

Heartfelt appreciation goes to the more than 80 veterinarians who offered their expertise for this book. I must also thank the countless veterinary teachers and researchers across the nation who gave freely of their time and talent to answer my endless questions over the years.

Grateful thanks to Matthew Hoffman, who shared my vision; to Ellen Phillips, who makes me look good; and especially to Meredith Bernstein, who does all the really hard stuff.

Finally, this book wouldn't be possible without all the cats and dogs who share our lives—and the caring owners dedicated to keeping their furry family members safe. Without you, this book would never have been written.

FIRST STEPS
IN FIRST AID

Your Pet's Essential Medicine Chest

It's impossible to predict what sort of emergency might happen to your pet. And when your cat or dog is injured, quick treatment is vital—you may not have time to conduct a search for the right remedy or tools. So it's best to be prepared for the most common injuries and have the necessary supplies ready to use at a moment's notice.

You can buy commercial first-aid kits from pet-supply stores and catalogs. These kits contain all the basic care items. Or you can put together your own, using the following list as a guide.

PET FIRST-AID KIT

- Information card with your veterinary emergency clinic phone number and the local or national poison-control number
- Information card indicating your pet's baseline temperature and weight
- Commercial muzzle or length of fabric to make one
- Bandaging materials
  - Sterile gauze pads and Telfa pads, various sizes
  - 1- to 2-inch rolls of stretchable and non-stretchable gauze
  - Elastic bandage (Ace bandage)
  - Plastic wrap (Saran Wrap) to seal wounds
  - Bandage tape
  - Blunt scissors for bandaging (also to trim fur away from wounds)
- Duct tape or other heavy tape (to immobilize your pet on a firm surface)
- Bubble wrap (for splinting)
- Blunt-tipped tweezers or hemostats (to remove splinters and other foreign objects)
- Electric clippers (to trim fur around wounds)
- Needle-nose pliers (to remove foreign objects)
- Large needleless syringe or eyedropper (to give liquid medicine)
- Rectal thermometer
- Clean towel or blanket (to restrain your pet, keep him warm, or use as a stretcher)
- Ready-made cold packs and hot packs, or a washcloth and a hot-water bottle to make your own
- Antiseptic liquid soap (Betadine Skin Cleanser)

(continued on page 6)

Human Medicines That Work for Pets

Some human medicines are also effective for dogs and cats, though the dosages are usually lower due to the smaller size of the animal. Here are the medications that vets recommend most often. It's always best to give your vet a quick call before giving your pet any type of human medicine, just to verify that it's safe for your pet and will work for his condition. Also, tell the vet if your pet is currently taking any other medications, in case there could be interactions.

Medication	Use
A & D Ointment	Antibacterial ointment for scrapes and wounds
Anbesol	Topical anesthetic for mouth pain
Aveeno Oatmeal Medicated Bath	For soothing itchy skin
Benadryl	Antihistamine
Betadine Skin Cleanser	Antiseptic liquid soap for cleansing on or around wounds
Betadine Solution	Antiseptic solution for flushing or soaking injured areas
Bufferin	Pain reliever
Burow's solution	Topical antiseptic
Caladryl	Soothing topical lotion for pain and itching
Cortaid	Anti-itch cream
Desitin	Soothing ointment
Dramamine	For car sickness, nausea
Dulcolax	For constipation
Epsom salts	Soothing soak for irritated, itchy skin
Hypo Tears	Eye lubricant
Iodine	Topical antiseptic
Ipecac Syrup	Emetic to promote vomiting
Kaopectate	For diarrhea
Lanacane	Topical anesthetic
Massengill Disposable Douche	Odor neutralizer for skunk spray, body odor
Metamucil (unflavored)	For constipation
Mylanta Liquid	For digestive upset, gas

For Dogs	For Cats
Apply thin coating 3–4 times a day for 7–10 days	Apply thin coating 3–4 times a day for 7–10 days
Dab on liquid with cotton swab once or twice a day for up to 2 days	Do not use more than one time
Use as bath rinse as often as 3 times a week	Use as bath rinse as often as 3 times a week
1 mg per lb every 6–8 hours	1 mg per lb every 6–8 hours
Use full strength to wash affected area	Use full strength to wash affected area
Dilute with distilled water to the color of weak tea, then apply	Dilute with distilled water to the color of weak tea, then apply
10–25 mg per 2.2 lb two or three times a day	DO NOT USE
Moisten cotton ball and apply to wound	Moisten cotton ball and apply to wound
Paint on sore area	Paint on sore area
Apply once or twice daily as needed	Apply once or twice daily as needed
Rub on affected area	Rub on affected area
2–4 mg per lb 3 times a day	¼ of 50-mg tablet (12.5 mg) once a day
5- to 20-mg tablet once a day or ½ to 2 pediatric suppositories (10 mg) once a day	5-mg tablet once a day or ½ pediatric suppository once a day
1 cup per gal of water, then soak affected area	1 cup per 2 gal of water, then soak affected area
Apply 4–12 times a day	Apply 4–12 times a day
Paint on wound	Paint on wound
1 tsp per 20 lb, up to 3 tsp	DO NOT USE
½–1 tsp per 5 lb, to a maximum of 2 Tbsp every 8 hours	½–1 tsp per 5 lb every 4–8 hours for 1 day only
Apply to sore area with gauze pad	DO NOT USE
Mix 2 oz per gal of water, use as a soak for 15 min, then bathe as usual	Mix 2 oz per gal of water, use as soak for 15 min, then bathe as usual
1 tsp per 10–25 lb, mixed in food	½ tsp (small cat) to 1 tsp (large cat), mixed in food
Dogs weighing 15 lb or less get 3 Tbsp, 16–50 lb get 4 Tbsp, and 51 lb or more get 6 Tbsp	DO NOT USE

(continued)

Human Medicines That Work for Pets (cont.)

Medication	Use
Neosporin	For preventing wound infection
Pedialyte or Gatorade	For dehydration
Pepcid AC	For vomiting
Pepto-Bismol	For diarrhea, nausea, indigestion, vomiting
Phillips' Milk of Magnesia	For constipation
Preparation H	For sore anal area
Robitussin Pediatric Cough Formula	Cough suppressant
Solarcaine	Topical pain reliever and anesthetic
Tylenol	Pain reliever
Vicks VapoRub	For congestion
Witch hazel	Astringent/topical antiseptic

■ Antiseptic solution (Betadine Solution) to soak or flush injured areas

■ Cotton balls

■ Clean washcloth

■ Lubricants (mineral oil, petroleum jelly, K-Y Jelly)

■ Sterile saline contact lens solution (to flush wounds)

■ Karo syrup or honey (for shock)

■ Antibiotic ointment (Neosporin) for wounds

■ Activated charcoal preparation (ToxiBan)

■ 3% hydrogen peroxide for poisoning

■ Syrup of Ipecac (to induce vomiting)

■ Buffered aspirin (for pain—for dogs only! Check with your vet for the correct dose if your dog has any other health problems)

■ Antihistamine (Benadryl) for itching (it's also a good sedative)

■ Anti-diarrheal (Kaopectate)

■ Styptic powder (Kwik-Stop) for minor bleeding

WHAT ABOUT HUMAN MEDICINES?

Veterinary medications designed for problem conditions in cats and dogs work very quickly. They're often flavored to go down more easily, and they're formulated in various strengths to fit the needs of tiny kittens or huge Saint Bernards. But people rarely have pet medications on hand.

Some human drugs are dangerous when given to pets. Too much Tylenol, for example, can kill

For Dogs	For Cats
Apply 3–4 times daily as needed	Apply 3–4 times daily as needed
Mix 50/50 with water, offer as much as dog wants	Mix 50/50 with water, offer as much as cat wants
5 mg per 10 lb once or twice a day	5 mg per 10 lb once or twice a day
0.5–1 ml per lb or ½–1 tsp per 5 lb, to a maximum of 30 ml or 2 Tbsp up to 3 times per day, or 1 tablet per 15 lb up to 3 times per day	DO NOT USE
2–4 tsp per 5 lb every 6 hours	½–1 tsp once a day
Apply up to 4 times daily	DO NOT USE
Ask your vet	Ask your vet
Apply to sore area once or twice a day for up to 2 days	DO NOT USE
Ask your vet	Ask your vet
Smear a small amount on your pet's chin for easier breathing	Smear a small amount on your pet's chin for easier breathing
Dab on affected area	Dab on affected area

a cat. But because many human medicines contain the same active ingredients as the pet versions, you can often relieve your dog or cat's symptoms with first aid using the right choices from your own medicine chest. It's always a good idea to get the okay from your vet first.

Most over-the-counter medications come in capsules, pills, or liquids and are labeled by the strength of the dosage. Liquids usually are dosed in milliliters (ml) or teaspoon and tablespoon measures, and they often come with a measuring cup or eyedropper. Pills are typically designated by strength in milligrams (mg) or micrograms (mcg).

Dogs and cats almost never should get the same dosage as people—they are, after all, much smaller creatures. And their bodies work differently than ours do and can't metabolize drugs in the same way. The dose for pets is usually based on their body weight, so you must know how much they weigh before medicating them. (Have your pet weighed the next time you're at the vet's office, record the results, and keep them in your pet's medicine chest.) Medicines designed for people usually contain way too much of the drug for pets, so it's vital to get out your calculator and figure out how much of that 325-milligram pill is right for your pet.

For instance, Benadryl is given to cats and dogs at a dose of 1 milligram for each pound they weigh. That means that a 50-pound dog needs 50 milligrams of the drug. If the Benadryl

Dose Division

Human medicines usually come in much larger doses than a pet needs. Liquids tend to be the easiest to scale down to a pet-size dose. Pills may be trickier when your dog or cat needs half a pill or less.

Commercial pill cutters are available from pet-supply stores or catalogs for about $5. When you don't have a pill cutter available, you can divide pills with guillotine pet nail trimmers. Just hold the pill in the opening where the toenail would rest and cut it to the size you need.

Another option is to powder the pill, then divide the crushed medicine into the appropriate dose. You can mix the powder into a tasty treat so that it goes down more smoothly. A mortar and pestle, which you may have in your kitchen anyway, is perfect. If you don't have one, you can put the pill between two pieces of foil and use a meat mallet or even the bowl of a spoon to crush it into a powder.

comes as a 100-milligram pill, you'll need to give half of that pill to your 50-pound pet.

The table on page 4 includes many common over-the-counter medications for humans and their dosage equivalents for pets. The chapter that covers your pet's specific condition may offer more detailed information on how much to give. If you are still uncertain about what and how much to give, check with the vet.

Pet-Supply Catalogs

R. C. Steele Pet Supplies
1989 Transit Way, Box 910
Brockport, NY 14420-0910
(888) 839-9420
Web site: www.rcsteele.com

Doctors Foster and Smith
2253 Air Park Road, PO Box 100
Rhinelander, WI 54501-0100
(800) 381-7179
Web site: DrsFosterSmith.com

That Pet Place Dog & Cat Pet Supplies
237 Centerville Road
Lancaster, PA 17603
(888) THAT-PET (842-8738)
Web site: www.thatpetplace.com

Pet Warehouse
PO Box 750138
Dayton, OH 45475-2138
(800) 443-1160
Web site: www.petwhse.com

New England Serum Company
PO Box 128
Topsfield, MA 01983-0228
(888) 637-3786
Web site: www.neserum.com

Omaha Vaccine Company
PO Box 7228
Omaha, NE 68107
(800) 367-4444
Web site: www.omahavaccine.com

The Dog's Outfitter
1 Maplewood Drive
Hazleton, PA 18201-9798
(800) 367-3647
Web site: www.dogsoutfitter.com

Appraising the Situation

Pet owners live with their dogs and cats 365 days a year and are in the best position—even more so than a veterinarian—to recognize what's normal and what's not. After all, if you're lucky, a veterinarian will see your dog or cat only once or twice a year. So at some point, when your pet is healthy and happy, create a baseline first-aid health chart that lists vital signs for each cat or dog in your home. These baseline readings should include:

- Temperature
- Color of skin and gums
- Capillary refill time
- Dehydration test
- Heart rate
- Pulse rate
- Respiration rate
- Responsiveness

Since each pet is an individual, a range of readings may be normal. But once you've determined what your pet's specifics are, anything outside this individual "normal" range will alert you to a problem that needs to be addressed. This will also help you assess how serious the condition might be, what first-aid steps you need to take, and if first aid is all that's needed or if treatment is best left to the veterinarian. Read on for more on how to evaluate each of these vital signs.

TEMPERATURE

Normal body temperature for cats and dogs ranges between 99° and 102.5°F. A pet who has played or

Taking your pet's temperature is a lot easier if someone else can hold her head and distract her. Lubricate the tip of a rectal thermometer. Lift the base of your pet's tail and slowly insert the thermometer into his rectum until half of it is inside. Keep it in for 3 minutes, then withdraw it and check the reading.

exercised strenuously often has a slightly elevated temperature of a degree or two, but it should return to a normal range with rest. And although a fever may not be dangerous by itself, it could point to underlying problems that need first aid. Here's how to take your pet's temperature.

■ Use a rectal thermometer. For a bulb thermometer, shake down the mercury until it reads about 96°F.

■ Lubricate the bulb tip of a rectal thermometer or the end of a digital thermometer with mineral oil, K-Y Jelly, or petroleum jelly.

■ Grasp the base of your pet's tail and lift it to access the anus. Insert the thermometer about halfway. Keep a firm grip on the tail to keep your pet from escaping or sitting down on the thermometer.

■ After 3 minutes, remove the thermometer, wipe it clean with a tissue, and read the silver column of mercury. (Follow the manufacturer's directions to read a digital thermometer.) Be sure to clean the thermometer with rubbing alcohol to avoid spreading disease.

SKIN AND GUM COLOR

Skin tone can be hard to see on a pet because of all the fur. Veterinarians use the color of the mucous membranes, like the "whites" of the eyes and the gums above the teeth, to gauge a pet's health. For gums, anything other than a normal pink color calls for immediate veterinary attention or first-aid care. If your pet's gums are pigmented (black or brown), try to find a non-pigmented pink spot on the gums or lips to as-

Taking Your Pet's Temperature

Once you take your pet's temperature, it's important for you to know when it's considered normal and when it signals an emergency situation. Check the chart below to determine when your pet's okay and when he needs immediate medical attention.

Temperature	What It Means	Call the Vet?
106°F or higher	Emergency! Cool your pet (page 238)	YES, immediately
105°F	High fever	YES, same day
104°F	Moderate fever	YES
103°F	Moderate fever	YES
102°F	Normal range	NO
101°F	Normal range	NO
100°F	Normal range	NO
99°F	Normal range	NO
99° to 95°F	Mild hypothermia (page 250)	YES, same day
Below 95°F	Emergency! Warm your pet (page 249)	YES, immediately

Mucous Membrane Color Test

Use this quick visual assessment to determine if your pet needs medical help.

Membrane Color	What It Means	Call the Vet?
Pink	Normal	NO
Pale to white	Anemia or shock (page 333)	YES, immediately
Blue	Smoke inhalation (page 347) or suffocation (page 366)	YES, immediately
Bright cherry red	Carbon monoxide poisoning (page 122) or heatstroke (page 237)	YES, immediately
Yellow	Liver problems (page 311)	YES, same day

sess her condition. If you can't find a pink spot there, you will need to find a nonpigmented spot on another mucous membrane, like the vulva or prepuce (the fold of skin covering the end of the penis).

CAPILLARY REFILL TIME

Capillaries are tiny blood vessels that lie near the surface of the skin. They're easiest to see in your pet's gums, above his teeth. The capillaries are what give this tissue its normal pink color. You can judge the condition of your pet's blood circulation by a capillary refill test. Here's what to do.

■ Lift your pet's upper lip, then press the flat of your finger against the nonpigmented, pink gum tissue. This temporarily squeezes blood in that spot out of the capillaries and blocks the normal flow.

■ Quickly remove the pressure, and you'll see a white, finger-shaped mark on the gum. Use the second hand on your watch to time how long it takes for the pink color to flood back into the white spot—that's the capillary refill time.

Capillary Refill Test

To assess the condition of your pet's circulation, consult the following chart.

Capillary Refill Time	What It Means	Call the Vet?
1–2 seconds	Normal	NO
2–4 seconds	Moderate to poor; possible dehydration (page 148) or shock (page 333)	YES
More than 4 seconds	Emergency! Severe problems; dehydration, shock	YES, immediately
Less than 1 second	Emergency! Severe problems; heatstroke (page 237), shock	YES, immediately

DEHYDRATION TEST

You can gauge a pet's degree of dehydration, or fluid loss, with a simple test. The first sign of a problem is loss of the skin's elasticity. Normally hydrated dogs and cats have extra loose skin at the tops of their heads and the bases of their necks—the scruff—that's easy to grasp. When the water balance of the body is normal, you can gently pull up the scruff, and when you release it, the skin will spring back immediately to a normal position. The skin at the top of the head is more likely to show this effect, so you might want to test there first.

The more severe the dehydration, though, the slower the skin will retract. With moderate dehydration, the skin will go back slowly. In severe cases, where the skin remains standing up in a ridge off the body even after you've released it, immediate first aid and veterinary care are required.

HEART RATE

To measure your pet's normal heart rate, have him sit or lie in a relaxed position and place the palm of your hand over his left side directly behind the point of his elbow. Feel for the heartbeat and count the pulses in 15-second bursts. Then multiply this number by 4 to get the beats-per-minute rate. To ensure an accurate reading, repeat the count two or three times and average them to find your pet's average normal rate.

With illness or injury, a slower-than-normal rate—bradycardia—can indicate heart disease or shock. A racing heart can also point to shock. Either requires prompt medical attention. And of course, a stopped heart is the most dire emergency of all and requires immediate CPR.

Check your pet's pulse rate as well to become familiar with how a normal pulse feels. It should be strong, and you should feel it at the same time as each heartbeat. An irregular pulse points to heart problems, while a "bounding" pulse or

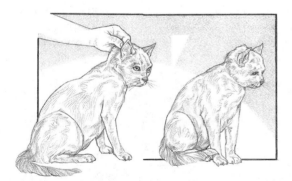

Here's how to use the scruff test to find out if your pet is dehydrated. First, grab a pinch of the skin on top of your pet's head, then release it. The longer it takes to spring back into place, the more severe the dehydration.

Your Pet's Normal Heart Rate

The chart below shows the average beats per minute based on your pet's size.

Pet	Normal heart rate (bpm)
Small dogs (up to 20 lb)	70–180
Medium and large dogs (more than 20 lb)	60–140
Cats	120–240
Puppies (up to 6 weeks)	Up to 220
Kittens (up to 6 weeks)	200–300

a very weak pulse can indicate shock, weak heart output, or a drop in blood pressure. All of these conditions require immediate medical attention.

Pets don't have very strong pulses in their "wrists" on the front legs or in the neck. The best place to find your pet's pulse is in the femoral artery, in the crease of the hind leg at the groin.

Have your pet lie on his side, then press the flat of your fingers in the area until you locate the pulse. Be aware that it may be much more difficult to find if your pet is depressed, dehydrated, or has a low blood pressure.

RESPIRATION

Most dogs breathe 10 to 30 times a minute; for cats, the rate is 10 to 40 times a minute.

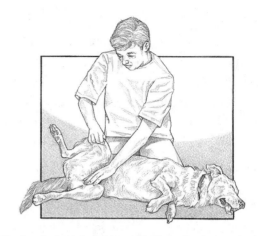

The best place to feel a pulse is in the femoral artery, located in the groin where the hind leg meets the body. Pressing gently, use your index, middle, and ring fingers to feel for the pulse. It's very strong at this point. If you can't feel it and you can't hear a heartbeat in the chest, the heart has probably stopped, and you'll need to start CPR.

Monitoring Respiration

When your pet is resting quietly, anything other than quiet, effortless breathing requires medical attention and possibly artificial respiration (see page 19). See the chart below for the warning signs.

Respiratory Signs	What They Mean	Call the Vet?
Effortless breathing, quiet to soundless	Normal	NO
Increased respiratory rate	First sign of breathing problems	YES, immediately, if condition is worsening. If respiratory rate is increased but problem is not worsening, call the vet the same day.
Excessive panting or gasping; dogs stand with elbows outward, cats sit crouched with head and neck extended	Emergency! Progression to early respiratory failure	YES, immediately
Labored, open-mouthed breathing and blue gums	Emergency! Pulmonary failure; pet is suffocating	YES, immediately
Slowed, shallow, or stopped breathing, unconsciousness imminent	Emergency! Respiratory collapse; prepare for artificial respiration	YES, immediately

Dogs who are hot or exercising breathe faster and may pant up to 200 breaths a minute. Panting and open-mouthed breathing are considered danger signs in cats because they don't use panting routinely as a means to cool off, the way dogs do. If your cat is panting or breathing with her mouth open, call the vet immediately.

RESPONSIVENESS

Healthy dogs and cats are alert and responsive to whatever is happening in their surroundings. When they are injured or ill, their behavior is affected to various degrees. The more serious the condition, the less response there will be.

TRIAGE

Besides knowing how to evaluate your pet's various vital signs and how they impact his health, you must also assess the seriousness of any problems. This is particularly important when there are multiple injuries.

This process is called triage—prioritizing injuries and body conditions in the order of their severity. Triage allows you to use first-aid to work on the most serious risks first to save your pet's life. Only then should you address any other conditions.

Before doing anything else, make sure that your surroundings are safe for both you and your pet. It won't do either of you any good if you perform first aid in the middle of a burning

Gauging Responsiveness

Normal, healthy pets are usually alert, curious, and responsive. See the chart below to determine if your pet's behavior is cause for concern.

Level of Consciousness	What It Means	Call the Vet?
Alert and responsive to owner and outside stimulation; if you call your pet for a treat, he should respond	Normal	NO
Depressed; response slow to sight or touch stimulation; may be sleepy or reluctant to move	Common to many illnesses	YES, next day, if the condition doesn't resolve with first aid
Disoriented; bumps into objects, stares blindly, walks with unsteady gait or in circles, falls over to one side	Probably neurologic or inner ear involvement	YES, same day
Stupor; can be aroused only by deep pain stimulation (i.e., pinched toes).	Neurologic or metabolic problem; serious	YES, immediately
Comatose (unable to wake) or having seizures	Emergency! Severe neurologic damage or disruption from injury, disease, or toxin	YES, immediately

Top 10 Triage Priorities

In order of urgency, treat these conditions before anything else in an emergency situation. Then take care of your pet's other problems.

1. Stopped breathing, no pulse (page 125)
2. Stopped breathing with pulse (page 126)
3. Loss of consciousness (page 396)
4. Shock: pale gums; rapid breathing; weak, rapid pulse; cold skin (page 333)
5. Difficulty breathing (page 19)
6. Chest puncture or gaping wound (page 128)
7. Severe bleeding (page 95)
8. Abdominal puncture or gaping wound (page 55)
9. Extremes of body temperature: too hot (page 237) or too cold (page 248)
10. Poisoning: stings (page 79), toxins (page 311), snakebites (page 350), etc.

building or busy highway. Once you are both in a secure place, assess your pet's vital signs to determine your next step. Is he responsive to your voice? Breathing okay? Does his gum color or capillary refill time point to shock?

As a general rule, internal or whole-body injuries like shock or poisoning take precedence over external injuries like cuts or a broken leg. Although certainly serious and painful, an eyeball out of the socket or a burn is not necessarily life-threatening and can be addressed after a pet's more serious injuries have been treated. For instance, a mouth burn from chewing an electrical cord won't matter if your pet has stopped breathing from the electric shock.

PLAYING DOCTOR

First aid is just that—a one-time emergency treatment that gets your dog or cat over the life-threatening event long enough to get the necessary medical help. When it comes to dog and cat care, the best first-aid book in the world cannot replace the expertise of a veterinarian who examines your dog or cat up close and personal. So don't try to save money or trouble by doctoring your pet at home. He deserves better from you.

Basic Techniques and How to Do Them

When we think of pet first aid, it's usually limited to emergencies, like being hit by a car or being electrocuted when a puppy chews through a light cord, for example. Luckily, most pet owners will never need to deal with such dramatic problems.

But all pet owners are faced with everyday problems like ear infections, cut paws, or upset stomachs. Time and again, you'll find first-aid techniques useful. These basic techniques apply to hundreds of dog and cat conditions, whether your pet suffers from a fractured leg, a bleeding wound, or just the sniffles or a splinter.

What's more, in really dramatic situations, they can save your pet's life.

SAFE RESTRAINTS

A humane restraint serves three major purposes. First, it protects you from being bitten or clawed by your injured pet while you're administering first aid. Second, restricting your pet's movements keeps him from making the injury worse. Finally, the restraint keeps him in one place so that the wound can be examined and treated. Here are some examples.

Muzzles

Even the most gentle and loving dog or cat will bite in reflex when he's hurt. Commercial muzzles are available from pet-supply stores and catalogs for all sizes and shapes of dog and cat faces. But when you don't have a commercial muzzle handy, you can make one.

Cats and short-nosed dogs like pugs are a challenge because there's not enough nose for you to tie shut. One of the best muzzles for these pets is a pillowcase. Fit the cloth bag over your pet's head and gently hold it around the neck. The fabric keeps the teeth engaged, and often, pets stop struggling once they can no longer see what's happening. You can pull the pillowcase down as low over your pet's body as necessary to contain his front paws and claws as well—allow just the affected body part to stick out of the pillowcase for easy access so that you can treat it. Some treatments, like a cool-water soak, can be done right through the pillowcase.

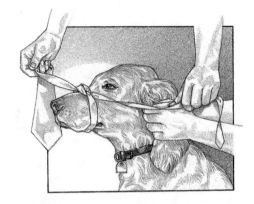

To make a muzzle, tie a loop in a necktie or a length of panty hose and slip it over your pet's nose. (Have someone help you, if possible.)

Tighten the knot, then loop the ends down under his chin and make another knot.

Draw the ends back over his neck and tie them in a knot or bow behind his ears.

Dogs with long noses are much easier to muzzle. You can use any long piece of material, from a necktie or length of gauze bandage to a leg from a pair of panty hose, or even an extra leash. Loop the material around your pet's jaw and tie it in a single knot (half hitch) on top of his nose. Then bring both ends of the tie back down under his jaw and tie another single knot. Finally, pull the ends behind the base of his neck and tie them in a bow or knot. The muzzle will hold his jaws closed so he can't bite.

Restraint Techniques

Each form of restraint works best for a specific type of injury. Choose a technique that leaves the injured area accessible for treatment. In most instances, one person restrains the pet while a second person performs first aid. In all cases, it's best to place small pets on a counter or tabletop so that they are at waist level. Medium-size to large dogs are best treated on the floor, with you kneeling beside them.

Reclining restraint: Place your pet on his side, with the injured area facing up. With one hand, grasp the ankle of the foreleg that's against the ground while gently pressing your forearm across his shoulders. With the other hand, grasp the ankle of the hind leg that's against the ground while pressing that forearm across his hips. This technique works particularly well with medium-size to large dogs and is also recommended for dog breeds with prominent eyes, like Pekingese. (Holding these types of dogs around the neck produces pressure that may pop out their eyeballs.)

Stretch restraint: With cats and small dogs, grasp your pet by the loose skin at the back of the neck—the scruff—with one hand. Capture both hind feet with the other hand. Gently stretch out your pet and hold him against a tabletop.

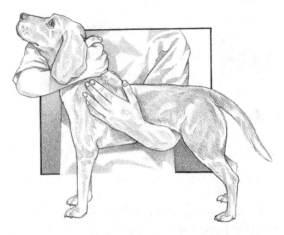

To restrain your dog for treatment, bring one arm underneath and around his neck, pulling him snug against your chest, while reaching with your other arm under and around his chest to immobilize him.

To examine or treat a small pet, put him on his side on a table. Hold the scruff of his neck with **one hand and his back feet with the other,** then stretch him out. You can wear a thick glove on the hand that holds the feet.

Hugging restraint: Bring one arm underneath and around your dog's neck in a kind of half-nelson to hug him to your chest. With the other arm, reach under and around his chest and pull him closer against you. This technique works best for dogs over 20 pounds and is most useful when trying to immobilize the abdomen, legs, chest, and back. (For women, a better alternative may be to reach *over* and around the dog's chest, as shown on page 272.)

Kneeling restraint: Pressure around the necks of dogs with prominent eyes, like Pekingese, may pop out their eyeballs. So with these breeds, instead of restraining with a neck grip or by the scruff, put your dog on the floor between

your knees and facing away from you as you kneel. Then put one hand on top of your dog's head and the other around or beneath his jaws to steady his head while another person treats the area. This form of restraint also works well for giving pills to cats.

To restrain a dog with prominent eyes, like a Pekingese or pug, hold him between your knees, facing out. Keep his head steady with one hand on top of his head and the other under his chin.

How to Make an Elizabethan Collar

Commercial cone-shaped collar restraints, called Elizabethan collars or e-collars because they surround a pet's head like the giant ruff of an Elizabethan lord, are available in a variety of sizes to fit any pet. They prevent dogs and cats from reaching injuries with their teeth, and they also protect facial sores from pawing or scratching toenails. You can get them at pet-supply stores, through catalogs, or from the veterinarian. In a pinch, you can even make one. Here's how.

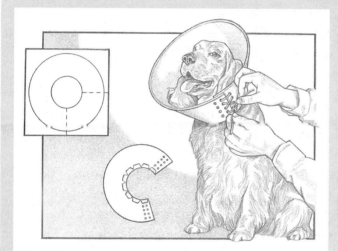

Measure your pet's neck and the distance from his collar to the tip of his nose, then mark these measurements on a piece of rigid cardboard or plastic. Make a V-shaped cut from the outer edge to the inner circle.

Use a knitting needle or awl to punch holes along both edges of the collar.

Lace a shoestring or yarn through the holes to secure the collar around your pet's neck.

ARTIFICIAL RESPIRATION AND CPR

Your pet's cardiopulmonary system works like a superefficient cargo train that circles the body and never stops. The lungs dump the cargo—oxygen—into the bloodstream, while the heart serves as the engine that moves the blood. By the time blood completes a full circuit around the body and returns to the lungs, the oxygen has been off-loaded where it's needed so that the train can take on a fresh oxygen supply and repeat the process. Anything that interrupts your pet's breathing or heartbeat stops him dead in his tracks. He'll lose consciousness, and failure to receive oxygen for even a few minutes causes irreversible brain damage.

Artificial Respiration

Pets usually go into respiratory arrest first; the heart may continue to beat for a short while even after a pet's breathing stops. You must begin artificial respiration within minutes to save your pet's life. Start rescue breathing immediately, but be prepared to continue in the car on the way to the hospital. Have somebody else drive while you work on your pet—it's not unusual for a cat or dog to be saved after an owner breathes for them for ½ hour or more.

A pet who is very cold may breathe much more slowly than normal, so be sure that he has stopped breathing. Watch for the rise and fall of his chest or feel for his breath on your palm. If he is not breathing, his gums will turn blue from lack of oxygen.

Before beginning artificial respiration, check to see if the airway is clear. Open your pet's mouth and look inside for a foreign object. If the airway is blocked, grab his tongue and pull it outward to dislodge the object, or reach in with your fingers or small pliers or tongs to grab it. If you can't reach it, use the Heimlich maneuver (see page 22). Once the airway is open, begin rescue breathing.

To give your pet artificial respiration, hold his mouth shut with one hand around his muzzle, cover his nose with your mouth, and blow gently into his nose until you see his chest rise.

- Lay a large pet on his side (you can cradle a small pet in your lap) and straighten his neck by lifting the chin so that his throat offers a straight shot into his lungs.
- Mouth-to-mouth breathing won't work because you can't seal your pet's lips with your mouth, and too much air escapes. Instead, close your pet's mouth with one or both hands to seal it.
- Put your mouth completely over his nose (with a small pet, your mouth will cover both his nose and mouth) and blow with two quick breaths, watching to see if his lungs expand. Air will go directly through the nose and into the lungs when the mouth is sealed correctly.
- Blow just hard enough to move his sides. For a very large dog, you'll need to blow pretty hard, but blow gently for cats and tiny dogs, or you could rupture their lungs. Between breaths, let the air naturally escape out of the lungs before giving the next breath. Give 15 to 20 breaths per minute until he begins breathing on his own or you reach the veterinarian.

Cardiopulmonary Resuscitation (CPR)

CPR combines artificial respiration with external heart compressions, which help move blood through the body when the heart has stopped beating. Follow the instructions for rescue breathing, and alternate with chest compressions. It's best to have two people perform CPR, with one breathing for the pet while the other does chest compressions.

To tell if your pet's heart has stopped, place your palm flat against his lower chest directly behind the left front elbow to feel for the heartbeat, or place your ear against the spot and listen. You can also feel for the pulse in the femoral artery that's located close to the surface on the inside of the thigh at the groin. Place three fingers flat against this area and press firmly, and you should feel it. Another clue: Pets with stopped hearts won't respond to anything. Pinch your pet firmly between his toes or tap his eyelid. If he doesn't blink or flinch, start CPR immediately.

To give CPR to a medium-size or large dog, first lay him on his side on a hard surface like a floor and, if you have one, place a small pillow under the lower part of his chest. Then position one hand near the highest point of the chest wall, place your other hand over the first, and use both hands to compress your dog's chest.

For Cats and Small Dogs (Less Than 20 Pounds)

- The "cardiac pump technique" calls for compressions directly over the heart to literally squeeze the heart to pump blood. Do this with all cats and with dogs weighing less than 20 pounds. To find the heart, gently flex your pet's front left foreleg backward. The center of the heart is located just where the point of the elbow crosses the chest.

- Place your pet on his side on a relatively flat, firm surface. Cup your hand over the point of the chest just behind the elbows. Squeeze firmly, pressing in about ½ inch, with your thumb on one side and your fingers on the other.

- You can also perform compressions between your fingers on kittens and puppies. Cradle your pet in the palm of your hand, with your thumb over the heart and your fingers on the other side. Squeeze rhythmically to make the heart pump.

- Veterinarians recommend 80 to 100 compressions a minute. That's a little more than one per second, which can be hard to do without training. If you can manage 60 to 100 per minute, you're doing fine.

For Medium and Large Dogs (More Than 20 Pounds)

- Dogs who weigh more than 20 pounds have such strong bones and so much space between the ribs and heart that compressions won't affect their hearts. Veterinarians recommend that instead of pumping above the heart, you use the "thoracic pump method," which places

The Heimlich Maneuver

Pets put all kinds of things in their mouths, and when something goes down the wrong way, it can block breathing. In these cases, a simple Heimlich maneuver may save your pet's life. Repeat the maneuver two or three times in succession, then check to see if the object has come loose in your pet's mouth. If it hasn't, you can continue the maneuver in the car while someone drives you to the veterinarian.

For a cat or small dog, hold his back against your stomach with his head up and his feet hanging down. Put your fist just underneath the rib cage—you can feel the soft, hollow place easily—and push inward toward your belly and upward toward your chin at the same time. Use a strong thrusting action to help dislodge the object.

If your large dog is choking, lay him on his side on the floor and kneel behind him so that his head points to your left and your knees are touching his back. Lean over him, fit your right fist just below his rib cage, and press sharply upward and inward toward his head.

compressions at the highest part of the chest. That changes the pressure most significantly within the chest cavity, and the increasing and decreasing pressure moves blood forward. Place one hand on top of the other against the chest and push down 25 to 50%.

■ For a barrel-chested dog like a bulldog, lay the dog on his back, cross his paws over his breastbone, and kneel with his abdomen between your legs. Hold his paws and perform chest compressions by pushing downward directly over the breastbone. If your dog moves a lot

Acupuncture Resuscitation

Chinese medicine has successfully used acupuncture on people and animals for more than 2,000 years. Veterinarians agree that a single acupuncture point could revive your pet because stimulating this point releases natural adrenaline (epinephrine), a drug used in cardiac arrests to stimulate the heart and breathing.

Acupuncture shouldn't replace CPR, but a series of sharp jabs to this point with a clean needle, pin, or even your sharp fingernail could revive your pet if CPR fails.

If your pet is unconscious and his heart has stopped, stick a needle or safety pin into the center of the slit in his upper lip. Insert the needle down to the bone and wiggle it back and forth.

while you are compressing his chest, put him on his side, then proceed as described above.

Alternate between compressions and breaths, giving one breath for every five compressions for any size pet. Continue CPR until your pet revives or you reach the animal hospital.

HOW TO CLEAN WOUNDS

Anytime the skin is broken, bacteria or other foreign matter—even the fur—can contaminate a wound and potentially cause infection. Bleeding is a natural cleansing mechanism that helps flush out dangerous material. Don't clean wounds that bleed excessively, as this will just make them bleed more. But for wounds that aren't bleeding, nothing beats first-aid cleansing to protect your pet from further harm.

If long fur is in the way, trim it with blunt scissors or electric clippers to keep it from sticking to the injury. If you're using scissors, first slip your index and second fingers through the fur and hold them against the wound. Cut the fur level with your fingers, leaving a 1-inch border around the wound. (This technique is illustrated on page 114.) If the skin is broken, dab on a water-soluble lubricant like K-Y Jelly; the trimmed fur will stick to the jelly and wash out easily.

Most of the time, the injury will be sore, and even the most gentle touch can cause pain. The best way to cleanse a wound is to flush it with cool water or sterile saline contact lens solution to float out debris. You can use the spray attachment from the sink, a garden hose, or even a squeeze bottle of saline solution (be sure to use saline solution only; other contact lens solutions can burn).

Follow the cleansing with a nonstinging antiseptic solution like Betadine Solution to disinfect the wound. Dilute it with distilled water until it's the color of weak tea, then put it in a plant sprayer and spray the area thoroughly. Once the wound has been disinfected, gently dab it dry with gauze pads or a clean, lint-free cloth.

BANDAGING TECHNIQUES

Many injuries heal best when they're allowed contact with the open air. But others benefit from bandages, particularly temporary bandages, as a part of first-aid treatment. Bandages serve a number of purposes. They:

■ Keep wounds dry
■ Absorb wound seepage to promote healing
■ Control bleeding with mild pressure
■ Keep a pet from licking or chewing an injury
■ Shield the wound from contamination

A bandage must be changed every day or two and kept clean and dry between changes. Swelling above or below the bandage means that it's too tight. If your pet suddenly starts licking and chewing the bandage or there's a bad smell, remove the bandage immediately to be sure that there's not an infection or another problem brewing. For first aid, a bandage is often applied on a temporary basis to provide protection until veterinary treatment is available.

Parts of a Bandage

A good homemade bandage contains three parts: an absorbent pad, gauze, and tape.

Absorbent pad: Sterile nonstick pads like Telfa pads work best, but any absorbent material that's clean and lint-free works for first aid. Paper towels and other paper products tend to stick to wounds and can be hard to remove later. If they're all that's available, apply a bit of K-Y Jelly to the injury first. It's water-soluble and easy to wash away later.

Gauze: Roll gauze wrapped over the pad holds it in place. Don't wrap too tightly, because injuries often swell, which can cut off blood circulation. If you can't easily slip one or two fingers under the bandage, it is too tight. Try to overlap the gauze by about a third of its width each time around. If you don't have roll gauze, you can use other elastic-type material to temporarily hold the pad in place. The leg from a pair of panty hose works well.

Tape: Elastic adhesive bandage like Elastoplast works best to secure the pad and gauze in place, but any adhesive tape is okay if that's all you have available. Be sure that the tape covers a portion of the fur on both sides of the bandage so that it will stay in place and your pet can't work it loose or remove it. If you don't have any tape, plastic wrap like Saran Wrap can work to temporarily hold the bandage on, and because it sticks to itself and not fur, your pet may tolerate it more readily. Be sure that you don't wrap the tape too tightly—check to see that you can slip at least two fingers between the bandage and the skin.

Special Techniques

There is a wide range of bandaging techniques designed for the various parts of a pet's body.

Paws and paw pads: After the injury has been cleaned, disinfected, and dried, place your pet's wounded paw on top of a gauze pad. Put a doubled length of roll gauze on the paw, from the front of the foot up over the toes and under the paw. Then use a single-ply wrapping of roll gauze around the paw, starting at the toes and moving up until it covers the folded gauze below. Overlap each layer slightly and use even pressure. Paw pads sweat, so to keep the bandage dry, let the gauze breathe by applying tape only at the top edge. Finish by slipping on a cotton athletic sock to protect the bandage (cut it to fit if necessary) and tape it at the top edge to your pet's fur.

Legs: Bandage the same way as a paw: Apply an absorbent pad to the wound and secure it by wrapping gauze around the leg. Tape the gauze to the fur on both sides of the wound. Slip a sock over the whole works and secure it with tape. The sock will help protect the bandage so that your pet can't pull it off with his teeth and will allow the rest of the limb to breathe.

Tail: When a specific area of the tail is injured, apply a pad and secure it with gauze. Then slip a cotton tube sock over the end of the tail so that it covers the pad and up to two-thirds of the length of the tail. Next, wrap tape over the sock, beginning at the tip of the tail and working toward the body in a diagonal pattern. Be sure to run the tape 2 inches beyond the cuff of the sock and directly onto the fur.

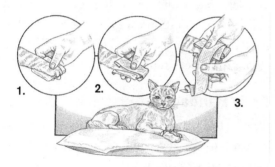

1. For a paw injury, first put a clean gauze pad over the wound.
2. Using roll gauze folded in half, extend a strip from the front of the foot over the paw and under the toes.
3. Wrap a single strip of gauze around the paw, starting at the toes and moving upward until it covers the gauze underneath.

The bandage needs to breathe, so secure only the top, using a strip of tape. After that, put a clean white sock over the foot and tape it at the top. The wrapping should be firm but not too tight. You've done it right if you can slip a pencil between the foot and the wrapping without having to work too hard.

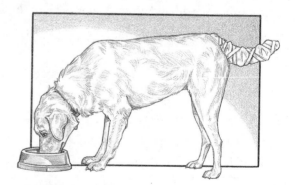

To protect your dog's injured tail, use a mummy-wrap technique. First, put a cotton tube sock over his tail. Wrap tape around the sock in a criss-cross pattern, beginning at the tip and working back toward his body. Continue to wrap 2 inches past the end of the sock to secure it, then work back toward the tip of the tail, being careful not to wrap too tightly.

Then run the tape back down from the body to the tail tip, again in a diagonal pattern. This creates a kind of Chinese finger puzzle that's difficult for a pet to pull off.

Ears: When one or both ears are injured, it's best to bandage the whole head to contain the injury. Fold the ears over the top of your pet's head, with a gauze pad or adhesive bandage covering the injured portion, and secure the ends together with tape. The ears should form a cap on top of your pet's head. Wrap roll gauze over the ears, around the head, and beneath the throat to hold the ears in place. If you don't have gauze, you can slip a tube of flexible material, such as a sleeve from a cotton T-shirt or a sock with the toe cut off, over your pet's head to hold the ears in place. Tape the gauze or fabric on both ends to your pet's fur to hold it in place.

Neck: Apply an absorbent pad to the cleaned wound and hold it in place by wrapping roll gauze over the pad and around your pet's neck

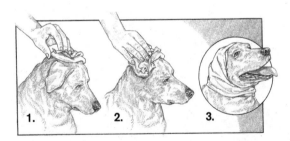

1. To bandage an injured ear, first apply a gauze pad to the wound, then fold the earflap on top of your dog's head.
2. Fold the other earflap over the first so that both ears form a "cap" on top of your dog's head.
3. Hold the ears in place by wrapping gauze or soft fabric around your dog's head and neck, then taping it in place.

in a loose pattern. Secure the bandage with tape, making sure that your pet's breathing is not restricted.

Chest and shoulders: Position an absorbent pad on top of the wound. Hold it in place by wrapping gauze in a figure-eight pattern over the top of the pad and alternating around the chest, behind and then in front of the forelegs. Use tape to secure the bandage.

Hips and flanks: Position an absorbent pad over the wound. Hold it in place by wrapping roll gauze in a figure-eight pattern over the top of the pad, alternating around the abdomen in front of and between or behind the rear legs. Secure with tape, following the same pattern and catching fur around the body. You can also use clean men's underwear to protect a wound in this area. Slip it on over the rear legs so that the tail sticks out the fly, and tape the waistband around your pet's tummy.

Body Bandages

Injuries to a pet's sides, back, or stomach can be difficult to bandage. There are a couple of techniques that are effective.

■ The easiest technique is to slip a clean cotton T-shirt onto your pet by putting his front legs through the armholes and his head through the neck. Tape the waist around his middle.

■ Make a many-tailed bandage using a rectangular length of material. Cut several slits in opposite sides of the rectangle to make "tails" in the fabric. Tie these over your pet's back or beneath the abdomen so that the fabric covers the affected area.

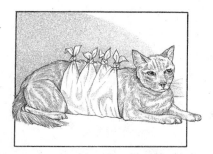

You can make a body bandage from a rectangle of material like T-shirt fabric or an old sheet or pillowcase. Cut slits in each side of the rectangle to make straps that you can tie over your pet's back.

■ Body bandages tend to slip one way or another as a pet walks. A more effective bandage is a body wrap, which works well to keep pets from chewing and scratching anywhere on the trunk. To make one, stand your pet on a towel or old sheet, mark the positions of his feet, remove him from the sheet, and cut holes for his legs at those points. Slide your pet's legs through the holes as you bring up the edges of the fabric to cover the trunk of his body and secure the fabric along the back

A homemade body wrap can protect an injury and keep your pet from chewing or scratching it. Stand him on a towel or sheet and mark the positions of his feet, then remove him and cut out the holes you marked. Put him back on the cloth, pull it up over his legs, and secure it at the top with safety pins.

For an injured leg or paw, put your pet in the body wrap, then cover the limb with a sock. Attach the sock to the body wrap with safety pins so that he can't pull it off.

with safety pins. This body wrap can also be used with cotton socks to protect your pet's feet or legs. Secure the socks to the body wrap with safety pins so that your pet can't remove them.

MAKING A SPLINT

If you suspect a leg fracture, you can use a splint to pad and protect the leg and keep it from moving. To do that, the joints both above and below the break must be immobilized. Therefore, only breaks of the lower leg can be easily splinted.

The splint should cover the entire leg and can be made of any rigid material: cardboard, rolled newspaper, or even a folded towel. One of the best splint materials is bubble wrap. It pads the leg and protects it at the same time. A splint does not correct the fracture; it just holds it as is to prevent further damage until help is available.

Handling Pain

Signs of pain in dogs and cats can be pretty subtle. To catch them, you must be alert to changes in their behavior. Dogs tend to be more vocal and may yelp, hold up a hurt paw, or limp. Cats more often simply hide and refuse to move. Other signs include panting, drooling, refusing to eat, "hunching" or tucking up a painful tummy, bowing a painful neck, flinching when touched, or squinting if an eye is painful or watery.

If you suspect spine problems or fractures, don't use any pain medicine for first aid. Also, since the most common pain relievers for dogs, like buffered aspirin, can make bleeding worse, they can be dangerous to give as first aid when you aren't sure about the extent of the problem. (You should never give aspirin to cats.) Veterinarians have much more effective and safer pain medicines that they can give to pets once a diagnosis has been made. But there are some effective and safe pain treatments that you can use as first aid. Here are the best.

- Cortaid contains steroids that reduce painful inflammation. It works well on minor cuts and scrapes or insect stings.
- Products containing benzocaine, like Lanacane and Solarcaine, contain topical anesthetics that numb the pain of sunburn and mouth sores. Benzocaine should not be used on cats.
- Hot compresses work wonders on sore, stiff joints caused by arthritis.
- Ice numbs the pain of nearly any skin injury, bruise, or burn within minutes.

For more on medications, see "Human Medicines That Work for Pets" on page 4.

To make one, gently place your pet's leg on the padded material, wrap the material around the leg, and tape it in place. Start from the foot and tape upward toward the body. Then take your pet to the vet.

SAFE TRANSPORT

Moving an injured pet must be done with care to avoid making the problem worse or causing more pain. With minor injuries, a dog may be able to walk to the car by himself, so let him. As a general rule, injured pets should not rest in your arms. That can cause them more stress from your emotional upset, and it can also cause breathing problems. It's also very difficult for you not to jostle your pet just by shifting in your seat or breathing. For more serious injuries, you must take specific precautions to:

- Support your pet's back
- Keep broken legs supported
- For a chest injury, lay your pet with his injured lung down on the seat or transport board and his uninjured or less injured lung up to aid breathing

■ Allow your pet to find his own most comfortable position for resting and breathing

Types of Conveyance

There are several ways you can transport your pet to the car and to the vet. Here are the best options.

Pet carrier: Small dogs and cats do best when they can be comfortably confined in a carrier or box. This allows you to move them when needed without jostling an injured leg or other body part, which can happen simply by shifting your weight if your pet is on your lap.

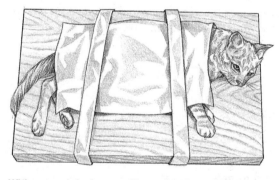

With some injuries, you'll need to immobilize your pet before transporting her to the vet. Carefully and without jostling her, gently slide your cat or dog onto a board or other rigid object, cover her with a towel or blanket, and use strong tape to secure the fabric to the board and immobilize her.

Rigid surface: A rigid surface is particularly important for suspected back injuries. Set a board on the ground next to your injured pet and slide her back-first onto the surface with one hand beneath her shoulders and one beneath her hips. You can move a cat or small dog on a cutting board, a large book, a cookie sheet,

or a trash-can lid, while a large dog may be carried on an ironing board or sheet of plywood. Be sure that the rigid surface will fit easily in your car's backseat. Cover your pet with a towel or blanket, then tape or tie her onto the board so that she doesn't slip off. You can use duct tape (or any other tape that's handy) and run it over her body just behind her front legs and in front of her hind legs over top of the cloth to strap her down. Or tie her down with panty hose. With a big dog, you'll need two people, one at each end of the board, to carry her to the car.

"Stretcher": When you don't have a board or other rigid surface that's big enough, you can put your dog on a blanket or towel and have two people lift it, one at each end, like a stretcher.

PRINCIPLES OF FOLLOW-UP CARE

First aid offers only the "first" care necessary to see that an injury is treated. In order for your pet to heal correctly and recover fully, follow-up care is sometimes necessary for a day or two, or even for weeks. This often is simply a continuation of the care that you began as first aid. It includes:

■ Monitoring the wound
■ Cleaning the injury
■ Changing bandages
■ Giving prescribed medicines—oral, topical, or injectable

Giving Liquid Medications

Liquid medicine is the easiest to give to unwilling pets. Often, a needleless syringe will accompany

To give your pet liquid medicine, tilt her head up, then insert a needleless syringe or eyedropper into the corner of her mouth and squirt the medicine into her cheek. Stroke her throat until she swallows.

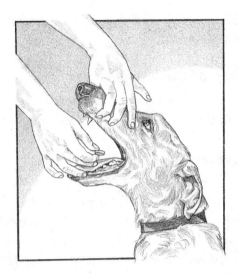

To give your pet a pill, press his lips against the sides of his teeth. Once he opens his mouth, place the pill on the back of his tongue, close his mouth, and stroke his throat until he swallows.

the liquid. Draw up the designated amount, then insert the tip into the corner of your pet's mouth and slowly squirt the medicine into his cheek. Keep his head tipped up so that gravity prompts the medicine to flow in the right direction. Stroke his throat until you see him swallow. You may need to give just a few drops at a time to be sure that he gets it all. If you don't have a needleless syringe, you can use an eyedropper.

Pilling

Dogs often take pills willingly when they're hidden in a tasty treat like peanut butter or cheese. But some dogs and most cats will swallow the treat and spit out the pill. You must make sure that your pet actually swallows the medicine for it to do any good.

To give a dog a pill, circle the top of his snout with your hand, pressing both sides of the jaw along the gum line just behind the large, pointed canine teeth. This action will prompt your dog to open wide. When he does, push the pill over the hill of his tongue with your other hand. Then close his mouth and gently stroke his throat until he swallows. Follow the pill with a treat to chase it down so that he's distracted and forgets to spit it out.

The same technique works with many cats, but if it doesn't, grasp the loose fur at the scruff of your cat's neck and pull his head back until his nose points at the ceiling. His mouth will automatically drop open—just pull down the jaw with one finger and drop the pill into his mouth at the back of the tongue. (It helps to put some butter or margarine on the pill to help it slide down.) Aim for the V-shape in the center of the cat's tongue. Then close his mouth and watch for him to swallow. Cats usually lick their

Pill Syringe

If you're afraid that you'll lose a finger trying to pill your pet, you can invest in a pill syringe, also called a pill gun or pill dispenser. It's a hollow plastic dispenser available at pet-supply stores, and it's easy to use to get a pill into your pet's mouth.

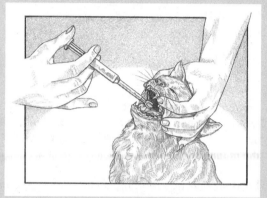

To use a pill syringe, place your cat on a table or countertop and put one hand on top of his head, circling his muzzle with your fingers. Press his lips back against the teeth behind the canine teeth to make him open wide. With the other hand, lay the pill-laden syringe on his tongue so that the exit end points at the back of his throat but doesn't quite touch it. Push the plunger to release the pill, then withdraw the syringe.

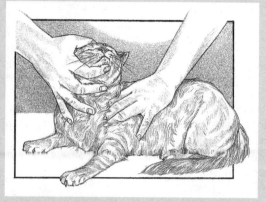

After administering the pill, hold your pet's mouth closed and stroke his throat (or gently blow on his nose) to prompt him to swallow.

noses after swallowing a pill. You can also crush the pill with the bowl of a spoon, mix it into a bit of strong-smelling cat food, and feed it to your cat.

Medicating Your Pet's Ears

Pets' ear canals are long and curved, so it takes a special technique to get medicine where it needs to go. Usually, ear medication is a liquid or ointment. To apply it, tip your pet's head so that the opening of the affected ear points upward. Put several drops of the medicine in the ear canal, then firmly grasp your pet's earflap so that he doesn't immediately shake his head and spew the medicine all over you. Use the other hand to massage the base of the ear. You should

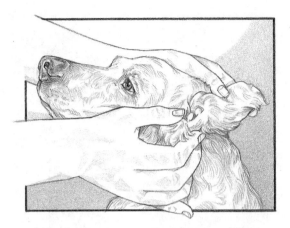

To treat ear problems, tilt your pet's head and drip or squeeze the medication into the ear canal. Then massage the base of the ear to work the medication in. Holding the earflap with the other hand will keep him still.

hear a squishing sound as the medicine spreads through the inner canal.

Medicating Your Pet's Eyes

Eye medication is usually a liquid or ointment, and you apply both the same way. Tip your pet's

To administer eye medication, pull down your pet's lower eyelid and squeeze a small amount of medicine into the cupped tissue. When your pet blinks, the medication will flow over the surface of his eye.

head so that he's looking at the ceiling. Gently pull down the lower eyelid on the affected eye and drip or squirt several drops of the medicine into the cupped tissue. Then release the eyelid and let your pet blink several times. This will naturally spread the medicine over the eye surface wherever it's needed.

Preventing Problems

Many of the accidents and emergencies that vets see most often could be easily prevented. First-aid can be a lifesaver when something unforeseen crops up, but the most important thing you can do for your beloved furry companion is to try to prevent injuries and illnesses to begin with. It's really just a matter of common sense. Here are some simple things you can do to keep your pet safe and sound.

SAFETY IN THE GREAT OUTDOORS

Don't Let Your Pet Run Free

Letting pets run loose in the neighborhood is not only unsafe; in many areas, it's also illegal. When you allow dogs or cats to roam around unsupervised, you put them at risk of being hit by a car, attacked by a rabid animal, mauled by another dog or cat, poisoned, stolen, shot, beaten, or lost. Doesn't your pet deserve more from you than that? Keep your pet safe: Keep him inside. There's no reason to ever let pets out unsupervised. Most cats are happy to stay in-doors all the time, and they're much safer that way. Your dog will be perfectly happy if you take him out with you—safely leashed, of course. And yes, cats can also be leash-trained.

Get a Good Fence

If you feel that you must let your pet out for un-supervised time outdoors, build a strong fence. It should be tall enough to keep your dog from climbing out (that can be 6 feet tall for a little, but adventurous, cocker spaniel) and to keep other animals from climbing in. Ideally, it should extend below ground level to keep your dog from burrowing out and other dogs from digging their way in. And it should be strong enough so that your dog can't just knock it down. Of course, cats are expert fence and tree climbers, but they can be foiled by using Cat Fence-In, a system of custom netting that attaches to existing wood, masonry, wire, or chain-link fences or around trees to keep cats safely confined to the backyard. To order, write to Cat Fence-In at PO Box 795, Dept. E, Sparks, NV 89432, call them at (888) 738-9099, or check their Web site at www.catfencein.com.

What about electric fences? They are designed to keep a boundary-trained pet confined to your yard, but they have no effect on anything that's not wearing a shock collar. They do nothing to keep other animals out, including squirrels, rabbits, cats, and other dogs. And if your pet is tempted or frightened beyond caution, he may ignore the shock and escape to chase or flee a furry invader. Finally, shock collars used incorrectly may actually cause a panic attack or even burn your pet.

Even if your fence is foolproof, remember that your pet can still get heatstroke if he can't escape to some shade on a hot day, or get hypothermia and frostbite if he's left out too long in the cold. He can dehydrate if he knocks over his water dish and has nothing to drink. A cat can fall and fracture bones while climbing trees, and a dog can engage in digging and other destructive behaviors if he's bored and doesn't have enough stimulation—like quality time with his human family.

Chains Aren't Humane

A dog tethered out in the yard is an emergency waiting to happen. He can wind himself around a tree and be unable to unwind himself, or become tangled up in something like shrubbery and choke. He can be attacked by other animals or by people. He can choke while straining to get to animals, cars, bicycles, or people. He can get heatstroke, frostbite, hypothermia, viruses, and allergies from being left out and exposed to the elements. He can pick up ticks, fleas, and worms. He may not be able to get away from his own excrement and could suffer from fly bites

> # Outdoor Basics
>
> To keep your pet as safe, healthy, and happy as possible if you leave him out for part of the day, make sure that he has everything on this list.
>
> - A completely and safely fenced enclosure
> - Plenty of room to run and play
> - A shady place to lie down
> - Shelter from the elements—a sturdy doghouse, "igloo," or similar structure
> - Several deep, sturdy water bowls that are diligently filled
> - Safe, durable toys and play structures like a large section of sewer pipe to run through and a tire suspended on a rope; for cats, something to climb works well
> - Flea, tick, and heartworm protection
> - A clean enclosure—pick up after him daily

or maggots. If he can't reach his water or knocks it over, or if it freezes, he can suffer from dehydration. He's bound to be bored and frustrated with such limited freedom, which again is a recipe for destructive behavior or even obsessive chewing and self-injury.

Get Your Pet Some ID

Even if you keep your pet indoors, he may accidentally become lost. A repairman may leave the door open, or your pet may jump out of the car before you can get a firm hold on his leash.

Don't Poison Your Pet

When pets, especially dogs, see something that looks like food, they eat it. This can lead to poisoning if what they see is rat bait or maybe a dead rat that died from poisoning. If you use poisoned bait, keep it and any victims out of the reach of your pets. It is a good idea to keep the number of a local or national poison-control center handy at all times. (For more information on poisoning, see page 311.) Other potential poisons include:

Antifreeze: Pets love the sweet taste of antifreeze, which is extremely toxic and often fatal. Don't leave antifreeze where your pet can get into it. And if your car leaks antifreeze, keep your pet out of the garage.

Chocolate and other stimulants: Chocolate contains a strong stimulant, theobromine, which can poison pets. A large dog may have to eat half a box to be poisoned, but a single piece can poison a cat. Keep all stimulants—candy, alcohol, tea, coffee, and soda—out of your pet's reach.

Household cleaners: Bleach, detergent, floor wax, and toilet-bowl cleaners can all be harmful to your unsuspecting pet. Again, try to use environmentally friendly alternatives, and always keep the toilet lid down.

Insecticides: Spraying chemical insecticides around your pet can make him sick. If you need to have your house "bombed" or treated for termites, roaches, ants, or fleas, board your pet for a week afterward, until the worst of the toxic fumes can air out. (This is a great time for you to go on vacation, too!) If you're spraying chemicals yourself, don't use them near your pet's eating area, and put his bowls away until you've finished spraying. For your health as well as your pet's, consider using a less toxic pest control.

Lawn and garden chemicals: If you use toxic controls such as herbicides, pesticides, fungicides, and similar products on your property, keep your pet away from them. Many are extremely toxic to pets. Keep your pet off the lawn for a week after it's been sprayed. Remember, there are safe, effective organic lawn and garden products. For your pet's sake, use them.

Medications: Keep all medicines—human and animal—out of your pet's reach. And don't give your pet a higher dose of any medication than your vet recommends. More is *not* better, and it could be fatal.

Plants: Some houseplants, especially tropicals like dieffenbachia (dumb cane) and dracaena, are poisonous. Check the plant list on page 316, and if you have any of the suspect plants, give them to a petless friend.

Tobacco: Nicotine is one of the most powerful natural poisons. If you smoke, keep your cigarette and cigar butts, pipe tobacco, and so on out of your pet's reach.

And the longer a pet stays lost, the more chance he'll be injured and need first-aid, so you want him returned as soon as possible.

To be safe, make sure that your pet has identification. Put a tag on his collar with your name and phone number and "Reward" on it—this apparently works much better than putting his name and your number on the tag. To have the best chance of getting your pet back, you can have your vet either tattoo him with an ID number on the ear or inner thigh or implant an ID chip just under the skin of his shoulder.

Neuter Your Pet

Reproductive disorders, unwanted litters, and a lot of undesirable behavior (like fighting, roaming, and caterwauling) can be prevented if you get your pet neutered or spayed. You'll reduce the risk for bite wounds, abscesses, or being hit by a car and virtually eliminate the chance of mastitis, birthing problems, uterine prolapse, and certain breast and uterine cancers.

Besides preventing medical emergencies, neutering is the responsible thing to do. Tens of millions of unwanted pets are euthanized every year, and they fill animal shelters to overflowing as they await their unhappy ends. Unless you are a professional breeder of purebred dogs or cats, neuter your pets. They'll lead longer, happier lives, and you'll be part of the pet overpopulation solution, not part of the problem.

Don't Leave Your Pet in the Car

You've heard it before, but it's worth repeating: Do *not* leave your pet in a closed car. With all that glass creating a hothouse effect, tempera-tures inside cars can climb higher and faster than you can possibly imagine, literally baking your poor pet. This is true even on a cold, sunny day. And cracking the window won't help, because leaving it open invites theft—of your car as well as your pet—and it offers a tempting escape hatch for that curious pup or kitty. Take your pet inside with you or leave him at home. And don't be tempted to tie him at the curb while you're inside shopping; he may not be there when you come out.

The backs of pickup trucks are not safe for children or for your pet, and in some areas, it's against the law to transport pets in the open beds of trucks. A bump in the road can toss your dog into oncoming traffic. Tethered pets may try to leap out and hang themselves or get dragged and suffer friction burns or other injuries. A pet carrier is the safest option for transporting pets, either inside the car (on the backseat so that an airbag won't crush the carrier) or in the truck bed. In either case, the carrier should be securely tied with a seatbelt or cross tie.

PET-PROOFING YOUR HOME

Machinery and Pets Don't Mix

Keep your pet away from machinery when it's in operation—that includes sewing machines and woodworking equipment as well as lawn-mowers and chainsaws. Your pet wants to be near you, and he may not realize the danger until it's too late. Keep your pet indoors when you're working on the lawn, and shut the door of the sewing room or woodshop. Be particularly alert for cats who like to sleep on (or inside) warm car engines during cold weather. Always honk the horn or bang on the hood of the car before you start the engine.

Office equipment can be dangerous, too. A prizewinning dog once shredded his tongue in a paper shredder that had been left on automatic. Even scissors, a stapler, and a letter opener can become hazards to an unsupervised pet. If your pet has access to your home office, keep sharp objects safely out of his reach. And turn off your equipment when you're not there and using it.

Kitchen and Laundry-Room Alert

We've all heard horror stories about pets who ended up in the stove, microwave, or refrigerator. A curious cat could get a paw caught in the garbage disposal, too. When you're using an appliance, make sure that your pet isn't in it before you turn it on or shut the door. Small pets may creep inside the dishwasher to lick leftovers. And don't leave the kitchen while you're cooking. Gas burners can be especially hazardous to cat tails, and electric stove tops are notorious for burning tender cat paws.

Cats also love the warmth of the clothes dryer and can sneak in when your back is turned. For your cat's sake, keep the dryer door closed when you're not using it, and check both it and the washer for signs of occupation before turning them on.

Make Sure That Your Pet's Collar Fits

This may seem obvious, but pets' bodies change over time just as ours do. A growing puppy may outgrow three collars before he reaches full size. Even an adult dog may put on weight that makes his collar too tight. Check your pet's collar for fit every week or so when he's still growing to keep the collar from choking him or even cutting into his flesh. And check your older pet's collar every month or so, too. If you can easily slip two fingers under it, it's loose enough.

Feed Your Pet Right

Your pet will be healthier and avoid a host of digestive disorders like vomiting and diarrhea or even food allergies if you feed him the best pet food you can afford, and not too much of it. Don't skimp on quality and buy cheap food packed with chemical fillers. It's like feeding your pet a diet of potato chips and expecting him to thrive. Instead, feed a high-quality pet food. You'll find that he needs less to feel full since he's getting more nutrition and fewer fillers.

For your pet's sake, ration his treats. However pleased he is to get them, a fat pet is not a happy pet. He feels bad, looks bad, and doesn't enjoy life nearly as much as his trimmer cousins. You can prevent stress to joints that causes hip and shoulder pain by keeping your pet slim and trim.

There are healthy treats that you can substitute for those dog "cookies"—crunchy carrots, snap peas, grapes, apples, and other fruits and veggies are good for your dog, and you'll be surprised how much he'll enjoy them. They may even reduce the chance of tooth problems. Cats often relish melon and canned pumpkin, which can help eliminate hairballs and intestinal blockages.

Resist the temptation to substitute food for play and affection. Your pet's best treat is time spent with you—and it's calorie-free! Best of all, regular exercise slows the signs of arthritis and can prevent painful joints.

"People food" that's loaded with fat and sugar isn't any better for your pet than it is for you. You may not be able to resist pizza, doughnuts, fries, and barbecue, but don't feed them to your pets. Cats and dogs don't get clogged arteries, but these foods can still rot their teeth and put on unnecessary pounds just as they do for their owners.

Keep Pets Away from Cords

Sharp teeth and electrical wires do not mix. Don't leave puppies, kittens, or adult pets who like to chew cords unsupervised in rooms where cords are accessible. If you must leave your pet, unplug all cords before you go out. There are cord covers available in both metal and plastic, and you can also slip cords into lengths of PVC pipe. It's not pretty, but neither is an electrocuted pet.

Pet-Proof Toys

Cats and dogs, especially youngsters, love to mouth objects, and nearly anything that doesn't move faster than they do is fair game. Anything that goes into a pet's mouth can potentially be swallowed and end up blocking the intestines, getting caught in the throat or mouth, or entrapping the jaws.

Supervise your pet's playtime to be sure that your cat doesn't swallow that feather toy and your dog doesn't break a tooth chewing your shoes, swallow a piece of a chewed-up toy or one that's too small to be safe for him, or poison himself by swallowing the change from your pockets. Also be sure to supervise him whenever he's chewing on bones, pig's ears, or small pieces of rawhide. And don't leave string, yarn, fishing line, or any stringlike object lying around where your pet could swallow it and ball up his intestines, requiring emergency surgery.

MODERATION IN ALL THINGS

For pets as for people, moderation is the key to a long, healthy, happy life. A moderate amount of high-quality food and moderate but regular exercise and playtime will go a long way to keep this book on the shelf and not in your hands. The only things your pet needs in immoderate doses are sleep and your loving attention!

The First-Aid Symptom Finder

Often, you may not know what's wrong with your pet. Turn to this First-Aid Symptom Finder as a first step. Look up your pet's symptoms (for diarrhea, for example, check under "Digestion and Elimina-

tion" on page 41), and you'll find at a glance the conditions that may be causing the trouble. Once you've identified the problem, just flip to the page that discusses it, and you'll see what to do to get your pet out of trouble fast.

APPETITE AND EATING

Symptom	Chapter and Page
APPETITE LOSS	Anal Gland Impaction (page 65), Birthing Problems (page 83), Foreign Object in Mouth (page 199), Foreign Object Swallowed (page 204), Frostbite (page 219), Incontinence (page 257), Jaw Swelling (page 266), Mastitis (page 287), Neck Pain (page 300), Puppy Strangles (page 322), Smoke Inhalation (page 347), Ticks (page 380), Tongue Swelling (page 390), Worms (page 413)
NOT EATING	Bee and Wasp Stings (page 79), Falls (page 175), Foreign Object in Mouth (page 199), Mouth Injuries (page 290), Mouth Sores (page 292), Neck Pain (page 300), Tooth Damage (page 393)

BEHAVIOR

Symptom	Chapter and Page
ACTING DAZED	Head Injuries (page 232)
ACTING DRUNK OR CONFUSED	Carbon Monoxide Poisoning (page 122), Low Blood Sugar (page 281), Smoke Inhalation (page 347), Snakebites (page 350), Ticks (page 380)
ACTING FRANTIC	Choking (page 131), Foreign Object in Mouth (page 199), Jaw Entrapment (page 263)
AGITATION	Birthing Problems (page 83), Foreign Object in Mouth (page 199)
ANXIETY	Electrical Shock (page 165), Seizures (page 330)
BITING FLANKS	Birthing Problems (page 83)

BEHAVIOR (cont.)

Symptom	Chapter and Page
CHEWING SKIN, COAT, OR TAIL	Flea Allergy (page 184), Frostbite (page 219), Hives (page 242), Hot Spots (page 245), Lick Sores (page 276), Skin Infections (page 336), Splinters (page 358), Tail Infections (page 371), Toe Cysts (page 387)
CRYING WHEN USING LITTER BOX	Constipation (page 140), Urinary Blockage (page 402)
DEPRESSION	Dehydration (page 148), Hypothermia (page 248), Mastitis (page 287), Shock (page 333), Ticks (page 380), Urinary Blockage (page 402)
DISORIENTATION	Clothes-Dryer Injuries (page 134), Ear Infections (page 160), Head Injuries (page 252), Low Blood Sugar (page 281), Seizures (page 330)
DROOLING	Foreign Object in Mouth (page 199), Head Swelling (page 234), Mouth Injuries (page 290), Mouth Sores (page 292), Poisoning (page 311), Scorpion Stings (page 327), Toad Poisoning (page 384)
HEAD SHAKING, TILTING, OR BOBBING	Earflap Injuries (page 157), Ear Infections (page 160), Foreign Object in Ear (page 193), Foreign Object in Mouth (page 199), Limping (page 278), Low Blood Sugar (page 281), Neck Pain (page 300)
HOLDING HEAD LOW OR STIFFLY	Back Injuries (page 75), Foreign Object in Throat (page 209), Neck Pain (page 300)
HOLDING MOUTH OPEN	Asthma Attacks (page 72), Foreign Object in Mouth (page 199), Mouth Injuries (page 290), Mouth Sores (page 292)
HOUSE SOILING	Diarrhea (page 150), Incontinence (page 257), Seizures (page 330), Urinary Blockage (page 402)
HYPERACTIVITY	Foreign Object in Mouth (page 199), Jaw Entrapment (page 253), Poisoning (page 311)
LEAVING BABIES	Birthing Problems (page 83), Mastitis (page 287)
LETHARGY	Anal Gland Impaction (page 65), Carbon Monoxide Poisoning (page 122), Dehydration (page 148), Heatstroke (page 237), Hypothermia (page 248), Poisoning (page 311), Puppy Strangles (page 322)
LICKING EXCESSIVELY	Airborne Allergies (page 63), Anal Gland Impaction (page 65), Flea Allergy (page 184), Hot Spots (page 245), Lick Sores (page 276), Toe Cysts (page 387)
MALAISE	Birthing Problems (page 83), Foreign Object Swallowed (page 204), Poisoning (page 311), Smoke Inhalation (page 347)
PADDLING WITH LEGS	Head Injuries (page 232), Seizures (page 330), Snakebites (page 350)
RELUCTANCE TO STAND OR WALK	Back Injuries (page 75), Collapse (page 137), Fractures (page 212), Heatstroke (page 237), Ticks (page 380)
RESTLESSNESS/PACING	Birthing Problems (page 83), Bloat (page 100)
RUBBING FACE	Airborne Allergies (page 63), Food Allergies (page 190)
SLEEPINESS	Head Injuries (page 232), Hypothermia (page 248)
STARING	Head Injuries (page 232), Seizures (page 330)

BEHAVIOR (cont.)

Symptom	Chapter and Page
TIRING EASILY	Back Injuries (page 75), Chest Injuries (page 128), Dehydration (page 148), Fever (page 180), Strangulation (page 363)
TOOTH GRINDING	Constipation (page 140), Foreign Object Swallowed (page 204), Seizures (page 330), Ticks (page 380)
TUCKING TUMMY IN PAIN	Foreign Object Swallowed (page 204)
WALKING IN CIRCLES	Ear Infections (page 160), Head Injuries (page 232)
WHINING OR CRYING	Abdominal Wounds (page 55), Birthing Problems (page 83), Burns from Heat (page 113), Collapse (page 137), Constipation (page 140), Dehydration (page 148), Ear Infections (page 160), Foreign Object in Mouth (page 199), Heatstroke (page 237), Neck Pain (page 300), Urinary Blockage (page 402)
WON'T LIFT HEAD	Back Injuries (page 75), Neck Pain (page 300)
WON'T MOVE	Abdominal Wounds (page 55), Collapse (page 137), Falls (page 175), Unconsciousness (page 390)
YELPING	Car Accidents (page 117), Porcupine Quills (page 319), Scorpion Stings (page 327)

DIGESTION AND ELIMINATION

Symptom	Chapter and Page
ABDOMINAL SWELLING/ POTBELLY	Bloat (page 100), Bowel Obstruction (page 103), Constipation (page 140), Foreign Object Swallowed (page 204)
BLOOD IN STOOLS	Ticks (page 380), Worms (page 413)
BLOOD IN URINE	Poisoning (page 311), Urinary Blockage (page 402)
DARK URINE	Poisoning (page 311), Ticks (page 380)
DIARRHEA	Bee and Wasp Stings (page 79), Carbon Monoxide Poisoning (page 122), Diarrhea (page 150), Fading Puppy or Kitten (page 172), Fever (page 180), Food Allergies (page 190), Foreign Object Swallowed (page 204), Heatstroke (page 237), Poisoning (page 311), Worms (page 413)
DIFFICULTY URINATING	Anal Gland Impaction (page 65), Rectal Prolapse (page 325), Urinary Blockage (page 402)
MALODOROUS STOOLS	Constipation (page 140), Diarrhea (page 150)
PUDDINGLIKE STOOLS	Diarrhea (page 150), Worms (page 413)
SPECKS IN STOOL	Worms (page 413)
STOMACH PAIN	Bloat (page 100), Bowel Obstruction (page 103), Constipation (page 140), Foreign Object Swallowed (page 204), Worms (page 413)
URINATING INVOLUNTARILY	Poisoning (page 311), Seizures (page 330)
URINATING LESS OFTEN	Urinary Blockage (page 402)

DIGESTION AND ELIMINATION (cont.)

Symptom	Chapter and Page
URINATING MORE OFTEN	Poisoning (page 311)
URINE DRIBBLING OR LEAKING	Incontinence (page 257)
URINE SCALDING	Incontinence (page 257)
VOMITING	Bowel Obstruction (page 103), Carbon Monoxide Poisoning (page 122), Food Allergies (page 190), Foreign Object Swallowed (page 214), Heatstroke (page 237), Poisoning (page 311), Urinary Blockage (page 402), Vomiting (page 410), Worms (page 413)

EARS

Symptom	Chapter and Page
BLEEDING FROM INSIDE	Car Accidents (page 117), Clothes-Dryer Injuries (page 134), Falls (page 175), Head Injuries (page 232)
CRUMBLY BLACK OR BROWN MATERIAL	Ear Infections (page 160)
CRUSTY MARGINS AND TIPS WITH LEAKING SERUM	Fly Bites (page 187)
DISCHARGE	Ear Infections (page 160), Foreign Object in Ear (page 193)
DROOPING TIPS	Frostbite (page 219)
HEARING LOSS	Carbon Monoxide Poisoning (page 122), Ear Infections (page 160), Foreign Object in Ear (page 193)
INFLAMMATION	Ear Infections (page 160), Frostbite (page 219)
ITCHING	Ear Infections (page 160), Ticks (page 380)
ODOR	Ear Infections (page 160), Foreign Object in Ear (page 193)
SCRATCHING OR PAWING EARS	Ear Infections (page 160), Foreign Object in Ear (page 193), Ticks (page 380)
SORENESS	Ear Infections (page 160), Foreign Object in Ear (page 193), Ticks (page 380)
SWELLING	Earflap Injuries (page 157), Ear Infections (page 160), Foreign Object in Ear (page 193)

EYES

Symptom	Chapter and Page
BLINKING RAPIDLY	Eye Infections (page 167), Foreign Object in Eye (page 196)
BLOODSHOT EYES	Eye Infections (page 167), Foreign Object in Eye (page 196)
DISCHARGE	Eye Infections (page 167), Foreign Object in Eye (page 196), Sties (page 361)
EYELID IRRITATION	Bites from Animals (page 90), Sties (page 361)
EYELID SWELLING	Bee and Wasp Stings (page 79), Sties (page 361)

EYES (cont.)

Symptom	Chapter and Page
GLASSINESS OR SUNKENNESS	Dehydration (page 148), Low Blood Sugar (page 281), Shock (page 333)
GRAY OR BLUE RIMS	Drowning (page 153), Hypothermia (page 248), Shock (page 333)
LOOKING IN TWO DIFFERENT DIRECTIONS	Head Injuries (page 232)
OUT OF SOCKET	Bites from Animals (page 90), Car Accidents (page 117), Eye Out of Socket (page 169), Falls (page 175)
PAWING EYES	Foreign Object in Eye (page 196), Sties (page 361)
REDNESS AND ITCHING	Sties (page 361)
SQUINTING	Eye Infections (page 167), Foreign Object in Eye (page 196)
TEAR GLAND SWELLING	Sties (page 361)
WATERING	Foreign Object in Eye (page 196), Poisoning (page 311)

HEAD, MOUTH, NOSE, AND TEETH

Symptom	Chapter and Page
AMMONIA-SCENTED BREATH	Incontinence (page 257)
BAD BREATH	Foreign Object in Mouth (page 199), Mouth Injuries (page 290), Mouth Sores (page 292)
BLOOD IN SALIVA	Foreign Object in Mouth (page 199), Mouth Injuries (page 290), Mouth Sores (page 292), Tooth Damage (page 393)
BLOOD IN VOMIT	Heatstroke (page 237), Poisoning (page 311), Worms (page 413)
BLOODY NOSE	Foreign Object in Nose (page 202), Head Injuries (page 232), Heatstroke (page 237), Nosebleeds (page 303), Snakebites (page 350), Ticks (page 380)
BURNS ON LIPS, CORNERS OF MOUTH, OR TONGUE	Electrical Shock (page 165)
DIFFICULTY SWALLOWING	Fishhook Injuries (page 182), Foreign Object in Throat (page 209)
DROOLING	Fishhook Injuries (page 182), Foreign Object in Mouth (page 199), Head Swelling (page 234), Jaw Swelling (page 266), Mouth Injuries (page 290), Mouth Sores (page 292), Poisoning (page 311), Scorpion Stings (page 327), Toad Poisoning (page 384), Tongue Swelling (page 390), Tooth Damage (page 393)
FACE DROOPING	Ear Infections (page 160), Head Injuries (page 232)
FACIAL SWELLING	Bee and Wasp Stings (page 79), Head Swelling (page 234), Hives (page 242)
GUM STICKINESS	Abdominal Wounds (page 55), Bites from Animals (page 90), Bloat (page 100), Burns from Heat (page 113), Collapse (page 137), Dehydration (page 148), Foreign Object Swallowed (page 204), Heatstroke (page 237), Shock (page 333), Smoke Inhalation (page 347)

HEAD, MOUTH, NOSE, AND TEETH (cont.)

Symptom	Chapter and Page
GUM SWELLING	Mouth Sores (page 292)
GUMS, BLUE	Drowning (page 153), Hypothermia (page 248), Mouth Injuries (page 290), Smoke Inhalation (page 347), Suffocation (page 366)
GUMS, BRIGHT RED	Carbon Monoxide Poisoning (page 122), Heatstroke (page 237)
GUMS, DARK PINK OR RED	Heatstroke (page 237)
GUMS, GRAY, WHITE, OR PALE	Arrow Wounds (page 69), Bee and Wasp Stings (page 79), Bites from Animals (page 90), Bloat (page 100), Drowning (page 153), Foreign Object Swallowed (page 204), Hypothermia (page 248), Shock (page 333), Smoke Inhalation (page 347), Toad Poisoning (page 384)
GUMS, PURPLE	Asthma Attacks (page 72)
HEAD SWELLING	Bee and Wasp Stings (page 79), Head Injuries (page 232), Head Swelling (page 234), Hives (page 242)
HEAD TRAPPED	Head Entrapment (page 229), Jaw Entrapment (page 263)
JAW BLEEDING	Fractures (page 212), Jaw Entrapment (page 263)
JAW SWELLING	Fishhook Injuries (page 182), Foreign Object in Mouth (page 199), Jaw Entrapment (page 263), Jaw Swelling (page 266)
LIP LESIONS (IN CATS)	Mouth Sores (page 292)
LIP SWELLING	Mouth Sores (page 292)
LIPS, BLUE OR GRAY	Drowning (page 153), Hypothermia (page 248), Shock (page 333)
MOUTH PAIN	Mouth Injuries (page 290), Mouth Sores (page 292), Tooth Damage (page 393)
MOUTH SORES	Jaw Entrapment (page 263), Mouth Sores (page 292), Tooth Damage (page 393)
MOUTH SWELLING	Jaw Entrapment (page 263), Mouth Sores (page 292)
MOUTH WOUNDS	Fishhook Injuries (page 182), Foreign Object in Mouth (page 199), Jaw Entrapment (page 263), Mouth Injuries (page 290)
NASAL DISCHARGE	Fishhook Injuries (page 182), Foreign Object in Mouth (page 199), Foreign Object in Nose (page 202), Nosebleeds (page 303)
NASAL DRYNESS	Foreign Object in Nose (page 202), Jaw Swelling (page 266)
OBJECT PROTRUDING FROM NOSE	Foreign Object in Nose (page 202)
PAWING MOUTH	Fishhook Injuries (page 182), Foreign Object in Mouth (page 199), Mouth Injuries (page 290), Mouth Sores (page 292), Toad Poisoning (page 384)
SALIVA, THICK	Dehydration (page 148), Toad Poisoning (page 384)
SALIVATING EXCESSIVELY	Mouth Sores (page 292), Poisoning (page 311), Toad Poisoning (page 384)

HEAD, MOUTH, NOSE, AND TEETH (cont.)

Symptom	Chapter and Page
TONGUE OR GUMS, BLUE	Asthma Attacks (page 72), Carbon Monoxide Poisoning (page 122), Cardiac Arrest (page 124), Smoke Inhalation (page 347), Suffocation (page 366)
TONGUE SWELLING	Bee and Wasp Stings (page 79), Foreign Object in Mouth (page 199), Mouth Sores (page 292), Tongue Swelling (page 390)
TONGUE, BRIGHT RED	Choking (page 131), Foreign Object Swallowed (page 204), Heatstroke (page 237)
TONGUE, PALE	Hypothermia (page 248), Shock (page 333)
TOOTH GRINDING	Foreign Object Swallowed (page 204), Seizures (page 330), Ticks (page 380)

HEART AND CIRCULATION

Symptom	Chapter and Page
BLEEDING	Abdominal Wounds (page 55), Arrow Wounds (page 69), Bites from Animals (page 90), Bleeding (page 95), Car Accidents (page 117), Chest Injuries (page 128), Cuts and Wounds (page 143), Earflap Injuries (page 157), Fractures (page 212), Gunshot Wounds (page 224), Head Injuries (page 232), Shock (page 333)
ERRATIC HEARTBEAT	Electrical Shock (page 165), Poisoning (page 311), Shock (page 333)
NO HEARTBEAT	Cardiac Arrest (page 124)

HINDQUARTERS AND TAIL

Symptom	Chapter and Page
ANAL SWELLING AND REDNESS	Anal Gland Impaction (page 65), Rectal Prolapse (page 325)
BITING REAR END	Anal Gland Impaction (page 65), Constipation (page 140), Worms (page 413)
LICKING REAR END	Anal Gland Impaction (page 65), Rectal Prolapse (page 325), Vaginal Prolapse (page 407), Worms (page 413)
OBJECT PROTRUDING FROM ANUS	Bowel Obstruction (page 103)
ODOR	Abscesses (page 60), Constipation (page 140), Maggots (page 284)
PUS	Abscesses (page 60), Tail Infections (page 371), Urinary Blockage (page 402)
RICELIKE OBJECTS NEAR TAIL	Worms (page 413)
SCOOTING	Anal Gland Impaction (page 65), Constipation (page 140), Worms (page 413)
TAIL SENSITIVITY	Anal Gland Impaction (page 65), Tail Infections (page 371), Tail Swelling (page 374)

HINDQUARTERS AND TAIL (cont.)

Symptom	Chapter and Page
TAIL SORENESS	Tail Infections (page 371), Tail Swelling (page 374)
TAIL SWELLING	Tail Infections (page 371), Tail Swelling (page 374)
TISSUE BULGING UNDER TAIL	Birthing Problems (page 83), Rectal Prolapse (page 325), Vaginal Prolapse (page 407)

LEGS, HIPS, AND PAWS

Symptom	Chapter and Page
BLEEDING	Bites from Animals (page 90), Car Accidents (page 117), Fractures (page 212)
BONE PROTRUDING	Fractures (page 212)
DIFFICULTY GETTING UP	Falls (page 175)
DRAGGING LEG	Back Injuries (page 75), Fractures (page 212), Ticks (page 380)
HOLDING PAW UP	Fractures (page 212), Ingrown Nails (page 260), Leg Swelling (page 273), Limping (page 278)
HOPPING GAIT	Falls (page 175), Ingrown Nails (page 260), Kneecap Slipping (page 271)
INABILITY OR RELUCTANCE TO STAND	Back Injuries (page 75), Fractures (page 212), Pad Burns (page 305), Paw Damage (page 308), Shock (page 333)
LEG DANGLING	Car Accidents (page 117), Fractures (page 212)
LEG AT ODD ANGLE	Fractures (page 212)
LEG SWELLING	Abscesses (page 60), Bites from Animals (page 90), Car Accidents (page 117), Fishhook Injuries (page 182), Frostbite (page 219), Ingrown Nails (page 260), Kneecap Slipping (page 271), Leg Swelling (page 273), Limping (page 278), Nail-Bed Infections (page 295), Ticks (page 380)
LICKING PAWS OR TOES	Airborne Allergies (page 63), Ingrown Nails (page 260), Nail-Bed Infections (page 295), Ticks (page 380), Toe Cysts (page 387)
LIMPING	Abscesses (page 60), Arrow Wounds (page 169), Bites from Animals (page 90), Bleeding (page 95), Car Accidents (page 117), Falls (page 175), Fishhook Injuries (page 182), Fractures (page 212), Frostbite (page 219), Ingrown Nails (page 260), Kneecap Slipping (page 271), Leg Swelling (page 273), Limping (page 278), Nail-Bed Infections (page 295), Pad Burns (page 305), Paw Damage (page 308), Ticks (page 380)
LOSS OF USE OF HIND LEGS	Back Injuries (page 75), Ticks (page 380)
PAD BLEEDING	Ingrown Nails (page 260), Paw Damage (page 308)
PAD BLISTERS	Pad Burns (page 305)
PAD CRACKS OR CALLUSES	Pad Burns (page 305), Paw Damage (page 308)
PAD INFLAMMATION	Fishhook Injuries (page 182), Ingrown Nails (page 260), Pad Burns (page 305), Paw Damage (page 308), Toe Cysts (page 387)

LEGS, HIPS, AND PAWS (cont.)

Symptom	Chapter and Page
PAD SWELLING	Ingrown Nails (page 260), Nail-Bed Infections (page 295), Paw Damage (page 308)
PAD WOUNDS	Fishhook Injuries (page 182), Pad Burns (page 305), Paw Damage (page 308)
PAW ABRASIONS	Burns from Friction (page 110), Paw Damage (page 308)
PAW BURNS	Burns from Friction (page 110), Pad Burns (page 305), Paw Damage (page 308)
PAW PUNCTURE	Fishhook Injuries (page 182), Ingrown Nails (page 260), Paw Damage (page 308)
PAW SWELLING	Nail-Bed Infections (page 295)
PUS DRAINING FROM PAWS	Nail-Bed Infections (page 295), Pad Burns (page 305), Paw Damage (page 308)
STRETCHING LEG BACKWARD	Kneecap Slipping (page 271)
TOE SORENESS	Nail-Bed Infections (page 295), Paw Damage (page 308), Toe Cysts (page 387)
UNSTEADINESS	Head Injuries (page 232), Seizures (page 330)
WALKING WITH BACK TOES TURNED UNDER	Back Injuries (page 75)
WALKING STIFF-LEGGED	Birthing Problems (page 83)
WALKING STRADDLE-LEGGED	Testicular or Scrotal Swelling (page 377), Urinary Blockage (page 402)
WOBBLY HIND LEGS	Back Injuries (page 75), Ticks (page 380)
WON'T LET PAW BE TOUCHED	Cuts and Wounds (page 143), Ingrown Nails (page 260), Nail-Bed Infections (page 295), Paw Damage (page 308), Splinters (page 358)

REPRODUCTIVE SYSTEM

Symptom	Chapter and Page
BREAST HARDNESS	Mastitis (page 287)
BREAST INFLAMMATION	Abscesses (page 60), Mastitis (page 287)
BREAST SWELLING	Bloat (page 100), Mastitis (page 287)
DECREASED MILK PRODUCTION	Mastitis (page 287)
FAILURE TO NURSE	Fading Puppy or Kitten (page 172), Mastitis (page 287)
LABOR WITHOUT DELIVERY	Birthing Problems (page 83)
NIPPLE DISCHARGE	Mastitis (page 287)
SCROTAL SWELLING	Frostbite (page 219), Testicular or Scrotal Swelling (page 377)
TESTICULAR HARDNESS	Testicular or Scrotal Swelling (page 377)
TESTICULAR INFLAMMATION AND SWELLING	Testicular or Scrotal Swelling (page 377)

REPRODUCTIVE SYSTEM (cont.)

Symptom	Chapter and Page
TISSUE PROTRUDING FROM VAGINA	Vaginal Prolapse (page 407)
VAGINAL DISCHARGE, MALODOROUS	Birthing Problems (page 83)

RESPIRATORY SYSTEM

Symptom	Chapter and Page
BREATH, SHORTNESS OF	Burns from Heat (page 113), Carbon Monoxide Poisoning (page 122), Collapse (page 137), Strangulation (page 363)
BREATHING DIFFICULT OR LABORED	Arrow Wounds (page 69), Asthma Attacks (page 72), Bee and Wasp Stings (page 79), Car Accidents (page 117), Chest Injuries (page 128), Choking (page 131), Collapse (page 137), Drowning (page 153), Electrical Shock (page 165), Falls (page 175), Food Allergies (page 190), Foreign Object in Throat (page 209), Fractures (page 212), Gunshot Wounds (page 224), Head Entrapment (page 229), Hives (page 242), Poisoning (page 311), Scorpion Stings (page 327), Smoke Inhalation (page 347), Strangulation (page 363), Suffocation (page 366), Ticks (page 380), Tongue Swelling (page 390)
BREATHING NOISILY	Asthma Attacks (page 72), Bee and Wasp Stings (page 79), Foreign Object in Nose (page 202), Foreign Object in Throat (page 209)
BREATHING RAPIDLY	Burns from Heat (page 113), Collapse (page 137), Fractures (page 212), Heatstroke (page 237), Shock (page 333)
BREATHING SHALLOWLY	Arrow Wounds (page 69), Chest Injuries (page 128)
BREATHING, STOPPED	Bites from Animals (page 90), Car Accidents (page 117), Cardiac Arrest (page 124), Clothes-Dryer Injuries (page 134), Foreign Object in Nose (page 202), Foreign Object in Throat (page 209), Fractures (page 212), Heatstroke (page 237), Jellyfish Stings (page 269), Low Blood Sugar (page 281), Poisoning (page 311), Shock (page 333), Smoke Inhalation (page 347), Snakebites (page 350), Strangulation (page 363), Suffocation (page 366), Toad Poisoning (page 384), Unconsciousness (page 396)
COUGHING	Asthma Attacks (page 72), Choking (page 131), Collapse (page 137), Electrical Shock (page 165), Foreign Object in Throat (page 209), Smoke Inhalation (page 347)
GAGGING	Choking (page 131), Collapse (page 137), Fishhook Injuries (page 182), Foreign Object in Mouth (page 199), Foreign Object in Throat (page 209), Head Swelling (page 234), Jaw Swelling (page 266), Mouth Injuries (page 290), Mouth Sores (page 292), Poisoning (page 311), Tooth Damage (page 393)
GASPING	Asthma Attacks (page 72), Carbon Monoxide Poisoning (page 122), Foreign Object in Throat (page 209), Smoke Inhalation (page 347), Suffocation (page 366)

RESPIRATORY SYSTEM (cont.)

Symptom	Chapter and Page
PANTING (IN CATS)	Birthing Problems (page 83), Heatstroke (page 237)
SNEEZING	Foreign Object in Nose (page 202)
SNORTING	Foreign Object in Nose (page 202), Foreign Object in Throat (page 209)
THROAT SWOLLEN SHUT	Bee and Wasp Stings (page 79), Heatstroke (page 237)
WHEEZING	Asthma Attacks (page 72), Bee and Wasp Stings (page 79), Foreign Object in Throat (page 209)

SKIN AND COAT

Symptom	Chapter and Page
BITE WOUNDS	Abscesses (page 60), Bites from Animals (page 90), Snakebites (page 350), Spider Bites (page 354), Ticks (page 380)
BLISTERS	Burns from Chemicals (page 106), Burns from Heat (page 113), Frostbite (page 219)
DISCHARGE	Abscesses (page 60), Burns from Chemicals (page 106), Burns from Heat (page 113), Frostbite (page 219), Skin Infections (336)
FLAKINESS	Skin Infections (page 336)
FUR LOSS, PATCHY	Flea Allergy (page 184), Hot Spots (page 245), Lick Sores (page 276)
FUR LOSS, SKIN RED TO GRAY	Airborne Allergies (page 63), Food Allergies (page 190), Skin Infections (page 336)
FUR, WET AND SMELLY	Abscesses (page 60), Diarrhea (page 150), Incontinence (page 267), Maggots (page 284)
GREASINESS	Airborne Allergies (page 63), Skin Infections (page 336)
HIVES	Bee and Wasp Stings (page 79), Hives (page 242), Jellyfish Stings (page 269)
INFLAMMATION	Cuts and Wounds (page 143), Suture Problems (page 369)
ITCHING	Airborne Allergies (page 63), Flea Allergy (page 184), Food Allergies (page 190), Hives (page 242), Hot Spots (page 245), Impetigo (page 254), Skin Infections (page 336), Suture Problems (page 369)
LOSS OF ELASTICITY	Dehydration (page 148)
MAGGOTS	Cuts and Wounds (page 143), Maggots (page 284)
OILINESS	Skin Infections (page 336)
PIMPLES (USUALLY IN PUPPIES/KITTENS)	Impetigo (page 254)
PUS	Abscesses (page 60), Skin Infections (page 336)
RANCID ODOR	Impetigo (page 254), Maggots (page 284)
RASH	Airborne Allergies (page 63), Flea Allergy (page 184), Hives (page 242), Impetigo (page 254)

SKIN AND COAT (cont.)	
Symptom	**Chapter and Page**
SCABS	Flea Allergy (page 184), Impetigo (page 254)
SKIN BUMPS, RED	Lick Sores (page 276)
SKIN, BLUE OR GRAY	Drowning (page 153), Frostbite (page 219), Hypothermia (page 248)
SKIN, COLD	Frostbite (page 219), Hypothermia (page 248)
SKIN, HARD AND NONPLIABLE	Mastitis (page 287)
SKIN, PALE OR WHITE	Frostbite (page 219), Hypothermia (page 248)
SORES	Abscesses (page 60), Flea Allergy (page 184), Hot Spots (page 245), Lick Sores (page 276), Puppy Strangles (page 322)
SORES, BULL'S-EYE	Skin Infections (page 336), Ticks (page 380)
SORES, RED AND SHINY	Skin Infections (page 336)
SORES, RED AND WET	Abscesses (page 60), Burns from Heat (page 113), Hot Spots (page 245)
SORES, WET AND WEEPING	Burns from Chemicals (page 106)
SPLOTCHES	Airborne Allergies (page 63), Hives (page 242), Hot Spots (page 245)
SWELLING	Abscesses (page 60), Bee and Wasp Stings (page 79), Bites from Animals (page 90), Food Allergies (page 190), Gunshot Wounds (page 224), Hives (page 242), Jellyfish Stings (page 269), Puppy Strangles (page 322), Scorpion Stings (page 327), Skin Swelling (page 341), Snakebites (page 350), Suture Problems (page 369)
WELTS	Hives (page 242)
WORMS IN WOUND	Abscesses (page 60), Maggots (page 284)

WHOLE-BODY SYMPTOMS	
Symptom	**Chapter and Page**
COLD TO TOUCH	Hypothermia (page 248)
COLLAPSE	Bee and Wasp Stings (page 79), Birthing Problems (page 83), Car Accidents (page 117), Collapse (page 137), Food Allergies (page 190), Jellyfish Stings (page 269), Low Blood Sugar (page 281), Poisoning (page 311), Seizures (page 330), Scorpion Stings (page 327), Toad Poisoning (page 384), Unconsciousness (page 396)
DIZZINESS	Ear Infections (page 160), Heatstroke (page 237), Low Blood Sugar (page 281)
ELEVATED BODY TEMPERATURE	Clothes-Dryer Injuries (page 134), Fever (page 180), Heatstroke (page 237), Seizures (page 330)
FAINTING	Asthma Attacks (page 72), Burns from Heat (page 113), Collapse (page 137), Ear Infections (page 160), Low Blood Sugar (page 281), Poisoning (page 311), Seizures (page 330), Smoke Inhalation (page 347), Unconsciousness (page 396)

WHOLE-BODY SYMPTOMS (cont.)

Symptom	Chapter and Page
FALLING OVER	Ear Infections (page 160), Seizures (page 330), Unconsciousness (page 396)
FEVER	Abscesses (page 60), Anal Gland Impaction (page 65), Bee and Wasp Stings (page 79), Fever (page 180), Puppy Strangles (page 322), Spider Bites (page 354), Ticks (page 380)
HUNCHED BACK	Abdominal Wounds (page 55), Back Injuries (page 75), Constipation (page 140)
LACK OF MOVEMENT	Collapse (page 137), Fading Puppy or Kitten (page 172)
LOW BODY TEMPERATURE	Drowning (pagee 153), Fading Puppy or Kitten (page 172), Frostbite (page 219), Hypothermia (page 248), Shock (page 333)
LUMPS, HARD OR SOFT	Abscesses (page 60), Mastitis (page 287), Skin Swelling (page 341)
NECK SWELLING	Abscesses (page 60), Neck Pain (page 300), Puppy Strangles (page 322)
PARALYSIS	Back Injuries (page 75), Scorpion Stings (page 327), Ticks (page 380)
RETCHING	Choking (page 131), Foreign Object Swallowed (page 204), Heatstroke (page 237), Ticks (page 380), Vomiting (page 410)
SEIZURES	Birthing Problems (page 83), Carbon Monoxide Poisoning (page 122), Electrical Shock (page 165), Head Injuries (page 232), Low Blood Sugar (page 281), Poisoning (page 311), Seizures (page 330), Snakebites (page 350), Toad Poisoning (page 384)
SHAKING, SHIVERING, OR TREMBLING	Bee and Wasp Stings (page 79), Hypothermia (page 248), Low Blood Sugar (page 281), Snakebites (page 350), Spider Bites (page 354)
STIFFNESS	Fading Puppy or Kitten (page 172), Poisoning (page 311), Ticks (page 380)
UNCONSCIOUSNESS	Asthma Attacks (page 72), Bites from Animals (page 90), Car Accidents (page 117), Cardiac Arrest (page 124), Clothes-Dryer Injuries (page 134), Fading Puppy or Kitten (page 172), Falls (page 175), Fractures (page 212), Head Injuries (page 232), Heatstroke (page 237), Hypothermia (page 248), Low Blood Sugar (page 281), Neck Pain (page 300), Poisoning (page 311), Seizures (page 330), Spider Bites (page 354), Strangulation (page 363), Suffocation (page 366), Unconsciousness (page 396)
WEAKNESS OR WOOZINESS/ GROGGINESS	Abdominal Wounds (page 55), Bee and Wasp Stings (page 79), Birthing Problems (page 83), Burns from Heat (page 113), Carbon Monoxide Poisoning (page 122), Clothes-Dryer Injuries (page 134), Collapse (page 137), Dehydration (page 148), Drowning (page 153), Ear Infections (page 160), Falls (page 175), Heatstroke (page 237), Low Blood Sugar (page 281), Poisoning (page 311), Seizures (page 330), Shock (page 333), Suffocation (page 366), Unconsciousness (page 396)

Advisors for Part One

■ Lowell Ackerman, D.V.M., is a veterinarian at Mesa Veterinary Hospital in Scottsdale, Arizona, and author of *Skin and Coat Care for Your Dog* and. *Skin and Coat Care for Your Cat.*

■ Shane Bateman, D.V.M., D.V.Sc., is a veterinarian board certified in the American College of Emergency and Critical Care Medicine and assistant professor of emergency and critical care medicine at Ohio State University College of Veterinary Medicine in Columbus.

■ John Brakebill, D.V.M., is a veterinarian at Brakebill Veterinary Hospital in Sherman, Texas.

■ Grace F. Bransford, D.V.M., is a veterinarian in Corte Madera, California.

■ Dale C. Butler, D.V.M., is a veterinarian at Best Friends Animal Hospital in Denison, Texas.

■ Lyndon Conrad, D.V.M., is a veterinarian at Noah's Landing Pet Care Clinic in Elkhart, Indiana.

■ Alvin C. Dufour, D.V.M., is a veterinarian at Dufour Animal Hospital in Elkhart, Indiana.

■ Deborah Edwards, D.V.M., is a veterinarian at All Cats Hospital in Largo, Florida.

■ Martha Gearhart, D.V.M., D.A.B.V.P., is a veterinarian at Pleasant Valley Animal Hospital in New York.

■ Grady Hester, D.V.M., is a veterinarian at All Creatures Animal Clinic in Rolesville, North Carolina.

■ Janie Hodges, D.V.M., is a veterinarian at Valley View Pet Health Center in Farmers Branch, Texas.

■ Jean C. Hofve, D.V.M., is a veterinarian and Companion Animal Program coordinator for the Animal Protection Institute in Sacramento.

■ Joanne Howl, D.V.M., is a veterinarian in West River, Maryland; secretary/treasurer of the American Academy on Veterinary Disaster Medicine; and past president of the Maryland Veterinary Medical Association.

■ Chris Johnson, D.V.M., is a veterinarian at Westside Animal Emergency Clinic in Atlanta.

■ Terry Kaeser, D.V.M., is a veterinarian at Goshen Animal Clinic in Indiana.

■ Mauri Karger, D.V.M., is a veterinarian at I-20 Animal Medical Center in Arlington, Texas.

■ Ron Lawrence, D.V.M., is a veterinarian at the Texoma Veterinary Hospital in Sherman, Texas.

■ Peter Levin, V.M.D., is a veterinarian at Ludwig's Corner Veterinary Hospital in Chester Springs, Pennsylvania.

■ Albert Mughannam, D.V.M., is a veterinary ophthalmologist at Veterinary Vision in San Mateo, California.

■ Thomas Munschauer, D.V.M., is a veterinarian at Middlebury Animal Hospital in Vermont and past president of the Vermont Veterinary Medical Association.

■ Margaret J. Rucker, D.V.M., is a veterinarian at Southwest Virginia Veterinary Services in Lebanon, Virginia.

■ Laura Solien, D.V.M., is a veterinarian at Maplecrest Animal Hospital in Goshen, Indiana.

■ Kevin Wallace, D.V.M., is an instructor in the department of clinical sciences at Cornell University College of Veterinary Medicine in Ithaca, New York.

■ Drew Weigner, D.V.M., is a veterinarian at The Cat Doctor in Atlanta.

■ Jeffrey Werber, D.V.M., is a veterinarian at Century Veterinary Group in Los Angeles.

■ H. Ellen Whiteley, D.V.M., is a veterinarian in Guadalupita, New Mexico, and author of *Understanding and Training Your Dog or Puppy* and *Understanding and Training Your Cat or Kitten.*

■ Dennis L. Wilcox, D.V.M., is a veterinarian at Angeles Clinic for Animals in Port Angeles, Washington.

■ David Wirth-Schneider, D.V.M., is a veterinarian at the Emergency Clinic for Animals in Madison, Wisconsin.

■ Sophia Yin, D.V.M., is a veterinarian in Davis, California, and author of *The Small Animal Veterinary Nerdbook.*

Part Two

COMMON INJURIES AND CONDITIONS

Abdominal Wounds

CALL YOUR VET: **IMMEDIATELY**

Only a thin layer of skin, fat, and muscle protects the stomach, intestines, liver, and other abdominal organs—called the viscera—from the outside world. Abdominal wounds are common and are nearly always serious because the organs are easily bruised and torn. Injuries from car accidents, falls, or kicks from horses may not show on the outside, while animal bites or torn spay incisions often split open the abdomen so that the organs spill out and are exposed to infection.

If your pet doesn't seem to be in pain and the wound hasn't penetrated the abdomen, you can treat it at home. But severe abdominal wounds are medical emergencies. They are painful whether the organs are exposed or not. Pets hunch their backs when their tummies hurt or flinch when touched and refuse to move.

Since it can be difficult to tell whether a wound has penetrated the abdominal cavity, have your vet examine *any* abdominal puncture or wound. Bite marks may look very minor, but they may have serious consequences, so make sure that you have them checked out, too.

The body produces chemicals like epinephrine (adrenaline) that help a pet survive the initial trauma, but they last for only 10 to 20 minutes. First aid will keep your pet alive until you reach medical help, and it can prevent life-threatening complications like infection.

 **DO THIS NOW**

For Penetrating Wounds

Check for signs of shock. Severe injury often causes shock, which makes the organs shut down from lack of oxygen. A pet in shock acts weak or woozy. His eyelids droop, and he may have a pale tongue or gums. Shock can kill a pet in as little as 10 to 20 minutes, and he'll need *immediate* veterinary care to survive. Wrap him in a blanket to keep him warm—this can slow down the shock process—then drive him to the clinic. You can also put a drop or two of Karo syrup or honey on your pet's gums to help keep him conscious. (For more information, about shock, see page 333.)

Apply pressure. If the injury bleeds, apply direct pressure to the wound with a clean cloth or gauze pad. If the blood seeps through, don't re-move the pad; just place a second one over the first and continue the pressure. (Removing the pad will disturb any clots that are forming.) If the bleeding comes from the intestines or another organ that's exposed, you may be able to squeeze a bit of the tissue at the site to stop the bleeding. Gently grasp the bleeding tissue between your thumb and the tips of two fingers, using a moistened sterile gauze pad, a clean moistened towel, or even a cotton makeup square over the wound. Apply as much pressure as you would expect to use to burst a ripened grape. (Organs tend to be so soft that pressure won't work as well as squeezing.) If the bleeding continues, maintain the pressure while someone transports you and your pet to the animal hospital.

Protect the wound. Cover the puncture or cut to keep germs from entering the wound. Cont-

 FIRST ALERT

Peritonitis

Peritonitis is an inflammation or infection of the abdominal cavity from bacteria that enter through a wound. Bites that puncture the abdomen from the outside often introduce germs. But trauma, swallowed objects, or uterine infections that rupture organs on the inside are also common causes because they allow germs to spill into the body cavity.

Peritonitis causes an extremely painful abdomen, and pets typically hunch their backs and tuck up their tummies to protect the area. They may walk with a stiff-legged gait or refuse to move at all. Sometimes the tummy swells with infection. A fever over 104°F is typical, and pets tend to refuse food and act depressed.

Peritonitis is extremely serious and can be hard to cure, so if your pet has these symptoms, get help right away. When the infection is caught in time, massive doses of antibiotic and antimicrobial medicine can help. Some pets require surgery to clean out their insides and repair the damage.

amination that infects the inside of the body can be deadly, even when the wound itself looks minor. It takes only about an hour for bacteria to get a foothold, so it's important to treat the injury very quickly. Use a thick pad of clean folded towels or sheets, then wrap an elastic bandage, such as an Ace bandage, around the body to hold it on. If you don't have an elastic bandage, you can use panty hose to tie the pad in place. Make sure that it's loose enough for you to slip your fingers between the bandage and your pet's back so he can breathe comfortably.

Rinse the organs. If the viscera are exposed outside the body and medical help is more than 20 minutes away, thoroughly but gently rinse the organs with sterile saline contact lens solution. If you don't have that, use clean lukewarm water. This helps reduce contamination by mechanically rinsing contaminants away and diluting them. It also helps keep tissues moist (organ tissue dies if it dries out).

Put the organs back. Protruding organs and intestines may be gently pushed back into your pet's abdominal cavity once they've been rinsed.

Soak gauze pads or a clean, lint-free pillowcase or a clean bath towel with sterile saline contact lens solution or lukewarm water and use it to place the organs inside. If you use your bare hands, wash them first in antiseptic or wear disposable medical gloves (available in drugstores) so you don't introduce bacteria into the body.

Hold the organs in place with a firmly applied belly band made from plastic wrap like Saran Wrap or a plastic garbage bag. Place it over the moist pads or cloth, wrap it around your pet's

With possible internal injuries, it's important to immobilize your pet before transporting her. For a cat or small dog, a sturdy trash-can lid can be a rigid transport if you don't have a carrier. Towels will keep her more comfortable during her trip.

body, and tape it in place. Make sure that the band is not wrapped too tightly; it just needs to hold the covered organs in place.

If you can't return the organs to the abdominal cavity, wrap them in a clean, wet bath towel like a sling around your pet's belly until you get him to the animal hospital. Make sure that all the organs are covered.

Numb the pain with ice. Don't give your pet pain medicine like aspirin, because it can interfere with the ability of the blood to clot and make the bleeding worse. Instead, you can apply an ice pack against the wound outside the protective bandage. The ice pack will help numb the pain, and the cold can also help slow bleeding.

Move your pet carefully. Transport your pet on a rigid, stable surface to keep from jostling the organs even more. Small dogs and cats do best in pet carriers or boxes. Don't carry your pet in your arms because that can increase her stress levels and make the shock worse. If you don't have a box or carrier, you can use a trash-can lid, as long as it is sturdy enough to bear your pet's weight without buckling. Line the lid with a clean towel first. Then move her carefully, keeping her as still as possible. Use an ironing board or a blanket stretcher to move a big dog.

For Nonpenetrating Wounds

Clip your pet's fur. To clean wounds that don't penetrate into the abdomen, first shave or cut the fur away from the injury. This will remove one of the biggest sources of bacteria and can help prevent infection. Use electric clippers or carefully clip the fur with blunt scissors. If you're using scissors, first slip your index and second fingers through the fur and hold them against the wound. Cut the fur level with your fingers, clipping a 1-inch border around the wound. (This technique is illustrated on page 114.) To keep the clippings from sticking to the wound, coat it with a thin layer of water-soluble lubricant like K-Y Jelly. The cut fur will adhere to the jelly, and you can wash it away with a gentle stream of water.

Cleanse the wound. You can use warm water and a clean washcloth to wipe off visible wounds as long as they haven't penetrated into the abdomen. If there is a lot of crusting or cheesy-looking white, green, yellow, or black debris, the best way to clean it off is with lukewarm tap water from a handheld showerhead or sprayer. Rinse the area gently with the water until the debris softens. Then, wearing a disposable medical glove, gently ease the crusty discharge away.

Do this once or twice daily as needed for the first 2 to 3 days, but don't wash the wound if it looks like a healthy scab is forming.

 ## SPECIAL SITUATION

If your pet is in pain: He may bite by reflex. To help him, you may need to safely restrain him and protect yourself. Muzzle dogs with a necktie or panty hose. Tie it around your dog's nose and knot it on top of his muzzle, then draw the ends beneath his chin and knot again. Finally, pull the ends back and tie them behind his ears. (For an illustration of this technique, see page 17.) For a cat or short-nosed dog like a pug, slip a pillowcase over his head. Do not do either, however, if your pet is having trouble breathing.

 ## FOLLOW-UP CARE

■ Nearly all pets with abdominal wounds need antibiotics to prevent or treat infection. Generally, you give the medicine two or three times a day for 10 to 21 days, depending on the situation. To pill your pet, gently press his lips against the sides of his teeth to prompt him to open his mouth, then quickly push the pill to the back of his tongue. Hold his mouth closed with one hand and stroke his throat with the other to help stimulate him to swallow, or gently blow into his nostrils so that he'll gulp. Often, a pet will lick his nose after he has swallowed. (This technique is illustrated on page 30.)

■ A cat can be tougher to pill, and you don't want her to struggle after a traumatic injury, so

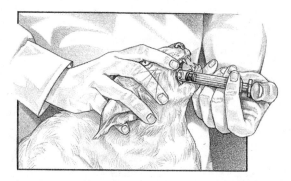

To give your pet liquid medicine, tip her head up. Then insert an eyedropper or syringe into the corner of her mouth and squirt the medicine into her cheek pouch. Stroke her throat until she swallows.

the veterinarian may prescribe liquid antibiotics. Give liquid medicine by inserting the pre-measured dropper (or needleless syringe) into the corner of your pet's mouth and slowly squirting into her cheek cavity. Tip her head up so she must swallow and so the medicine doesn't dribble out. Stroke her throat until you see her swallow; you may need to give just a few drops at a time to be that sure she gets it all.

■ Open abdominal wounds need stitches and often a drain to get rid of infectious material. Keep the area clean by gently sponging it off with a cloth or gauze pad soaked in warm water. Cats usually don't bother sutures, but dogs often lick and chew the stitches and can reopen the wound. Paint on Bitter Apple, a vile-tasting liquid, to stem the chewing or use a cone-shaped collar restraint called an Elizabethan collar so that your pet will let the wound heal. Remove it at mealtimes so he can eat.

■ Depending on the severity of the wound, you may need to limit your pet's activity and prevent him from climbing stairs or running and jumping. Crate or cage rest may be required for pets with extensive internal injuries. Walk pets only on a leash and prevent roughhousing, even if your pet wants to play, because any vigorous activity could cause reinjury or tear internal stitches.

THE BEST APPROACH

Plastic Wrap

One of the easiest, most effective, and safest first-aid bandaging techniques for open abdominal wounds is wrapping the trunk of the pet's body in plastic wrap like Saran Wrap. The plastic won't stick to the wet towel holding the internal organs, it seals out germs, and it sticks to itself so you don't have to tape it to hold it in place. It's also elastic enough that it shouldn't interfere with your pet's breathing. And it's easy for veterinary staff to remove because it won't stick to the fur and is removed easily with scissors. As your pet heals, you can also use plastic wrap to keep his bandages dry when he goes outside.

Advisors

■ Deborah Edwards, D.V.M., is a veterinarian at All Cats Hospital in Largo, Florida.

■ Al Schwartz, D.V.M., is a veterinarian at Moorpark Veterinary Hospital in California.

■ Lenny Southam, D.V.M., is a house-call veterinarian at Targwood Animal Health Care in West Chester, Pennsylvania; manager of CompuServe's VetCare Forum; and coauthor of *The Pill Book Guide to Medication for Your Dog and Cat*.

■ David Wirth-Schneider, D.V.M., is a veterinarian at the Emergency Clinic for Animals in Madison, Wisconsin.

Abscesses

CALL YOUR VET: **SAME DAY**

MEDICINE CHEST

Hot pack or compress
Washcloth
Towels
Pillowcase
Blunt scissors or electric clippers
Water-soluble lubricant (K-Y Jelly)
Warm water
Mild dishwashing detergent (Dove)
Pill syringe
Gauze pads
Elizabethan collar

An abscess develops when germs get caught beneath the skin and there's nowhere for the infection to drain as it festers. Any injury or sore that breaks the skin can cause an abscess.

Dogs aren't affected as often as cats, although they do get abscessed anal glands more often than cats. When a cat is bitten or scratched by another cat, the wounds leave tiny holes that seem designed to abscess, because cat skin heals very fast and seals in the bacteria from these injuries. Cat abscesses are almost always on the head, rump, or paw, depending on whether the cat won or lost the fight. Often, you won't even notice the abscess until the pet limps; you see a hot, red, swollen area; or the sore ruptures and drains smelly yellow, green, or bloody pus. Pets often develop fevers of 104° to 106°F.

Abscesses aren't usually dangerous, but they are extremely painful. They can also eat away the surrounding tissue and leave nasty scars if they aren't treated promptly. In rare cases, an abscess can rupture inward instead of outward and infect the entire body. But usually, after a trip to the vet, you can take care of abscesses at home.

🔥 DO THIS NOW

Draw out the infection. When the abscess is soft and swollen but hasn't yet begun to drain, you can apply hot compresses to the sore. That will help bring the infection to a head, open the wound, and speed up the healing process. Soak a washcloth in water as hot as you can stand, wring it out, and place it on top of swollen tissue. If you're using a premade hot pack or hot-water bottle, wrap it in a towel before applying. Apply the compress two to five times a day for 5 minutes on, 5 minutes off until it cools. Do not put a hot pack in the armpits or groin area.

FIRST ALERT

Bubonic Plague

Fleas can carry a type of bacteria that causes bubonic plague, the dreaded medieval disease that can make people—and cats—deathly ill. The name comes from the bubo, a painful infected swelling that appears as a symptom of the disease. In cats, a bubo forms under the chin or in the loose skin where the jaw turns into the neck around the lower jawbone. It looks exactly like an abscess. Dogs rarely get bubonic plague, but cats are exposed to plague when they eat infected rodents. The usual treatment is antibiotics, and cats tend to recover completely if treated in time.

People can get sick from handling an infected cat if they come in contact with pus. So if you live in a high-risk state—New Mexico, Arizona, Colorado, Iowa, Texas, or California—and your cat develops a suspicious swelling, don't treat it yourself. Wrap the cat in a towel and alert your veterinarian so that the veterinary staff can give proper treatment and take appropriate precautions.

Restrain your pet. Abscesses are excruciating, and your pet won't want you to touch the sore. She may even bite you unless she is safely restrained. Unfortunately, cats are hard to muzzle because their faces are so short, and often, the abscess is on the head. For head sores, have a second person grasp the cat by the scruff with one hand and by the hind feet with the other and gently hold her down against a tabletop while you treat the wound. When the abscess is on the rump or a single paw, wrap the pet's front end up in a thick towel or a pillowcase, with the back end exposed. Cats who continually fight your attempts to restrain them will probably need to be sedated or anesthetized by a vet before they can be helped.

Clip the fur. Once the abscess has begun to drain, the fur will get wet and smelly. It can stain upholstery and carpeting. Besides being messy,

fur holds the bacteria in place and can slow down the healing and make it harder to keep the area clean. Use blunt scissors or electric clippers to cut away the fur that surrounds the abscess. If you're using scissors, first slip your index and second fingers through the fur and hold them against the abscess. Cut the fur so that it's level with your fingers, clipping a 1-inch border all the way around the abscess. (This technique is illustrated on page 114.) If the skin is broken, fill the wound with a water-soluble lubricant like K-Y Jelly before you clip. Then thoroughly rinse the abscess with lukewarm water after you've finished trimming. The trimmed fur sticks to the jelly and washes out.

Clean the area. The tissue inside a ruptured abscess looks red and granular. This means that the sore is starting to heal, but you still need to clean the pus away as it drains. Wash the area with lukewarm water. You can use a mild dish-washing detergent like Dove to get pus out of the fur. If the fur is really matted with pus, try holding a warm, very wet cloth on the area for 10 to 15 minutes to soften the crust. Then wash with soap and rinse gently.

FOLLOW-UP CARE

■ Most pets with abscesses need antibiotics for 10 days or longer. It's important that they take *all* the medicine to be sure that the infection is cured. For dogs, you can hide pills in a treat like cheese and they'll wolf it down, but cats tend to eat the treat and leave the pill. To pill a cat, put the palm of your hand on top of the cat's head so that your thumb is on one side and your index or middle finger is on the other. Press the cat's lips against his teeth. Usually, this is enough to prompt him to open wide so you can push the pill to the back of his throat. Or use a pill syringe—a hollow plastic dispenser available at pet-supply stores—to get the pill into your cat's mouth. Then close his mouth and stroke his throat until you see him swallow. (This technique is illustrated on page 31.)

■ Depending on how deep or large the abscess is, your vet may stitch the wound or put a soft latex tube drain under the skin. The drain ensures that the wound won't heal over and reab-scess. Stitches should stay in place for 1 to 2 weeks; drains generally should be removed in 24 to 72 hours, depending on the amount and type of drainage. During this time, you need to keep the area clean. Moisten a clean cloth or gauze pad with warm water and wipe away the drainage as often as needed. Cats often keep themselves clean, and that's fine as long as they don't pull out the stitches or the drain.

■ Dogs who have stitches or drain tubes tend to chew at the incision and pull out the sutures. You can put a cone-shaped collar restraint called an Elizabethan collar on your dog to keep him from reaching the sore until it heals. Remove it at mealtimes so he can eat.

THE BEST APPROACH

Pillowcase Restraints

Cats are notoriously hard to hold when they don't want to be touched. You can be bitten or clawed when the cat struggles to break your hold, even if she's normally gentle. Veterinarians who specialize in cats say that using a pillowcase is the perfect way to restrain a cat. Cats often stop struggling if they can't see what's happening, and the fabric helps confine those sharp claws. To work on the cat, you can keep the injured body part exposed at the open end of the pillowcase.

Advisors

■ Deborah Edwards, D.V.M., is a veterinarian at All Cats Hospital in Largo, Florida.

■ Larry Edwards, D.V.M., is a veterinarian at Canyon Creek Pet Hospital in Sherman, Texas.

■ Lenny Southam, D.V.M., is a house-call veterinarian at Targwood Animal Health Care in West Chester, Pennsylvania; manager of CompuServe's Vet Care Forum; and coauthor of *The Pill Book Guide to Medication for Your Dog and Cat.*

Airborne Allergies

CALL YOUR VET: **IF NEEDED**

Pets can develop allergies to the same things that cause people to have hay fever. Airborne particles like house dust, plant pollen, and molds are invisible, but breathing them can make your pet's life miserable if he's allergic to them. Unlike people, who have sneezing fits and teary eyes, allergic pets get itchy skin.

Here's why: Specialized cells called mast cells react to the substance and produce histamine, which causes the allergic reaction. People have the greatest concentration of mast cells in their respiratory tracts, which is why they get runny noses, asthma, and hay fever. But dogs and cats have most of their mast cells in their skin, so they break out.

Usually, dogs with inhalant allergies suffer itchiness in the front halves of their bodies. They react with face rubbing, foot licking, armpit scratching, and neck and chest itchiness. Some cats break out with tiny bumps all over the head and neck, while others develop big, flat, red patches of thick skin on the thighs and groin.

 DO THIS NOW

Try an antihistamine. Antihistamines like Benadryl may help soothe your pet's itchy skin until you can get him to the vet. It also has the side effect of causing drowsiness, which can stop the scratching as well. The liquid usually comes in a dose of 12.5 milligrams per teaspoon; pills are usually 25 milligrams each. Pets will need 1 milligram for each pound of body weight every 6 to 8 hours. That means a 10-pound cat or dog should get about ¾ teaspoon of liquid or half a pill.

Soak your pet. The most effective first aid for itchy skin is a cool-water soak. Hot water aggravates the itch, but cool to cold water reduces the inflammation. Fill the tub or sink (or use the hose outside) and gently rinse your pet's skin for 10 to 20 minutes. If a daily bath for 3 to 4 days doesn't do the trick, call your vet.

An oatmeal bath is very effective at reducing itchiness. Use a product like Aveeno or fill a cotton sock with oatmeal and run the bathwater over it, although this may not be as effective as a specially formulated product.

 ## FOLLOW-UP CARE

■ Dogs and cats with inhalant allergies have a real problem avoiding allergy triggers because their fur traps pollen and mold spores and holds them close to their skin where they can breathe them. Some of these pollens can actually be absorbed through the skin and cause a reaction. One of the best home treatments is shampooing to wash debris out of the fur. Frequent baths— up to three times a week—are very helpful, and the cool bathwater is soothing.

■ Use shampoo that contains oatmeal or other natural ingredients. Pets with allergies are often sensitive to perfumes, dyes, and animal proteins, so check the ingredient list and avoid them.

■ Dogs with inhalant allergies often have very itchy feet, and they'll lick and chew their toes constantly. The footpads and webs of the toes have an enormous number of blood vessels near the skin surface, so anything that the dog steps in—like grass pollen—can potentially be absorbed. Soak your dog's feet in an oatmeal conditioner solution three times a week. You can find oatmeal products at pet-supply stores.

■ Dogs and cats respond very well to essential fatty acid (EFA) supplements, which are important to healthy skin. Look for those that contain omega-3 and omega-6 fatty acids. Many EFA products are available from pet-supply stores, but the best ones are sold over the counter at veterinary offices. You can sprinkle a powder onto your pet's food or use the capsule form. EFA will help moisturize your pet's skin and give a sheen to his coat, plus, he will benefit from their anti-itch properties.

THE BEST APPROACH

Allergy Shots

When your pet is allergic to something he breathes, the first step in curing the allergy is to identify the culprit. To do that, veterinary dermatologists use allergy tests similar to those used with people.

Once your veterinarian has identified the allergens, he will vaccinate your pet with tiny amounts of the substances on an ongoing basis. He may start out with three or more injections a week, then taper to one a week or less frequently. Improvement from this immunotherapy can be slow, and treatment usually must continue for at least a year before there's marked improvement.

Advisors

■ Lowell Ackerman, D.V.M., is a veterinarian at Mesa Veterinary Hospital in Scottsdale, Arizona, and author of *Skin and Coat Care for Your Dog* and *Skin and Coat Care for Your Cat.*

■ Steven A. Melman, V.M.D., is a veterinarian and dermatological consultant at Derma Pet, a pet skin-care products company in Potomac, Maryland.

■ Susette Nygaard, D.V.M., is a veterinarian at East Lake Veterinary Hospital in Dallas.

Anal Gland Impaction

CALL YOUR VET: **IF NEEDED**

MEDICINE CHEST

Blunt scissors or electric clippers
Disposable medical gloves
Hemorrhoid cream (Preparation H)
Elizabethan collar
Clean cloth
Warm water
Unflavored psyllium supplement (Metamucil)
Washcloth

Dogs and cats have two glands, or sacs, beneath the skin near the anus—one on each side. They are similar to a skunk's scent glands, and they give each pet's anal region and feces a distinctive odor—kind of a smelly business card that other animals can recognize. The glands secrete a liquid that's usually pressed out, or expressed, during each bowel movement. When the feces are too soft and don't exert enough pressure to empty the glands as they pass, or if the glands produce too much, the liquid can thicken and clog up the glands. Cats almost never have anal gland problems, but dogs do, and toy dog breeds have anal gland impaction more often than bigger dogs.

Pets with anal gland problems tend to lick themselves a lot, or they may "scoot" or drag their bottoms against the floor in an effort to open up the impaction. A clogged anal gland is tender and swollen. It can eventually abscess and rupture, with lots of bloody or pussy drainage. This requires a visit to the vet right away. You can use first aid to empty clogged glands and fix the problem, but once the sacs are infected, your pet needs medical help to clear up the infection. You'll know that your pet's glands have become infected if they are red, discolored, and very painful. Other signs include fever, loss of appetite, and lethargy. First aid can speed up the healing process and relieve the discomfort.

DO THIS NOW

Get a good grip. When you treat the rear end of your pet, you have very little control over the biting end—you can't lift his tail and hold his head at the same time. You'll need to hold him firmly because treating sore anal glands can be very painful, and he'll struggle and try to get away. So enlist another pair of hands to restrain your dog. Set a small dog on a table or coun-

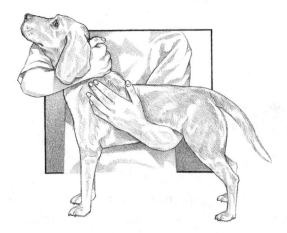

Have a second person restrain your dog before you try to express his anal sacs. The best way is to bring one arm underneath and around your dog's neck while reaching with the other arm under and around your dog's chest to immobilize him.

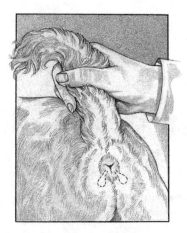

To find your dog's anal sacs, lift his tail over his back. The anal sacs are located at the 5 and 7 o'clock positions near the anus. If they feel round like peas or marbles, they may be impacted and need to be expressed.

tertop; kneel beside a large dog on the floor. Bring one arm underneath and around the dog's neck in a kind of half-nelson to snug him to your chest. Use the other arm to reach under and around his chest, pulling him even closer against you.

Clip your pet's fur. If the fur beneath your pet's tail is long, clip it off carefully using either blunt scissors or electric clippers. This will help you see what's going on and also make the area easier to treat and keep clean. If an anal gland is abscessed or has ruptured, the weeping sore tends to deposit matter in the fur, and your dog can leave stains wherever he sits.

Drain the glands. When your dog has been scooting or licking a lot, try emptying the glands manually to give him some relief. You'll want to wear disposable medical gloves (available in drugstores) and an old T-shirt for this because the contents of the sacs have a very strong, nasty odor that you don't want squirted on good clothes.

To empty the sacs, first lift the tail up and gently pull it over the dog's back. This will expose the rectal area and pull the skin taut over the sacs. The anal sacs are located at the 5 and 7 o'clock positions on the anus, and you should be able to feel them if they are full—they'll feel a bit like peas or marbles under the skin. The ducts that empty them to the outside are higher—at 4 and 8 o'clock. Using your thumb and forefinger, squeeze in a C-shaped sweeping arc to literally milk the substance out. Start below the 5 and 7 o'clock positions and milk upward. The material will be dark brown to clear. If it's yellow or blood-streaked, your dog may have an infection and need antibiotics from a veterinarian.

FIRST ALERT

Perianal Tumors

A swollen spot on one side of a dog's anus may look similar to an anal gland impaction or abscess, but instead, it may be a growth called a perianal gland tumor. These grow from specialized sebaceous glands in the skin of the tail area. They are stimulated to grow by a male hormone, probably testosterone, which is why they are three times more common in unneutered male dogs than in females. Most affected dogs are older than 7 years, and Siberian huskies, Samoyeds, Pekingese, and cocker spaniels are affected most often.

The tumors at first look like small, rubbery, rounded warts. They grow slowly but can get very large, break through the skin, ulcerate, and bleed. Perianal tumors make it hard for a dog to keep himself clean, and they can get in the way of normal bowel movements. Most are benign, although the less frequently occurring malignant growths can spread and potentially kill a pet. The usual treatment is to surgically remove the tumor and neuter the male dog to eliminate the hormone that prompts the tumor growth.

Any growth that appears on your pet should be examined by your vet. Once he examines it, he can determine whether it should be removed or left alone.

Soothe him with a cream. For mild irritations that are red and itchy but not infected, use hemorrhoid cream (like Preparation H) to help your dog feel better. You can apply the cream up to four times a day, but don't use a suppository more than once a day. Keep him from licking off the cream until it's absorbed—give him a treat to keep him busy or fit him with a cone-shaped collar restraint called an Elizabethan collar so that he can't reach his nether regions. (Remove it at mealtimes so he can eat.) If the area doesn't clear up in a couple of days, you'll need to take him to the vet.

Give him a compress. Use a warm, wet compress on the area if it's too sore to touch. Even when your dog has a severe infection, you can slip a compress beneath his tail and let him sit on it. Simply soak a clean cloth in warm tap water and squeeze out the excess water. When the cloth cools off, repeat the soaking process. Most dogs welcome the treatment as soon as they realize that it feels good. The warmth and moisture bring blood into the area and help relieve the inflammation. Use the compress for at least 10 minutes at a time, three times a day.

 FOLLOW-UP CARE

■ If there is an infection, your vet will prescribe antibiotics, and you'll need to give them to your dog for at least 10 days. You can hide pills in tasty treats like a hunk of cheese, or you can pill the dog. To give a dog a pill, grasp his muzzle with one hand, pressing his lips gently against the teeth on each side to prompt him to open his mouth. Then push the pill to the back of his tongue in the center—if it lands on the side of his tongue, he'll probably hold it in his cheek and spit it out later. Once the pill is in the center of his tongue and as far back as possible, close his mouth with your hand and stroke his throat until you see him swallow. You can also immediately follow the pill with a treat so that he'll swallow the pill automatically. (This technique is illustrated on page 30.)

■ Continue to treat the area with warm, wet compresses as often and for as long as the dog will take it—an hour or more at a time would be great, especially if the impacted gland is starting to come to a head. The warm packs speed up the healing process and can help open up the infection, and they also help it drain.

■ Keep the area clean. Use a clean washcloth with warm water to gently clean the infected area.

THE BEST APPROACH

Fiber Cure

Increasing fiber in their diets is an easy and safe way to help most dogs express their anal glands naturally with each bowel movement. Any of the commercial "lite" formula diets contain higher amounts of fiber and will work, but the dog will need to eat a larger amount of a lite food compared with a "regular" diet to maintain his body weight.

Most canned foods have less fiber than their dry counterparts, although you can talk to your vet about the therapeutic high-fiber canned foods that are now available. If your dog eats a canned diet, you can mix in a tablespoon of an unflavored psyllium supplement like Metamucil per cup of food to increase the fiber. Whatever food your dog eats, you could also offer him some fresh vegetables as treats to increase the fiber in his stool —many dogs like raw carrots, cabbage, or celery. Be aware, though, that adding fiber to your dog's diet will not only help express his anal glands but will also increase the volume of his deposits.

Advisors

■ Larry Edwards, D.V.M., is a veterinarian at the Canyon Creek Pet Hospital in Sherman, Texas.

■ Martha S. Gearhart, D.V.M., D.A.B.V.P., is a veterinarian at Pleasant Valley Animal Hospital in New York.

■ Chris Johnson, D.V.M., is a veterinarian at Westside Animal Emergency Clinic in Atlanta.

Arrow Wounds

CALL YOUR VET: **IMMEDIATELY**

Arrow wounds in cats and dogs aren't terribly common, but they can happen if people misuse weapons either accidentally or maliciously. Free-roaming pets are at highest risk. Dogs sometimes will run sticks or posts into themselves accidentally by misjudging a leap, and these injuries are treated in the same way as arrow wounds.

Hunting arrows are designed to bring down deer or larger animals and can cause tremendous damage in a dog or cat, especially if the arrow enters the chest or abdomen. (For more information about abdominal wounds, see page 55; for chest wounds, see page 128.)

Arrows can break bones and cause limping and internal or external bleeding, and they can puncture the lungs and cause labored or shallow breathing from the pain. Pets can collapse from the shock and die within a very short time. Immediate medical attention is vital, and first-aid can reduce further injury during the trip to the hospital.

🩹 DO THIS NOW

Don't remove the arrow. A hunting arrow is often very sharp or even barbed, and you'll hurt your pet by trying to pull it out or push it through the body. You could cut an artery or blood vessel, do more damage to the tissues, or even injure an organ. So leave the arrow in place.

Muzzle your pet. Pets who have been injured with an arrow are often in pain and tend to bite out of reflex, not because they are vicious. Protect yourself and your pet by muzzling him so that you can help. For long-nosed dogs, you can use a long scarf, panty hose, or necktie. Loop the material around his muzzle and knot it on top of his nose, then tie once more under his chin. Finally, draw the ends of the material back and tie them firmly behind the ears. (This technique is illustrated on page 17.) For short-faced pet like a pug or a cat, you can fit a pillowcase over his head to give him something else to use his teeth on. If your pet appears to be having trouble breathing, however, don't muzzle him or attempt to cover his face in any way.

Cut off the arrow shaft. Once your pet has been muzzled and you can safely help him, cut off the long exposed shaft so that it won't be bumped or jiggled during the trip to the hospital. If the arrow has a wooden shaft, try using a small pruning tool to cut it. Rather than cutting the shaft flush with your pet's body, leave a couple of inches exposed so that the veterinarian can easily see the wound and grasp the shaft, if needed.

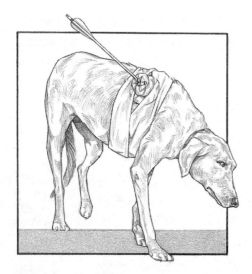

Stabilize an arrow in your pet's body by twisting a small towel to form a rope, coiling it around the base of the arrow, and fastening it with a safety pin. Then wrap plastic wrap in layers around your pet's body and over the towel to immobilize the arrow until you can get to the vet.

Immobilize the arrow. Many commercial hunting arrows are made of a composite material or metal that's not easy to cut without jiggling the shaft, and that risks further injury to your pet. You can usually look at the arrow to determine if the shaft is made of wood or something else. If it's not wood and you can't cut it, stabilize it by bandaging around it. Wrap a clean kitchen towel, hand towel, or bubble wrap gently around the base of the shaft where it enters the skin and bind it with a piece of plastic wrap like Saran Wrap. Then get your pet to the vet immediately, with as little jostling as possible.

Control the bleeding. An arrow can penetrate deeply, and if it cuts an artery, there can be severe bleeding, especially when it enters the chest or abdomen. Apply direct pressure and elevate the wound to help control and slow the bleeding until you can get help. Use a sterile gauze pad, a clean cloth like a washcloth, or even a sanitary napkin, and hold it against the injury with your hand. (You'll have to put pressure on the edges of the wound, around the arrow shaft.) If the blood soaks through, put another pad on top of the first and keep up the pressure; removing the first pad could disrupt the clot that's forming and make the bleeding worse. (Fore more information about bleeding, see page 95.)

Keep your pet still. Transport your pet on a stable object so you don't jiggle the arrow and cause more injury. An arrowhead is usually razor-sharp, and any movement could saw into the flesh and cause more serious bleeding. Medium to large dogs can rest on the backseat or cargo area of the car, with the arrow wound up. Put small pets in a box or pet carrier. You could even use a trash-can lid lined with a soft towel to transport cats or small dogs. It doesn't matter if the lid is plastic or metal; just be sure that it's sturdy enough to bear the pet's weight without buckling.

Watch for shock. The pain and bleeding from an arrow wound can cause shock, which disrupts the normal flow of blood and can kill a pet in 10 to 20 minutes. Shock will make your pet's gums turn pale, and he could lose consciousness. If his gums are still pink, you may still have a little time to get him help. Cover him with a blanket to keep him warm and quiet to help slow down the process. You can also put a drop or two of Karo syrup or honey on your pet's gums to help keep him conscious. (For more information about shock, see page 333.)

 FOLLOW-UP CARE

■ Puncture wounds caused by arrows plant bacteria deep beneath the skin. That's a prime opportunity for infection. Most pets will need antibiotics prescribed by the vet for a couple of weeks after they come home. For dogs, you can hide pills in a hunk of cheese or another treat. Cats tend not to be fooled so easily, though, so use a pill syringe and follow it with the treat to reward the cat. (This technique is illustrated on page 31.)

■ Some pets will have stitches or drains to keep the wound open, and it's important to keep the wound clean and dry until it heals. Use a cotton ball or gauze pad soaked in warm water to wipe away any discharge.

■ Keep your pet quiet until the injury has begun to heal, and avoid too much exercise, which could break open the wound or stress the damaged muscle. Your pet shouldn't run, jump, or climb stairs unless okayed by your veterinarian. You may need to confine him in a small room and carry him up and down the stairs until he's more mobile. Ask your vet exactly how and for how long your pet should be kept quiet.

■ Dogs can be bad about licking or chewing sutures. You can paint or spray Bitter Apple on the area—it tastes nasty, and it helps prevent your pet from bothering the wound. Or you can fit your dog with a cone-shaped collar restraint called an Elizabethan collar that keeps him from reaching the tender place with his teeth. It is almost impossible for a dog to eat while wearing this collar, though, so remove it for meals and replace it afterward.

Advisors

■ Deborah Edwards, D.V.M., is a veterinarian at All Cats Hospital in Largo, Florida.

■ James M. Harris, D.V.M., is a veterinarian at Montclair Veterinary Hospital in Oakland, California.

■ Mike McFarland, D.V.M., is a veterinarian at the Emergency Animal Clinic in Dallas.

■ Lenny Southam, D.V.M., is a house-call veterinarian at Targwood Animal Health Care in West Chester, Pennsylvania; manager of CompuServe's Vet Care Forum; and co-author of *The Pill Book Guide to Medication for your Dog and Cat*.

Asthma Attacks

CALL YOUR VET: **IMMEDIATELY**

Asthma is very rare in dogs but common in cats, especially Siamese. It usually comes on slowly, and you may not notice the first few attacks. Coughing is the main symptom. You'll see your cat crouched low, with her head extended and elbows away from her body. Cats having more serious attacks will visibly struggle to breathe. They'll strain and gasp, and their mouths will hang open. In some cases, the gums will turn purple because of a lack of oxygen.

Asthma usually needs to be treated with medications. Here's how to handle an attack until you can get your cat to a veterinarian.

DO THIS NOW

Get your cat into a cool place. Cool temperatures reduce the body's need for oxygen.

Get her into a quiet place. Noise and turmoil in the environment speed the metabolism, increasing the body's demand for oxygen. Try to get your cat to a quiet place, preferably away from other pets or noisy children.

Give her fresh air. Asthma attacks are usually triggered by something in the environment. It could be cigarette smoke. It could be dust. It could be paint fumes. Whatever the cause, taking your cat out of the area and giving her fresh air to breathe can reduce the severity of the attack. If the attack occurs in a room that you're remodeling, for example, put her in another room and set up a fan on a low speed to keep fresh air flowing.

Get her to the vet. Severe asthma attacks can restrict breathing completely, causing a cat to faint. When that happens, she needs to see a veterinarian immediately. Try not to touch or hold your cat more than you need to, because physical contact will increase her overall stress and make it harder for her to breathe. Use a pet carrier or box to transport her to the vet.

Help her breathe. Cats who lose consciousness may or may not start breathing on their

How to Give a Shot

For cats with severe asthma, attacks can be life-threatening. You won't have the luxury of waiting to get to a veterinarian. You'll need to know how to give the proper medicines by injection. (Talk to your vet about doing this yourself at home.)

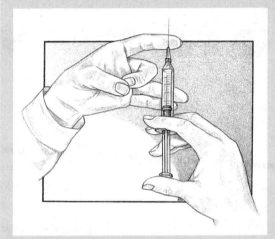

Draw the specified amount of medication into the syringe. Point the needle at the ceiling while thumping the syringe with your finger. This will shake air bubbles into the top of the needle. Slightly press the plunger to squeeze out the air. When a tiny drop of fluid comes from the needle, the air is out.

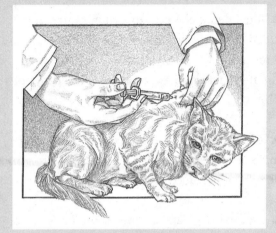

To give your cat an injection, first put her on a countertop or table. Pull up the loose skin over her shoulders with one hand while inserting the needle horizontally with the other.

own. Be prepared to give artificial respiration. Since an asthma attack makes it difficult for cats to exhale, you'll have to help with that as well. Close your cat's mouth with your hands, give two quick breaths into her nose, and watch to see if her chest rises. Give 15 to 20 breaths a minute, gently pressing on the chest after each breath to help her exhale. Keep breathing for your cat until she starts breathing again on her own or until you reach medical help.

While you're doing artificial respiration, stop every minute or so to check for a heartbeat by either feeling or listening to your cat's chest. If her heart stops beating, you'll need to start CPR. (Fore more information on these techniques, see page 19.)

✎ FOLLOW-UP CARE

■ Cats with asthma will keep having attacks as long as they're exposed to whatever it is they're sensitive to. Each cat is different. Chemical scents from carpet freshener, hair spray, and paint commonly trigger attacks. So do pollen and dust. You'll need to figure out what your cat is reacting to, then keep her away from it.

■ You'll definitely want to switch to unscented and dust-free litter. Litter boxes with lids can be a problem because they trap dust when cats use them. You'll also want to avoid feather toys or pillows.

■ Run a humidifier during the winter, when the air is dry. Breathing cool, humidified air can significantly reduce the risk of attacks.

■ Cats with severe asthma sometimes need emergency medicine to help them breathe. Inhalers work for people, but not for cats. Your veterinarian may give you a prescription for injectable asthma drugs such as epinephrine (EpiPen), aminophylline (Slo-bid), or terbutaline (Brethine). You'll be given syringes and taught how to give an injection when your cat needs emergency help.

■ Nearly all cats with asthma need to take medications several times a week. Drugs such as prednisolone (Prelone), given orally, help fight inflammation in the lungs. At first, your cat may need to take the medications daily, but once the asthma is under control, she may be able to take them as little as once a week. (See page 30 for instructions for pilling a cat.)

THE BEST APPROACH

Air Purifiers

Dust, pollen, and other airborne particles are among the most common triggers of asthma in cats. Veterinarians often recommend using an air purifier. One of the best is the Pure Air 2500, which can handle an area as large as 2,500 square feet.

Unlike many purifiers, which depend on filters, the Pure Air 2500 uses catalytic oxidation. Gas inside a sealed quartz tube is electrically stimulated. This generates ultraviolet radiation, ions, and ozone that are similar to the radiation in sunlight. The ions collect the dust, pollen, and other particles in the room and eventually settle them on the ground, leaving the air free of pollutants. You can purchase the Pure Air 2500 from the manufacturer's Web site, www.rgf.com, or call (800) 842-7771.

Advisors
■ Gerald Brown, D.V.M., is a veterinarian at City Cat Doctor in Chicago.

■ Melissa A. Gates, D.V.M., is a veterinarian at Cordova Veterinary Hospital in Rancho Cordova, California.

■ James M. Harris, D.V.M., is a veterinarian at Montclair Veterinary Hospital in Oakland, California.

■ H. Ellen Whiteley, D.V.M., is a veterinarian in Guadalupita, New Mexico, and author of *Understanding and Training Your Cat or Kitten.*

Back Injuries

CALL YOUR VET: **IMMEDIATELY**

Back injuries are particularly dangerous because often, a pet's spinal cord is so damaged that the pet becomes paralyzed. Most back injuries happen from car accidents or other severe trauma. A tiny dog could suffer a back injury from a dictionary that falls on him. But dogs also injure their backs by jumping on and off furniture the wrong way. This is especially true of breeds that have short legs and long bodies, like dachshunds, basset hounds, and corgis. Poodles and cocker spaniels also have a high incidence of back injury.

The most severe back injuries cause loss of feeling below the injury. Typically, the pet can't use his hind legs or stand up. Even if the pet still has feeling left, he'll be in such extreme pain that he won't want to stand or walk and may cry out and yelp when touched. Pets with other types of spinal injuries may walk with a wobbly gait or "toe-under" the back feet (walk on the tops of the paws instead of the pads) because they've lost the feeling in their hind paws.

Pets with injured backs need emergency medical attention as soon as possible. First aid helps get them that help without causing further injury.

DO THIS NOW

Keep your pet as quiet and still as possible. Don't encourage him to try to stand or walk, and calm him down with petting so that he doesn't struggle; any movement can damage the spinal cord even more.

Move your pet cautiously. It's most important to get your pet to the clinic as quickly as possible, but in a safe way that doesn't jar or move his back. Putting your pet on a rigid surface like a board is best, but for small pets, you

FIRST ALERT

Wobbler's Syndrome

Dogs can develop a relatively rare condition called cervical spondylopathy, or wobbler's syndrome, that causes a misalignment of the bones in the neck. This puts pressure on the spinal cord, so the dog gradually loses sensation in his rear end, and his hind legs "wobble" when he walks.

Great Danes and Doberman pinschers are most often affected. The disease gets worse and worse until the dog becomes paralyzed, first in the rear legs, then in the front limbs. The cause remains a mystery, and though there's no cure, some dogs are helped by steroid therapy or surgery.

If you suspect that your pet has this condition, take him to the vet to be examined. You don't have to make a frantic trip to the emergency room, but you should get to your vet as soon as possible. If your dog exhibits these neurological symptoms suddenly, however, and they quickly worsen, it's an emergency, and you should head for the clinic right away.

can use a large book, a cookie sheet, or even the blade of a snow shovel or the lid of a trash can, as long as it is sturdy enough to hold your pet's weight without buckling. Set the carrier object directly beside your pet. Gently slide a sheet or towel under him, then use the fabric to gently pull him horizontally onto the rigid surface. The goal is to get your pet on or in the carrier with as little jostling as possible. A box or pet carrier that you can easily place the pet inside is also a good choice for small pets.

If you have a larger dog who has a crate, simply take the lid off the crate (you will probably have to take the door off first) and then gently ease your pet into the crate by sliding the towel or sheet. You can also use a sheet of plywood or even an ironing board to

transport bigger dogs. Two people should move a big pet onto the carrier surface, with one lifting at the shoulders and neck and the other at the hips. Coordinate your movements so that both of you lift and move the dog at the same time and keep his back as motionless as possible. Or better yet, slide a towel or sheet under the dog, then both of you lift at the same time. If you don't have a rigid object, put the dog on a blanket and use it as a stretcher. Once the dog is on the board or blanket, each person should pick up an end to carry him to the car. One of you should sit with your pet and try to keep him calm and still during transport.

If you can't find anyone to help, gently work a sheet or blanket under your dog, trying to

If your pet has suffered a back injury, it's important to immobilize him before transporting him to the vet. One way is to place your cat or dog on a board, cover him with a towel, and use strong tape to secure the towel to the board to immobilize him.

move him as litttle as possible. Then drag the sheet or blanket onto the flat, rigid object. Carry the dog to your car with minimal jostling. If the flat object won't fit in your car, use it as a ramp. Hold two corners of the blanket in each hand and gently drag your dog off the ramp and onto the car seat or cargo area.

Keep your pet still. When moving a pet on a flat, rigid surface, be sure that he doesn't fall or struggle and move too much. Loosely put a towel or blanket over him to hold him on the surface. You can use duct tape (or any other strong tape that you have handy) and tape the towel or blanket down over his body just behind his front legs and in front of his hind legs to strap him down. If your pet struggles or fights at the attempt to restrain him, stop immediately so that he doesn't hurt himself even more. Then just try to let him lie quietly on the board with someone supervising him.

Guard against shock. A pet who has been hit by a car often will go into shock, a condition that shuts his circulation down and can kill him in 10 to 20 minutes. Keeping your pet covered with a blanket will help combat shock. You can also put a drop or two of Karo syrup or honey on your pet's gums to help keep him conscious.

FOLLOW-UP CARE

■ The standard care for spinal bruising and inflammation is keeping the pet quiet. Confine your pet for 4 to 6 weeks, with no running, jumping, climbing stairs, or sudden jarring activity allowed. It is important, however, to continue some physical activity, like gentle walking, to prevent muscle weakness or other problems.

■ Most pets with back injuries are prescribed medication like steroids to reduce the inflammation in the spinal cord. Dogs often get pain medicine like carprofen (Rimadyl) from the vet. If you hide pills in peanut butter, cheese, or a piece of hot dog, your dog will eat it like a treat. Be sure to talk to your vet about any medications that your pet currently takes to avoid adverse drug reactions.

Many pain medications are toxic to cats (although they can tolerate some of the newer anti-inflammatory medications). More commonly, your vet will prescribe narcotic drugs like butorphanol tartrate (Torbugesic) or an opiate drug like fentanyl (Duragesic) that's applied as a skin patch. You'll need to keep your cat from licking the drug patch, or it could make him sick. To prevent your pet from licking the area, you can have him wear a cone-shaped collar restraint called an Elizabethan collar. He won't be able to eat while wearing the collar, though, so be sure to remove it during feedings.

■ Pets who have surgery to correct back problems will need to have their sutures kept clean. Often, they'll have stitches nearly the length of their backs. Use a gauze pad dampened with warm water to wipe away any drainage or crusty discharge near the wound edges.

■ If your pet tries to chew his sutures, you can fit him with an Elizabethan collar.

■ Despite prompt first aid and medical care, spinal damage can leave pets partially paralyzed. Some dogs and cats can maintain a quality lifestyle by using special carts that allow them to get around almost as well as they did before the injury. The pet wears a harness attached to a wheeled cart where the rear legs rest, and he pulls himself around with his front legs. It's a good idea to visit your vet so that he can take the necessary measurements to ensure that the apparatus fits properly and does not chafe your pet's skin.

THE BEST APPROACH

Swimming Rehabilitation

Pets who have had back injuries take a long time to heal because any movement can redamage the spinal cord. At the same time, exercise is important to strengthen the muscles, which protect the spine and help the pet regain mobility. Swimming is one of the best ways to help recovering pets regain their strength and mobility because the water helps support their weight and also gives their leg muscles a safe workout. Some veterinary institutions have hydrotherapy pools, but the majority of clinics don't. If your dog is little, have him swim in the bathtub. For a bigger animal, talk to a friend who has a pool and see if your dog can swim there if you supervise him.

Pets who have stitches must wait for a week or so until the incision has begun to heal before heading for the pool. The water must be warm—about 88° to 92°F. Water therapists suggest that you support your pet's body with your hand beneath his chest. His feet shouldn't touch the bottom of the pool or bathtub while he paddles. A 10-minute swim session for 3 days in a row helps pets recover faster and better from back injuries. The longer the swim therapy continues, the faster your pet will recover.

Advisors

■ Shane Bateman, D.V.M., D.V.Sc., is a veterinarian board certified in the American College of Emergency and Critical Care Medicine and assistant professor of emergency and critical care medicine at Ohio State University College of Veterinary Medicine in Columbus.

■ Charles DeVinne, D.V.M., is a veterinarian at Animal Care Clinic in Peterborough, New Hampshire.

■ Billy D. Martindale, D.V.M., is a veterinarian at the Animal Hospital of Denison, Texas, and chairman of the board of directors of the Texas Veterinary Medical Association.

■ Thomas Munschauer, D.V.M., is a veterinarian at Middlebury Animal Hospital in Vermont and past president of the Vermont Veterinary Medical Association.

Bee and Wasp Stings

CALL YOUR VET: **IF NEEDED**

MEDICINE CHEST

Blanket
Karo syrup or honey
Antihistamine (Ben-
    adryl)
Credit card, dull knife,
    or fingernail file
Cold, wet washcloth
Cold pack or compress
Baking soda
Ammonia or calamine
    lotion (Caladryl)
Cotton balls
Ice cubes or ice water
Turkey baster or squirt
    gun
Oatmeal bath (Aveeno)

Dogs and cats are often stung on the face, head, or inside the mouth when they try to play with bees and wasps. Fur protects most of their bodies, but pets can be bitten or stung on their sparsely furred stomachs or flanks when they blunder into a hive or a fire-ant nest. Most of the time, the sting or bite causes minor swelling and redness that can be hard to see under the fur and is itchy or painful. First aid is usually all you'll need to relieve your pet's discomfort.

Some pets, however, can have serious allergic reactions to otherwise harmless insects. It may take only one sting for a pet's muzzle to swell up like a cantaloupe, even if he has been stung on the tail. And in rare instances, the reaction happens on the inside, too, so that a pet's throat swells and shuts off his air. Usually, this happens suddenly, and symptoms include fever or low body temperature, wheezing, trembling, weakness, pale gums, vomiting, diarrhea, rapid breathing, and collapse. This is a medical emergency called anaphylactic shock that requires immediate veterinary attention. First aid can buy you time until you reach medical help.

DO THIS NOW

For Anaphylactic Shock

Look for symptoms of shock. Anaphylactic shock is a condition in which the blood circulation shuts down. Symptoms can include pale gums, trembling, weakness, fever or low body temperature, vomiting, diarrhea, wheezing, fast breathing, and collapse. Pets can die from shock in 10 to 20 minutes unless they get veterinary help. Wrap your pet in a blanket to keep him warm and turn on the car heater if the weather is cool. You can also put a drop or two of Karo syrup or honey on your pet's gums to help keep him conscious.

FIRST ALERT

Spider Bites

Most spider bites cause painful swelling only at the site, and they're treated just like bee or wasp stings. But a handful of spiders are venomous, and after the initial sharp pain from the bite, pets can develop chills, fever, labored breathing, and shock within 30 minutes to 6 hours. First aid helps, but an injection of antivenin may be necessary, and pets may suffer partial paralysis for days until they recover.

If you suspect that your pet has been bitten by a poisonous spider, apply ice immediately to slow the spread of the venom. Put him in a pet carrier or right in the car—don't let him walk, or it could hasten the spread of the poison. Your pet needs medical treatment as soon as possible. (For more information about spider bites, see page 354.)

Treat the swelling with an OTC remedy. If your pet is conscious and able to swallow, the best thing to do is give him an over-the-counter antihistamine like Benadryl to counteract the swelling. The liquid usually comes in a dose of 12.5 milligrams per teaspoon; pills are usually 25 milligrams each. Pets will need 1 milligram for each pound they weigh; that means that a 10-pound cat or dog should get about ¾ teaspoon of liquid or half a pill. Then get your pet to the vet as soon as possible.

Drain your pet's lungs. Your pet can make gurgling noises as he struggles to breathe if his lungs fill up with fluid. Pick up a small pet by his hind legs, or lift a larger one around the hips; hold him upside down for 10 seconds or so to help drain fluid from the lungs.

Be prepared to perform artificial respiration. If your pet stops breathing, wrap your hand around his muzzle to close his mouth and blow two quick breaths into his nose, watching to see his chest rise. You may need to blow quite hard to force air past his swollen throat into his lungs. Give 15 to 20 breaths a minute until your pet begins breathing again or until you reach medical help. (This technique is illustrated on page 20.)

Check your pet's pulse or heartbeat. Place your palm or ear against the left side of your pet's chest directly behind the elbow to detect the heartbeat. You can also feel the pulse in the crease where his hind leg joins his body, because that's where the large femoral artery runs near the surface. (This technique is illustrated on page 13.)

If his heart is not beating, start CPR. For a cat or small dog, cup a hand over the point of the chest just behind the elbows. Squeeze firmly in a "coughlike" manner between your fingers and thumb, pressing in about ½ inch, about 80 to 100 times a minute. Alternate one breath for every five compressions.

For a larger dog, put him on a firm, flat surface on his side and use both hands on top of each other to compress his chest by 25 to 50%, giving a breath into the nose after every fifth compression until your pet revives or until you reach medical help. (This technique is illustrated on page 21.)

For Routine Stings and Bites

Remove the stinger. If you can see the stinger, it's best to remove it. Bees leave their stingers behind, and a stinger may continue to pump venom into the body as long as it remains in the skin. Scrape it free with a credit card, blunt knife blade, or the edge of a fingernail file.

Try an over-the-counter remedy. As long as your pet is breathing properly, he probably won't need to see a veterinarian even if his face or head swells quite a bit. An over-the-counter antihistamine like Benadryl usually takes down the swelling within 20 minutes or so. The liquid usually comes in a dose of 12.5 milligrams per teaspoon; pills are 25 milligrams. You can give 1 milligram per pound of body weight; this means that a 10-pound cat or dog would get about ¾ teaspoon of liquid or half a pill. For minor swelling, you can use a Benadryl ointment directly on the wound.

Use a cold pack or compress. This will soothe the pain and help reduce the swelling and inflammation. Rinse a clean washcloth in cold water and hold it against the swollen area, then place a cold pack or plastic bag of ice on top of the wet cloth. Apply the cold to the swelling for 10 to 30 minutes several times a day. A bag of frozen peas or corn works well as a cold pack and molds to the body contours.

Make a baking soda poultice. A poultice of baking soda will help neutralize the sting, but this can be messy in fur and isn't very practical unless the sting is on a sparsely furred area. Make a poultice by mixing 1 tablespoon of baking soda with enough water to create a thick paste and dab it on the swelling.

Give your pet relief with ammonia. Dampen a cotton ball with ammonia and dab it on fire-ant bites to relieve itching and pain. (Or you can use a calamine lotion like Caladryl.)

Try ice or baking soda. Stings inside the mouth can be hard to treat, and your pet may not allow you to touch them. You can offer ice cubes for him to lick or a bowl of ice water for him to drink. Or flush your pet's mouth with a teaspoon of baking soda mixed in a pint of water. Use a turkey baster or a squirt gun to target the sting, but be careful that your pet doesn't inhale any liquid.

✏ FOLLOW-UP CARE

■ One dose of an antihistamine like Benadryl probably won't be enough, and the swelling may come back. You can repeat the dose every 6 to 8 hours as needed.

■ Some pets develop hivelike reactions all over their bodies that cause severe itching. And any sting tends to itch as it heals. Hives usually go away in about 24 hours—sooner when treated with an antihistamine—but you can relieve the itching with cold-water soaks or oatmeal baths. Aveeno Soothing Bath Treatment works well to soothe itchy skin. A 20-minute soak twice a day will help.

■ To relieve pain in dogs, you can give acetaminophen like Tylenol. Check with your vet for dosage instructions.

■ Tylenol and aspirin-type pain relievers can be dangerous for cats. Your vet can prescribe a pain medication, or you can use an ice pack for 10 to 20 minutes a day as needed. This will work nearly as well as medication and is safe for your cat.

■ Stings inside the mouth can make pets refuse to eat because it hurts to chew. Soften food with warm water or low-fat, no-salt chicken broth, or make a puree in the blender. Feed soft food for 2 days, or until your pet can manage a regular diet again. If he hasn't eaten after 2 days, take him to the vet.

■ Pets who have experienced anaphylactic shock from an insect sting will be at risk in the future for life-threatening reactions. Your veterinarian may give you epinephrine, a drug given as an injection beneath the skin to counteract the problem, in a device such as an EpiPen.

THE BEST APPROACH

Pill Cutters

Pills for people usually come in much larger doses than a pet needs, and half a pill or less may be more than enough. You can find commercial pill cutters at pet-supply stores or in catalogs, but a quick and easy way to divide pills without buying another gadget is to use the pet nail trimmers that you may already have. Simply hold the pill in the opening where the toenail would rest and cut it to the size you need.

Advisors
■ Dale C. Butler, D.V.M., is a veterinarian at Best Friends Animal Hospital in Denison, Texas.
■ Patricia Hague, D.V.M., is a veterinarian at the Cat Hospital of Las Colinas in Irving, Texas.
■ Ken Lawrence, D.V.M., is a veterinarian at the Texoma Veterinary Hospital in Sherman, Texas.
■ Julie Moews, D.V.M., is a veterinarian at Bolton Veterinary Hospital in Connecticut.

Birthing Problems

CALL YOUR VET: **IF NEEDED**

Dogs and cats usually have few birthing problems. But dog breeds with large heads and narrow hips, like bulldogs, are prone to problems, and older, overweight, or nervous pets have more trouble. A first-time mother may not know what to expect or what to do and can create problems for herself. And if the birth canal is too small, if the pet's contractions are weak or stop, or if a baby is positioned oddly or is very large, the birth can be interrupted. This can not only become dangerous for the puppies or kittens, who may die, but it can also be painful or even life-threatening for the mother.

The birth process for dogs and cats occurs in stages, and timing is everything. The first stage is restlessness, panting, maybe vomiting or the shakes, and nesting behavior, where the dog or cat looks for the perfect place to have her babies. Contractions begin in the second stage, and the mother should deliver the first puppy or kitten within about 1 hour of the first active contractions. A translucent, amber, golf ball–size placenta emerges first, then breaks open to release amniotic fluid, and the first baby should be born within an hour or so. Dogs may take as long as 24 hours from the first stage to deliver all their babies, and cats may take about 36 hours. Once regular and frequent contractions have started or there is amniotic fluid, or both of these happen, it will usually take 4 to 6 hours for all the babies to be born. The mother may rest between births.

In most instances, you can use first aid to help the new mother have a successful birthing if she starts to have problems. But if your dog or cat acts weak, depressed, bites at her flanks in pain, labors for about an hour without a birth and is still having regular and frequent contractions, or if there's a black, yellow, or bloody vaginal discharge that smells rotten, she'll need immediate medical help. (The smell of the discharge is especially important, since there is similarly colored discharge in a normal birth.)

DO THIS NOW

Take your dog's temperature. With dogs, take the mother's temperature with a rectal thermometer lubricated with petroleum jelly. This will help pinpoint when the first stage of labor is due to begin, since the body temperature always drops a degree or two below normal (99° to 102.5°F) about 24 hours before the dog goes into labor. Once you know that the mother's temperature has dropped, you can predict that she'll be in labor within 24 hours, and the first puppy should appear about 30 to 90 minutes after regular and frequent contractions begin.

In some pets, it may be difficult to detect when these active contractions begin, so watch your pet carefully. The mother-to-be will generally become more agitated and will be working hard to get the process going. You probably won't be able to take your cat's temperature. Cats tend to be reclusive when they are going to give birth, and you may not notice behavioral changes as easily as with a dog.

Clip the fur. With longhaired dogs and cats, trim the hair around the rear end with blunt scissors or electric clippers. This not only prevents some of the mess of birthing fluids from collecting in the fur but also gets fur out of the way to prevent a puppy or kitten from becoming entangled.

✚ FIRST ALERT

Milk Fever

When a mother dog or cat does not have enough calcium in her body to support the drain from producing milk, she can develop a life-threatening condition called eclampsia, or milk fever. This usually develops during the first couple of weeks after the birth of the babies, and small-breed dogs with large litters are at highest risk.

The affected pet will become very agitated, leave the babies, pace, pant excessively, tremble, walk with a stiff-legged gait, and even develop seizures and collapse. Often, she'll develop a fever of 106°F or higher. Milk fever can cause her lips to stretch back in a bizarre grin because the low calcium causes a kind of tetany that affects the nerves and pulls the muscles in odd ways. Without treatment, the mother can die within only a few hours, so she needs emergency medical treatment as soon as possible.

The treatment involves intravenous replacement of calcium, like calcium gluconate. When given in time, it can reverse all the signs within 15 minutes. The puppies or kittens should be removed from nursing for at least 24 hours, or until the mother is stabilized, and they may need to be fed by hand until they're weaned.

Give her privacy. A hormone called oxy-tocin is released by the brain and signals your pet's body to begin labor and milk release. But the stress of having spectators, like a first-grade class or the neighborhood kids, watching the process can shut off the flow of oxytocin and stop normal uterine contrac-tions, so that what otherwise would have been a normal delivery may require cesarean surgery. The best way to get things started again is to give the mother some privacy. Shoo away the spectators, shut the door, and let your dog or cat settle down.

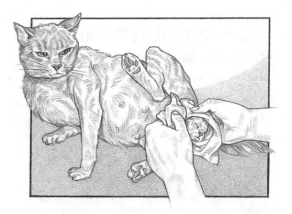

If the mother cat or dog needs help, gently guide the baby out of the birth canal in a curved motion, drawing it out and down toward the mother's legs.

Watch for problems. Puppies and kittens don't change position during the birthing process—after conception, they develop in the "horns" of the Y-shaped uterus for about 63 days and move into the birth canal from that position, either forward or backward. Puppies and kittens are very flexible, so a breech birth usually isn't an emergency. Wait to see that the puppy or kitten is progressing out—it's safe to wait up to 15 to 20 minutes while the baby is visible in the birth canal.

🥫 SPECIAL SITUATIONS

If there's no birth after 20 minutes of pushing: If the mother pushes and the baby is not born after 20 minutes, you'll need to help.

Before anything else, make sure that some-body the new mother trusts is there to talk to her and soothe her so that she remains calm while you help with the birth. Newborns are covered with a wet membrane, and they can be very slippery. So wrap a dry cloth or towel around the puppy or kitten and apply gentle pressure to pull it out.

Imagine that the baby is C-shaped, with the head at one end of the C and rear legs at the other. Don't pull straight out from the vaginal area but rather in a curve downward toward the mother's legs, in a C-shape. Time your gentle pulling to coincide with the mother's pushing—don't fight her body. It may help to have the mother standing so that gravity helps with the process.

Rotate the baby as you pull, first to one side, then to the other, with each contraction. A bit of lubricant like K-Y Jelly or petroleum jelly, applied with clean fingers to the vulvar lips and to the baby, can help a big baby slip out. Don't worry that you'll injure the baby—puppies and kittens are pretty resilient. If the puppy or kitten isn't delivered after a few minutes of your gentle assistance, you'll need to get medical help.

What about the Afterbirth?

Nature intended that mother cats and dogs eat the placentas for a couple of reasons. First, the material contains nutrients that can help fuel the mother's body and help produce milk. Second, it helps clean up the birth area and prevents odors from developing that in the wild might attract predators.

But our domestic dogs and cats don't always do what nature intends. It's a good idea for the mother to eat one or two, but it probably won't matter too much one way or another if she refuses to eat any. In fact, mothers can develop diarrhea from eating too many of the placentas. And as long as the mother is eating a highly nutritious commercial food designed for reproduction (puppy and kitten formulas are perfect—they contain more carbohydrates and fat than adult foods so that Mom doesn't have to eat so much to meet her needs), she should be in fine shape whether she eats several or none.

If the mother doesn't remove the newborn's membrane: The afterbirth that's connected to the umbilical cord contains oxygen-rich blood that will sustain the baby for a very short time. Usually, the mother will immediately begin licking the baby all over. This removes the membrane sac and stimulates the baby to start to breathe. But if the mother doesn't remove the membrane within 30 seconds, you need to at least break it open and peel it away from the kitten's or puppy's face so that the baby can breathe. The membrane will gather around the umbilical cord—take care not to pull on the cord, or it could rupture too close to the body and cause bleeding or herniation (a tear in the abdominal muscles that allows internal organs to protrude outside the body).

If the newborn doesn't start breathing: If the puppy or kitten doesn't begin breathing on his own within 10 to 30 seconds, pick up the baby in a clean towel and vigorously rub him all over, across and on both sides of the chest. This stimulates both the circulation and the lungs to start working. Stop the treatment when the baby starts to move, breathe, or cry, and return him to his mother.

Newborns may have fluid inside the mouth

To clear fluid out of a newborn's lungs, wrap her in a towel and hold her upside down, swinging her in an arcing motion to let gravity remove the fluid.

and nose that interferes with breathing. If the vigorous toweling doesn't do the trick, you can use a bulb-suction syringe that you'd use for an infant to help clear his nose.

The bulb syringe may not reach far enough inside the body. If necessary, you can clear any fluid from the baby's lungs by holding him upside down while keeping him folded safely in a towel.

Swing the puppy or kitten head-down between your legs, starting at shoulder height. Repeat the rapid arcing motion several times. That allows gravity to help clear fluid out of the lungs and respiratory tract. Be sure to grasp the baby firmly so that you don't lose your grip.

If the mother doesn't cut the umbilical cord: The mother usually will cut the umbilical cords with her teeth. Sometimes, though, there are so many babies that she doesn't get around to all of them, or she becomes distracted and

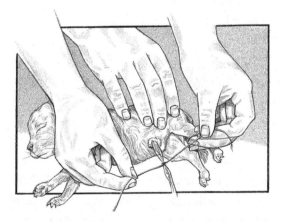

To keep a newborn's umbilical cord from bleeding, tie it off with thread before you cut it. It helps to have someone else steady the baby so you have both hands free.

neglects to cut them loose. You'll need to cut them if Mom doesn't do it herself within 2 to 3 minutes.

You can wear disposable medical gloves (available in drugstores), or at least be sure that your hands are very clean.

The cord will bleed when you cut it with scissors, so use a hemostat (clamp), which you can get at medical supply stores and from some pet-supply catalogs, or tie it off with thread before you cut it.

You can keep the thread, clamp, and scissors blades soaking in rubbing alcohol to keep them clean until you're ready to use them. Be sure to dry them with sterile gauze or a clean towel before using them.

Put the clamp or tie thread about ½ to 1 inch away from the puppy's or kitten's body. Then use very sharp scissors to cut through the cord on the far side of the tie (the order is body, clamp, and cut). Dip the end of the cord in iodine to prevent bacteria from entering through this open area. If you use thread, leave it tied onto the stump of the umbilical cord, which will eventually dry up and fall off the body. The end attached to the placenta may bleed slightly, but the placenta will detach soon from the uterus, if it hasn't already, and this bleeding is normal. However, if there is a constant dripping of blood from the mother for more than 5 to 10 minutes, she should be checked by a vet right away.

If you don't have a clamp or thread, once the placenta has passed, use gloved or very clean fingers to pinch the umbilical cord about ½ to 1 inch away from the baby's body between your

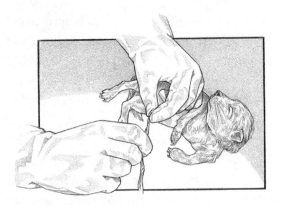

If you don't have a clamp or thread, you can crimp the blood vessels before cutting the cord by pinching it with your thumbnail and index finger.

thumbnail and first finger. Pinching firmly, saw gently across the cord with your thumbnail for 30 to 60 seconds. You're not trying to sever the cord, but this gentle sawing action will crimp and close off the blood vessels inside and make it easier to cut. Then use scissors soaked in rubbing alcohol and dried as described above to gently snip the cord on the placenta side of where you pinched the cord.

🩹 FOLLOW-UP CARE

■ Once all the puppies or kittens are born, give the mother some privacy. That will reduce her stress and allow her body to prompt milk release to feed the newborns. It's important for puppies and kittens to drink this "first milk," called colostrum, because it contains all kinds of immune factors that help protect the babies from disease.

■ If the puppies or kittens seem to have trouble getting milk after about ½ hour, the mother may be having trouble relaxing enough to release milk and may suffer from caked breasts. You can help by stimulating the nipples with a warm, wet washcloth and massaging them gently.

■ If the mother refuses to let the babies nurse from one or more breasts, she may have an infection called mastitis. If you suspect mastitis, call your veterinarian immediately. (For more information, see page 287.)

■ If the mother isn't able to nurse her babies, you'll need to provide milk for them. Commercial bitch or queen milk replacers are the best—Just Born makes both puppy and kitten formulations, or you can get KMR for kittens or Esbilac for puppies. They are available at pet-supply stores and from catalogs or from your veterinarian. The amount to feed depends on the size of the babies and the product content, so follow the directions on the package. Be sure to warm the formula as directed on the package label so that it doesn't upset the babies' tummies.

Nursing bottles are available, or you can use an eyedropper or needleless syringe. If you use a nursing bottle, check the size of the hole in the nipple by holding the filled bottle upside down without squeezing it. The formula should drip from the nipple; if it doesn't, heat a sewing needle and enlarge the hole slightly. Test the bottle again before using it to be sure that the opening is not too large. Again, the formula should drip slowly from the nipple. You can also purchase a nursing kit at pet stores that contains everything you'll need to nurse newborn puppies or kittens. When feeding, be sure to keep the puppy or kitten in a normal nursing position—on his tummy—for best results.

■ After puppies or kittens are born, the mother will have a normal vaginal discharge for up to 4 weeks, and it can be any color from red to green or even black. But if the discharge develops a foul odor or there's still lots of blood in it 3 weeks following the birth, it could signal a vaginal or uterine infection, a retained placenta, or failure of the ovaries to return to normal. She'll need medical attention as soon as possible, and the vet may prescribe antibiotics.

■ When the mother has a vaginal infection, the infants may get bacteria from the discharge. The puppies and kittens who nurse may develop diarrhea, cry, become weak, or even die. The most important steps are to remove them from the mother, feed them yourself, and keep them warm. You can fill a plastic soda bottle with hot water, wrap it in a clean towel, and let the puppies or kittens snuggle around that. (For more information about fading puppies or kittens, see page 172.)

THE BEST APPROACH
Soda-Bottle Body Warmers

Newborn puppies and kittens have no internal thermostats to keep themselves warm, and their normal body temperature ranges between 92° and 97°F. They are kept alive only by snuggling up with each other or next to their mother so they are warmed by her body temperature, which stays at about 99° to 102.5°F. Because the babies can't regulate their temperatures, they can also easily become burned from outside warming sources like heat lamps or electric pads. But one of the most effective and inexpensive ways to keep the newborns warm is with 20-ounce plastic soda bottles.

Fill the bottles with hot water and wrap each in a dry, thick kitchen towel. The towels will buffer the heat source so that the babies don't get burned. Hold the wrapped bottles on your skin—if you can comfortably tolerate the heat, they're the right temperature. The wrapped bottles will keep the puppies or kittens warm, even when Mom has to leave them alone for short periods. You can also use towel-wrapped hot water bottles to provide warmth to the babies.

Advisors
■ Lorrie Bartloff, D.V.M., is a veterinarian at Three Point Veterinary Clinic in Elkhart, Indiana.
■ Kevin Doughty, D.V.M., is a veterinarian at Mauer Animal Clinic in Las Vegas.
■ Alvin C. Dufour, D.V.M., is a veterinarian at Dufour Animal Hospital in Elkhart, Indiana.
■ A. Michelle Miller, D.V.M., is a veterinarian at Animal Aid Clinic South in Elkhart, Indiana.
■ Jeff Nichol, D.V.M., is the hospital director and a veterinarian at the Adobe Animal Medical Center in Albuquerque.

Bites from Animals

CALL YOUR VET: **SAME DAY**

Cats and dogs are sometimes bitten by wild animals like raccoons, but they're more likely to be bitten by other pets. Dogs tend to be bitten by other dogs and cats by other cats, usually over territorial disputes. Cats can also be bitten by dogs who consider them prey. Even minor bites are serious because they may become infected.

A bite from a cat punctures like a needle, so you won't notice the wound until it swells with infection and your cat limps or licks the wound. Dog bites are always serious because the long canine teeth poke a single hole in the skin but then rip the muscle underneath when the dog shakes his victim. Internal organs can tear, bones can break from the trauma, and eyes can pop from the sockets. If your pet gets bitten, take him to the vet, even if the damage appears minor. Nearly all cat bites get infected, so your vet will probably prescribe antibiotics to prevent an abscess from forming.

It takes bacteria about 1 hour to multiply enough to cause problems, so first aid during this golden period may help prevent infection. You'll also need first aid for serious wounds to control bleeding or breathing problems until you can reach help.

🩹 DO THIS NOW

Break it up. If you see your pet attacked, don't try to pull the animals apart. Instead, grab a hose and spray both animals on their heads with a blast of water until they stop. You can also use a bucket of water or some other distraction like a whistle, or just scream to make them stop.

Check your pet's breathing and heartbeat. Animal bites can puncture or bruise the lungs

FIRST ALERT

Abscesses

Dogs don't get abscesses as often as cats, because cat skin heals so quickly that it seals over puncture wounds within an hour or so of the injury. Sharp teeth plant bacteria deep beneath the skin, and with nowhere to go, bacteria fester into an abscess—a pocket of infection.

Animal bites are nearly invisible under the fur until they swell. The swelling feels hot, and the pet often develops a fever of 104° to 106°F, acts depressed, and won't eat. An abscess is very painful, and pets flinch with pain when the wound is touched. An abscess needs to be opened and cleaned out; often, it swells so much that the skin ruptures by itself. When that happens, you'll see wet fur oozing white to green, blood-tinged, smelly liquid.

Cut away the long fur from the wound (see page 92 for instructions) and clean off the infected matter with mild soap and water. Then visit your veterinarian. Deep abscesses may need surgical repair as well as antibiotics. (For more information about abscesses, see page 60.)

and heart, and pets can lose consciousness and stop breathing. You may need to give artificial respiration.

To give artificial respiration, close your pet's mouth with your hands, place your lips over her nose, and give two quick breaths. Watch to see if her chest rises. Then give 15 to 20 breaths a minute until she begins breathing again on her own or until you reach medical help. After each breath, watch for her chest to rise, then remove your lips and let the air escape. (This technique is illustrated on page 20.)

Feel or listen for a heartbeat by placing your palm or ear against her left side behind the "elbow." You can also feel the pulse in the crease where her hind leg joins her body, because that's where the large femoral artery runs near the surface. (This technique is illustrated on page 13.) If her heart stops beating, start CPR.

Perform CPR. CPR can jump-start a heart when it has stopped beating. For a small pet, cup a hand over the point of the chest just behind the elbows. Squeeze firmly in a "coughlike" manner, pressing in about ½ inch, with your thumb on one side and fingers on the other, about 80 to 100 times a minute. Alternate one breath for every five compressions.

Put a larger dog on a firm, flat surface on his side and use both hands on top of each other to compress his chest 25 to 50%. Give one breath into the nose after every fifth compression until your pet revives or you reach medical help. (This technique is illustrated on page 21.) It's best to have someone else drive to the vet's office while you're performing CPR.

Watch for signs of shock. If your pet has pale gums and is losing consciousness, it can mean a severe loss of blood either on the outside or on the inside, where you can't see it. And that can lead to shock, a condition in which the organs eventually shut down. Shock can kill your pet in as little as 10 to 20 minutes. Wrap her in a warm blanket to slow the shock process, put her in a pet carrier or on the backseat of the car, and get her to the vet immediately. You can also put a drop or two of Karo syrup or honey on your pet's gums to help keep her conscious. (For more information about shock, see page 333.)

Control bleeding. Animal bites don't bleed a lot unless a blood vessel is cut. To control bleeding, put a clean cloth or gauze pad against the wound and apply pressure. The bleeding should stop in 5 minutes or less. If the pad soaks through, put another pad on top of the first and keep up the pressure. Don't lift off the first pad or you'll disturb the clot. You can use a pressure bandage by wrapping the pad with an elastic bandage like an Ace bandage, strips of cloth, or tape.

Seek medical attention. When a leg wound continues to rapidly drip blood despite a pressure bandage, get to your vet as quickly as possible. Ask a friend to drive or to continue first aid while you drive, and apply pressure with your hand on top of the bandage until you reach the animal hospital. (For more information about bleeding and how to apply a pressure bandage, see page 95.)

Restrain your pet. Bite wounds are so painful that you usually must restrain your pet before you can treat her so that you aren't bitten, too. Wrap cats and small dogs in a towel or pillowcase that allows access to the wound. Put larger

dogs on a tabletop or kneel beside them on the floor. Bring one arm up around your dog's neck and the other arm under and around her tummy and hug her to your chest. (This technique is illustrated on page 18.)

As long as she's breathing normally, you could muzzle her to protect yourself while you treat the wound. A necktie or the leg from a pair of panty hose works well. Tie it around your pet's muzzle over her nose, then knot it again beneath her chin. Pull the ends back behind her ears and tie them. (This technique is illustrated on page 17.) For cats and snub-nosed dogs like pugs, you can use a pillowcase as described above. As with muzzling, don't do this if your pet is having trouble breathing.

Protect wounds on your pet's belly or chest. Wrap a large, clean bath towel around the wound, keeping it loose so that you don't restrict your pet's ability to breathe. Secure the towel with an elastic adhesive bandage like Elastoplast.

Keep eyes moist. If your pet has an eye out of the socket, soak a gauze pad with plain water or sterile saline contact lens solution and cover the eyeball to keep it moist until you can reach your veterinarian. (For more information, see page 169.)

Clear the area. Don't clean bites that bleed a lot, because that could keep them from forming a clot. Once wounds have stopped bleeding, you can gently clean the area. For longhaired pets, clip away the fur around the bite first so that bacteria on the fur won't infect the wound. Use

Rabies Risk

Rabies is spread through germs in the saliva of infected animals, and it affects all mammals, including people. In the 20th century, an average of 1 to 2 people a year died from rabies in the United States. Bites from wild animals like raccoons, skunks, bats, and foxes account for nearly 93 percent of cases, but domestic animals, including cats and dogs, also can infect your pet or you. In fact, 610 cases of rabid pets were reported in 1997, with twice as many cats as dogs infected. Iowa and Pennsylvania report the most cases, probably because of the wild animals in those areas that infect cats and dogs.

In most states, rabies vaccination is required by law for cats and dogs because it protects pets even if they get bitten by a rabid animal. It's important to find out if the animal that has bitten your pet has had a vaccination. The bitten pet should be revaccinated and quarantined to be sure that she's not infected. Once an animal develops symptoms, rabies is always fatal.

the wound with warm water after you've finished. The trimmed fur sticks to the jelly and washes out.

Clean the area with peroxide. Use a small amount of 3% hydrogen peroxide on a clean washcloth to wipe off the area surrounding visible wounds; warm water also works fine. Don't pour straight hydrogen peroxide on open wounds, however, because it will damage living cells and make healing more difficult. Hydrogen peroxide will also effectively bleach blood from fur, the floor, or furniture.

Numb the pain with ice. Pain medicine like aspirin can interfere with clotting and make bleeding worse. Instead, apply an ice pack within the first half-hour after the bite to dull the pain. It will also help reduce swelling and bruising from crushing bites. Rinse a clean washcloth in cold water and hold it against the injury, then place a cold pack or plastic bag of ice on top. Do this for 10 to 30 minutes several times a day. A bag of frozen peas or corn works well as a cold pack to mold to the body contours.

FOLLOW-UP CARE

■ It's important to keep puncture wounds like cat bites open so that they'll drain and avoid sealing in bacteria that cause infection. Apply cold compresses several times a day for 10 to 30 minutes (depending on how long your pet will tolerate it). If you were late in detecting the bite and an infection seems to be developing, use hot packs wrapped in a towel two to five times daily, for 5 minutes on, 5 minutes off until it cools.

electric clippers if you have them, or clip carefully with blunt scissors. If you're using scissors, first slip your index and second fingers through the fur and hold them against the wound. Cut the fur so that it's level with your fingers, clipping a 1-inch border all the way around the wound. (This technique is illustrated on page 114.) If the skin is broken, fill the wound with K-Y Jelly before you clip. Then thoroughly rinse

Don't apply a hot pack to a fresh wound, though; it can make the bleeding worse. And do not put a hot pack in the armpit or groin area.

■ Nearly all pets who have animal bites need antibiotics to fight infection. Your veterinarian may give your pet an injection, but often you'll need to give pills every day for 7 to 10 days.

To give a pill, you can try hiding it in something tasty, like peanut butter or cheese. This works better for dogs than cats, though. Dogs and cats will open their mouths if you gently press their lips against the sides of their teeth. Once your pet's mouth opens, push the pill to the back of her tongue with your finger or use a commercial pill syringe (available at pet-supply stores). Then close her mouth and stroke her throat until you see her swallow. Watch for her to lick her nose—that generally means she has swallowed. If you haven't given your pet a pill before, handle her carefully—she may bite. (For more on how to pill a cat, see page 31.)

■ Animal bites often need stitches and a soft latex drainage tube put under the skin to keep serum and infected fluids from collecting. Keep the area clean and dry by wiping away any

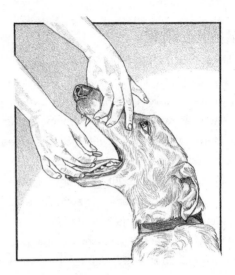

To give your pet a pill, press his lips against the sides of his teeth. Once he opens his mouth, place the pill on the back of his tongue, close his mouth, and stroke his throat until he swallows.

drainage with a little 3% hydrogen peroxide or warm water along the suture line.

■ Some pets lick at or chew their wounds or stitches, and that interferes with healing. A protective bandage won't work, because it's best to leave bite wounds open to the air to speed healing. Prevent your pet from bothering the wound with an Elizabethan collar, a cone-shaped restraint that fits over her head. You'll need to take it off when she eats.

Advisors

■ James M. Harris, D.V.M., is a veterinarian at Montclair Veterinary Hospital in Oakland, California.

■ Al Schwartz, D.V.M., is a veterinarian at Moorpark Veterinary Hospital in California.

■ Daniel Simpson, D.V.M., is a veterinarian at West Bay Animal Hospital in Warwick, Rhode Island, and spokesperson for the Rhode Island Veterinary Medical Association.

■ Lenny Southam, D.V.M., is a house-call veterinarian at Targwood Animal Health Care in West Chester, Pennsylvania; manager of CompuServe's Vet Care Forum; and coauthor of *The Pill Book Guide to Medication for your Dog and Cat*.

■ Elaine Wexler-Mitchell, D.V.M., is a veterinarian at the Cat Care Clinic in Orange, California, and president of the Academy of Feline Medicine.

Bleeding

CALL YOUR VET: **IF NEEDED**

Bleeding often looks more serious than it really is. Clotting usually begins in 60 to 90 seconds, and a scab will form after a few hours. Some of the "safest" wounds, in fact, are those that bleed heavily at first, because the blood flushes away debris and bacteria.

Deep wounds, however, or wounds involving a covered vein or artery, are more serious. Neck and leg wounds tend to be the worst because large veins and arteries lie near the surface in these areas. Blood from a damaged vein is dark red and flows evenly. Blood from a damaged artery spurts with each heartbeat, is bright red, and is generally much more serious.

Bleeding from shallow cuts and scrapes can be stopped with simple first aid. Deeper wounds always need medical attention, even when you're able to stop the bleeding at home.

DO THIS NOW

Control the bleeding. Don't wash wounds that are bleeding heavily—it will make it harder for clots to form. You need to control the bleeding first. Apply a gauze pad or a clean piece of cloth to the wound. Or use a sanitary napkin—it's perfect because the material is highly absorbent. If blood soaks through the pad, apply a second pad on top of the first one and continue the pressure. (Removing the first pad will remove the clot that's trying to form.) The bleeding should stop in 5 minutes or less.

When you can't stop bleeding with finger pressure alone, you'll need to apply a pressure bandage. With the original pad still in place, wrap it with several layers of roll gauze, an elastic bandage like an Ace bandage, or even duct tape or masking tape. The pressure bandage should be firm but not too tight. If you can't easily slip the end of a cotton swab under

The Pressure Points

There are places in the body where arteries are very near the surface. Pressing on a specific area will partially close the artery, reducing the flow of blood and allowing clots to form.

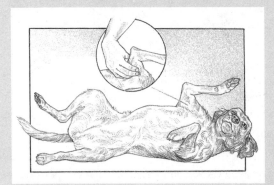

To control bleeding in a front leg, press the pressure point located in the armpit. Put your thumb on the outside of the upper leg and your fingers on the inside.

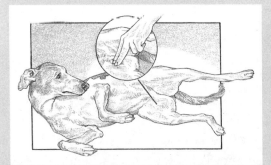

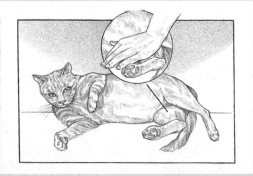

To stop bleeding in a dog's rear leg, turn him on his back on a stable surface so that his groin area (lower belly) is exposed. Find the pressure point over the femoral artery on the inside of his leg and apply firm pressure with the first two fingers of your hand.

To stop bleeding in the rear leg of a cat, turn him on his back on a stable surface so that his groin area is exposed. Find the pressure point over the femoral area on the inside of his leg and apply firm pressure with the heel of your hand.

The Pressure Points (cont.)

If your dog's tail has been injured and it's bleeding, steady him by running your left arm under his belly and pressing him against you. Use your right hand to lift his tail. With your left hand, apply pressure near the base of the tail by pressing firmly with your thumb on the top of tail and your fingers underneath.

If your cat's tail is bleeding, hold him on your lap, with your left arm circling his chest. To stop the bleeding, use your left hand to lift his tail and your right hand to apply pressure between the injury and the body. Put your thumb on top of the tail and your fingers underneath and press firmly.

the bandage, it's probably too tight. For small pets, cover the absorbent pad with plastic wrap like Saran Wrap and keep pressure on the pad.

Look for signs of shock. Pets who have lost a lot of blood also lose their ability to retain heat, and they may go into shock—a condition in which the body's organs shut down. Shock can kill a pet in as little as 10 to 20 minutes. Wrap him in a towel or blanket and get him to a veterinarian immediately. You can

also put a drop or two of Karo syrup or honey on your pet's gums to help keep him conscious. (For more information on shock, see page 333.)

If he has gone into shock, you may need to perform artificial respiration. Wrap your hand around his muzzle to close his mouth and blow into his nose with two quick breaths. Watch for his chest to rise, then give 15 to 20 breaths a minute until he begins breathing again on his own or until you reach medical help. After each breath, watch for his chest to rise, then remove

FIRST ALERT

Hidden Blood

Bleeding isn't caused only by wounds. Rodent baits often contain an ingredient called warfarin or other compounds that may cause internal bleeding by blocking the body's production of proteins needed for clotting. This is the most common cause of poisoning in pets. Every year, many dogs and cats, especially those who live on farms, are poisoned by warfarin, either because they ate the bait or because they ate rodents that ate the bait.

Pets who have eaten warfarin may bleed from the mouth, nose, or anus. They may also bleed internally, or there may be traces of blood in the urine or stools. These symptoms may take 1 to 2 days to appear because it takes that long for the body to use up its supply of clotting proteins. If you see your dog or cat eating a poison containing warfarin, you'll need to induce vomiting by squirting 3% hydrogen peroxide into the back of his mouth with a needleless syringe. (See page 30 for an illustration of this technique.) For both dogs and cats, give 1 to 2 teaspoons for every 10 pounds of body weight. Repeat two or three times until your pet vomits, allowing 5 minutes between doses. Then get to a veterinarian immediately and take along the packaging from the bait.

Your vet can treat pets with warfarin poisoning with vitamin K, which restores the blood's ability to clot. Sometimes oral vitamin K therapy may be necessary for several weeks. (See page 318 for more information.)

your lips and let the air escape. (This technique is illustrated on page 20.)

Raise the injured part. Elevating the injured area will help slow bleeding. This isn't essential, however. In fact, it can be harmful if a bone has been broken. If your pet holds one of his limbs in an awkward way or doesn't move it at all, if one of his limbs dangles at a strange angle, if he seems to be in extreme pain when moving, or if you can feel his bone crunch as he moves a limb, he may have a broken bone and needs to see the vet right away. (For more information about fractures, see page 212.)

 SPECIAL SITUATION

If your pet's ears are bleeding: Ears have a vein near the surface that can bleed a lot. And since pets shake their heads when an ear is injured, the bleeding gets worse. To put pressure on the ears, first apply an absorbent pad or cloth. Cut a length from a pair of panty hose and slip it over your pet's head behind his ears. Then move the panty hose forward over the absorbent bandage to hold it in place. Make sure that his eyes and mouth are not covered. Use the thigh portion of the panty hose for big dogs and the toe end for smaller pets. (For more information on ear injuries, see page 157.)

FOLLOW-UP CARE

■ Whether or not a wound requires stitches, it's essential to keep it clean for at least a week afterward. Sponge off discharge and crust from around the wound edges several times a day. Do not disturb the wound itself unless directed by your veterinarian. Follow this with an application of an antibiotic ointment like Neosporin.

■ Dogs and cats instinctively lick their wounds, and in some cases, this can reduce the risk of infection. But more than a few gentle licks may be too much. Pets who lick their wounds too much can dramatically slow the healing time. If the area around the wound seems moist or wet and the scab never seems to dry out, you may need to fit your pet with a cone-shaped restraint collar called an Elizabethan collar, which will keep him from licking his wounds. The collar can make it hard to eat, however, so you'll want to remove it at mealtimes.

THE BEST APPROACH

Ouch-Free Tape

The first-aid tape that's used to secure bandages on people can be a nightmare for pets because of their fur—changing the bandages can be more painful than the wound itself. A product called Vetrap Bandaging Tape, available at pet stores, is designed to stretch and stick to itself rather than sticking to hair and skin. It stays in place and doesn't absorb moisture, so it stays clean longer.

Advisors

■ Shane Bateman, D.V.M., D.V.Sc., is a veterinarian board certified in the American College of Emergency and Critical Care Medicine and assistant professor of emergency and critical care medicine at Ohio State University College of Veterinary Medicine in Columbus.

■ Joanne Howl, D.V.M., is a veterinarian in West River, Maryland; secretary/treasurer of the American Academy on Veterinary Disaster Medicine; and past president of the Maryland Veterinary Medical Association.

■ Thomas Munschauer, D.V.M., is a veterinarian at Middlebury Animal Hospital in Vermont and past president of the Vermont Veterinary Medical Association.

■ John Rush, D.V.M., is a veterinarian board certified in the American College of Emergency and Critical Care Medicine and section head of emergency and critical care service at Tufts University School of Veterinary Medicine in North Grafton, Massachusetts.

■ Daniel Simpson, D.V.M., is a veterinarian at the West Bay Animal Hospital in Warwick, Rhode Island, and spokesperson for the Rhode Island Veterinary Medical Association

■ Kevin Wallace, D.V.M., is an instructor in the department of clinical sciences at Cornell University College of Veterinary Medicine in Ithaca, New York.

■ David Wirth-Schneider, D.V.M., is a veterinarian at the Emergency Clinic for Animals in Madison, Wisconsin.

Bloat

CALL YOUR VET: **IMMEDIATELY**

Information gathered from veterinary hospitals across the country shows that a potentially deadly kind of indigestion called bloat is on the rise. The cause of bloat isn't clear, but it may have to do with dogs gulping air when they eat too fast or get excited.

As the stomach swells, it presses against other organs and large blood vessels, which interferes with bloodflow. The trapped gas can also make the stomach twist—a condition called volvulus, or torsion—so that the built-up pressure can't escape up the throat or out through the bowels. The twist also compresses the vein that returns blood to the heart and cuts off blood supply to the stomach and other organs like the spleen, so tissue dies.

Any dog can get bloat, but big dogs—especially Great Danes—are affected most often. A dog with bloat has a painful, distended abdomen, acts restless, and may try to vomit or defecate. If the stomach twists, he may die from shock. So if your dog shows symptoms of bloat, get him to the vet *immediately.* His life depends on it. If you live more than ½ hour away from a veterinary clinic, call your vet immediately and ask for instructions for at-home emergency procedures.

🩹 DO THIS NOW

Guard against shock. A dog will go into shock very quickly when his stomach twists, and shock can kill a pet in as little as 10 to 20 minutes. Besides the distended abdomen, you'll see that his gums are pale, and he may be weak and woozy. It's important to keep him warm to combat the shock. Wrap him in a warm blanket and turn the heat on in the car while you transport him to the vet. You can also put a drop or two of Karo syrup or honey on your pet's gums to help keep him conscious. (For more information about shock, see page 333.)

Give your dog a liquid antacid. As long as your dog can belch or vomit, the condition probably isn't caused by a twisted stomach. Problems from overeating usually get better by themselves once the gas passes out of the system. To speed up the process, give him Mylanta by mouth. This liquid antacid contains simethicone, which absorbs gas. Give dogs weighing 15 pounds or less 3 tablespoons, 16- to 50-pound dogs 4 tablespoons, and dogs 51 pounds or more 6 tablespoons. Squirt the medicine into his mouth with a needleless syringe. (See page 30 for an illustration of this technique.) The stomach swelling should start to subside in 20 minutes or so. If it doesn't, or if the condition gets worse, see your veterinarian immediately.

Take your dog for a walk. When your dog has eaten something he shouldn't have—maybe a whole loaf of yeast bread or something from the garbage—gentle exercise may help move the gas through his system. Try walking your dog until he's able to pass stool or gas; this should work in about 20 minutes. If it doesn't, or if you are not sure what's happening, see your veterinarian immediately.

Plan ahead. The quickest way to relieve the gas pressure is with a stomach tube, but this can be hard to do at home when your dog is alert because he'll be in pain and hard to restrain. But it may be worth planning ahead for this kind of emergency if veterinary help is more than ½ hour away and you have a dog that is at risk. Ask your vet to demonstrate techniques you can use in an emergency situation.

 FOLLOW-UP CARE

■ If your dog needs emergency surgery to untwist his stomach and remove damaged tissue, usually the surgeon attaches the stomach to the body wall to help prevent a relapse. You'll need to keep the incision line clean. Dampen a gauze pad with warm water and wipe away any drainage from the area surrounding the incision, but don't wipe the incision itself.

■ Some dogs may need to be fitted with an Elizabethan collar—a cone-shaped device that keeps them from bothering their stitches. Dogs won't be able to eat while wearing the collar, though, so be sure to remove it during feedings.

■ If your dog has had surgery, it's a good idea to take his temperature every day for the first week just to make sure that no infection develops. Insert a rectal thermometer lubricated with petroleum jelly or K-Y Jelly about halfway into your dog's rectum and wait 3 to 5 minutes. (See page 9 for an illustration of this technique.) Normal dog temperature ranges from about 99° to 102.5°F. A fever means that your veterinarian may need to prescribe antibiotics.

■ About 6 percent of dogs who suffer one episode of bloat will relapse, even after surgery. Reduce the chance of a repeat by feeding your dog very small amounts of food spread over the entire day. This will reduce his tendency to gorge. Do *not* feed one giant meal at a time.

■ Change your dog's diet to low-fiber food. Some kinds of fiber tend to ferment and release gas once in the stomach, and this may increase the risk of a relapse.

■ Dogs who worry about other animals stealing their food tend to gulp it quickly and swallow air. Feed your dog by himself, away from competition. Try adding water to dry food so that it swells before it's swallowed and won't expand so much once it's in your dog's stomach.

■ Happy, well-adjusted dogs tend to have a decreased incidence of bloat. Try to spend more quality time with your dog in petting or play sessions. Dogs are very social creatures and need to interact with their family in a positive way. This positive interaction can relieve stress, which seems to predispose dogs to recurring bouts of bloat.

■ Restricting water and exercise just before and after meals doesn't decrease the risk of bloat, so it's best to give your dog moderate portions of food and exercise throughout the day. This may also cut down on emotional stress brought on by binge behavior—drinking lots of water at one time or exploding with pent-up energy when he is finally allowed to play.

■ Keep your dog's food bowl on the floor. In the past, experts recommended setting big dogs' food bowls off the ground so that they didn't have to reach so far to eat, but this has been shown to considerably increase the risk of bloat.

THE BEST APPROACH

Hypodermic Needle

To decompress the dangerous buildup of gas in a dog with bloat, a hollow but razor-sharp tool is best. Veterinarians use large-bore hypodermic needles that are 14 to 16 gauge or larger. If you have an at-risk dog and live more than ½ hour away from medical help, ask your veterinarian for such a needle and for a demonstration of how to use it in an emergency.

Advisors

■ Shane Bateman, D.V.M., D.V.Sc., is a veterinarian board certified in the American College of Emergency and Critical Care Medicine and assistant professor of emergency and critical care medicine at Ohio State University College of Veterinary Medicine in Columbus.

■ Peter Levin, V.M.D., is a veterinarian at Ludwig's Corner Veterinary Hospital in Chester Springs, Pennsylvania.

■ Billy D. Martindale, D.V.M., is a veterinarian at the Animal Hospital of Denison, Texas, and chairman of the board of directors of the Texas Veterinary Medical Association.

■ Julie Moews, D.V.M., is a veterinarian at Bolton Veterinary Hospital in Connecticut.

Bowel Obstruction

CALL YOUR VET: **IF NEEDED**

MEDICINE CHEST

Mineral oil or
  petroleum jelly
Disposable medical
  gloves
K-Y Jelly
Blanket
Karo syrup or honey
Blunt scissors
Clean cloths or gauze
  pads
Warm water

Dogs experience bowel obstruction more often than cats because they love to chew, so they end up swallowing nondigestible objects like sticks and stones. Cats tend to have problems with string-type toys like ribbons or with pieces of toys or feathers that break off. And both dogs and cats can get clogged up from eating cooked bones or swallowing coins, pacifier nipples, tampons, or other objects. Fortunately, when the object is small enough to make it to the colon, it usually passes normally into the litter box or the yard, and your pet is fine.

But sponges and rubber-type materials that swell in the intestinal tract or large or sharp-pointed items that lodge in the intestines cause blockages or lacerations and need to be surgically removed as soon as possible, or they could kill your pet. When the blockage is high up in the intestinal tract, projectile vomiting will occur, and your pet may not be interested in eating. A blockage lower down also causes vomiting, but it will be less frequent, dark brown, and smell like feces, and the abdomen will swell. If you notice these symptoms, or if the vomiting is severe or prolonged and his condition is worsening, take your pet to the vet immediately.

Bear in mind, though, that not all of these symptoms need to be present to signify trouble. Look out for any unusual behavior or signs that your pet may have ingested something that he shouldn't have.

DO THIS NOW

Let nature take its course. When you know that the swallowed object is small, you can wait 24 hours to let nature work it out. As long as your pet still feels well enough to eat and drink without vomiting, try feeding her a jumbo-size meal. Dish up 1½ times her normal serving size. This should encourage increased bowel activity and help the object pass.

FIRST ALERT

Bloat

Very large dogs with deep chests, like Great Danes and Labrador retrievers, are prone to bloat, a condition in which the stomach swells up with gas and/or fluid. The signs look very similar to those of bowel obstruction.

The excessive gas and stomach pain of bloat make the dog restless, and he drools and may try to vomit or may pass feces by mouth.

In severe cases, he won't be able to vomit or belch because his stomach has twisted. Signs of shock—pale, cold gums and collapse—develop, because the blood supply is cut off from the stomach and spleen. This is called torsion or volvulus and is an emergency that requires *immediate* veterinary help, or your dog could die. (For more information about bloat, see page 100.)

Keep an eye on your pet. Make sure your pet is eating and especially drinking normally and watch vigilantly for signs of intestinal upset.

Lubricate the object. Give a dose of mineral oil or petroleum jelly to help slick down the mass and help it pass. Give about 1 teaspoon of mineral oil for every 10 pounds of your pet's weight and mix it well into his food. *Do not* give mineral oil by mouth, because it's easy to inhale and can cause life-threatening pneumonia.

If you are using petroleum jelly for your cat, you can stick it on a paw and she'll lick it off when she cleans herself. You can give the petroleum jelly to your dog the same way you give him a pill, or you can try wiping it on the roof of his mouth and letting him lick it down himself. Give one dollop on a finger (about a tablespoon) for a cat, and the same dose per every 10 pounds of body weight for a dog. Consider doing this in a room that's easy to clean up in case your pet decides to shake it all over the place.

Remove the object if you can. You may see the object partially protruding from your pet's anus. If you can tell that it's hair, grass, or a solid nonstring object, put on disposable medical gloves (available in drugstores), grasp the object, and pull gently. If the object does not move, lubricate your gloved fingers and your pet's anus with K-Y Jelly, gently insert your index finger, and try to position it in front of the object. Then gently try to pull the object out. You may need another person to hold and restrain your pet during the procedure because the object will most likely be uncomfortable or even painful to pass. Have your helper hug your pet's body to his chest, with one arm around his neck and the other under and around his abdomen. (This technique is illustrated on page 18.)

If your pet objects to any of this or if you

meet resistance in trying to remove the object, see your vet right away. Your pet may need to be sedated to allow safe removal.

Watch for signs of shock. Untreated bowel obstruction becomes particularly dangerous if the blood supply in the intestines is cut off. This happens when the tissues around the obstruction swell and hinder the flow of blood. Without free bloodflow, the tissues can die. A pet in this situation has a very tender tummy that can feel hard like a board. After a while, he goes into shock, his gums become pale, and he may collapse. To fight the shock, wrap your pet in a blanket to keep him warm and put a drop or two of Karo syrup or honey on his gums to help keep him conscious. Then get veterinary help immediately. (For more information on shock, see page 333.)

 SPECIAL SITUATION

If string dangles from the anus: *Do not* pull it out. It may be attached to a fishhook embedded inside or wrapped around intestinal tissue. Tugging on string, yarn, or any similar material could cut up your pet's organs and kill him. Use blunt scissors to carefully cut off the dangling end as close to the anus as safely pos-

sible so that your pet doesn't pull at it, either. Your veterinarian may need to take x-rays before attempting to remove the string.

 FOLLOW-UP CARE

■ A pet who has had surgery for bowel obstruction has an incision that you'll need to keep clean. Dampen a clean cloth or gauze pad with warm water and wipe off drainage only as needed. Check the incision several times daily initially for redness, swelling, obvious discomfort or pain, and discharge. If any of these are present, have your veterinarian check it.

■ Dogs and cats who have had one bowel obstruction are at risk for a repeat. They tend to either have a habit of swallowing the wrong thing, or they develop scar tissue inside the intestines that makes it more difficult for even small items to pass. So avoid giving them bones or rawhide chews that can be swallowed. "Pet-proof" your home by picking up anything that your pet might swallow or by making potentially troublesome areas off-limits with a baby gate or closed door. Be very careful in choosing toys for your pet. Wine corks, corn cobs, chewed-up squeaky toys, and small balls are some of the most common causes of obstructions.

Advisors

■ Peter Levin, V.M.D., is a veterinarian at Ludwig's Corner Veterinary Hospital in Chester Springs, Pennsylvania.

■ Susan Little, D.V.M., is a veterinarian at Bytown Cat Hospital in Ottawa, Ontario, Canada.

■ Billy D. Martindale, D.V.M., is a veterinarian at the Animal Hospital of Denison, Texas, and chairman of the board of directors of the Texas Veterinary Medical Association.

Burns from Chemicals

SEE YOUR VET: **IMMEDIATELY**

Chemical burns tend to be more serious than simple heat burns because chemicals continue damaging the skin and flesh for as long as they make contact. No matter how painful and serious they are at first, they usually get worse within a day or two.

Many chemicals, including toilet cleaners, chlorine, swimming pool cleaners, weed killers, and battery acid cause burns. A heavy coat of fur doesn't protect dogs and cats from chemicals. In fact, it often makes the burns worse because fur holds onto liquids and powders and keeps them in contact with skin longer.

DO THIS NOW

Protect your skin and eyes. First, put on disposable medical gloves (available in drugstores) and make sure your eyes and skin are covered. The same goes for anyone else who is nearby. If your pet begins to shake his coat and tail, the chemical will go everywhere.

Remove your pet's collar. Leather collars absorb moisture and will hold chemicals against the skin. Even metal and nylon collars are dangerous because they trap liquids. In addition, chemical burns can swell quickly, making collars or harnesses so tight that they interfere with breathing.

Use a muzzle. Don't let your pet lick the area, because licking will spread chemicals from the outside of the body to the inside. The fastest way

An Instant Muzzle

Dogs and cats instinctively lick their wounds, including wounds caused by chemicals. Even when chemicals are strong enough to burn the mouth, pets will keep licking because it's the only remedy they know. Veterinarians recommend putting muzzles in first aid-kits, but you can also make a muzzle in an emergency. Before you start to make the emergency muzzle, have someone firmly grasp your pet's neck skin behind and just below the ears. Dogs don't enjoy being muzzled, especially when they're hurt and frightened. Holding the head in place this way will steady it and prevent bites. To make an emergency muzzle, follow these easy instructions.

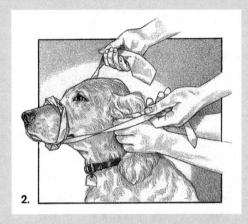

2.

Tighten the knot, then loop the ends down under the chin and make another knot.

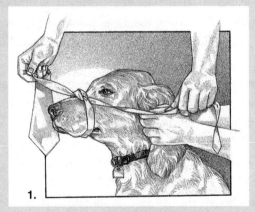

1.

Tie a loop in a necktie or a length of panty hose and slip it around your pet's mouth.

3.

Draw the ends back over the neck and tie them in a knot or bow behind your dog's ears.

to stop licking is to tie his mouth closed. Don't waste time looking for materials, however. Chemicals can do a lot of damage very quickly, especially on the tongue or the inside of the mouth. You may be better off holding your pet to keep him from licking while someone else looks for panty hose or a necktie to tie his mouth or—for a short-nosed pet like a cat or a pug—a pillowcase to slip over his head. Don't use a muzzle if your pet is having trouble breathing, however.

Have a large needleless syringe filled with water readily available in case you need to gently rinse out your pet's mouth.

Remove the chemical. If the chemical is a powder, brush off your pet thoroughly with a stiff-bristled brush. Then rinse off his coat with water as described below. Before brushing your pet, put on a mask or wrap a bandanna around your nose and mouth so that you don't inhale potentially dangerous chemical powder.

Flood the areas with a lot of cool to luke-warm water. (Water that is too hot may speed up the absorption of the chemical through the skin, while water that is too cold may cause hypothermia.) Keep rinsing for at least 20 minutes. Try to direct the stream of water away from the rest of the body to prevent spreading the chemical. Water is the best first aid there is, so keep flushing even if the water appears to be making the damage worse. Don't use antibiotic or other ointments because they'll trap residues of the chemical next to the skin.

Look for symptoms of shock. Pets who have been exposed to large amounts of chemicals sometimes go into shock. Signs of shock include rapid breathing, pale tongue or gums, or passing out. Shock is an emergency, and it can kill your pet in as little as 10 to 20 minutes. Wrap your pet in a towel or blanket to keep him warm and slow the progression of shock, then get him to a veterinarian immediately. You can also put a drop or two of Karo syrup or honey on your pet's gums to help keep him conscious. (For more information on shock, see page 333.)

Help your pet breathe. You may need to give artificial respiration if your pet goes into shock. Put your mouth over his nose (make sure that there is no chemical residue on his nose first) and blow with two quick breaths, watching to see his chest rise. Continue breathing, giving 15 to 20 breaths a minute, until he starts breathing on his own or until you get to a vet. (This technique is illustrated on page 20.)

FOLLOW-UP CARE

■ Chemical burns are often protected with bandages called wet-to-dry, available in drugstores and from vets. They're applied wet, then allowed to dry against the wound. When they're peeled off, they remove dead tissue at the same time. Wet-to-dry bandages need to be changed several times a day. Your vet will show you how.

■ Burns often cause sores that are wet and weepy. Once the burn starts healing, switch from wet-to-dry bandages to absorbent non-stick pads such as Telfa pads. They help keep wounds dry and allow air to circulate.

■ Change the bandages according to your veterinarian's instructions. As the burns heal, you can start changing the bandages every second or third day. As soon as a bandage starts getting damp, it needs to be changed. Once a durable layer of new skin, called epithelium, has nearly covered the area, you may be able to remove the bandage altogether. Check with your vet to see how soon you can do this. For large wounds, your pet may have to keep bandages on for weeks.

■ Even though it's dangerous to apply ointments right after pets have been burned by chemicals, you do want to use an antibiotic ointment like Neosporin as the burn heals. A good rule of thumb is if your pet is still wearing bandages at your vet's instruction, apply the ointment. Once the bandages have been removed and a healthy new layer of skin has formed, stop applying it.

■ It's pretty obvious when chemical burns are healing properly. When there's a problem, the first sign is likely to be a bad smell. Every time you change the bandage, give it a sniff. An odor that's unusually bad probably means that an infection is brewing, and you'll want to call your vet right away. Other warning signs include sudden decrease in appetite, decreased activity level, pain, or fever. Also, if your pet is chewing at the burn site, it could mean that it's getting infected.

■ Check for swelling, warmth, pain, and the other warning signs within a few hours of applying any new bandage. These signs could signal that the bandage is too tight and needs to be loosened. You must also protect any bandaged area from becoming soiled or wet. Taping a thick plastic bag temporarily over the bandaged site before your pet goes out can help if it is wet outside. Just be sure to remove the plastic bag when he comes back in.

THE BEST APPROACH

Pet Shower

Dogs and cats are always getting into something that needs to be washed off. Putting them under a faucet doesn't work, and using a hose isn't always practical, especially in winter. A very effective device is the Pet Shower Delux. Available in pet supply stores, it attaches to bathtub or shower plumbing. It has an 8-foot hose with an on-off spray nozzle that you can operate with one hand. This allows you to put water where you need it while holding your pet still with the other.

The Pet Shower Delux isn't cheap—it costs about five times more than other sprayers—but it's worth the extra cost. The hose is much longer, which makes it easier to use. And because the mounting hardware is permanently affixed to the plumbing (you remove the hose between uses with a quick-release fitting), it won't pull off the faucet as slip-on models do.

Advisors

■ Shane Bateman, D.V.M., D.V.Sc., is a veterinarian board certified in the American College of Emergency and Critical Care Medicine and assistant professor of emergency and critical care medicine at Ohio State University College of Veterinary Medicine in Columbus.

■ Joanne Howl, D.V.M., is a veterinarian in West River, Maryland; secretary/treasurer of the American Academy on Veterinary Disaster Medicine; and past president of the Maryland Veterinary Medical Association.

■ Kevin Wallace, D.V.M., is an instructor in the department of clinical sciences at Cornell University College of Veterinary Medicine in Ithaca, New York.

Burns from Friction

SEE YOUR VET: **IF NEEDED**

Bicyclists refer to friction burns as road rash, and they're among the most painful injuries that people—and dogs and cats—get. Pets usually get friction burns when they've fallen out of cars or pickup trucks or when they've been hit or dragged by cars. The friction of pet against pavement scrapes away fur and skin. These injuries usually aren't deep, but they cover a large area, which makes them painful and slow to heal.

Small friction burns are easy to treat with first-aid. Larger burns, especially those covering more than 5 to 10 percent of the body (about the size of the surface covering the pet's thigh), are more serious. That's because they often get infected and may progress to shock, a life-threatening condition in which the body's organs begin to shut down.

DO THIS NOW

Rinse the burn. The best treatment for friction burns is water, and lots of it. Place your pet in a tub and flood the affected area with gently running cool to lukewarm water for 5 to 10 minutes. This flushes away grit and helps reduce pain and swelling.

Remove the debris. Pets who have been dragged on dirt, grass, or pavement invariably have a lot of debris packed into the wound. Water will remove some of it, but not all. You may need to use blunt-tipped tweezers to remove larger particles. Try not to touch wounds with your bare hands; use disposable medical gloves (available in drugstores) so you don't contaminate the wound further. Having wounds cleaned is painful, and some pets won't put up with it. Don't struggle too much. If you are not able to completely clean the wound at home so that no debris is visible, you should call the vet. He may recommend bringing your pet in so that the wound can be treated professionally, probably under sedation.

Take off your pet's collar. Since friction burns can swell very quickly, be sure to remove your pet's collar if the burn is on her head or neck.

Look for signs of shock. Friction burns involving more than 5 to 10% of the body must be treated by a veterinarian. In the meantime, watch out for shock. A pet going into shock often has trouble breathing because her circulatory system isn't distributing blood and oxygen efficiently. A pet in shock acts weak or woozy. Her eyelids droop, and she may have a pale tongue or gums. She may lose consciousness as well.

Don't bother cleaning the wound if you suspect that your pet is going into shock. That will waste valuable time, and cool water can make shock progress more rapidly. Wrap her in a blanket and get her to an emergency clinic as fast as you can. You can also put a drop or two of Karo syrup or honey on her gums to help keep her conscious. (For more information on shock, see page 333.)

If you are alone, try to put your small pet in a carrier. Put the carrier on the seat beside you. A large pet should go on the backseat or in the cargo area of the vehicle. If your pet is unconscious or barely conscious, gently stretch her head and neck out a little to help breathing. If she's conscious, she won't hold her head and neck in place, so don't worry about it. If someone can go with you to the vet, though, have him hold your pet's head and neck out straight on the way.

 FOLLOW-UP CARE

■ Because friction burns remove large amounts of skin, the wounds weep a lot. Dry the area several times a day with a clean, soft cloth. Don't use cotton balls, because they will stick to the wound.

■ Apply aloe vera ointment, available in drugstores and pet-supply stores, three times a day. Aloe vera reduces pain and has been found to speed healing.

■ Friction burns heal more quickly when they're kept dry, which means that you'll want to apply a bandage to keep your pet from licking the area. For a burn on a lower leg, slip a white cotton sock onto the leg, then wrap gauze and tape around the top to hold it in place. It's harder to bandage wounds elsewhere on the body because tape won't stick to fur. After you've covered the wound with a nonstick dressing like a Telfa pad, slip your pet's head through the neck and her front feet through the arms of a T-shirt. Then wrap a little roll gauze around her body to hold the shirt in place, but be careful not to wrap too tightly.

■ Veterinarians usually don't recommend topical anesthetics, but friction burns are unusually painful. If your pet appears to be in a great deal of pain, consult your veterinarian about topical anesthetics.

■ Unwrap the bandage and check the burn at least three times the first day, applying aloe vera ointment each time. If the wound seems clean and dry, you'll need to change the bandage only once a day. But if the wound is weeping so much that the bandage is sticking, you'll need to change it more often.

■ If you don't have aloe vera ointment, you can apply a thin layer of antibiotic ointment like Neosporin to the bandage when you change it. Another choice is silver sulfadiazine (Silvadene). Veterinarians often prescribe it because it keeps burns and other wounds healthy. Apply the cream once or twice a day.

■ You can keep bandages clean and dry when your pet goes outside by wrapping the area with plastic wrap like Saran Wrap. For a leg burn, slip a plastic bread bag over the foot and tape it in place. Don't keep a burn wrapped for a long time, since plastic will prevent air from getting to the burn and slow healing. Wrap the bandages only when your pet is going outside, then take the wrapping off when she comes back in.

THE BEST APPROACH

Antiseptics

Veterinarians suggest using antiseptic solutions like diluted Betadine Solution for friction burns because they are gentle to the healing tissues.

Before using an antiseptic, make sure that the wound has been cleared of debris. If there is a lot of debris or crusting, or if the wound is discharging material that is white, yellow, black, or green, the best thing is to rinse first with lukewarm water from a handheld showerhead or sprayer. Then, wearing a disposable medical glove, gently ease the softened material away. (Do not do this if a healthy-looking scab is forming. A healthy scab is dry and hard, with minimal amounts of redness around the edges, and is not pussy or weepy.) Then add Betadine Solution to a few cups of distilled water until the solution is the color of weak tea and use it to flush the burn. This can be done daily or twice daily, if needed, for the first 2 to 3 days.

Advisors

■ Shane Bateman, D.V.M., D.V.Sc., is a veterinarian board certified in the American College of Emergency and Critical Care Medicine and assistant professor of emergency and critical care medicine at Ohio State University College of Veterinary Medicine in Columbus.

■ Joanne Howl, D.V.M., is a veterinarian in West River, Maryland; secretary/treasurer of the American Academy on Veterinary Disaster Medicine; and past president of the Maryland Veterinary Medical Association.

■ Kevin Wallace, D.V.M., is an instructor in the department of clinical sciences at Cornell University College of Veterinary Medicine in Ithaca, New York.

■ Elaine Wexler-Mitchell, D.V.M., is a veterinarian at the Cat Care Clinic in Orange, California, and president of the Academy of Feline Medicine.

Burns from Heat

CALL YOUR VET: **IF NEEDED**

MEDICINE CHEST

- Cool water
- Blunt scissors
- Mild soap
- Antiseptic solution (Betadine Solution)
- Ice
- Plastic bag or washcloth
- Blanket or towel
- Karo syrup or honey
- Soft cloth
- Aloe vera ointment or antibiotic ointment (Neosporin)
- Nonstick absorbent pad (Telfa pad), cloth, or gauze pad
- Sterile saline contact lens solution
- Roll gauze or elastic bandage (Ace bandage)
- Wet-to-dry bandage
- Elizabethan collar
- Plastic wrap (Saran Wrap)

Dogs don't get burned very often because they instinctively shy away from heat. Cats, on the other hand, love heat and will lounge on surfaces as hot as 126°F. All they feel is the comfort—they don't feel themselves getting burned. They're also attracted to candles and gas-stove flames.

Burns are hard to see because fur tends to hide the damage. Mild burns, called first-degree burns, affect the top layer of skin and usually appear as angry red marks. Second-degree burns go deeper into the skin and may raise blisters. If they cover small areas of the body (less than 1 percent), you can easily treat them at home, although they're often slow to heal. Large first- and second-degree burns (covering more than 2.5 percent of the body surface area) should be examined by a veterinarian. (To help in your estimates of body surface area, each limb represents about 10 percent of the pet's total.) Third-degree burns must always be treated by a veterinarian. These burns go through all the layers of skin and into the flesh underneath. The skin turns brown and leathery. They're less painful than other burns because they destroy nerve endings, but they're much more serious.

 DO THIS NOW

Flush the burn with cool water for 5 to 10 minutes. Cool water acts as a temporary anesthetic and cleans the burn. Burns continue to "cook" even without heat. The flow of cool water reduces temperatures below the surface and helps prevent further damage. You can

A Close Trim

Pets often get infected burns because their fur makes it difficult to clean the area well. For all but the mildest burns, you'll want to trim the fur short enough so that you can see (and clean) the entire area.

If your pet has been burned, have a second person hold her still so that you can clip the fur around the burn. Use blunt scissors and slip your fingers under the fur to make it stand up so you don't cut your pet.

wash small burns with a garden hose, although a spray bottle or handheld showerhead also works. For cats and small dogs, it may be easiest to hold them under the faucet in the tub or sink.

Large burns may cause shock, and cold water would make things worse, so don't use it if the burn covers more than 2.5% of your pet's body.

Trim the fur surrounding the burn. Use blunt scissors and cut your pet's fur short enough to let you see the whole burn, but not so short that you're close to the skin.

Cleanse the burn. Burns get infected easily, so wash the area well with mild soap and cool water. If you have it, an antiseptic solution like Betadine Solution is better. Add it to a few cups of distilled water until the solution is the color of weak tea, then flush the burn.

Take off his collar. If your pet has been burned on the head or neck, remove his collar immediately. Burns cause tissues to swell, and this can make a collar tight enough to cause choking.

Watch for shock. Burns that cover more than 25% of a pet's body can cause the body to lose huge amounts of fluid. This can lead to shock, a dangerous condition in which the body's circulation shuts down. Signs include fast breathing, weakness, pale gums, and ultimately, loss of consciousness. Pets who are going into shock need to see a veterinarian immediately.

If you suspect shock, don't wash the burn, because this can slow circulation. Instead, put ice in a plastic bag or wrap it in a washcloth and hold it against the burn. Wrap your pet in a blanket or towel to keep him warm, then get help right away. You can also put a drop or two of Karo syrup or honey on your pet's gums to help keep him conscious. (For more information about shock, see page 333.)

FOLLOW-UP CARE

■ After cleaning mild burns, pat the area dry with a soft cloth. Don't use cotton balls; the fibers will stick to the wound.

FIRST ALERT

Delayed Damage

Puppies and kittens sometimes get mouth burns when they chew through electrical cords. The burns may raise blisters, generally visible on the gums, lips, and tongue, and they can be painful, but the real danger is what happens afterward. Even minor electrical shocks can damage blood vessels in the lungs. This causes a slow leak of fluids that can interfere with breathing. The way electricity affects the heart is even more serious. While severe shocks can stop the heart immediately, sometimes the damage is delayed for a few hours. Although pets will seem fine, their hearts may be beating erratically. It could take several hours before the symptoms—shortness of breath, difficulty breathing, loss of appetite, lethargy—appear.

Don't assume that electrical burns will get better, even if they seem to be minor. Call your vet right away, even if there are no visible symptoms. Bite marks on an electrical cord and a burning odor in the room or from the pet are also signs that he may have gotten a burn or shock.

■ Apply an aloe vera ointment three to five times a day. This can dramatically shorten healing time. Most aloe vera ointments also contain vitamin E, which can also speed healing.

■ Very mild first-degree burns don't need to be covered with a bandage. Apply the aloe vera or an antibiotic ointment like Neosporin several times a day until a scab forms. At that point, the burn is almost healed, and you can leave it alone.

■ Since second-degree burns get infected so easily, and because pets tend to lick them non-stop, veterinarians usually recommend covering them with a nonstick bandage. A good choice is a Telfa pad, although a sterile gauze pad or a clean, white cloth is also fine. If a second-degree burn is really blistered and oozing a lot— to the point where the dressing becomes stuck and difficult to remove—be sure to have your veterinarian look at it. In the meantime, continue to use nonstick dressings. If the bandage still sticks, you may want to soften it with a bit of sterile saline contact lens solution before removing it, so you don't start new bleeding.

■ Spread a thin coat of antibiotic ointment like Neosporin on the pad. This will prevent infection and keep the pad from sticking to the burn. Don't use ointments containing hydrocortisone, because steroids make burns heal more slowly. Hold the pad in place by wrapping it with roll gauze or an elastic bandage like an Ace bandage.

■ Burns take a long time to heal and generally need different bandages at various stages. For the first several days, check with your vet to see if you can use a wet-to-dry bandage. These are applied wet and allowed to dry, which creates a tight seal over the burn. Soak a sterile gauze pad in distilled water or saline solution, then press it over the wound. Cover this with a larger dry pad and hold everything in place with a strip of roll gauze.

■ For the first few days, change the wet-to-dry bandage four or five times a day. This allows you to inspect the burn for signs of infection, and removing the bandage also removes dead tissue that can contaminate the burn.

■ After a few days, switch to a dry nonstick bandage like a Telfa pad. Continue coating the bandage with antibiotic ointment. Telfa pads protect the burn while allowing liquids to drain out. If you don't have them, you can substitute a sanitary napkin or a disposable diaper. Change the bandage whenever it feels damp on the outside. This should be once a day at first. If the bandage needs changing more frequently, consult your vet. Later, you'll need to change it only every few days.

■ To keep bandages dry when your pet goes outside, cover them with a plastic bag or plastic wrap like Saran Wrap. Burns need air to heal, so remove the plastic when he comes inside.

■ Dogs and cats instinctively lick their wounds, which can add to the healing time. A pet who won't leave the area alone or is licking or chewing at the bandage will need to be fitted with a cone-shaped device called an Elizabethan collar to keep him from reaching the burn. He won't be able to eat while wearing the collar, though, so be sure to remove it during feedings.

THE BEST APPROACH

Silver Sulfadiazine

Burns are dangerous because they damage large areas of skin. This makes it easy for bacteria to get in and cause infection. And because burns heal from the inside out, the surface of the skin is the slowest to heal. This means that infections have a lot of time to get started.

Veterinarians often prescribe a medicated cream called silver sulfadiazine (Silvadene). It's a very powerful antiseptic and inhibits the growth of bacteria. You apply the cream two or three times a day.

Advisors

■ Shane Bateman, D.V.M., D.V.Sc., is a veterinarian board certified by the American College of Emergency and Critical Care Medicine and assistant professor of emergency and critical care medicine at Ohio State University College of Veterinary Medicine in Columbus.

■ Joanne Howl, D.V.M., is a veterinarian in West River, Maryland; secretary/treasurer of the American Academy on Veterinary Disaster Medicine, and past president of the Maryland Veterinary Medical Association.

■ Kevin Wallace, D.V.M., is an instructor in the department of clinical sciences at Cornell University College of Veterinary Medicine in Ithaca, New York.

■ Elaine Wexler-Mitchell, D.V.M., is a veterinarian at The Cat Care Clinic in Orange, California, and president of the Academy of Feline Medicine.

Car Accidents

CALL YOUR VET: **IMMEDIATELY**

MEDICINE CHEST

Length of fabric or pillowcase for muzzling
Small pillow
Clean cloth or sanitary napkin
Blanket or towel
Karo syrup or honey
T-shirt
Gauze pads
Sterile saline contact lens solution
Newspaper, magazine, or bubble wrap
Tape
Pet carrier or other rigid object
Plastic wrap (Saran Wrap)
Bitter Apple
Antiseptic liquid soap (Betadine Skin Cleanser)

Dogs and cats often survive car accidents because they're protected to some extent by thick layers of fur and their rather remarkable flexibility. But their fast recovery times are deceiving. One reason that car accidents are so dangerous is that many pets do walk away from them, seemingly with nothing worse than a torn nail or a few scrapes. People assume that they're fine and don't take them in for checkups. All the while, however, they may have internal injuries that won't show up for hours or days. And by that time, it's much harder for them to recover.

If your pet spends time outside, you should suspect the worst if he comes home with a limp or is having trouble breathing. These are among the most common symptoms of car accidents, and they can make their appearance even when pets look just fine on the outside.

Pets who have been hit by cars don't always walk away, of course. Knowing emergency first aid is the best way to increase the odds that you can get them to the veterinarian in time.

DO THIS NOW

Muzzle your pet. Dogs and cats who have been injured will often bite the first person who tries to help. First, be sure your pet is not having difficulty breathing. If his breathing is okay, tie a loop in a necktie or length of panty hose and slip it over his nose. Tighten the knot on top of his nose, then knot the fabric under his jaw. Make a third pass by pulling the ends behind the ears and tying them again. For a cat or short-nosed dog like a pug, you can slip a pillowcase over his head. (For an illustration of muzzling, see page 17.)

Check breathing. The force of being hit by a car often damages the lungs, causing breathing to stop, and getting the dog or cat to begin breathing again is the first priority. Hold your pet's mouth closed with one hand, put your mouth over his nose, and give two quick breaths. Watch to see if his chest rises, then continue by giving 15 to 20 breaths a minute until your pet begins breathing on his own or until you reach medical help. (This technique is illustrated on page 20.)

Check for a heartbeat. Press your ear or palm against the chest behind the left elbow. Or use your index and second fingers to feel for a pulse in the femoral artery, located in the groin where the hind leg meets the body.

Give CPR. If you can't find a pulse or hear a heartbeat, you'll need to give chest compressions to force blood through the body. For cats and small dogs, cup your hand over the point of the chest just behind the elbows. Squeeze firmly, with your thumb on one side and your fingers on the other and pressing in about ½ inch, 80 to 100 times a minute. Alternate one breath for every five compressions.

A medium to large dog needs to be lying on his side on a firm, flat surface. If you have one, put a small pillow or rolled-up coat or blanket under your dog's lower chest. (This will eliminate any dead space and improve the compressions.) Place both hands on top of each other against his chest. Try to compress the chest by

Finding a Pulse

Your pet's heart is well-protected, but the extreme force of car accidents can cause it to stop. Before giving CPR, you have to determine if the heart is beating. It's much easier to hear the actual heartbeat than to feel a pulse, so listen to his chest as well.

The best place to feel a pulse is at the femoral artery, located in the groin where the hind leg meets the body. Pressing gently, use your index, middle, and ring fingers to feel for the pulse. If you can't feel it and can't hear a heartbeat in the chest, the heart has probably stopped.

about 25 to 50% with each compression. Alternate compressions with breaths at the same rate as for small dogs. The goal is 80 to 100 compressions per minute. (This technique is illustrated on page 21.)

Continue with artificial respiration and CPR until your pet revives or until you can get him to a veterinarian. It's best to have someone drive you so you can treat your pet on the way.

FIRST ALERT

Hidden Injuries

People are often amazed when they watch pets get up, shake themselves, and walk away from car accidents. It's possible that they were very lucky, but it's just as possible that there's a hidden injury waiting to knock them back down.

Even low-speed collisions pack a tremendous amount of force. Blunt force may not break bones or skin, but it can bruise the lungs. This condition, called pulmonary contusion, won't clear up on its own. In fact, the bruise spreads, causing the lungs to slowly fill with blood. Pets can literally drown, sometimes 24 hours or more after the accident occurred.

Lung damage is easy to recognize because pets struggle to breathe. This is always an emergency, especially because artificial respiration won't help when the lungs are filled with fluid. You'll have to get your pet to a veterinarian as quickly as possible.

Stop the bleeding. The next priority is to stop bleeding. The fastest way to do this is to press directly on the wounds with a clean cloth, gauze pad, or even your hand. (A sanitary napkin is perfect because it is highly absorbent.) The idea is to slow the flow of blood and give clots a chance to form. Hold the pad in place for about 5 minutes. Even serious bleeding will usually stop within this time if you maintain pressure.

It's common for blood to soak through the pad or cloth before the bleeding stops. Don't remove it, because that will disturb the clots that are trying to form. Instead, apply a second pad on top and continue the pressure. (For more on bleeding, see page 95.)

Check the gums. If the bleeding won't stop, take a moment to look at your pet's gums. They should be pink or dark-colored. If they appear unusually pale, there's been a lot of blood loss, and you're going to need expert help quickly because your pet is going into shock. Wrap him in a towel or blanket for warmth. You can also put a drop or two of Karo syrup or honey on his gums to help keep him conscious. (For more information on shock, see page 333.)

Cover and protect the wounds. Whether you're giving first-aid at the side of the road or driving to a veterinarian, covering open wounds will keep them clean and help prevent infection. You don't need anything fancy—even throwing a T-shirt over a wound will help keep it clean.

Protect your pet's eyes. Eye injuries are common in car accidents, and to prevent blindness, you need to protect the eyes if they have been injured. Soak a clean cloth or gauze pad in sterile saline contact lens solution or clean water and hold it gently over the injured eye without applying any pressure. (See page 169 for instructions on how to give first aid to a pet whose eye is out of its socket.)

Check for broken legs. If you suspect that a leg is broken (your pet holds the limb abnormally or doesn't use it at all, he's in extreme pain when moving, the limb dangles at a strange angle, or you can feel the bone crunching as your pet moves that limb), you don't have to do a lot. If you can get to a veterinarian within 20 minutes, touch the area as little as possible. Dogs and cats instinctively know how to move to protect the injury.

Immobilize a broken leg. If you can't get to a veterinarian quickly, you have to immobilize the injured leg. Use gauze or cloth to protect any visible wounds, then put a towel around the leg. Immobilize the leg by wrapping it inside a newspaper, magazine, or bubble wrap, or put something long and stiff, like a wooden spoon, on top of the towel. Then tape the "roll" closed. Work from the leg out—use something clean to protect the wound, something soft to pad it, something stiff to immobilize it and, finally, tape to hold it all together.

Move your pet carefully. Any broken bone needs to be handled gingerly, but it's especially important when the break is in the pelvis or spine. The best way to move pets with fractures is on a rigid surface. A board will work; so will an ironing board. For small pets, you can use a pet carrier or even a cookie sheet or the blade of a snow shovel. As long as it's rigid and prevents the spine or pelvis from flexing, it will work.

Oblivious to Danger

People often wonder why dogs and cats run straight into traffic. It's not because they're stupid. Pets learn from experience, and car accidents, unfortunately, are lessons that they don't always survive. In addition, they simply don't see moving objects the same way people do. They run into traffic because they don't realize that they are in danger.

Dogs and cats have limited ability to focus on moving objects. They really can't tell whether a car is moving away from them or toward them, and they have difficulty judging the speed of oncoming traffic. Pets experience very little in the natural world that moves as quickly as a car.

The idea is to drag—not lift—your pet onto the surface by sliding a sheet or towel under him and gently pulling him onto the flat surface, then cover him and tape him down. Put one strip of tape across his body just in front of his hind legs and another strip just behind the front legs. Then get him in the car and drive to the vet's office. (See page 28 for more on moving pets safely.)

FOLLOW-UP CARE

■ Pets who have been hit hard enough to need first aid are going to need quite a bit of follow-up care, beginning with bandages. They should always be dry and clean. Your veterinarian will tell you how to change them to reduce the risk of reopening a wound.

■ Check your pet's toes several times a day to see if they're swollen, cold, or tender. These are signs that bandages are too tight and need to be loosened.

■ Smell the bandages once or twice a day. A distinctly bad smell means that an injury is getting infected. Another sign of trouble is licking. Pets who ignore their bandages for several days, then suddenly start licking or biting at them are probably having more pain, and this may mean that an infection is getting started. Fever, loss of appetite, or sudden behavior changes might also mean that there's an infection beneath the bandages. Call your vet if you note any of these signs.

■ Keep bandages clean by wrapping them with plastic wrap like Saran Wrap when your pet goes outside. Wounds need to breathe, though, so remove the plastic as soon as he comes back in.

■ Dogs and cats often view bandages as a challenge—things to be removed with their teeth. Veterinarians recommend coating bandages with a nasty-tasting substance. Bitter Apple, a pet repellent sold in pet stores, is a good choice.

Your veterinarian may give you a product called Variton, which also has a terrible taste that pets dislike.

■ Pets who have been badly injured need a lot of time to recover. Their natural instinct is to lie around all day, which is not good. Check with your vet to make sure that your pet doesn't need to be strictly confined. With the vet's okay, gently encourage your pet to get up, go outside, and move around a little bit. Movement helps increase blood circulation in the injured area and removes toxins. Lying around all day increases the risk of infection, pneumonia, or other complications. If your pet is unwilling to move, he may be in pain. Contact your vet if you think that's the case.

■ Your veterinarian may prescribe medication for pain. Don't use over-the-counter painkillers after a serious injury. Even though aspirin is safe for dogs, it can be toxic to cats. And because aspirin thins the blood and inhibits clotting, it can cause increased bleeding later on.

■ Clean minor cuts and scrapes once a day with an antiseptic liquid soap like Betadine Skin Cleanser.

Advisors

■ Shane Bateman, D.V.M., D.V.Sc., is a veterinarian board certified in the American College of Emergency and Critical Care Medicine and assistant professor of emergency and critical care medicine at Ohio State University College of Veterinary Medicine in Columbus.

■ Thomas Munschauer, D.V.M., is a veterinarian at Middlebury Animal Hospital in Vermont and past president of the Vermont Veterinary Medical Association

■ Sandra Sawchuk, D.V.M., is clinical instructor at the University of Wisconsin School of Veterinary Medicine in Madison.

■ Kevin Wallace, D.V.M., is an instructor in the department of clinical sciences at Cornell University College of Veterinary Medicine in Ithaca, New York.

■ David Wirth-Schneider, D.V.M., is a veterinarian at the Emergency Clinic for Animals in Madison, Wisconsin.

Carbon Monoxide Poisoning

CALL YOUR VET: **IMMEDIATELY**

Carbon monoxide is commonly found in car exhaust, improperly vented furnaces, and smoke from fires, because it's a natural by-product of fuel combustion. The colorless, odorless, tasteless gas is dangerous because when it is inhaled, it competes with and replaces oxygen in the bloodstream. Pets act drunk or confused and lethargic as the brain becomes starved for oxygen. The classic sign of carbon monoxide poisoning is bright cherry-red gums, but pets may also have labored breathing, deafness, and seizures.

The only antidote to the poison is oxygen therapy, which allows the body to get rid of the gas. First aid followed by immediate medical care may save your pet's life.

🩹 DO THIS NOW

Remove your pet from the source of the carbon monoxide. Get him into fresh outside air. When only a small amount of blood has been contaminated—less than 10%—pets recover simply by breathing clean air. Most of the time, these dogs and cats may act sleepy and woozy, but they remain conscious and return to normal within a day. If your cat or dog has any of these symptoms, take him to the vet.

Be ready to help your pet breathe. A blood gas level of 25% carbon monoxide or higher is potentially deadly. Cats and dogs often lose consciousness or stop breathing. Pets who stop

To give your dog artificial respiration, hold his mouth shut with a hand around his muzzle, cover his nose with your mouth, and blow gently into his nose until you see his chest rise. Give 15 to 20 breaths per minute.

FIRST ALERT

Antifreeze Poisoning

Dogs and cats like the sweet taste of antifreeze, which is actually a chemical called ethylene glycol. Lapping up a spill on the garage floor can be lethal—as little as 1 tablespoon can kill a cat, and ½ cup can kill a 20-pound dog. Besides drunken behavior, the poison can cause vomiting, diarrhea, and, rarely, seizures, usually within an hour or two of drinking it. The symptoms usually go away within 12 hours, but meanwhile, the digested antifreeze travels to the liver, where it is broken down into toxic by-products. These toxic by-products travel to the kidneys, where they can cause a complete shutdown, and the dog or cat will stop urinating. By the time the animal stops urinating, it is probably too late to reverse the damage, and he'll go into a coma and die.

A drug called 4-methylpyrazole (Fomepizole) is the antidote, but it must be given within an hour or two of the poisoning. If you see your pet drink antifreeze, make him vomit, and then get him medical attention. You can prompt your pet to vomit by giving him 1 to 2 teaspoons of 3% hydrogen peroxide for every 10 pounds of body weight (the foaming action will trigger a gag reflex). You may repeat this procedure two or three times, waiting about 5 minutes between doses. The hydrogen peroxide may work better if there is a little food in your pet's stomach, so try offering a small meal beforehand. If you don't have a needleless syringe, use a turkey baster or a squirt gun to squirt the peroxide into the back of your pet's mouth. If he acts depressed or drunk, however, vomiting could cause dangerous problems, so just get him to the vet.

breathing need oxygenated air immediately, so be prepared to give artificial respiration.

Hold your pet's mouth closed with one hand, cover his nose with your mouth, and blow into his nostrils until you see his chest expand. Try two quick breaths and watch to see if his chest rises. (Be sure that you don't breathe in the air that your pet exhales.) You'll need to give 15 to 20 breaths per minute until your pet starts breathing on his own again or until you reach medical help.

FOLLOW-UP CARE

■ No follow-up care is usually necessary once your pet returns from his hospital stay or office visit.

Advisors
■ Ken Lawrence, D.V.M., is a veterinarian at the Texoma Veterinary Hospital in Sherman, Texas.
■ Peter Levin, V.M.D., is a veterinarian at Ludwig's Corner Veterinary Hospital in Chester Springs, Pennsylvania.
■ Julie Moews, D.V.M., is a veterinarian at Bolton Veterinary Hospital in Connecticut.
■ Sandra Sawchuk, D.V.M., is clinical instructor at the University of Wisconsin School of Veterinary Medicine in Madison.

Cardiac Arrest

CALL YOUR VET: **IMMEDIATELY**

Dogs and cats don't have heart attacks, but several conditions can stop their hearts. A blow to the chest from a fall or car accident, temperature extremes like heatstroke, suffocation from drowning or choking, and even diseases like heartworms cause cardiac arrest.

Dogs and cats stop breathing before cardiac arrest occurs, and their gums may be pale or bluish. They'll completely lose consciousness, with no signs of life. You must immediately use CPR to try to restart the heart and breathing, then get medical help as soon as possible. Often, CPR isn't very successful without specialized veterinary equipment, but first aid at least gives your pet a chance.

DO THIS NOW

Check for a pulse. Determine if your pet's heart has stopped by taking his pulse. You won't be able to feel it in the carotid artery in the neck as you can with people. Instead, press the fingertips of your index, middle, and ring fingers into the crease where the inside of his thigh meets his body and feel for a pulse in the femoral artery, which is very big and near the surface. (This technique is illustrated on page 13.) If you can't feel the pulse, put your ear or hand flat against your pet's left side directly behind the elbow to listen or feel for the heartbeat.

Check his reflexes. Sometimes a pulse can be hard to find, so check for responsiveness.

- Call his name and watch for a response—even an ear twitch.
- Pull gently on his leg to see if he pulls back.
- Watch his eyes as you pinch hard between his toes; he'll blink if he's even partially conscious.
- Tap the inside corner of his eyelid to prompt a blink reflex.

No response means that he's unconscious. If he's unconscious but breathing and his heart is beating, continue to monitor for signs of cardiac arrest. Control any bleeding on the way to the clinic and treat for shock by wrapping him in a blanket. If you have it available, you can put a drop or two of Karo syrup or honey on his gums. This will help raise his blood sugar levels in case low blood sugar is the reason for his unconsciousness. (For more information on bleeding, see page 95; for shock, see page 333.)

If Your Pet's Heart Has Stopped

Begin artificial respiration. If your pet's heart has stopped and he has stopped breathing, start artificial respiration (see page 126), then begin chest compressions. If his heart restarts, control the bleeding, treat shock, and go to the vet.

Start CPR. Different CPR techniques are needed to get the circulation going, depending on the size of your pet.

To give CPR to a cat or small dog, cup your hand over the point of the chest, just behind the elbows. Squeeze firmly, pressing in about ½ inch, with your thumb on one side and your fingers on the other. This not only pumps the heart but also makes the pressure inside the chest (and against the heart) rapidly increase and decrease and helps move the blood. Ideally, one person gives chest compressions while a second performs artificial respiration. Give one breath for every 5 compressions. The goal is 80 to 100 compressions and 15 to 20 breaths per minute until your pet revives or you reach medical help.

Lay a medium-size or large dog on his side on a hard surface and, if it's readily available,

How CPR Works

CPR in people compresses the heart between the backbone and the flat breastbone, using sharp downward thrusts on the chest as the person lies on his back. The anatomy of flat-chested and very big dogs is similar. But in smaller pets, the chest is more pointed, so the heart "floats" inside the body between the breastbone and back. For pets larger than 10 pounds, chest compressions don't actually compress the heart but squeeze the blood vessels in the chest, causing the blood to flow.

place a small pillow or rolled blanket under the lower part of his chest. This will eliminate any dead space and improve the compressions. Put one hand on his chest at a comfortable position near the highest point of the chest wall. Place your other hand on top of the first, then press down firmly and vigorously with both hands, compressing the chest by 25 to 50%. (You may need to exert a lot of force with larger dogs, but don't worry about breaking bones—they'll heal.) Alternate compressions with breaths at the same rate as for small dogs. (This technique is illustrated on page 21.)

For a barrel-chested dog like a bulldog, lay the dog on his back, cross his paws over his breastbone, and kneel with his abdomen between your legs. Hold his paws and perform chest compressions by pushing downward directly over the breastbone. If your dog moves a lot while you are compressing his chest, put him on his side, then proceed as described above.

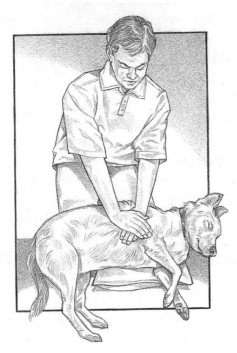

To give CPR to a medium-size or large dog, first lay him on his side on a hard surface and, if you have one, place a small pillow under the lower part of his chest. Then position one hand near the highest point of the chest wall, place your other hand over the first, and use both hands to compress your dog's chest.

Every minute, stop CPR to check for a pulse or breathing. If the heart starts again, stop the compressions but continue artificial respiration until your pet breathes on his own or you reach medical help. It's best to have someone drive you so you can continue the first aid while you're en route to the vet.

If all else fails, try acupuncture. Stick a needle or safety pin directly into the middle of the slit in your pet's upper lip beneath the nose. Insert it down to the bone and wiggle it back and forth. This will stimulate the release of a dose of adrenaline (epinephrine), a natural chemical that veterinarians use to jump-start the heart. (This technique is illustrated on page 23.)

If Your Pet Is Not Breathing

Open the airway. If your pet is not breathing but his heart is beating, continue to monitor for cardiac arrest while you try to start his breathing.

Before rescue breathing can help, the airway must be clear. Open your pet's mouth and look inside for a foreign object. If the airway is blocked, use a piece of gauze or cloth to grip his tongue and pull it outward to dislodge the object, or reach in with your fingers or small pliers or tongs to grab it. If you can't reach it, use a modified Heimlich maneuver.

For a cat or small dog, hold him with his back against your stomach, his head up, and his feet hanging down. Fit your fist into the soft hollow right under his rib cage and pull in and up toward your belly and chin with a strong thrusting action.

Put a larger dog on his side and kneel behind him, with your knees against his backbone. Lean over him and put your fist into the hollow beneath the rib cage, then push sharply upward and inward, toward the dog's head and your knees. (This technique is illustrated on page 23.)

Repeat the maneuver two or three times in succession, then check to see if the object has come loose in the mouth. If it hasn't, you can continue the maneuver in the car while someone drives you to the veterinarian.

Start artificial respiration. Once the airway is clear, close your pet's mouth, make sure that

FIRST ALERT

Heart Failure

Heart disease occurs often in dogs and cats, and one of the most common signs is a cough. When the heart isn't working efficiently—because of age, a hereditary weakness, or heartworms—fluid collects in the lungs and makes it difficult to breathe. Your pet may cough a lot in attempts to expel the fluid. He may seem agitated or distressed, and he may have trouble catching his breath, breathe more quickly than normal, or tire easily after minimal exertion. These are all potential signs of heart failure, so if your pet has these symptoms, take him to the vet right away.

Dogs with heart disease assume a characteristic posture when they breathe or cough. They'll stand with their elbows out as though they're holding themselves up. What they're really doing is giving the chest more room to expand.

his neck and head are in line with his back, and blow two quick breaths into his nostrils. Watch to see if his chest expands, then give 15 to 20 breaths a minute. You'll have to blow pretty hard to fill the lungs of really big dogs, but with cats and small dogs, be careful to just puff into the lungs so they don't rupture. The key is to blow only until the chest rises. (This technique is illustrated on page 20.)

Sometimes, air collects in the stomach when it goes down your pet's throat. Every few minutes, push on his stomach with your hand on the left side behind his ribs to expel it.

 ## FOLLOW-UP CARE

■ No follow-up care is usually necessary once your pet returns from his hospital stay or office visit. Your vet will instruct you if he thinks follow-up care is needed.

Advisors

■ Dale C. Butler, D.V.M., is a veterinarian at Best Friends Animal Hospital in Denison, Texas.

■ Martha S. Gearhart, D.V.M., D.A.B.V.P., is a veterinarian at Pleasant Valley Animal Hospital in New York.

■ Julie Moews, D.V.M., is a veterinarian at Bolton Veterinary Hospital in Connecticut.

Chest Injuries

CALL YOUR VET: **IMMEDIATELY**

Chest injuries are often due to blunt trauma—a pet is hit by a car, falls, or gets kicked by a horse or malicious human. Bites, bullets, arrows, or running into stationary objects can also cause terrible chest injuries. Cuts and lacerations may happen when pets encounter power grass trimmers or try to run through a glass door or wire fence. (For more information about cuts and wounds, see page 143.)

A chest injury is always painful, and dogs and cats may struggle to breathe. A hard blow to the chest can bruise the lungs or heart, and that also interferes with breathing. The animal may stretch his neck out to make breathing easier, respirations may become shallow or may be very labored and fast, and you'll probably see more motion in the abdomen with each breath. A broken bone can also pierce the lung and cause it to collapse. And any kind of wound that penetrates into the chest cavity will interfere with breathing, even if no other injury is present.

Any chest injury is an emergency that needs immediate medical attention. First aid can keep your pet more comfortable—or even keep him alive and breathing—until you can get help.

DO THIS NOW

Control the bleeding. Before doing anything else, stop any bleeding. The best method is direct pressure to the wound. Hold a clean cloth, gauze pad, or sanitary napkin against the wound and put firm pressure over the area with the palm of your hand or fingers. If the pad soaks through, don't remove it—that could disrupt clotting. Instead, just add another pad on top of the first and continue the pressure.

Treat your pet for shock. Shock can kill your pet in as little as 10 to 20 minutes, so prompt treatment can buy you time to get medical help. Keep your cat or dog as quiet as possible and wrap him in a blanket or towel to keep him warm. You can also put a drop or two of Karo syrup or honey on your pet's gums to help keep him conscious. (For more about shock, see page 333.)

Look for wounds. Check to see if your pet has an open chest wound that exposes the lung, or if there is a puncture that allows intermittent or continuous "sucking" of air into the chest when he inhales. In this case, you should get your pet to the vet as quickly as possible. In the meantime, there are a few techniques you can use to help your pet breathe.

If the wound has a tiny entry, like a puncture wound from a bite, you can seal it with a big wad of petroleum jelly or K-Y Jelly. Then put a clean cloth or clean plastic sandwich bag against the ointment on top of the opening and hold it in place with tape wrapped around the torso. If the wound is too large for ointment, cover it with a piece of plastic wrap like Saran Wrap to form a seal. Hold it in place with your hand or

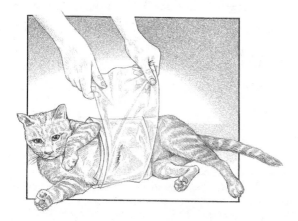

Wrap an open chest wound with plastic wrap to help protect the wound until you can get to the vet.

very lightly wrap it around your pet's chest while someone else drives you to the vet. (See "Sealing Sucking Wounds" on page 130.)

Once the wrap is in place, have your pet lie on the injured side. That keeps pressure on the bleeding, helps seal the hole, and also offers rigid structure to the chest wall if your pet has broken ribs.

FOLLOW-UP CARE

■ Most chest wounds are so serious that pets are hospitalized for treatment until they are out of danger. When surgery is necessary to repair torn internal structures or fix broken ribs, the dog or cat may have a large incision down one side of his body or down the breastbone. Keep the sutures clean by wiping away any drainage as needed, using a gauze pad soaked with sterile saline contact lens solution.

■ Some pets with massive chest wounds will still be bandaged when they come home. It's important to keep the bandage clean and dry because it will cause itching and infection if it gets wet. Protect the area by wrapping it with plastic wrap before your pet goes outside in rainy weather.

■ As the incision starts to heal, it may itch, and dogs especially may lick or chew at the sutures. Use a cone-shaped collar restraint like an Elizabethan collar to keep him from bothering the sutures. He can't eat while wearing the collar, though, so remove it during feedings. Or you can smear a tiny bit of Vicks VapoRub or Bitter Apple on the skin around the sutures. The odor and taste keep most pets from licking and chewing. Reapply as needed, usually once a day.

■ Depending on the injury, you may need to give antibiotics to prevent infection. Sticks and other foreign objects can put bacteria or even fungi deep inside a wound. It's pretty easy to hide a pill in a dab of peanut butter or cheese so that your dog will take it willingly. For cats, you can crush most medicines with the bowl of a spoon and mix them with wet cat food. If your cat refuses the medicated food, try grasping the back of her neck and pointing her nose at the ceiling—the trick is getting her nose perpendicular. This will prompt her to open wide. Drop the pill on the center dip of her tongue and close her mouth, keeping her nose pointed up. Gravity will do the rest, and she should swallow. Give her a treat to wash the pill down the rest of the way.

THE BEST APPROACH

Sealing Sucking Wounds

The area inside the chest is normally a vacuum that allows the lungs to easily expand when your pet inhales air. But when a wound punches through the chest wall, it's like switching on a vacuum cleaner inside the body. Air gets pulled into the cavity, and that pressure collapses the lungs so that they can't expand. Once the lungs collapse, your pet can suffocate. These injuries to the chest are commonly described as sucking wounds because of the way the air is pulled into the hole. Blood from the opening may bubble as air rushes in and out.

You can make a one-way valve that seals the wound to keep air from being sucked into your pet's chest yet allows the air inside to escape. This can help reestablish the normal vacuum, prevent the lungs from collapsing, and ease your pet's breathing until medical help is available.

Cut a section of plastic wrap or any clean plastic material (a sandwich bag or part of a clean garbage bag also works). Using first-aid tape, tape the plastic over the open wound so that it completely covers the injury, but tape it on only three of the four sides so that you can lift the open side, if necessary, to allow air to escape. As your pet inhales, her inflating lungs push air out of her chest cavity and back through the hole—the plastic will lift on that side and let it escape. But when she exhales and the lungs deflate, the sucking of the wound pulls the plastic against the hole and keeps any additional air from entering the chest cavity.

Advisors

■ Patricia Hague, D.V.M., is a veterinarian at the Cat Hospital of Las Colinas in Irving, Texas.

■ Barry N. Kellogg, V.M.D., is a veterinarian at the Center for Veterinary Care in Great Barrington, Massachusetts, and the head of VMAT 1 (Veterinary Medical Assistance Team), the national disaster team for veterinary medicine.

■ Mike McFarland, D.V.M., is a veterinarian at the Emergency Animal Clinic in Dallas.

■ Lenny Southam, D.V.M., is a house-call veterinarian at Targwood Animal Health Care in West Chester, Pennsylvania; manager of CompuServe's VetCare Forum; and coauthor of *The Pill Book Guide to Medication for Your Dog and Cat*.

Choking

CALL YOUR VET: **IF NEEDED**

Like people, dogs and cats choke if something lodges in their throats or wind-pipes. They gag, retch, and cough to try to expel the object, and they can be-come frantic when it won't move. Dogs are affected most often because they love to play catch and chew, and balls or pieces of toys or sticks can get caught in their throats.

Choking can quickly turn dangerous if the stuck object cuts off the air supply. Even a partial blockage can cause a pet to pass out, and if a ball sticks in her throat like a cork in a bottle, she may suffocate without prompt first aid.

🩹 DO THIS NOW

Quickly try to pull the object out. If your pet can't force breath past the object, she'll pass out and will die within minutes. You won't have time to wait for medical help or to restrain her. Make a quick attempt to reach the object. Pull her tongue out of the way first—use a cloth to grip it—then reach in and pull the object out. Balls are hard to grasp, but spoon-shaped tongs may work. If you can't get the object after one or two quick tries, use the Heimlich maneuver described on page 132.

If you can see the object and your pet will allow you, use a hemostat (a long, thin clamp available from pet-supply catalogs), blunt-tipped tweezers, or needle-nose pliers to grasp

the object and draw it out. Try once or twice, but don't prolong the struggle, or the stress could make her breathing worse until she col-lapses. As long as you can hear wheezing or some noise with the breathing, she's still getting air past the object, and you have time to get medical help.

Restrain your pet. If your pet is still conscious but having trouble breathing, you'll also need to remove the object manually. A panicked pet may bite out of fear, so don't try to look in her mouth until you have help to restrain her. Have the other person wrap her in a towel to contain her flailing legs or hug her around the neck and

FIRST ALERT

Rabies

Unless you know the animal, never attempt to help a dog or cat who appears to be choking, because it could expose you to rabies. The "dumb" form of the disease includes throat paralysis that makes animals salivate and drool. They can't swallow, so it looks as if something is stuck in their throats and they're choking. Pets with dumb rabies usually become comatose and die in 3 to 10 days. Those with the "furious" form act insane, attack with no warning, eat and chew inedible objects like wood and stones, and eventually become paralyzed and die within 4 to 7 days.

There is no cure for rabies, and it is extremely contagious to people. If you suspect that a strange dog or cat may be infected, *avoid all contact.* Call your veterinarian, the animal control office, or the county health department for advice.

---

body in a kind of half-nelson hold. Then you can grasp the top of her muzzle and gently press her lips against her teeth with your thumb and fingers on either side of the mouth to prompt her to open wide.

Try gentle compressions. You could try putting your hands on either side of the widest point of her chest while she's in a standing position and give three or four firm, gentle compressions to see if that will knock the object loose. If she's lying on her side, make sure that her neck is level with her chest, then use your cupped palm to clap against her side at the highest point of the chest.

Use a modified Heimlich maneuver. This can dislodge objects that you have trouble gripping. For a cat or small dog, hold her back against your stomach with her head up and feet hanging down. Fit your fist into the soft hollow immediately beneath her rib cage and pull in and up toward your belly and chin with a strong thrusting action.

For a larger dog, put her on her side as you kneel behind her with your knees against her backbone. Lean over and put your fist into the hollow beneath the rib cage, then push sharply upward and inward, toward the dog's head and your knees. Repeat this maneuver two or three times in succession, then check to see if the object has come loose in the mouth. If it hasn't, you can continue the maneuver in the car while someone drives you to the veterinarian. (This technique is illustrated on page 22.)

Be ready to give artificial respiration. When the object is dislodged, most pets start breathing again and may quickly revive, but you may need to give artificial respiration to jumpstart the system again. Close your pet's mouth with your hand, blow two quick breaths into her nose and watch to see if her chest rises. Continue giving 15 to 20 breaths a minute until she starts breathing or until you reach the veterinarian. (This technique is illustrated on page 20.)

Transport your pet. Carry your pet in your arms or in a pet carrier, whichever makes her more comfortable. Turn on the air conditioner in the car. (Dogs cool off by panting, and when something is stuck down their throats, they can become overheated very quickly.)

 FOLLOW-UP CARE

■ If the foreign object has injured your pet's throat, it will need a week or more to heal, and it may hurt to swallow regular food. Feed her a soft diet for at least a week. You can make gruel (a thin porridge) by running food through a blender with warm water or low-fat, no-salt chicken broth.

■ Your vet will prescribe antibiotics if your pet's throat has been injured or if she bit her tongue trying to get rid of the object and needed stitches. You'll usually have to give her pills two or three times a day for about 10 days. For a dog, you can hide pills in the soft food you're giving her. For a cat, put her on a tabletop, grasp the scruff of her neck, and gently arch her neck backward—her mouth will automatically fall open. Use your other hand to pull down her chin until you can see the V-shaped indentation in the center of her tongue. Drop the pill on the V, close her mouth, and she'll swallow it right down. Offer a treat immediately so she won't spit out the medicine.

THE BEST APPROACH

Hemostats

Veterinarians rely on specialized instruments to remove foreign objects from a pet's mouth or throat. Although needle-nose pliers or tongs work in a pinch, the ideal choice is a long, thin tool called a hemostat.

A hemostat works like scissors and has a similar handle, but instead of blades, the "jaws" come together like very long, thin pliers. They can be either straight or curved. The handle also has a locking mechanism so that once the jaws grip an object, they won't let go until they're mechanically released. You can find a variety of hemostats in pet-supply catalogs.

Advisors

■ Ken Lawrence, D.V.M., is a veterinarian at the Texoma Veterinary Hospital in Sherman, Texas.

■ Peter Levin, V.M.D., is a veterinarian at Ludwig's Corner Veterinary Hospital in Chester Springs, Pennsylvania.

■ Billy Martindale, D.V.M., is a veterinarian at the Animal Hospital of Denison, Texas, and chairman of the board of directors of the Texas Veterinary Medical Association.

■ Kevin Wallace, D.V.M., is an instructor in the department of clinical sciences at Cornell University College of Veterinary Medicine in Ithaca, New York.

Clothes-Dryer Injuries

CALL YOUR VET: **IMMEDIATELY**

Cats love heat. They seek out warmth whenever possible, and one of the most attractive places is inside the dryer. Clothes-dryer injuries happen almost exclusively to cats rather than dogs, when a cat ends up spinning with the clothes.

Most of the time, the cat is too disoriented and occupied with trying to keep her balance to cry or scream. But you'll hear a horrendous thumping noise as her body is battered around inside the machine—kind of like the noise a sneaker makes when it is tossed about in the dryer. Battering injuries that include bruises and head trauma are the most serious problems. Cats with concussion can lose consciousness or have seizures, but more often, they'll act drunk, cry a lot, and won't be able to walk in a straight line. Their pupils may be unequal in size if there's a head injury. (For more information about head injuries, see page 232.)

The high temperature of the dryer can also cause overheating and problems with breathing, and battering can cause shock. All cases of clothes-dryer injuries need medical attention. But first aid can delay the onset of shock and keep your injured cat alive until help is at hand.

DO THIS NOW

Get your pet to the vet. Head injury is almost inevitable. If your cat is unconscious, wrap her in a sheet, leaving her head uncovered, and transport her to the clinic as soon as possible. The sheet will help contain her struggles if she regains her senses in the car on the way there.

It's best to keep your cat in pet carrier or box because carrying her on your lap can increase stress.

Check for signs of shock. Shock can develop very quickly following a clothes-dryer injury,

FIRST ALERT

Burns

Burns caused by the clothes dryer are rare, but they can happen. Usually, though, you won't notice them until several days after the accident, when the top surface of the skin starts to die. The skin in these areas starts to thicken and feels very firm, and the fur over the area becomes matted from the leaking of fluid.

Once the skin has died, the flesh will slough away, and you'll need to keep the raw area clean so that it can begin to heal. Use blunt scissors or electric clippers to trim away fur beyond the margins of the injured area so that it's easier to treat. If you're using scissors, first slip your index and second fingers through the fur and hold them against the affected area. Cut the fur so that it's level with your fingers, clipping a 1-inch border all the way around the burn. (This technique is illustrated on page 114.) A stream of plain water with a mild antiseptic liquid soap like Betadine Skin Cleanser will help clean the area. Aloe vera products such as ointments can help speed healing, but deep or extensive burns may need special bandages and take a long time to heal. Any serious burn should be treated by your vet. (For more information about heat burns, see page 113.)

from the battering, the heat, or a combination of the two. Usually, it's a good idea to keep shock victims warm, but in this case, your cat is probably too warm, if anything. Put a drop or two of Karo syrup or honey on your pet's gums to help keep her conscious.

Make sure she's still breathing. Pets with head injuries who have lost consciousness may also stop breathing. If your pet is not breathing, first gently pull her tongue forward to make sure that it's not blocking her throat. Then close her mouth with one hand, sealing her lips closed, and completely cover her nose with your mouth. Give two breaths and watch to see if her chest rises. Continue to blow gently, with just enough pressure to make her chest rise, then let

the air escape before giving another breath. Give 15 to 20 breaths a minute until your cat starts breathing again on her own or until you reach medical help. (This technique is illustrated on page 20.)

 SPECIAL SITUATION

If you suspect heatstroke: Heatstroke can develop if your cat was in the dryer for any length of time. If she's not too upset, take her temperature to be sure that she's in the normal range of 99° to 102.5°F. Gently grasp her tail and insert a lubricated rectal thermometer into the rectum, just as you would for an infant. You can use petroleum jelly or vegetable oil to grease it up. (This technique is illustrated on page 9.)

If her temperature is up to 104°F, sponge the pads of her feet with rubbing alcohol, and the evaporative action will cool her down. If her temperature is higher than 104°F, it's quickest to dip her in cool water. Take her temperature every 5 minutes and stop the cooling-off process when the thermometer shows 103°F, because her body will continue to cool down on its own to normal—and you don't want her temperature to fall too far. (For more information about heatstroke, see page 237.)

 ## FOLLOW-UP CARE

■ Cats who survive clothes-dryer injuries will be pretty beaten up and will probably have many dark red bruises that are easiest to see around the head and ears, where the fur is shortest. Because bruises can develop anywhere on the body, systematically part the fur all over and inspect the skin. The sooner you apply cold packs to the sore areas, the better. The cold not only numbs the pain but also helps constrict blood vessels and reduce bruising. It takes about 15 minutes of application to do the best job. Apply cold packs two or three times a day for the first 2 days. First, place a cold, wet washcloth on the area. Then apply a ready-made cold pack, a plastic bag of ice, of a bag of frozen vegetables.

■ The injured cat may act a bit woozy and disoriented for hours to days after the clothes-dryer encounter. With head injuries, the veterinarian may prescribe medication. How long it will be needed depends on the extent of the injury. To give a pill, place one hand on the top of your cat's head, with your index finger and thumb gently pressing each side of the cat's lips against her teeth. This prompts her to open wide, and when she does, drop the pill to the back of her tongue, then close her mouth and watch for her to swallow. Follow the pill with a tasty treat, like a tidbit of smoked turkey sandwich meat. She'll forget to try to spit out the pill and it will go down with the treat. (This technique is illustrated on page 30.)

■ Your cat probably won't go near the dryer again after one encounter. But to be sure, bang loudly on the top of the machine and check inside before you close the door and turn it on.

Advisors

■ Shane Bateman, D.V.M., D.V.Sc., is a veterinarian board certified in the American College of Emergency and Critical Care Medicine and assistant professor of emergency and critical care medicine at Ohio State University College of Veterinary Medicine in Columbus.

■ Bernadine Cruz, D.V.M., is a veterinarian at Laguna Hills Animal Hospital in California.

■ Kenneth J. Drobatz, D.V.M., is a veterinarian and associate professor of critical care emergency service at the Veterinary Hospital of the University of Pennsylvania in Philadelphia.

■ Karen Hoffman, V.M.D., is a veterinarian at Delaware Valley Animal Hospital in Fairless Hills, Pennsylvania.

■ Jean C. Hofve, D.V.M., is a veterinarian and Companion Animal Program coordinator for the Animal Protection Institute in Sacramento.

Collapse

CALL YOUR VET: **IMMEDIATELY**

When your cat or dog suddenly falls over and can't get up, you must be a detective to figure out what caused the collapse. Pets who chew electrical wires can have delayed reactions to the shock and collapse up to an hour later when their lungs fill up with fluid. And some ingested poisons can knock pets out. A collapsed lung, internal bleeding from injury or from a cancerous growth, getting too hot or too cold, an allergic reaction to a bug bite, heart disease, and many other things can stop pets in their tracks.

It may take specialized tests to figure out the cause and get the right treatment. But first aid will help no matter what the reason, and it can save your pet's life.

DO THIS NOW

Help your pet breathe. When a pet has collapsed, be prepared to perform artificial respiration and/or CPR if she stops breathing or her heart stops. For artificial respiration, put your mouth directly over your pet's nose and breathe into her nose. Give two quick breaths, then wait to see if her chest rises. Then continue to give 15 to 20 breaths a minute until she starts breathing on her own or you reach medical help. (This technique is illustrated on page 20.) While you are breathing for her, check every 30 seconds or so to see if her heart is still beating.

Be ready to perform CPR. Listen or feel for the heartbeat behind your pet's left elbow. If you can't hear or feel it, begin CPR. Perform 5 heart compressions and then give a breath. For cats and small dogs, cup your hand over the point of the chest, with your thumb on one side and fingers on the other, and squeeze in a "coughlike" manner, compressing the chest about ½ inch. The goal is 80 to 100 compressions per minute.

Lay a larger dog on her side on a hard surface and press on the highest part of her chest. This changes the pressure most significantly within the chest cavity, and it's this increasing and decreasing

FIRST ALERT

Heart Disease

Pets can develop different kinds of heart disease, especially as they grow older. Dogs most commonly develop congestive heart failure. They tend to tire easily with exercise and may faint, and they may cough or have labored breathing or a swollen abdomen. Cats can have these signs, too, but they also commonly suffer sudden rear-leg paralysis from a blood clot formed due to cardiomyopathy, a disorder of the heart muscle that may involve thickening and obstructive damage to the heart. Both cats and dogs can collapse and die without warning from heartworms, parasites that infest the heart and lungs.

Many pets can be helped and their heart disease controlled with drug therapy that gets rid of excess fluid, adjusts the heart rate, or kills the parasites. Most heart diseases can be successfully treated with medication for extended periods of time. If you suspect heart trouble, see your veterinarian immediately.

pressure that actually moves blood forward. Place your hands on top of each other against the chest, then press down to compress about 25 to 50%. (CPR is illustrated on page 21; for more information about cardiac arrest, see page 124.)

Try something sweet. If your pet is breathing and her heart is beating but she is still collapsed after 2 to 3 minutes, offer her 2 to 3 tablespoons of Karo syrup or honey and go to the vet. This will help counteract low blood sugar, which can develop with many kinds of organ failures, heatstroke, hypothermia, and even shock, any of which can cause collapse. If she can't swallow, rub a small amount of Karo or honey on the inside of her lips and gums so that her body will absorb it through the mucous membranes. If the collapse is due to low blood sugar alone, you'll see a dramatic improvement in only 10 minutes or so, but in any case, have your pet ex-

amined as soon as possible. (For more information about low blood sugar, see page 281.)

Watch for shock symptoms. Any kind of accident or bleeding injury can plunge your pet into shock so that she collapses as her circulation fails. She'll also have pale gums and rapid breathing. Wrap her in a blanket to keep her warm. You can also put a drop or two of Karo syrup or honey on your pet's gums to help keep her conscious. (For more information about shock, see page 333.)

Keep your pet warm. Pets who get very cold collapse when their body temperatures fall below normal. They may get so cold that they stop shivering, and their gums turn gray or blue. Wrap your pet in a warm blanket and get her to the veterinarian immediately. (For more information about hypothermia, see page 248.)

Keep your pet cool. Heatstroke may also cause collapse. This typically happens on a very hot day. Pets pant, feel very hot, and have bright red gums. Use a rectal thermometer lubricated with petroleum jelly to take your pet's temperature. If it's 105°F or lower, you can treat her at home, and she probably won't need medical attention as long as her temperature is lowered quickly. You may want to take her to the vet just in case. Temperatures in excess of 106°F need emergency treatment even after first aid. Cool your pet off to 103°F before you head for the veterinarian by using cool (not cold!) water from the sink or hose. (For more information about heatstroke, see page 237.)

Check for ticks. Pets who are bitten by ticks can suffer paralysis from a neurotoxin in the tick saliva. Dogs are affected most often, but cats and people aren't immune. Dogs first become weak, then collapse and are unable to walk. If your pet collapses, go to the vet immediately; don't take the time to remove the ticks. (For more about ticks, see page 380.)

Be alert for back injury. Move your pet as little as possible to prevent further damage to the spine. Put a small pet on a rigid surface like

Reading Gum Color

Different health conditions may turn your pet's gums various colors. Watch for these signs.

- White gums: shock, anemia
- Blue gums: smoke inhalation, suffocation
- Red gums: carbon monoxide poisoning, heatstroke
- Yellow gums: liver problems

a TV tray or bread board or inside a rigid box or pet carrier if you can manage it. A large dog also should be moved on a rigid surface like a wooden plank or ironing board. The next best thing is a blanket stretcher. Put the dog on the blanket so that two people can lift him by grasping the ends of the material to make a hammock-type conveyance. (For more information about back injury, see page 75.)

FOLLOW-UP CARE

■ No follow-up care is usually necessary once your pet returns from her hospital stay or office visit. Your vet will instruct you if he feels that follow-up is needed.

Advisors

■ Gary Block, D.V.M., is a veterinarian in Coventry, Rhode Island.

■ Dale C. Butler, D.V.M., is a veterinarian at Best Friends Animal Hospital in Denison, Texas.

■ Bernadine Cruz, D.V.M., is a veterinarian at Laguna Hills Animal Hospital in California.

■ Ken Lawrence, D.V.M., is a veterinarian at the Texoma Veterinary Hospital in Sherman, Texas.

■ John Rush, D.V.M., is a veterinarian board certified in the American College of Emergency and Critical Care Medicine and section head of emergency and critical care service at Tufts University School of Veterinary Medicine in North Grafton, Massachusetts.

Constipation

CALL YOUR VET: **IF NEEDED**

Dogs can develop constipation from eating wads of grass or from swallowing bones, and cats may get plugged with hairballs. Very furry dogs and cats can get constipated when soft stool forms mats in the long fur around the rectum and mechanically blocks the opening. Waste held for a long time against the skin leads to irritation and infection, which can make pets so sore that they don't even want to try to defecate. Dogs with this problem often try to defecate while standing up, or they may whine, "scoot" (drag their bottoms against the floor), or bite at their rear ends. You'll also notice a terrible smell.

If it doesn't seem that your pet has this type of constipation, but he has not had a bowel movement in several days, contact your vet for instructions on how to give an enema. Then, once your pet is "unblocked," you can use a laxative, stool softener, or high-fiber diet to help keep him regular. Enemas meant for humans could be dangerous to your pet, so ask the vet about appropriate enema and laxative products.

Older pets are more prone to develop problems because they may not have frequent bowel movements. The longer waste sits in the body, the more water the colon pulls out of it, making it drier and harder to pass. Sometimes, the rectum stretches with this hard fecal mass and damages the nerves and muscles. This is called mega-colon, and pets with this condition require medical management for the rest of their lives. Pets with severe constipation stop eating, vomit, develop painful tummies, and may need to be sedated for the veterinarian to remove the impaction. But most cases of constipation are easy to treat at home.

DO THIS NOW

Cover the work area. Dealing with constipation can be a nasty job. Prepare your work area by spreading absorbent towels on a table or on the floor. You'll also want to wear disposable medical gloves (available at drugstores).

Restrain your pet. Dogs and cats with mechanical constipation get very sore, so have a second person gently restrain your pet before you begin to treat him. For a dog, slip one arm around his neck and the other arm around his chest to hug him to you.

To restrain a cat, grasp the scruff of her neck with one hand, capture both rear paws with the other hand, and gently stretch her on her side on a tabletop. (Both of these techniques are illustrated on page 18.)

Clip his fur. For longhaired pets with mats, clip away the fur under the tail. Carefully use blunt scissors or electric clippers to get rid of the furry mess. Then, dampen a washcloth with warm water and clean off anything on the outside of the anal area that's blocking the way. A warm-water rinse with a sink sprayer attachment or spray bottle may soak matter free more comfortably and also prompt your pet to move his bowels.

If your pet doesn't defecate within 12 to 24 hours after clipping, take him to the vet. There is probably some underlying cause of the constipation that should be treated. The longer you wait, the more serious the problem can become.

 ## FOLLOW-UP CARE

■ Adding fiber to your pet's food will prevent constipation in most pets who have a mild problem from time to time. A high-fiber commercial food will work, or you can mix unflavored Metamucil into canned food. Check the label for the type that supplies 2.4 grams of sol-

✚ FIRST ALERT

Urinary Blockage

We often assume that dogs and cats who strain to go to the bathroom or make frequent unproductive visits to the litter box or yard are constipated. More often, however, it's a sign of urinary blockage, especially in cats.

The minerals in urine can crystallize and plug up the urethra so that the pet can't pass urine. When urine can't escape, the bladder fills to bursting. Urine backs up to the kidneys and can cause irreversible damage. Pets can die very quickly once they become blocked, from a combination of shock and the toxins that build up in the body. Urinary blockage is a medical emergency that needs veterinary care immediately. (For more information, see page 402.)

Corkscrew Tail Risk

Dog breeds that have corkscrew tails, like Boston terriers and bulldogs, often have anatomical structures that can interfere with normal defecation. Spiral tail bones tend to extend downward and press against the anal canal, pinching the rectum nearly closed against the pelvis. Besides the typical signs of constipation, these dogs may produce flat, ribbonlike stools. Most cases of these "tied-down" tails require surgery.

uble fiber per dose. For dogs, use 1 teaspoon per meal for each 10 to 25 pounds of body weight. Use ½ teaspoon for a small cat and 1 teaspoon for a large cat. For pets who eat dry food, mix the Metamucil with a little canned food as a daily treat. Sprinkling it on the dry food and mixing in a little water might also work.

■ The skin around the rectum often is raw or weepy after you've clipped the fur and washed the area. Apply an antibiotic ointment like Neosporin three times a day for several days until the inflammation goes away. It's best to keep the rear ends of furry pets clipped close. Rinse them off after bowel movements when necessary.

■ Some pets have problems with chronic constipation because their intestines don't work normally. One type of prescription medication, Lactulose, may help by increasing the amount of water retained by the fecal material, allowing for softer bowel movements. Give the medication as directed by your vet.

THE BEST APPROACH

Pumpkin Prevention

One of the best and healthiest ways to prevent constipation is to mix pumpkin into your pet's food. Pumpkin is very high in fiber and has a high water content, and both of these factors help keep pets regular. Even better, most dogs and cats love the taste, especially of canned pumpkin. It takes only 1 to 2 teaspoons per meal for a cat or dog who weighs less than 15 pounds or 1 to 2 tablespoons for a dog who weighs 15 to 35 pounds. Larger dogs will need 2 to 5 tablespoons.

To make it simple to use, buy jumbo-size cans when they go on sale, then freeze the right amounts in muffin papers and thaw them as needed. You'll know that you've given too much if your pet's feces aren't formed and they have a puddinglike consistency. If this happens, just cut back on the amount of pumpkin.

Advisors

■ Clint Chastain, D.V.M., is a veterinarian at Preston Road Animal Hospital in Dallas.

■ Jean C. Hofve, D.V.M., is a veterinarian and Companion Animal Program coordinator for the Animal Protection Institute in Sacramento.

■ Peter Levin, V.M.D., is a veterinarian at Ludwig's Corner Veterinary Hospital in Chester Springs, Pennsylvania.

■ Kate Lindley, D.V.M., is a veterinarian and owner of Kitty Klinic in Lacey, Washington.

Cuts and Wounds

CALL YOUR VET: **IF NEEDED**

The skin is the largest organ of the body, and its three layers protect pets from bacteria and other germs. Wounds open the gate to infection in both dogs and cats, and a cut blood vessel can cause life-threatening bleeding. Cuts and wounds can often be hard to see because they are hidden by fur.

Pets get cuts for all kinds of reasons, from car accidents and animal bites to tears from thorns or barbed wire or even running through plate-glass windows. Pet owners often cut their pets' skin accidentally when they try to trim out matted fur. Cats are more prone to cuts than dogs because their skin is thinner.

Deep wounds that cut through the skin into the flesh need stitches within 2 to 4 hours to heal most effectively. Shallow wounds and minor cuts may need only home care, but even those that need medical attention can be helped by first aid. Surface cuts can look more dangerous than they are when they bleed a lot, but they're usually less prone to infection than puncture wounds.

DO THIS NOW

Muzzle your pet. An injured pet may bite you when he's in pain, so don't try to help him without safe restraints. Unless there's a head injury or breathing problem, use a length of fabric like a necktie to muzzle your dog. (See page 17 for an illustration of this technique.) If your dog has a pushed-in nose or it's your cat who has been cut, put a pillowcase or towel over his head to prevent him from biting. It helps to have one person restrain and gently talk to your pet while the second person performs first aid.

Stop the bleeding. Put direct pressure against the wound with a gauze pad or clean cloth. If blood soaks through, just add another pad on top and continue the pressure. If you lift the pad, you could disturb the clot. (For more information about bleeding, see page 95.)

Control bleeding from the paws. Lacerations to foot pads bleed a lot because paws have a big blood supply. Put a pressure bandage on the paw to control the bleeding. (This also keeps bloody paw prints off your floor until you can get medical help.) Put a gauze pad against the wound, slip a cotton sock over the foot, and tape a plastic bag on top of the sock. The bags that newspapers come in work well. For pets with small paws, an even better alternative is to cover the paw bandage with a condom. Make sure that whatever covering you choose fits snugly enough to apply pressure to the wound without restricting circulation. You should be able to slip one or two fingers under the bandage. If your pet starts biting at it or seems excessively bothered by it, it may be too tight. Try the two-finger test and loosen it if necessary.

Get to the vet if bleeding won't stop. If heavy bleeding continues for more than 5 minutes, the injury has probably cut a vein or artery. Continue to apply direct pressure and head for

---

⊕ **FIRST ALERT**

Maggots

Flies are more than a filthy nuisance, especially for pets who have draining cuts or wounds. Flies lay eggs in open wounds, and within 12 to 24 hours, the tiny larvae, called maggots, hatch. It takes only 4 to 5 days for maggots to grow from 1 to 2 millimeters to an inch or more, because they eat so much. They live off the drainage and dead tissue from infected wounds. Maggots also tend to develop when feces soil the area around the tail and flies lay eggs in it.

Maggots burrow into the skin and are extremely painful. Because antibiotics may be necessary, visit your vet at the first sign of maggots. To help make your pet more comfortable until the appointment, try a 15-minute flush with plain, lukewarm water. This may encourage some of the maggots to leave the area in search of air. (For more about maggots, see page 284.)

your veterinarian's office right away. If possible, have a friend drive so that you can keep up continuous pressure.

Trim your pet's fur. Once the bleeding has stopped, use blunt scissors or electric clippers to trim the fur around the wound. If you're using scissors, first slip your index and second fingers through the fur and hold them against the wound. Cut the fur so that it's level with your fingers, clipping a 1-inch border all the way around the wound. (This technique is illustrated on page 114.) That helps you judge how serious the wound is and also removes bacteria and potential contaminants in the fur from contact with the wound. If the skin is broken, fill the wound with a water-soluble lubricant like K-Y Jelly before you clip. Then thoroughly rinse the area with warm water. The trimmed hair sticks to the jelly and washes out.

Clean shallow wounds. Wash shallow cuts that don't go completely through the skin with an antiseptic liquid soap like Betadine Skin Cleanser and water or a mild soap and water, then pat dry with a clean, soft cloth. You can also use a bit of 3% hydrogen peroxide on a clean cloth to wipe off the area around the wound. Hydrogen peroxide can damage skin cells, though, so don't pour or dab it directly on the wound. Use antibiotic cream like Neosporin or antiseptic spray like Bactine to help prevent infection.

Flush out deep wounds. Cuts and wounds need stitches if they're so deep that they gape open or if they're located near joints, which will put tension on the wound and interfere with healing. Use

lukewarm water to flush deep wounds. Flushing helps wash out germs and debris so that you can see how extensive the wound is. Then, wearing disposable medical gloves (available in drugstores), use your finger or hand to dislodge any stubborn material. Once dried blood, fur, or other debris is gone, you can gently wash the area with mild soap and water and pat it dry.

For puncture wounds like animal bites, call your vet. He will probably want to check the wound that day and will probably prescribe antibiotics. Until you get to the vet's office, keep the injury open so that it doesn't seal in bacteria that can cause infection. If you can't see your vet for several hours, apply a hot compress. You can use a ready-made hot pack wrapped in a towel or a washcloth soaked in hot water. Two to five times a day, hold it against the puncture, 5 minutes on, 5 minutes off, until it cools. (For more information about animal bites, see page 90.)

Apply some antibiotic ointment like Neosporin to minor cuts and wounds to help fight infection, but don't medicate deep wounds until after the vet has stitched them closed.

Bandage gaping wounds. You should leave puncture wounds open, but protect gaping wounds with a bandage. Press a gauze pad, a clean towel, or even a sanitary napkin or disposable diaper against the wound and secure it in place with an elastic bandage like an Ace bandage and tape. Make sure that the bandage is not too tight by slipping two fingers beneath the wrapping. If you don't have an Ace bandage, plastic wrap like Saran Wrap works well as a temporary measure, especially on body

When Your Cat Hurts Himself

Accidental cuts and bites are bad enough, but some cats actually give themselves bloody wounds. Hyperesthesia syndrome is a type of psychological disorder, an obsessive-compulsive problem that seems to affect Siamese, Burmese, Himalayan, and Abyssinian cats most often.

It usually first appears when the cat is between 1 and 4 years of age. As many as 4 percent of cats seen for behavioral problems suffer from mild to severe hyperesthesia syndrome. In the mildest form, the cat simply becomes a grooming fanatic and may lick off big patches of his fur. Other cats show inexplicable aggression and may go from friendly purring and rubbing to attack mode when their owners pet them. But some cats become so agitated that they bite and mutilate themselves and cause bloody wounds. Sometimes, this condition is triggered by itchy skin from an allergy or from fleas or other parasites, or it can result from stress from things like loud noises, traffic, or a new baby in the house. The extreme version of this malady is very rare. More likely, your cat will groom himself excessively, leading to hair loss but not to a wound.

This syndrome can be hard to diagnose and may take specialized testing like an MRI (magnetic resonance imaging) or SPECT (single photon emission computed tomography) scan to look at the cat's brain. A few cats can be jarred out of their mutilating behavior by distracting them with a loud hand clap or a squirt of water from a spray bottle. Others may be helped by drugs like fluoxetine hydrochloride (Prozac), which put a damper on self-destructive impulses. Your veterinarian or animal-behavior specialist can determine the root of your cat's problem and the best treatment.

wounds—you won't even need tape because it sticks to itself. Shoulder wounds are hard to bandage, but a T-shirt slipped onto your pet will give good protection. While your vet is checking out the wound, ask for a demonstration of how to protect the area as it heals and ask for appropriate bandage materials.

FOLLOW-UP CARE

■ Clean all wounds once or twice a day. Use a gauze pad with water and Betadine Skin Cleanser to cleanse the wound, and keep washing until you can see all the edges as well as the bottom of the wound clearly.

■ If your pet has stitches and there is a lot of blood and crust around the cut, wipe off any drainage and clean the area with a small amount of 3% hydrogen peroxide on a gauze pad.

■ Pets who have been bitten or suffered other types of puncture wounds may need oral antibiotics, prescribed by the vet, several times a day. The easiest way to pill your dog is to circle the top of his snout with your hand, pressing both sides of the jaw along the gums just behind the large, pointed canine teeth. Then use your other hand to push the pill over the hill of the tongue, close his mouth, and gently stroke his throat until he swallows. (This technique is illustrated on page 30.)

With a cat, put her on a tabletop, grasp the scruff of her neck, and gently arch her neck backward—her mouth will automatically fall open. Look for the V-shaped indentation in the center of her tongue. Drop the pill on the V and close her mouth, then offer a treat so she is more interested in that than in spitting out the medicine.

■ Bruising is a sign of broken blood vessels. Applying cold packs wrapped in a cold, wet washcloth for 10 to 30 minutes at a time several times a day will reduce inflammation and pain, and they're actually more effective than many drugs.

■ Watch for a fever, swelling, heat, obvious pain, or discharge (especially if it's foul-smelling or puslike) from the wound, which could indicate an infection. Infection can turn into an abscess, which may need to be cleaned out by a veterinarian. (For more information about abscesses, see page 60.)

■ Keep your pet indoors except for bathroom trips. When he goes outside, cover the injury with a temporary bandage. Most wounds heal better if left open to the air, though, so don't leave the bandage on for more than a couple of hours at a time.

■ Dogs often lick and chew stitches or sores, and that interferes with healing. Use a foul-tasting product like Bitter Apple on the area around the wound or fit your pet with a collar restraint called an Elizabethan collar. He won't be able to eat while wearing the collar, though, so be sure to remove it during feedings.

THE BEST APPROACH

Skin Glue

For most shallow wounds (not penetrating wounds or bite wounds), you can glue the skin together to help speed healing. Veterinary products like Nexaband S/C tissue glue are available from pet-supply catalogs. Products like New-Skin Liquid Bandage, available in drugstores, also work well for minor cuts. You don't need a bandage, and the glue sloughs off in about a week. Before using it, clean and disinfect the cut thoroughly to avoid sealing in infection. Apply the glue in a thin line to the edges of the cut, then hold them together with your fingers for about 10 seconds, until they bond together.

Advisors

■ Shane Bateman, D.V.M., D.V.Sc., is a veterinarian board certified in the American College of Emergency and Critical Care Medicine and assistant professor of emergency and critical care medicine at Ohio State University College of Veterinary Medicine in Columbus.

■ Bernadine Cruz, D.V.M., is a veterinarian at Laguna Hills Animal Hospital in California.

■ James M. Harris, D.V.M., is a veterinarian at Montclair Veterinary Hospital in Oakland, California.

■ Carin A. Smith, D.V.M., is a veterinarian in Leavenworth, Washington, and author of *101 Training Tips for Your Cat.*

■ Elaine Wexler-Mitchell, D.V.M., is a veterinarian at The Cat Care Clinic in Orange, California, and president of the Academy of Feline Medicine.

■ H. Ellen Whiteley, D.V.M., is a veterinarian in Guadalupita, New Mexico, and author of *Understanding and Training Your Cat or Kitten* and *Understanding and Training your Dog or Puppy.*

Dehydration

CALL YOUR VET: **IF NEEDED**

MEDICINE CHEST

Needleless syringe or
    turkey baster
Water
Ice cubes
Rehydration fluid
    (Pedialyte)

Cats' and dogs' bodies are made up of 60 percent water. That means there's more than 7 pounds of liquid in your 12-pound pet. When the water ratio falls even 5 percent below normal, pets start to show signs of dehydration. Pets are prone to dehydration when the weather is very hot and not enough water is available, but more often, vomiting and diarrhea cause the problem.

If your pet's eyes look different than they normally do and he is showing signs of weakness or lethargy, dehydration is probably becoming severe. Mild cases of dehydration, when the pet has no fever, diarrhea, or vomiting and is still interacting with the family, can be helped with first aid at home, but moderate to severe problems need medical attention as soon as possible.

DO THIS NOW

Offer your pet some water. As long as your cat or dog isn't vomiting continuously, offer him some water to drink. Dogs tend to be willing to lap up the water they need from a bowl, but cats can be reluctant to drink as much as they need. You can make the water more attractive by flavoring it with a bit of low-fat, no-salt chicken broth or the juice from water-packed tuna and warming it slightly before offering it to your cat. You can also use a needleless syringe or turkey baster to give him water.

Try ice. Some pets, especially dogs, like ice cubes as a treat, and that can be a way to give them more fluid. This works especially well when dehydration is a result of hot weather. Float ice in a bowl of water or just offer a cube to your pet to crunch.

SPECIAL SITUATION

If your pet has severe dehydration: Pets who have more severe dehydration will benefit from a rehydration fluid for children, such as Pedialyte. The solution replaces some of the electrolytes that the body loses through dehydration. You can mix it 50/50 with water or, if your pet will accept it, offer it straight. Usually, however, you'll need to give the Pedialyte like a liquid medicine. A needleless syringe or a turkey baster works well. Insert the tip of the syringe or baster into the center of your pet's mouth. Keep his head tilted up and squirt the solution into the pouch of his cheek. Hold your pet's mouth closed with your other hand and stroke his throat or gently blow in his nose to prompt him to swallow. Give him a little liquid (1 to 2 ounces) every 1 to 2 hours. If things have not improved after 6 to 8 hours, call your vet. (This technique is illustrated on page 30.)

 ## FOLLOW-UP CARE

■ Pets with moderate to severe dehydration probably will get intravenous fluid therapy at the veterinary hospital. But pets with chronic conditions like kidney failure, liver disease, or intestinal problems often need ongoing fluid therapy on a daily basis. Your veterinarian will advise you if this is necessary for your pet.

THE BEST APPROACH

Diagnosing Dehydration

"Tenting" the skin—gently lifting the skin on the top of your pet's head and gauging how quickly it springs back—is a good way to tell if your pet is dehydrated. (This technique is illustrated on page 12.) But you can more accurately tell just how dehydrated he is with the capillary refill time test.

Capillaries are tiny blood vessels that lie near the surface of the skin. They are easiest to see in your pet's gums above his teeth; the capillaries are what gives this tissue its normal pink color. Lift your pet's upper lip, then press the flat of your finger against the tissue. This temporarily squeezes blood in that spot out of the capillaries and blocks the normal flow so that when you quickly remove the pressure, you'll see a white, finger-shaped mark on the gum. In a normally hydrated dog or cat, the blood will flood back into the area and turn the white back to pink in less than 2 seconds. If the time is longer than 3 to 4 seconds, it is likely that your pet is dehydrated to some degree (especially if all the other signs—weakness, lethargy, and loss of skin elasticity—are also present) and needs to be treated by your vet, not with first aid.

Advisors
■ Janie Hodges, D.V.M., is a veterinarian at Valley View Pet Health Center in Farmers Branch, Texas.
■ Peter Levin, V.M.D., is a veterinarian at Ludwig's Corner Veterinary Hospital in Chester Springs, Pennsylvania.
■ Jeffrey Werber, D.V.M., is a veterinarian at Century Veterinary Group in Los Angeles.
■ Dennis L. Wilcox, D.V.M., is a veterinarian at Angeles Clinic for Animals in Port Angeles, Washington.

Diarrhea

CALL YOUR VET: **IF NEEDED**

Diarrhea—abnormally loose or frequent bowel movements—is very common in cats and dogs. Most cases are caused by "garbage-gut syndrome," when a pet eats something that he shouldn't. But diarrhea can also be a sign of more serious diseases like distemper or parvovirus, which usually also include vomiting and a fever, and these need medical care as soon as possible.

One of the most dangerous things about diarrhea is the loss of water from the body, which leads to dehydration. The more fluid the diarrhea contains, the more likely that dehydration will occur, especially if the pet is not eating or drinking and the episodes are frequent. If your pet is having frequent bouts of watery diarrhea, take him to the vet right away.

Puppies and kittens less than 8 to 10 months of age are much more likely than older pets to contract infectious diseases. If you have a young pet with diarrhea, call your vet for specific advice on what kind of first aid you can administer safely at home.

DO THIS NOW

Give your adult pet a break from food. Withhold food for 12 to 24 hours to rest the gut and give the inflammation time to heal. If there's nothing in the intestines, there won't be anything to come out. In rare cases, there are adult dogs and cats who cannot maintain blood sugar concentrations appropriately when fasting. If your pet seems very lethargic, sleepy, or weak during a fast, you should rub a sugar solution like Karo syrup or honey on his gums and get to your veterinarian right away. (For more information about low blood sugar, see page 281.)

Keep your pet hydrated. Make sure that water is available at all times so that your pet doesn't become dehydrated. An explosive, watery stool can pull huge amounts of fluids and

FIRST ALERT

Inflammatory Bowel Disease

Diarrhea with a puddinglike consistency that lasts for weeks or months at a time won't be helped by first aid. Both cats and dogs can develop inflammatory bowel disease, which is thought to be a type of allergic reaction to certain foods. The only way it can be diagnosed is with an internal examination of the intestinal tract after the pet is anesthetized. Veterinarians can do either a surgical biopsy of the tissue, in which they take a sample of the lining of the gut and have it analyzed, or use a viewing instrument called a colonoscope inserted into the rectum to take a look at the surface of the intestines and take tiny biopsies.

Pets can't be cured, but they can be helped with treatment. Because allergy is a type of overreaction of the immune system, drugs that dampen this reaction, like corticosteroids, are often prescribed to help ease the symptoms. There are also special diets available that pets may be able to tolerate. These diets have unusual ingredients like venison and potato that aren't as likely to cause an allergic reaction. Talk to your vet about what type of diet is best-suited to your pet. He will be able to give you specific instructions on types of ingredients and the best quantity for your pet.

important minerals out of the body. You can counter that with rehydration fluid like Pedialyte or Gatorade—mix it 50/50 with plain water and offer it in your pet's water bowl. You can also talk to your vet about a product called Ritrol, which has the same effect as Pedialyte and can be given either straight from the bottle or diluted 50/50 with water. (For more information on dehydration, see page 148.)

Use OTC medicines to help control diarrhea until you can see your vet. Unfortunately, dogs and cats tend to hate the taste of Pepto-Bismol and Kaopectate, so you may need help restraining your pet to get a dose down him. You can use a needleless syringe or a turkey baster to squirt the medicine into his mouth. (This technique is illustrated on page 30.)

The dose for both Pepto-Bismol and Kaopectate for dogs is ½ to 1 teaspoon per 5 pounds of body weight, to a maximum of 2 tablespoons up to three times a day, or 1 tablet per 15 pounds of body weight up to three times a day.

Cats shouldn't take Pepto-Bismol without a veterinarian's recommendation because it contains aspirin-like compounds that can be dangerous to cats. Kaopectate is the best choice for cats, but it doesn't work as well in dogs. You can give ½ to 1 teaspoon once every 6 hours for every 5 pounds your cat weighs. Don't give your cat this medicine for more than a day. If either medicine doesn't help after a day, take your pet to the veterinarian.

When to See the Vet

Take your pet to the vet immediately if he exhibits any of the following signs.

- Black stool with a tarlike consistency
- Extremely foul-smelling stool
- Stool that contains large amounts of red blood
- Diarrhea accompanied by vomiting
- Severe pain during defecation
- Fever
- Loss of appetite
- Lethargy

More minor kinds of diarrhea—where your pet still feels well and acts normally, and where the diarrhea is more puddinglike in consistency or contains only flecks of blood—can often be cured with first aid at home. But even then, if the diarrhea persists for longer than 3 days with no improvement, make an appointment with the veterinarian.

 FOLLOW-UP CARE

■ It may take a day or two for your pet's tummy to settle down after a severe upset, so ease the recovery period with some bland food and small meals. Cook plain white rice or macaroni until it's very soft. Mix it 50/50 with boiled skinless, boneless chicken breast or lean browned and drained ground beef. You can flavor it with a bit of low-fat, no-salt chicken broth or stir in a tablespoon of plain yogurt or cottage cheese. Yogurt has "good" bacteria that can help rebalance the intestinal upset that caused the diarrhea.

Like people, however, some pets can develop lactose intolerance. In these cases, giving milk products can worsen their diarrhea. If your pet routinely eats milk products with no problems, yogurt or cottage cheese shouldn't harm him. If he doesn't routinely eat milk products or is known to have lactose intolerance, you should not give him these foods.

Offer small but frequent meals of the rice mixture—about three or four a day for 24 hours. If the diarrhea is gone, increase the quantity and decrease the frequency of the meals for an additional 1 to 2 days. After that, gradually begin mixing your pet's regular food in with the rice and meat until he is back to his old feeding pattern. Start with a ration of 30 percent regular food and 70 percent bland diet. Each day, increase the amount of the regular food while reducing the amount of the bland diet—50/50, 70/30, and so on. After 4 to 5 days, your pet should be back on his regular diet.

Advisors
- Patricia Hague, D.V.M., is a veterinarian at Cat Hospital of Las Colinas in Irving, Texas.
- Janie Hodges, D.V.M., is a veterinarian at Valley View Pet Health Center in Farmers Branch, Texas.
- Peter Levin, V.M.D., is a veterinarian at Ludwig's Corner Veterinary Hospital in Chester Springs, Pennsylvania.

Drowning

CALL YOUR VET: **IMMEDIATELY**

MEDICINE CHEST

Pool skimmer, rake, or
  other long-handled
  tool
Towel, blanket, or hot-
  water bottle
Rectal thermometer
Petroleum jelly
Karo syrup, honey, or
  sugar water
Needle or safety pin

Dogs and cats are born with the ability to swim, so drowning is rare. What usually happens is that they jump or fall into water and then are unable to get out, either because they get too tired or because of steep pool sides or other obstacles. Should they lose strength and slip underwater, they literally breathe water into their lungs, which damages the lungs, prevents oxygen intake, and can lead to suffocation.

Pets who have drowned will sometimes drift onto dry ground, so it's not always obvious what has happened. Look at the lips, the rims of the eyes, or the gums: In drownings, the lack of oxygen makes these tissues gray or blue instead of their usual pink.

You may be able to revive your pet with CPR. Realistically, it's extremely difficult to get a stopped heart going again without specialized equipment. You can still save your pet's life, however, by restarting her breathing. Pets who start breathing on their own will usually recover, but they'll still need to see a veterinarian immediately. Pets who have almost drowned often have delayed breathing problems. They'll seem perfectly fine, but then seem to develop difficulty breathing within hours or up to a day later.

DO THIS NOW

Before you start first aid, get your pet out of the water. Unless you have a cat or a small dog or the water is very shallow, it's safest not to get in the water yourself. Veterinarians recommend using a pool skimmer, a fishing pole, a rake, or whatever implement you can grab to hook the collar and pull your pet within reach.

Get the water out of your pet's lungs. Once your pet is out of the water, you'll need to remove water from her lungs, windpipe, and mouth by

FIRST ALERT

Pneumonia

Pets who have been revived after drowning aren't out of the woods entirely. The water that rushed into the lungs may have contained dirt or germs that can cause pneumonia, an inflammation of the lungs. A pet with pneumonia usually has a fever and difficulty breathing. The breathing may sound moist or "bubbly" as well.

Pneumonia is serious, and pets can die within days if they don't get oxygen therapy, antibiotics, or other medical treatments. See your vet as soon as you notice symptoms. It may also be a good idea for any pet who has come close to drowning (even if she hasn't lost consciousness) to make a trip to the vet. He will perform a checkup and possibly take an x-ray to determine if any damage has been done or if water has been inhaled. If caught early, pneumonia can usually be treated much more effectively. Any pet who has been unconscious or had to be revived in any way should be seen by a vet despite successful resuscitation.

holding her upside down. Pick up a small pet by her hind legs or a larger pet by her hips, hang her upside down, and give her a good shake. If possible, have someone else thump her briskly on both sides of the chest for 10 to 15 seconds. Sometimes, this is all it takes to restart breathing.

If your dog is too large to lift, put her on her side, making sure that her head is lower than her tail. Put the heel of your hand in the dip behind the last set of ribs and thrust up sharply toward her head three or four times. Wait 1 to 2 seconds to see if water comes out, then try again. Don't spend more than a minute doing this, because the lungs absorb water very quickly. Water that doesn't come out quickly probably isn't going to. In fact, water may not be the problem at this point. Some pets experience a condition called dry drowning, in which fear (or frigid temperatures) causes the larynx—the airway to the lungs—to go into spasm. There may not be water in the lungs, but the pet still won't be able to breathe.

Start artificial respiration if your pet isn't breathing on her own. Hold your pet's mouth closed and put your lips over her nose. Give two quick breaths, then wait to see if her chest rises. Then keep giving breaths, either until she revives or until you can get medical help. Give about 15 to 20 breaths a minute, blowing until you see the chest rising to a normal height. (This technique is illustrated on page 20.)

After giving the first breaths, listen or feel for a heartbeat by putting your ear or palm against the left side of her chest. Or feel for a pulse, preferably in the groin where the hind leg joins the body. If her heart is beating, keep giving breaths. If there isn't a heartbeat, you'll need to do CPR, giving one breath for every five chest compressions. It's best to do

First Aid for the Heart

Veterinarians can get a heart beating again with an injection of epinephrine. If your pet has drowned, her heart has stopped, and you can't get to a veterinarian in time, you may be able to get a similar effect by trying this acupuncture technique. It stimulates the body to release adrenaline, a natural substance very similar to epinephrine.

If your pet is unconscious and his heart has stopped: Stick a needle or safety pin into the slit in the upper lip beneath your pet's nose. Insert it down to the bone, then wiggle it back and forth.

CPR while someone else drives you to the vet's office.

When giving CPR to small pets, cup your hand over the point of the chest, just behind the elbows. With your fingers on one side and your thumb on the other, squeeze the chest in a "cough-like" manner, pushing it down about ½ inch.

Put a larger dog on her side on a flat surface. Put one hand on top of the chest above the heart and your other hand on top of the first. Use both hands to thrust firmly down, compressing the chest by 25 to 50%. (This technique is illustrated on page 21.)

 FOLLOW-UP CARE

■ After your pet starts breathing, dry her off and wrap her in a blanket or towel. It's important to know how chilled she is, so use a rectal thermometer lubricated with petroleum jelly to quickly but gently take her temperature. (This technique is illustrated on page 9.) Most pets drown in water that's colder than their body temperatures, and the resulting chill makes the organs work less efficiently and slows recovery.

A pet whose core body temperature has been below 90°F for more than 30 minutes needs to be rewarmed from the inside out, using special medical techniques that your vet is trained to perform. Trying to rewarm her yourself in this situation can be dangerous. If your pet's temperature is less than 90°F and has probably been this low for longer than 30 minutes, *do not* apply external heat sources. Keep her wrapped in a blanket, put her into a heated car, and get to the vet quickly.

If your vet is more than 30 minutes away or your pet's temperature has dropped below 90°F within the past 30 minutes, however, you should apply external heat. Wrap a hot-water bottle in a towel and apply it to her belly or the insides of her thighs, where large arteries are near the surface. This warms the blood, which then helps warm the rest of the body. (For more on hypothermia, see page 248.)

Frigid Protection

Drowning is always an emergency, but pets who fall into icy water may have an advantage: Extremely cold water can help protect them from brain injury.

The brain may be damaged whenever oxygen is cut off for more than 5 minutes or so. Pets who stop breathing for longer than that can be revived, but they may never fully recover or act exactly the same.

Research has shown that water that is cold enough to chill the body and brain to less than 90°F can slow the rate at which brain cells die. This means that even pets who have spent a long time in cold water may have a good chance of making a full recovery.

■ Pets who are chilled burn a lot of energy trying to stay warm and will quickly deplete their body's blood sugar. You can replenish it almost instantly by dipping your finger in honey, Karo syrup, or sugar water and rubbing it on their gums.

■ Some pets can't stay away from the water even when they've had close calls. Swimming pools and hot tubs are especially dangerous because pets can jump or fall in, but the sides are too high and steep for them to climb out. Or they get trapped underneath pool covers and can't find their way out. Veterinarians recommend putting something conspicuous, like a patio table or a potted plant, near the steps leading out of the pool. This will help pets find their way out if they get disoriented.

■ Dogs and cats who go sailing need the same protection that people do. The U.S. Coast Guard recommends a product called the Pet Life Preserver, which comes in several colors and sizes. It consists of flotation material that covers most of a pet's back, sides, and chest and is secured with two adjustable quick-release buckle straps. It includes a "grab strap" on the back, which makes it easier to pluck pets from the water.

THE BEST APPROACH

Super-Absorbent Towels

Fur can absorb a lot of water, which means that dogs and cats who get wet tend to stay wet, and moisture removes heat from the body. Pets who like the water (or at least have to endure the occasional bath) will appreciate a towel called Moisture Magnet. Used by groomers, these towels, which are available from pet-supply catalogs, can absorb 10 times their weight in water—more than any other towel made.

Advisors
■ Thomas Munschauer, D.V.M., is a veterinarian at Middlebury Animal Hospital in Vermont and past president of the Vermont Veterinary Medical Association.
■ Sandra Sawchuk, D.V.M., is clinical instructor at the University of Wisconsin School of Veterinary Medicine in Madison.
■ Daniel Simpson, D.V.M., is a veterinarian at West Bay Animal Hospital in Warwick, Rhode Island, and spokesperson for the Rhode Island Veterinary Medical Association.

Earflap Injuries

CALL YOUR VET: **IF NEEDED**

A tremendous supply of blood flows through the earflap, which is the visible part of a cat's or dog's ear. So any injury to the earflap, even the tiniest cut, tends to be very bloody. One shake of the head can splatter blood everywhere, until the room looks like a slaughterhouse.

Outdoor cats are very prone to having their ears torn in fights with other animals. But it's dogs with thin coats and big floppy ears, like Labrador retrievers and beagles, who have the worst problems with earflap injuries. Hanging ears are injured more easily than upright ears, and dogs reinjure the wound when they shake their heads. The thin coat of fur on these breeds' ears doesn't offer much protection; dogs with thick coats are less likely to get earflap injuries.

A bruise on the earflap, usually from scratching or shaking the ears, can make the tissue swell like a balloon, resulting in an aural hematoma. (For more information, see "Aural Hematoma" on page 161.) This requires medical attention as soon as possible and minor surgery to repair. Most earflap injuries look worse than they really are, and they can often be successfully treated at home. But if your pet has a laceration on both the inside and outside of the earflap (longer than 1 inch in large dogs or ½ inch in cats or small dogs), if the bleeding does not stop within 15 to 20 minutes, or if the wound was caused by a bite from another animal, call your vet right away.

🐾 DO THIS NOW

Trim the fur. Furry-eared dogs don't often have earflap injuries, but if they do, you'll need to trim off any long fur on the earflap to expose the injury so that you can clean and treat it more easily.

If you use blunt scissors, do so very carefully so that you don't cut the skin. Electric clippers and even a mustache trimmer are safer choices. If you're using scissors, first slip your index and

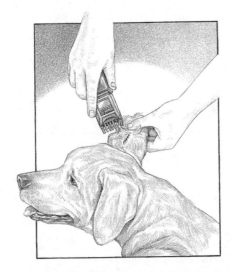

If you need to trim the fur on your dog's ear to treat an injury, electric clippers are much safer than scissors, since they're unlikely to cut into your dog's skin. Even a mustache trimmer works well.

second fingers through the fur and hold them against the wound. Cut the fur so that it's level with your fingers, clipping a 1-inch border all the way around the wound. (This technique is illustrated on page 114.) If the skin is broken, fill the wound with a water-soluble lubricant like K-Y Jelly before you clip. After clipping, thoroughly rinse the area with warm water. The trimmed hair sticks to the jelly and washes out.

Clean the earflap. If the injury is an animal bite, it is important to wash the earflap with mild soap and water, then pat it dry.

Stop the bleeding. Cuts, tears, or bites to the earflap usually bleed a lot because of the extensive blood supply to the area. Use a clean, soft cloth or a sterile gauze pad and apply pressure di-

rectly to the injury. The bleeding should stop in 5 minutes or less. Keep your pet quiet during that time, perhaps by feeding her tiny bits of a favorite treat while you talk calmly to her. (For more information on bleeding, see page 95.)

Tape the ears. Many dogs with floppy ears won't tolerate a bandage taped to the earflap; they'll shake their heads once, the bandage will fly off, and the ear will spray blood. A better option is to bandage the wound by taping both ears on top of your dog's head. That keeps her from breaking open the scab by flopping her ears around, and it's much more comfortable for your dog.

Use a gauze pad or small adhesive bandage to completely cover the injury. Then fold the earflap up over the top of your dog's head. Fold the other earflap over the top of the first so that both ears form a cap on top of your dog's head. Finally, hold the ears in place by wrapping roll gauze or a towel around your dog's head and throat, and tape it. You could also use the sleeve from a T-shirt or cut the toe off an athletic sock or length of panty hose and slip the tube of material over your dog's head to hold her ears in place, as long as it's not too tight and doesn't restrict breathing.

Use a topical ointment. Most of the time, dogs and cats will lick off any topical medicine, but they can't easily reach earflap injuries. Apply antibiotic ointment such as Neosporin, but don't use it for injuries with lots of bleeding. It's more important to bandage the injury to stop the bleeding, and the blood will actually help clean out the wound. But for less bloody injuries

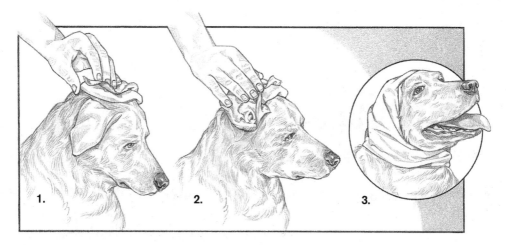

1. Cover an ear injury with a gauze pad or adhesive bandage.
2. Fold the earflap up on top of your dog's head.
3. Fold the other earflap over the first so that both ears form a cap on top of her head. Hold the ears in place by wrapping gauze or a towel around your dog's head and neck and taping it in place.

like fly strike, or when you can't get medical attention for more than 24 hours, an antibiotic is a good idea. Wait until any heavy bleeding has stopped, then apply the ointment and bandage the ear.

 ## SPECIAL SITUATIONS

If the bleeding doesn't stop: If after 15 to 20 minutes of direct pressure, the bleeding doesn't stop, see your vet right away. An artery may be damaged, or there may be a clotting problem. On the way there, keep applying direct pressure. Or place a wad of gauze or a small clean cloth on the inside of the earflap, roll the ear over it, and bandage it like a tube instead of a flap.

If your pet has a fly bite: Earflap injuries from fly strike (fly bites) don't bleed too much, but they look crusty and painful. Usually, fly bites affect dogs with upright ears. Gently clean off the crust with warm water and any mild antibacterial soap, then pat dry. (For more information about fly strike, see page 187.)

 ## FOLLOW-UP CARE

■ Torn earflaps or repairs to aural hematomas will probably need stitches, and your dog may come home with her ears bandaged to her head to keep the wound clean and dry. You may need to change the bandage every day and keep the suture site clean with a cotton ball soaked in warm water.

Advisors

■ Michael G. Abdella, D.V.M., is a veterinarian at Aliso Viejo Animal Hospital in Aliso Viejo, California.
■ Mauri Karger, D.V.M., is a veterinarian at I-20 Animal Medical Center in Arlington, Texas.
■ A. Michelle Miller, D.V.M., is a veterinarian at Animal Aid Clinic South in Elkhart, Indiana.

Ear Infections

CALL YOUR VET: **IF NEEDED**

Ear problems, usually involving inflammation of the ear canals, are estimated to affect up to 20 percent of all dogs and up to 7 percent of cats. Dogs with floppy or hairy ears like cocker spaniels are affected most often because their ears don't air out as well as erect ears such as a German shepherd's.

Ear infections are common because cats' and dogs' ear canals are shaped like an L and can trap moisture, which creates a perfect environment for bacteria, fungi, and parasites like ear mites. Clean, dry ears stay healthy. But water, soap, excess wax, or foreign objects like seeds or wads of hair can lead to infections. And sore, itchy, swollen ears can be a sign of allergy. Dogs and cats commonly shake their heads or scratch their ears from the intense itching.

Most dog ear problems are caused by an overgrowth of yeast, a kind of fungus that's normally found inside the ear canal. But when the yeast grows too rapidly, the ears get hot and inflamed and look kind of "goopy." They may have a strong dog odor or a sweet yeasty scent.

Ear mites, tiny spiderlike parasites that suck lymph from the skin of the ear canal, are another common cause of infections. Mites make pets' ears itchy and sore, and though you may not see the bugs, you'll notice crumbly brown or black material, which is a mixture of mite waste and wax that is a reaction to irritation. Ear mites and mild yeast infections can be helped with first aid.

Constant scratching or head shaking can damage the normal protective skin surface so that bacteria can infect the ears. Bacterial infections need medical attention, because putting the wrong medicine in your pet's ears could make the problem worse or even cause hearing loss. Be alert for any type of discharge that's light brown, yellow, greenish yellow, or dark and bloody, with or without head-tilting or loss of balance. The more serious infections can smell like fermenting fruit or chocolate.

DO THIS NOW

Treat yeast and fungal infections. A dark brown to black waxy material that's runny and smells rancid probably is a yeast overgrowth. Yeast and fungal infections are very common in dogs but less often diagnosed in cats. Return your pet's ears to their normal acidic pH with a 50/50 vinegar-and-water solution twice a day. Put the mixture in a spray bottle, lift the ear flap, and spritz the ears with the solution. Then wipe out the portion of the ear that you can see with a cotton ball. If you don't see improvement in 24 to 48 hours, take him to the vet.

Look for signs of ear mites. When the ears are very itchy and you can see a dark, crumbly material, chances are good that your pet has ear mites, tiny spiderlike critters that bite and live in the ear canal. There is a wide range of over-the-counter ear-mite medicines sold at pet stores, and your veterinarian may prescribe ointments containing neomycin sulfate, like Tresaderm. They have ingredients that kill the mites, and the ointments also soothe the inflammation.

SPECIAL SITUATIONS

If your pet has a chronic condition: Some dogs with seborrhea, a dandruff-like skin disease, also develop a condition called ceruminous otitis that causes a buildup of oily yellow wax in the ears. This is the perfect environment for infection to develop. These dogs need lifelong treatment to keep ear infections under control. A wax-dissolving cleaner like Cerumene or Epi-Otic, available in pet-supply stores and from catalogs, can help keep the wax buildup from causing problems.

If your pet has furry ears: With dogs who have lots of fur around or in their ears, you can reduce the incidence of infection by keeping the fur trimmed so that air can circulate more easily.

⊕ FIRST ALERT

Aural Hematoma

Violent head shaking or scratching at the ears, which often happens with ear infections, can bruise the tissue of the leatherlike flap that forms the outside portion of your pet's ear. The bruise causes the earflap to fill with fluid on either the inside or the outside, creating a bubble-like swelling. It's not an infection: The fluid inside is blood and serum, like a giant blood blister.

A hematoma isn't particularly dangerous, but it is uncomfortable for your dog or cat. The weight of the blood deforms the shape of the ear, and the disfigurement can become permanent without prompt treatment. It takes surgery to clean out the material and special bandages that help reshape the ear as it heals.

Dizzy Dogs and Cats

Most ear infections affect only the outer part of the ear. They can be treated at home or with a little help from your vet, and they are more aggravating than dangerous. But infections that come back over and over again can spread into the middle ear. That's because the pet's constant scratching and head shaking can rupture the eardrum. Chronic ear infections frequently result in a ruptured or destroyed eardrum, and that can open up the entire ear to severe damage.

The middle ear houses a chain of delicate bones that transmit sound, and chronic infection can cause permanent hearing loss. Middle-ear infection can also invade the facial nerves, which can leave your pet with a droopy face on the affected side or problems with an eye that won't focus. Pets with these serious infections often tip their heads to one side because of the pain. But if the infection travels beyond the middle ear to the inner ear, where the balance organs are found, pets can lose all sense of equilibrium, walk in circles, or fall over.

Hearing damage and balance problems are minor compared with the danger of meningitis, however. The inner ear is directly connected to the brain, and infection that travels by that route causes depression, fever, and sometimes death. It may take surgery to clean out all the infection, and even when your pet is successfully treated, he may be left with permanent damage to his balance so that he can no longer see the world straight. Clearly, it pays to control ear infections early on.

This will also help heal existing infections more quickly. Use blunt scissors or electric clippers to trim the fur close to the skin on the underside of your dog's earflap and around the ear opening. Be sure to gently restrain your dog so that he doesn't wiggle and poke himself with the scissors.

If there is fur in the ear canal: This is a problem with some breeds, including poodles, cocker spaniels, and Lhasa apsos, and it's helpful to pluck the fur out periodically to increase air circulation. Every 2 to 3 months, you can use your fingers or a hemostat (a long, thin clamp available from pet-supply catalogs) to remove the fur. Be sure to restrain your dog first,

and afterward, apply a 1% cortisone cream such as Cortaid or an over-the-counter hand cream that contains lanolin. If you aren't comfortable plucking your dog's ears, however, you can have your veterinarian or a groomer do it.

If your dog has floppy ears: With dogs who have floppy ears, it's helpful to tape them up so that they'll dry out and heal faster. Fold the ears over the top of your dog's head and secure the ends together with tape. Use white adhesive bandage tape or any other kind that will keep your pet's ears together and can be easily removed from his fur. You can also clip the long fur on the ear tips together with a clothespin, bobby pin, or hair clip. (Be sure that you clip just the hair.) Then play gently with your dog so that he won't think about it. Keep his ears up for at least 30 to 40 minutes or as long as 1 to 2 hours. You can help prevent a recurrence of infection by giving the ears a weekly airing out.

FOLLOW-UP CARE

■ The ear must first be cleaned for medication to be effective. A 50/50 vinegar-and-water solution works well for general cleaning, or your veterinarian may recommend a commercial cleanser like Oti-Clens that helps cut through wax. For bacterial infections, preparations like Nolvasan Otic, available from pet-supply stores and catalogs, contain an antiseptic called chlorhexidine that's particularly helpful.

Wear an old shirt or cover yourself with an apron or towel to protect your clothes because your pet is very likely to fling the ear cleaner on you when he shakes his head. If his ears are very sore, he may not want you to touch them, and your vet may need to sedate him prior to ear cleaning.

Place a cat or small dog on a counter or tabletop, or kneel on the floor next to a medium-size or large dog. Have your pet stand, sit, or lie down—whatever position is most comfortable for him. Stand or kneel beside or behind him.

If he won't stay still, you will need to use a little more restraint. Wrap your cat's legs with a towel, then kneel on the floor and place him between your legs with his head facing out. For a dog who won't cooperate, you'll need someone to help you. Lay your dog on his side, then grasp the ankle of the foreleg that's against the ground with one hand while gently pressing your forearm across his shoulders. Use your other hand to grasp the ankle of the hind leg that's against the ground and press your forearm across his hips. Have your helper clean and treat the exposed ear, then turn your pet over and reverse the restraint to treat the other ear.

■ To clean the ear, fill up the ear canal with the vinegar-and-water solution or Oti-Clens. Firmly grasp your pet's earflap to help hold him still, then vigorously massage the base of the ear. If his ears are itchy, your pet will enjoy this because it helps relieve some of that deep-seated irritation. Massage moves the cleanser into the bottom part of the L-shaped canal and flushes out hidden debris. The ear will make a squishing sound. Cotton swabs tend to push more wax and dirt down into the ear rather than pulling it out, so use a cotton ball to wipe the ear surfaces that you can easily reach.

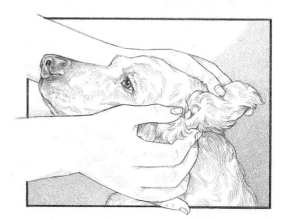

Clean your pet's ears by pouring liquid cleanser into the ear canal, then massaging the base of the ear to work the cleanser in. Holding the earflap with the other hand will help keep him still.

■ Ear medication may be in liquid form, which is easily dripped into the canal. Or it may be ointment in a tube with a long nozzle that you insert just into the vertical leg of the "L" of the ear canal. Ask your vet to show you exactly where to place it. To use a nozzle applicator, restrain your pet's head so that the tip of the tube doesn't poke the sides of the ear canal. Once the prescribed amount of medication is applied, massage the base of the ear to make sure that the medicine gets back into the bottom part of the canal, where most infections originate.

■ Yeast infections can be tough to cure. You need to continue treatment twice a day for at least a couple of weeks. An antifungal agent like nystatin, found in prescription medications like Panolog ointment, can be helpful.

■ Treat bacterial infections with prescription medications like Panolog, Gentocin, Tresaderm, or Liquichlor, depending on the type of bacteria and inflammation involved. Administer them according to your veterinarian's instructions.

■ When the infection is deep inside the ear, pets need oral antibiotics, too, for at least a month and sometimes for 6 to 8 weeks. Your vet will prescribe them. To give your pet a pill, open his mouth by gently pressing his lips against the sides of his teeth, then push the pill to the back of his tongue. Close his mouth and stroke his throat until he swallows. (This technique is illustrated on page 30.)

THE BEST APPROACH

Swimmer's Solution

Dogs such as retriever breeds who love to swim get more ear infections because they get water in their ears. For these pets and any others who seem to have ongoing ear problems, one of the best ways to prevent ear infections is to use "swimmer's solution."

This solution won't control an active infection, but it will help keep the natural balance of the inner ear healthy and keep bacteria or yeast from getting a foothold. Make the solution by mixing 1 cup of plain water with 2 cups of vinegar and 1 tablespoon of rubbing alcohol. Straight alcohol in the ears is too irritating, but a dash in the mixture helps cut through and dissolve any wax. The vinegar creates an acidic environment where yeast and bacteria can't grow.

Put the solution in a spray bottle and squirt the mixture on the outside of the ear canal as needed—once or twice a week is good, and also after every swim or bath. Swimmer's solution is also great for gentle routine cleaning of the ears. Squirt some of the solution on a cotton ball and wipe out the visible portion of the ear.

Advisors
■ Ann Buchanan, D.V.M., is a veterinarian at Glenwood Animal Hospital in Tyler, Texas.
■ Martha S. Gearhart, D.V.M., is a veterinarian at Pleasant Valley Animal Hospital in New York.
■ Susan Little, D.V.M., is a veterinarian at Bytown Cat Hospital in Ottawa, Ontario, Canada.

Electrical Shock

CALL YOUR VET: **IMMEDIATELY**

MEDICINE CHEST
Rubber gloves
Dark towel
Pet carrier or box

Electrical shock usually happens to puppies because they chew just about anything, including electrical and telephone cords. At their most severe, electrical shocks can trigger seizures or stop the heart. And the damage can be insidious because it comes on slowly, sometimes causing an erratic heartbeat or difficulty in breathing several days after the accident.

Most household shocks are nowhere near this serious. Dogs and cats will typically get burned on the lips, the corners of the mouth, or the tongue. In fact, veterinarians sometimes see a characteristic burned strip across the tongue, a mark that they call an electrical bite.

DO THIS NOW

Shut off the power. Electrical current often causes muscles to go into spasm, making it impossible for dogs or cats to let go once they've bitten into a cord. In fact, they'll usually bite down harder. You *must* disconnect the power before touching your pet. Otherwise, you'll get shocked as well and won't be able to help. The safest way to cut the power is to throw the main circuit breaker. If you are not sure where it is or you can't get to it quickly, you'll have to disconnect the cord. If you can find rubber gloves quickly, put them on before pulling the plug. Be very careful not to get too close to your pet; if you touch him, you'll get shocked, too.

Perform CPR if needed. Electricity can damage blood vessels in the body, causing a leakage of fluid that fills the lungs. This will cause coughing, difficulty in breathing, and extreme anxiety. Electricity can also cause an abnormal heartbeat when it disrupts the heart's normal electrical impulses. You'll need to perform artificial respiration and CPR if your pet collapses and stops breathing.

Wrap your hand around your pet's muzzle to close his mouth, then blow into his nose with two quick breaths. Watch to see if his chest rises, then give 15 to 20 breaths per minute until your pet begins breathing again on his own or until you reach medical help. (This technique is illustrated on page 20.) After each breath, watch for his chest to rise, then remove your lips and let the air escape.

After giving the first couple of breaths, place your palm or your ear against his chest just behind the left elbow and check for a heartbeat. (Or check the pulse at the femoral artery, where the inside of the hind leg joins the body.) If you can't detect a beat, you'll need to do chest compressions to help start the heart.

For a cat or small dog, cup a hand over the point of the chest just behind the elbows. Squeeze firmly in a "coughlike" manner, pressing in about ½ inch, with your thumb on one side and fingers on the other, about 80 to 100 times a minute. Give one breath per 5 compressions, or 15 to 20 breaths per minute.

Put a medium or large pet on his side on a firm, flat surface. With one hand on top of the other on his chest behind the elbow, push down, compressing the chest by 25 to 50%. Give compressions and breaths as described for small pets. (This technique is illustrated on page 21.)

Treat seizures with dark and quiet. Seizures aren't as serious as they appear, and they'll usually stop in 2 to 3 minutes. In the meantime, cover your pet's face with a dark towel to shut out light and noise. This can help end the seizure more quickly. Try not to touch or even talk to pets who are having seizures. Even though they're unconscious, the sound of your voice and physical contact will stimulate the brain, possibly causing the seizure to last longer.

Keep your pet quiet. Stress increases oxygen needs. Pets who have been shocked often suffer lung damage, and that makes it even harder for them to get enough oxygen. Moving them around or even holding them will increase the stress. If you can, put your pet in a dark pet carrier or a box, put it in the car, and run the air-conditioning on high until you get to the vet.

Give him ice. You can ease the pain of mouth burns by putting ice in his drinking water—the cold will act as a temporary anesthetic. Or you can put ice directly on the burns.

FOLLOW-UP CARE

■ Mouth burns take a long time to heal because they're always wet and tend to get infected. This can make it hard for pets to eat. Until the burns heal, plan to run your pet's usual food through the blender, adding enough low-fat, no-salt chicken broth to make it soupy.

Advisors

■ Debra M. Eldredge, D.V.M., is a veterinarian in Vernon, New York.

■ Joanne Howl, D.V.M., is a veterinarian in West River, Maryland; secretary/treasurer of the American Academy on Veterinary Disaster Medicine; and past president of the Maryland Veterinary Medical Association.

■ Kevin Wallace, D.V.M., is an instructor in the department of clinical sciences at Cornell University College of Veterinary Medicine in Ithaca, New York.

Eye Infections

CALL YOUR VET: **SAME DAY**

You can make a good guess about what's causing eye infections by looking to see if one or both eyes are infected. If just one eye is swollen or has a green or yellow discharge, it's probably a result of an injury from a poke with a stick, a fight with another animal, or even an embedded grass seed. If both eyes are infected, it's probably because of a virus.

Eye infections are easy to treat, but they can cause blindness if they aren't treated quickly and correctly. See a veterinarian as soon as you notice symptoms.

🩹 DO THIS NOW

Hold your pet steady. Eye infections are painful, and pets will struggle when you try to clean and treat them. This is a problem because holding them still, especially by the neck, increases pressure within the eye itself. In an eye that's infected, the additional pressure could damage its internal structures. Before treating the eye, you'll want to recruit someone to keep your pet still.

The easiest way to hold a cat or small dog is to wrap him in a towel or pillowcase, leaving only his head exposed. After he's wrapped, you can steady him even more by holding his muzzle. If you're treating a bigger dog, have him sit or lie between your legs with his back to your chest. Loop one arm around his chest (never the neck) and hold his muzzle with your other hand.

Wipe away discharge. Since eye infections are accompanied by a discharge, you'll need to wash it off. Start by holding a warm, damp washcloth over the eye to loosen the crust. Once it has softened, you can wipe it away fairly easily. You may have to repeat the soaking several times to clean the area around the eyes thoroughly.

Flush the eyes with sterile saline contact lens solution. Hold your pet's eye open with your thumb and forefinger and gently squirt the solution to bathe the surface of the eye. This

167

FIRST ALERT

Distemper

Dogs who haven't been vaccinated are at risk for canine distemper, a life-threatening viral infection that causes a white or yellow discharge from the eyes. Distemper is highly contagious. It usually occurs in puppies, but adult dogs can get it, too. Apart from the discharge, dogs with distemper will lose their appetites, develop diarrhea and coughs, and possibly have seizures. Once dogs develop distemper, there's no guarantee that they'll recover, but quick diagnosis and prompt medical treatment may save them.

will wash away debris and also ease the pain. You can even buy a saline solution made for pets, such as Opticlear Eye Wash, and keep it in your pet first-aid kit.

 FOLLOW-UP CARE

■ Eye infections can take 2 weeks or longer to clear up entirely. In the meantime, the eye will be irritated and sore. Washing the eye daily—both to remove crust and to rinse the surface of the eye—will reduce pain and help the infection heal more quickly. You can use distilled water, but saline solution is a better choice. Thoroughly dry the fur around the eyes after washing them.

Newborn Eye Problems

Even before kittens or puppies first open their eyes—usually between 9 and 12 days after birth—their eyelids may become infected and swell from an accumulation of pus. You can apply a warm, wet compress three or four times a day, but if the pus doesn't drain within 24 hours, see your veterinarian.

Advisors

■ Gerald Brown, D.V.M., is a veterinarian at City Cat Doctor in Chicago.

■ Debra M. Eldredge, D.V.M., is a veterinarian in Vernon, New York.

■ Dennis Hacker, D.V.M., is a veterinary ophthalmologist in El Cerrito, California.

■ Albert Mughannam, D.V.M., is a veterinary ophthalmologist at Veterinary Vision in San Mateo, California.

■ Kevin Wallace, D.V.M., is an instructor in the department of clinical sciences at Cornell University College of Veterinary Medicine in Ithaca, New York.

Eye Out of Socket

SEE YOUR VET: **IMMEDIATELY**

The eyeballs are tightly anchored in sockets of protective bone, and tension from the eyelids holds them in place. But a blow to the head or a fight with another animal can cause a cat's or dog's eye to pop out. This is especially common in flat-faced dogs such as Pekingese and Shih Tzus because their eye sockets are so shallow.

A displaced eyeball looks awful—it usually remains attached and just protrudes, although trauma such as a car accident can force it out so it lies upon the cheek—but it isn't life-threatening. In fact, as long as the muscles and optic nerve aren't damaged too badly, more than half of dogs will keep their sight as long as they get quick treatment.

DO THIS NOW

Protect the injured eye. An eye that's out of the socket must be treated by a veterinarian. Before leaving the house, place a gauze pad or lint-free cloth that's been soaked with lukewarm sterile saline contact lens solution—or, in a pinch, tap water—on the eye. Keep moistening the pad while someone drives you and your pet to your vet. Don't remove the pad to moisten it.

Another option is to apply a sugar solution, which protects the covering of the eye. Mix 3 tablespoons of Karo syrup in ½ cup of warm water. Soak a piece of gauze or cloth in the solution and hold the pad on your pet's eye. Keep moistening the pad and get to a veterinarian right away.

If your pet resists letting you apply the dressing, fill a spray bottle with saline solution or water and gently spray the eye every minute or so during the ride to the veterinarian.

Replace the eye within 1 hour. An eye that's out of the socket must be replaced within 1 hour to ensure the best chances of recovery. It's not difficult for veterinarians to replace an eye, but this isn't something you want to do yourself. If you're more than an hour away from help, how-

169

FIRST ALERT

Uveitis

The eyes are delicate, and trauma from any injury, especially one in which the eye pops out of the socket, frequently causes other problems. The most common is uveitis, an inflammation within the eyeball that may occur days after the initial problem.

Symptoms of uveitis include squinting and watery eyes. The surface of the eye may appear rough or cloudy, and the color may lighten or darken. Often, the pupil of the injured eye is smaller than the healthy one and reacts more slowly to changes of light.

Uveitis can cause blindness if it isn't treated quickly by a veterinarian, but it usually responds well to professional treatment.

ever, you may have no other choice. When an eye comes out of the socket, tissue behind the eyeball starts swelling, so you'll have to work quickly. Here's how to do it.

Tightly grip the skin of both the upper and lower eyelids. The eyelids tend to roll inward on themselves behind the eye, so try using a moistened cotton swab to gently ease the lid edges out, then grasp them with your fingers. Apply a generous amount of lubricant like K-Y Jelly to the eye; the more lubricated it is, the better the chance of replacement. Give the lid edges a strong pull forward. If you're lucky, the lids will wrap around the eye and snap it back into place. Or have someone help you hold the lid edges while you gently push on the eye with a *clean* finger. Then get to the vet as soon as you can.

If your first attempt to replace the eye doesn't work, don't try again. If you are having trouble doing this or you are at all uncertain about how to proceed, don't. Cover the eye and get to the vet immediately. There's probably too

much swelling behind the eyeball for it to pop back in.

 FOLLOW UP CARE

■ Most pets are fine once the eyeball has been replaced. However, those who have lost an eye once often do it again, so you'll have to be careful how you handle them. In addition, the eye may need home treatment after it has been put back.

■ Veterinarians sometimes stitch the eyelid temporarily to protect the eye, so you'll need to keep the sutures and surrounding area clean. Moisten a clean cloth with warm water and gently wipe away crusts or discharge. If your pet paws at his eye and removes his sutures, he will cause even more damage. He will need to wear a collar restraint called an Elizabethan collar to keep him from reaching the injured area. He won't be able to eat while wearing the collar, though, so be sure to remove it during feedings.

Almost Natural

Dogs and cats who have permanently lost an eye usually recover quickly and get around just fine. They can look pretty ugly, however, which is why many people ask their veterinarians to implant a prosthesis, or artificial eye.

Actually, it's not entirely artificial, and in some ways, it works better than its human counterpart. People often have eyes replaced with prostheses that look nearly the same as the originals. But these artificial eyes don't actually move like normal eyes. In dogs and cats, however, a veterinary eye surgeon can create a living, moving prosthesis from the damaged eye itself.

The surgeon removes the inner parts of the eyeball and replaces them with a silicon sphere. The eyeball retains its shape, and the vessels and muscles are still connected. This means that the eye stays alive and moves just like the other eye, even though it can't see. A repaired eye looks a bit different from the normal one, though, because the colored portion of the eye—the iris—has been removed.

■ Should the eye swell, fold a cold, wet washcloth in half and place it over the eye, then apply an ice pack for 15 minutes every 2 to 3 hours.

■ Your veterinarian may recommend using a prescription antibiotic for 1 to 2 weeks after the stitches have been removed. To apply it, pull down the lower lid, squirt a small amount of medication into the cupped tissue, then hold the eyelid closed to help the medicine spread. (This technique is illustrated on page 32.) Use only antibiotics prescribed by your vet.

■ Most people restrain their dogs by gripping their collars, hugging their necks, or holding the scruff. For dogs who have popped an eye, however, gripping the neck raises pressure in and around the eye, which can cause it to pop back out. A better means of restraint is to grip the dog's muzzle with one hand and put your other arm around his shoulders or on top of his head. And trade in his collar for a harness that fits around his chest.

Advisors

■ Shane Bateman, D.V.M., D.V.Sc., is a veterinarian board certified in the American College of Emergency and Critical Care Medicine and assistant professor of emergency and critical care medicine at Ohio State University College of Veterinary Medicine in Columbus.

■ Joanne Howl, D.V.M., is a veterinarian in West River, Maryland; secretary/treasurer of the American Academy on Veterinary Disaster Medicine; and past president of the Maryland Veterinary Medical Association.

■ Albert Mughannam, D.V.M., is a veterinary ophthalmologist at Veterinary Vision in San Mateo, California.

■ Daniel Simpson, D.V.M., is a veterinarian at West Bay Animal Hospital in Warwick, Rhode Island, and spokesperson for the Rhode Island Veterinary Medical Association.

Fading Puppy or Kitten

CALL YOUR VET: **IMMEDIATELY**

Puppies and kittens are very susceptible to illness, and they can go from being healthy, squirmy babies to near death within hours. A range of problems can cause them to "fade," from parasites and blood compatibility problems to viruses and maternal neglect. Hypothermia, dehydration, and hypoglycemia are the major causes of death in young pets, and there's no time to waste when a nursing puppy or kitten shows signs of distress.

Diarrhea and vomiting quickly dehydrate tiny puppies and kittens. This can make them move around less, so they lose body heat and can suffer hypothermia as a result. Low blood sugar develops if they fail to nurse regularly. They'll need medical attention immediately and can die without help. Pets who are 8 to 20 weeks old have a little more reserve, but they can become severely dehydrated in a short amount of time. If they are losing fluid through vomiting or diarrhea, becoming less active, not nursing aggressively, or crying frequently, take them to your veterinarian within 4 to 6 hours of seeing these signs. First aid can support them until you can reach the veterinarian. If the babies are vomiting or have diarrhea but are still active and nursing, call your veterinarian for advice.

DO THIS NOW

Keep him warm. The most important step is to keep the puppy or kitten warm. Young pets do not have built-in thermostats to regulate their own body temperatures, and they quickly get chilled if separated from the litter or their mother. Be sure to buffer the heat source so that the puppy or kitten doesn't get burned. You can use a hot-water bottle wrapped in a towel. But a 20-ounce plastic soda bottle filled with hot water and wrapped with a dry, thick kitchen towel works just as well, and it holds the heat for a long time. Judge the temperature of the wrapped bottle on your skin—you should be able to comfortably tolerate the heat.

You can also put plain, uncooked rice in a thick sock and microwave it for a couple of minutes. Let it sit for at least 5 minutes so that the heat is distributed evenly, and be very careful to check the temperature all over the sock so that you don't burn your pet.

Keep giving fluids. Giving your puppy or kitten fluids will fight possible dehydration. Nearly any kind of fluid will work—kitten and puppy milk replacers are available from pet-supply stores and catalogs or your veterinarian's office. If nothing else is available, dissolve 1 tablespoon of sugar in a cup of warm water and give that. The fluid not only fights dehydration but also helps keep the baby's blood sugar level on an even keel.

Use an eyedropper or needleless syringe and see if the animal will swallow. Be careful that he doesn't choke. Remember that puppies and kittens shouldn't be held on their backs to nurse like human babies. They'll take the nourishment more readily and naturally—without the danger of choking—when they're allowed to rest on their tummies as they would when nursing from their mother.

SPECIAL SITUATION

If he won't nurse: If your puppy or kitten refuses to nurse or is unconscious, dab a little Karo syrup or honey on his gums and get to the veterinarian right away. It will be absorbed through the tissue and help to keep his blood sugar levels normal.

 FOLLOW-UP CARE

■ Some puppies and kittens will be so dehydrated that your veterinarian may recommend that you give them fluids when they come home from the hospital. Subcutaneous fluid therapy—injecting fluid under the skin—can be tricky with these babies because their skin is so thin that the needle often goes clear through and comes out the other side. Puppies and kittens also have a very limited amount of space to hold fluid under their skin, so only tiny amounts can be given at a time, depending on the size of your pet.

Your veterinarian will give you the syringe and fluid and demonstrate how to use it the first time. To inject the fluid, draw the recommended amount into the syringe. Gently "tent" the skin on your pet's shoulders, then insert the needle and gently depress the plunger. Watch for leakage; if you see any, withdraw the needle slightly so that the fluid goes beneath the skin and not outside the body. You may need to give a dose of subcutaneous fluid several times a day.

■ When intestinal parasites are diagnosed, your puppy or kitten will probably be treated once at your vet's office and then several times at home with medication prescribed according to his weight. With very young pets, this usually is a liquid medication like Nemex-2 (pyrantel pamoate) or Piperazine. For liquids, draw up the prescribed amount in an eyedropper or needleless syringe, insert the tip into your pet's mouth between the cheek and gum, tip his head up, and slowly squirt in the liquid. (This technique is illustrated on page 30.) Give only a small amount at a time to make sure that your pet doesn't choke—puppies and kittens can't take a lot all at once.

■ Puppies or kittens who don't nurse well or who have been rejected by the mother will need to be fed commercial puppy or kitten milk replacer. Just Born is made in both puppy and kitten formulations. There's also Esbilac for puppies and KMR for kittens. It should be warmed to about 100°F so that it won't upset their stomachs. How often to feed and how much varies by the age and size of the pet. Check the package or ask your vet for specific instructions. Usually, puppies and kittens need to eat every 2 hours for the first 2 weeks, then every 4 hours for another couple of weeks, and finally, about every 6 hours or so.

You can also get nursing bottles for puppies and kittens at pet-supply stores, but you need to be sure that the opening in the nipple is large enough for the milk replacer to pass through easily. Fill the bottle with the milk replacer, then hold it with the nipple end down. The milk should drip slowly without the bottle being squeezed. If it doesn't, heat a sewing needle with a match and use it to enlarge the opening. Be careful not to make the opening too big, though—if the hole is too large, the pet can aspirate the food into his airway and down into his lungs. Test the bottle again before using it.

You can also purchase a nursing kit that contains everything you'll need to nurse newborn puppies or kittens at pet stores or from pet-supply catalogs.

■ Once puppies and kittens are 4 weeks old, they can begin eating mushy solid food. Run a quality commercial puppy or kitten food through the blender with water or a commercial milk replacer to make a gruel. Avoid cow's milk because it can be hard to digest and can cause diarrhea. Offer food in a shallow pan so that it's easy for your puppy or kitten to eat.

THE BEST APPROACH

Tube Feeding

There are times when puppies or kittens are so sick and weak that they aren't able to suck or swallow and will starve without being helped to eat. Experienced breeders routinely tube-feed puppies and kittens who need help by threading a flexible, hollow tube down each baby's throat into the stomach, then injecting the food with a syringe. It saves time when feeding a whole litter because it takes only about 2 minutes to feed each baby. No air is swallowed (so no burping is required), and you know that each baby is getting the right amount of food. If your veterinarian advises you to tube-feed your little ones, he will give you complete instructions and a demonstration.

Advisors
■ Lorrie Bartloff, D.V.M., is a veterinarian at Three Point Veterinary Clinic in Elkhart, Indiana.
■ Alvin C. Dufour, D.V.M., is a veterinarian at Dufour Animal Hospital in Elkhart, Indiana.
■ Grady Hester, D.V.M., is a veterinarian at All Creatures Animal Clinic in Rolesville, North Carolina.
■ A. Michelle Miller, D.V.M., is a veterinarian at Animal Aid Clinic South in Elkhart, Indiana.

Falls

CALL YOUR VET: **IMMEDIATELY**

Tiny dogs often are injured in falls when they jump from an owner's arms or off high furniture. They usually break one or both front legs. And although cats are considered surefooted creatures, they can be injured if they misjudge a leap or lose their balance. A fall from a short distance doesn't give a cat time to use her "righting mechanism" and land on her toes. And because cats can climb so high, their falls can cause broken bones, ruptured organs (males can rupture their bladders), or even death.

Even if you didn't see your pet fall, a limp or refusal to move could alert you to a broken bone or internal injuries. Cats may refuse to eat when injured from a fall because they often hit the ground with their chins and break their jaws. And pain from a fracture or lung or heart bruising can make pets struggle to breathe. Cats may safely leap from heights of 6 feet or more, but a fall from that distance or higher needs medical attention as soon as possible. Injuries may not be obvious right away, but they can become dangerous in as little as 1½ hours.

DO THIS NOW

Watch for stopped breathing. If your pet stops breathing, you'll need to breathe for him by blowing air into his lungs. Wrap your hand around his muzzle and cover his nose with your mouth. Give two quick breaths into his nose, watching to see if his chest rises. Then give 15 to 20 breaths per minute until your pet starts breathing again or until you reach medical help. (This technique is illustrated on page 20.)

Be alert for possible internal injuries. Broken ribs can cut the lungs or poke holes (hernias) into the tissue that separates the abdominal organs from the heart and lungs. Diaphragmatic hernias are common with falls. Pets have trouble breathing when the stomach, intestines, and other organs spill into the wrong space. The resulting shock can cause organ failure and blood loss that could

175

FIRST ALERT

Ear Infections

Three tiny fluid-filled balance organs called the utricle, saccule, and semicircular canal are found deep inside the inner ear. They are lined with tiny hairs that telegraph balance information to the brain when chalklike material suspended in the fluid touches them as your pet's head moves about. An infection that invades the inner ear can disrupt your pet's sense of balance so much that she can't tell up from down, walks in circles, keeps her head tilted, or misjudges spatial relationships. Pets who fall a lot may have ear infections.

Ear infections tend to cause a discharge along with a bad smell. Crumbly, dark brown to black debris usually indicates parasites; yellow, greenish, dark brown, or bloody discharge points to a bacterial infection; and a yeasty smell could indicate a fungal infection.

Left untreated, ear infections can lead to hearing loss or sometimes permanent damage to the pet's sense of balance. Affected pets may see the world as crooked and hold their heads tilted for the rest of their lives. If you notice any or all of these symptoms, see your vet immediately. (For more information about ear infections, see page 160.)

kill your pet rapidly. Get him to the vet immediately.

Control bleeding. Falls often punch broken bone through the skin and cause bleeding. Put direct pressure on the bleeding with a gauze pad, clean cloth, or sanitary napkin that will absorb the blood. Usually, bleeding will stop in 5 minutes or less. If the pad soaks through, don't remove it, or you could disrupt the forming scab. Instead, just put another pad on top of the first and continue the pressure. (For more information on bleeding, see page 95.)

Cover open wounds. Any open wound, whether it's from a bone that pokes through the skin or a punctured abdomen, should be covered to protect it from further contamination. Wrap a clean towel over and around the injury.

Keep pets with broken ribs still. If you can see that your pet has broken ribs, try to get him to lie down on a soft towel placed in a pet carrier or on a rigid surface and carefully transport him to the vet. If he is uncomfortable lying on his side and fights to remain upright, more damage may result. If he will sit quietly in the carrier or on the board, don't try to force him to lie down.

Seal "sucking" chest wounds. If there is a sucking chest wound, you'll see bubbling and

High-Rise Syndrome

Cats who fall from balconies or windows of tall buildings suffer a recognizable group of injuries depending on the height from which they fall. In fact, cats tend to survive falls from higher than nine stories with fewer injuries than when they plunge from the fifth floor, a phenomenon referred to as high-rise syndrome.

Falls from the first through fourth floors are least dangerous because the cat doesn't reach extreme speeds during the fall. A cat picks up speed as she falls until she reaches 60 miles per hour—she won't fall any faster. Called terminal velocity, this speed is reached during any fall from higher than the fifth story.

Falls from the fifth through ninth floors cause the worst injuries: Cats turn in the air as they fall so that they land on their feet with their legs braced and rigid, and they can end up with multiple leg fractures, chest injuries, broken jaws, concussions, spinal injuries, and ruptures of the bladder or other organs.

Falls from higher than the ninth floor, however, apparently give cats time to "parachute" the loose folds of skin under their legs, empty their bladders, and relax so that the abdomen and chest absorb most of the impact rather than the head and legs.

If you live in a high-rise building, make sure that you have screens securely in place on all windows, and don't ever leave the door to the balcony open.

hear the air rushing into the body through the hole as your pet strains to breathe. Wrapping plastic wrap like Saran Wrap over the wound and around your pet's body works well to seal the wound. Wrap lightly to seal the area, but not tightly enough to restrict breathing, and transport your pet with the injured side down. (For more information on chest wounds, see page 128.)

Protect chest or abdominal wounds. You need to keep bacteria away from the injury. Use a clean plastic garbage bag or plastic wrap to cover the injury and have your pet lie on the in-

jured side. That helps maintain the internal vacuum of the chest so that the lungs won't collapse and can work efficiently. (For more on abdominal wounds, see page 55.)

Look for head and back injuries. Any blood in the eyes, nose, or mouth means possible head injury. A pet who can't get up or refuses to get up could have a back injury. In either case, move him as little as possible. Don't pick him up to move him. Instead, slide a flat, rigid object like a cookie sheet, large book, or board under him. Then place a towel or blanket over him to help hold him in place. (For more information on back injuries, see page 75; for head injuries, see page 232.)

Use care with fractures. A small pet with a broken leg can be gently laid on a rigid surface and covered with a blanket or towel. He will do best in a pet carrier or a box. Don't carry your pet in your arms, because it can increase his stress level. If you don't have a box or carrier, you can use a trash-can lid, as long as it is sturdy enough to bear your pet's weight without buckling. Try to move the injured limb as little as possible as you transport your pet to the vet. You can also use the blanket or towel or a pillowcase to cover your pet's face so that he can still breathe but isn't able to bite you when you try to help him. (For more information on fractures, see page 212.)

Protect yourself. Larger dogs may need to be muzzled before they'll let themselves be helped. Use a necktie, panty hose, or other length of material to hold the dog's mouth closed. Tie it around his nose and knot it on top of his muzzle, then draw the ends beneath his chin and knot again. Finally, pull the ends back and tie them behind his ears. (This technique is illustrated on page 17.)

✎ FOLLOW-UP CARE

■ Pets' fractures may heal in as little as 6 weeks, but they often take longer, depending on the severity of the fracture and the age of the animal. They must rest the injured part during that time for it to heal properly. Keep your pet from jumping, climbing, or running until the splint or pin is removed.

■ Your veterinarian may prescribe a drug like tartrate butorphanol (Torbugesic), which you'll have to administer several times a day. Discuss your pet's pain management choices with your vet.

■ Cats with broken jaws will have trouble eating solid food for several weeks, especially if the fracture has been wired together. Mix the food with warm water or low-fat, no-salt chicken broth to form a soft gruel or paste that they can lick up and don't have to chew.

■ Pets who have suffered ruptured bladders, diaphragmatic hernias, or other internal injuries have incisions and stitches that need to be kept clean. Use a sterile gauze pad and warm water to wipe away any discharge.

THE BEST APPROACH

Pill Syringe

Giving pills to cats and short-faced dogs like pugs can be difficult because they don't have muzzles to hang onto, and their teeth are particularly sharp. One of the best tools is a pill syringe that dispenses the medicine safely into your pet's mouth without the risk of your fingers being bitten. They're inexpensive and are available from most pet-supply stores and catalogs. You must use the syringe carefully, though, so that you don't injure the back of your pet's throat.

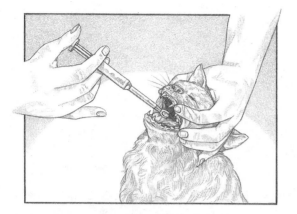

To use a pill syringe, place your pet on a table or countertop. Put one hand on top of her head, circling her muzzle with your fingers. Press her lips back against her teeth to make her open wide. With the other hand, aim the pill syringe toward the back of your pet's mouth and fire away.

Hold the syringe in one hand, place your other hand on top of your pet's head, and circle her muzzle with your thumb and middle fingers so that your fingertips press her lips against her teeth just behind the long canine teeth. This will prompt her to open her mouth.

After administering the pill, hold your pet's mouth closed and stroke her throat (or blow gently on her nose) to prompt her to swallow.

Lay the pill-laden syringe on your pet's tongue so that the exit end points at the back of her throat but doesn't quite touch. Quickly push the plunger to release the pill, withdraw the syringe, and hold your pet's mouth closed with your other hand. Stroke her throat or gently blow on her nose to prompt her to swallow.

Advisors

- Dale C. Butler, D.V.M., is a veterinarian at Best Friends Animal Hospital in Denison, Texas.
- Charles DeVinne, D.V.M., is a veterinarian at Animal Care Clinic in Peterborough, New Hampshire.
- Ken Lawrence, D.V.M., is a veterinarian at the Texoma Veterinary Hospital in Sherman, Texas.
- Peter Levin, D.V.M., is a veterinarian at Ludwig's Corner Veterinary Hospital in Chester Springs, Pennsylvania.
- Susan Little, D.V.M., is a veterinarian at Bytown Cat Hospital in Ottawa, Ontario, Canada.
- Julie Moews, D.V.M., is a veterinarian at Bolton Veterinary Hospital in Connecticut.
- Lenny Southam, D.V.M., is a house-call veterinarian at Targwood Animal Health Care in West Chester, Pennsylvania; manager of CompuServe's Vet Care Forum; and coauthor of *The Pill Book Guide to Medication for Your Dog and Cat*.

Fever

CALL YOUR VET: **IF NEEDED**

Fever is an elevated temperature that is generated by the body to fight disease. Normal cat and dog body temperature ranges between 99° and 102.5°F. A fever of 104°F in dogs and cats that's accompanied by lethargy, vomiting, diarrhea, or refusal to eat needs medical attention. If you can't get a veterinary appointment for your pet the same day, it's a good idea to give first aid to help him feel more comfortable.

🐾 DO THIS NOW

Take your pet's temperature. The only accurate way to tell if your dog or cat has a fever is to take his temperature. Taking the temperature rectally is simple to do. First, have another person steady the front end of your pet, hug his neck, or otherwise distract him from biting. For a bulb thermometer, shake down the column of mercury until it reads about 96°F. Then lubricate the bulb tip with a lubricant like petroleum jelly. Grasp the base of your pet's tail and lift it to give yourself a clear target. You can also steady your pet and keep him from escaping with a firm grip on his tail. This will also keep him from trying to sit down during the procedure, which could injure him if the thermometer breaks.

Insert the lubricated end of the thermometer

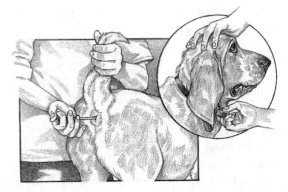

Taking your pet's temperature is a lot easier if you have a second person to steady and distract him. Lubricate the tip of the thermometer, then grip and lift your pet's tail. Slowly insert the thermometer into your pet's rectum until about half of it is inside. Keep him still for 3 minutes, then withdraw the thermometer to check the reading.

FIRST ALERT

Heatstroke

When hot weather raises a pet's body temperature to dangerous levels, he can suffer heatstroke. Hot weather isn't the only culprit. Being enclosed in a car, trapped in a clothes dryer, or kenneled without good air circulation are common and dangerous situations that could lead to heatstroke. Body temperature climbs to 105°F or higher—even 110°F isn't unusual. It's important to know the temperature level, so be sure to record it.

Heatstroke is a medical emergency that needs veterinary treatment as soon as possible. Unless the temperature is brought down very quickly, your dog or cat will suffer permanent brain and organ damage and may die, so first aid is essential to save his life.

Get your pet into a tub of cold water immediately or spray him down with a garden hose and put ice packs wrapped in a thin cloth between his back legs in the groin area and in the armpits of the front legs. Then wrap him in a cold, damp towel and get him to the animal hospital. (For more information about heatstroke, see page 237.)

about halfway into your pet's rectum and hold it in place for 3 minutes. Remove the thermometer, wipe it clean with a tissue, and read the silver column of mercury. (Follow the manufacturer's directions to read a digital thermometer.) Once you've finished, be sure to clean the thermometer with alcohol to avoid spreading disease.

Get to the vet immediately if body temperature is above 105°F. If it is over 107°F, mix rubbing alcohol 50/50 with water and spray or dab the solution on his armpits, groin, the insides of his earflaps, and the pads of his feet on your way to the vet. As it evaporates, it will cool your pet. The footpads and ears carry lots of blood vessels near the surface, so cooling the blood can help cool off the whole body.

 FOLLOW-UP CARE

■ No follow-up care is usually necessary once you've taken care of the emergency situation, unless your vet gives you specific instructions.

Advisors
■ Michael G. Abdella, D.V.M., is a veterinarian at Alisa Viejo Animal Hospital in Alisa Viejo, California.
■ John Brakebill, D.V.M., is a veterinarian at Brakebill Veterinary Hospital in Sherman, Texas.
■ Susette Nygaard, D.V.M., is a veterinarian at East Lake Veterinary Hospital in Dallas.

Fishhook Injuries

CALL YOUR VET: **IF NEEDED**

Fishhooks smell like bait and are attractive to any dog or cat, but it's usually young pets who play with them and end up with injuries. Often, the hook ends up in the pet's lips or inside her mouth, but it's not uncommon for a playful paw to be impaled.

A pet with a hook in his paw will limp, while a hook in the mouth can cause gagging, drooling, pawing at the mouth, or trouble swallowing. Hooks inside the mouth or down the throat need immediate medical attention. They can cause life-threatening injuries when swallowed, and the hook and fishing line may need to be surgically removed.

DO THIS NOW

Restrain your pet. It's best to have someone else to help either restrain or treat your pet. To hold a cat or small dog, grasp the scruff of her neck with one hand and her hind feet with the other. Lay her on her side on a flat surface and gently stretch her out. Bigger dogs do better on the ground while you kneel beside them. Put one arm under and around your dog's chest and your other arm around her neck. (Both of these techniques are illustrated on page 18.)

Muzzle her. If she is not having difficulty breathing, muzzle her with a length of panty hose or fabric, leaving the injured area exposed. (This technique is illustrated on page 17.) If you can't use a muzzle without disturbing the hook, however, go to the vet immediately.

Remove the hook. Most fishhooks have barbs on the ends to keep the hook from moving backward. They also have an "eye" at the end of the shaft to hold the line, and that stops the hook from moving forward. To remove a hook, either the barb or the shaft must be cut off so that the metal can pass through the flesh unimpeded.

If the barb of the hook has already passed all

FIRST ALERT

Swallowed Fishing Line

Swallowed fishing line can not only wad up your pet's intestines, it can also cut tissue and cause peritonitis—inflammation and infection of the abdomen—which can be deadly.

Don't try to pull out the exposed end of the line—it may be attached to a hook that's anchored in your pet's tummy. Swallowed fishing line is an emergency that needs immediate medical attention. (For more information about swallowed objects, see page 204.)

To remove a fishhook, get a second person to hold your pet. If the barbed end is visible, clip it off close to the skin with wire cutters. Finally, pull it out gently at the point of entry.

the way through the flesh so that it is easy to see, use a pair of wire cutters to clip it off close to the skin. Then gently back the hook out.

If the barb hasn't passed all the way through, use pliers to grasp the shaft, then push the barb through the flesh. Remember that it's curved, so push in the direction of the hook. Once you can see the barb, cut it off with wire cutters and remove it as described above. If the hook is embedded deeply, however, you may prefer to wait until your veterinarian can remove it.

FOLLOW-UP CARE

■ Most mouth wounds heal quickly with no further care. Clean foot wounds a couple of times a day with gauze pads and antiseptic liquid soap like Betadine Skin Cleanser until they start to heal.

■ Usually, a foot bandage must be changed daily, or at least every 3 days. Wrap the bandaged foot in plastic wrap like Saran Wrap to protect it when your pet goes outside. Be sure to remove the plastic when she comes back in.

Advisors

■ Kenneth J. Drobatz, D.V.M., is a veterinarian and associate professor of critical care emergency service at the Veterinary Hospital of the University of Pennsylvania in Philadelphia.

■ Jean C. Hofve, D.V.M., is a veterinarian and Companion Animal Program coordinator for the Animal Protection Institute in Sacramento.

■ Chris Johnson, D.V.M., is a veterinarian at Westside Animal Emergency Clinic in Atlanta.

Flea Allergy

CALL YOUR VET: **IF NEEDED**

Some pets can be bitten by a swarm of fleas and never be bothered. But when a pet is allergic, it takes only a bite or two for them to itch all the time.

Allergic pets react to the flea saliva: They break out with sores and itchy skin. Dogs are usually most affected on their rear ends, while cats often get tiny scabs all over. Pets who are allergic to fleas very often won't have any fleas on their bodies at all because they're so aggressive at licking and grooming them away.

If your dog or cat has scratched or chewed herself bloody, she'll need medical attention right away. But in most cases, first aid is all that's needed until you can get rid of the fleas.

DO THIS NOW

Treat with an antihistamine. To help reduce itching in the short term, you can give your pet an over-the-counter antihistamine like Benadryl. The antihistamine helps counteract the inflammation and can also make pets a bit sleepy so that they don't scratch so much. The liquid usually comes in a dose of 12.5 milligrams per teaspoon; pills are 25 milligrams each. You can give 1 milligram per pound of body weight every 6 to 8 hours until the reaction subsides. This means that a 10-pound cat or dog would get about ¾ teaspoon of liquid or half a pill.

To give a pill to a dog, circle the top of his snout with your hand, pressing his lips against his teeth on both sides of the jaw along the gum line, just behind the large, pointed canine teeth. Then use your other hand to push the pill over the hill of the tongue, close his mouth, and gently stroke his throat until he swallows. (This technique illustrated on page 30.)

For a cat, put her on a tabletop, grasp the scruff of her neck, and gently arch her neck backward—her mouth will automatically fall open a bit. Use your other hand to pull down her chin until you can see the V-shaped indentation in the center of her tongue. Drop the pill on the V, close your cat's mouth, and usually, she'll swallow it right down. Offer a treat immediately so that she is more interested in swallowing the treat than in spitting out the medicine. It can be helpful to kneel on the floor with the cat held between your knees so that she can't escape.

Soak your pet in cold water. For immediate relief from itchy skin, give your pet a cold-water soak in the bathtub or sink, or use the garden hose. Cool water reduces inflammation on contact. A 10- to 20-minute treatment will provide the most benefit, and you can repeat the soaking up to three or four times a day. (Cats tend not to appreciate water soaks, though. It's helpful to put a nonskid surface like an old towel or a small window screen in the bottom of the tub or sink. That gives the cat something besides you to claw and hang on to.)

Because bacteria grow in moist conditions, be sure to dry your pet carefully between soaks to avoid further irritation and discomfort.

Use an oatmeal bath. Many times, scratching just makes the skin itch worse, so your pet will continue to scratch. You must break this itch cycle so that your pet can get relief and allow her skin to heal. Oatmeal works well to stop the itch cycle. You can add an oatmeal-based product like Aveeno to the bathwater or use a pet shampoo and conditioner that contain oatmeal. An oatmeal bath once a day should give your pet relief until the allergic reaction goes away.

A cool bath with plain water or an oatmeal shampoo not only helps the itch but also drowns and rinses away fleas. A flea shampoo for dogs and cats may kill the fleas faster, but any plain shampoo that's safe for pets will work. Be sure to dunk your pet up to her neck and lather the suds around her neck to trap the fleas as they head for higher ground.

FOLLOW-UP CARE

■ Essential fatty acid (EFA) supplements—those containing omega-3 and omega-6 fatty acids—are very good for flea-allergic pets, not only because they moisturize the coat but also because they can actually reduce itching in some pets. The best ones are available over the counter, from pet-supply catalogs, or from your vet. Usually, you just add the EFA supplements to your pet's food.

■ Some flea-allergic pets need a prescription antihistamine or cortisone to get the itching under control. Give the pills as recommended by your vet. Cortisone tablets usually are tiny and easily hidden in a treat like a cube of cheese.

■ A conditioner containing oatmeal that's designed to be left on the coat and skin is very soothing to allergic skin. You can use this up to three times a week after a cool-water rinse or oatmeal bath.

■ There are now allergy shots (referred to as immunotherapy) that are designed for flea-allergic pets. These are a series of vaccinations that help pets build up a resistance to flea bites. The injections usually must continue for at least a year, and you can learn to give the injections yourself. To do so, draw up the serum into the syringe and jar loose any bubbles by holding the syringe with the needle pointed up, then tapping the syringe with your finger. Carefully press the plunger to get rid of the air. Grasping the loose skin of your pet's scruff, insert the needle beneath the skin and depress the plunger. Be sure to rub the injection site a bit once you take out the needle to reduce stinging and keep any serum from leaking out of the exit hole. (This technique is illustrated on page 73.)

■ To keep ahead of fleas in the environment, vacuum the entire house, especially the furniture, baseboard cracks, and your pet's sleeping and resting areas. This collects the eggs and larvae that are hidden around your house. Be sure to throw out the vacuum bag or the pests can hatch inside, and you'll spread them all over the next time you vacuum.

■ Throw your pet's bedding into the wash each week to get rid of any adults and immature fleas. The soap and hot water kill them.

THE BEST APPROACH

Once-a-Month Flea Treatments

The absolute best way to conquer flea allergies is to get rid of the fleas, and veterinarians agree that once-a-month preventives like Frontline, Program, and Advantage are the best choices. Look-alike products from pet-supply stores are less expensive, but they're not always as safe or effective as brand-name products. These products come as chewable tablets or liquid drops in premeasured doses that you squeeze onto the skin at the back of your pet's neck. The medicine is absorbed into the body and provides protection for up to a month by killing fleas when they bite and keeping immature fleas from maturing into egg-laying adults.

Advisors

■ Lowell Ackerman, D.V.M., is a veterinarian at Mesa Veterinary Hospital in Scottsdale, Arizona, and author of *Skin and Coat Care for Your Dog* and *Skin and Coat Care for Your Cat*.

■ Lyndon Conrad, D.V.M., is a veterinarian at Noah's Landing Pet Care Clinic in Elkhart, Indiana.

■ Grady Hester, D.V.M., is a veterinarian at All Creatures Animal Clinic in Rolesville, North Carolina.

■ Steven Melman, V.M.D., is a veterinarian and dermatological consultant at Derma Pet, a pet skin-care products company in Potomac, Maryland.

■ Susette Nygaard, D.V.M., is a veterinarian at East Lake Veterinary Hospital in Dallas.

Fly Bites

CALL YOUR VET: **IF NEEDED**

Cats are almost never bothered by flies, but dogs—especially those with upright ears, like German shepherds—often have bites on the inside tips of their ears. The stable fly, often called the biting housefly, looks like a regular housefly, but it has bayonet-like, needle-sharp mouthparts that it uses to obtain blood meals. Stable flies prefer horses, and they live primarily in the midwestern and southeastern states.

Dogs with fly bites on the ears won't have much bleeding, but the ear margins and tips will be crusty from the inflammation and serum that leaks from the bites. Little dogs are rarely bothered, but big dogs more often live outside, where they are exposed to summer flies. And larger dogs mean greater amounts of feces, which tends to draw flies. Fly-bite problems can be easily controlled with first aid.

DO THIS NOW

Soften the scab. Hold a washcloth soaked with warm water against your pet's sore ear margins to soften the scabs and crusty material. It may take 2 to 3 minutes until the material softens enough to be wiped away.

Wash the area. Once the crusty material is gone, wash the raw areas with an antiseptic liquid soap like Betadine Skin Cleanser, and be sure to rinse off the soap. Using plain warm water with a gauze pad is safest for cats.

Apply an antibiotic ointment. Use an over-the-counter antibiotic ointment like Neosporin to help soothe the inflammation and prevent the ears from getting infected.

FOLLOW-UP CARE

■ Fly bites make ears very sore, and they'll continue to leak serum and crust up for several days, even without more bites. Keep the sores clean by wiping off the excess crust at least once

Name That Fly

There are many kinds of flies besides the common stable fly, or biting housefly. Most of them target primarily livestock like horses and cattle, but they can also plague people and pets. Adult flies feed on blood, saliva, tears, or mucus, while larval forms (maggots) usually grow in wet or damp areas. Fly bites are not only painful, they can also spread diseases like anthrax and tularemia. Most flies can be killed or repelled by the same insecticides that are effective against fleas. Here are the types of flies that you and your pet are most likely to encounter.

Blackflies: Also called buffalo gnats because of the humps over their heads, blackflies are small (2 to 5 millimeters, or about ⅛ inch long) bloodsuckers. There are more than 1,000 species of blackfly. They tend to swarm near fast-moving rivers or streams.

Biting midges: Also called no-see-ums and punkies, these tiny (1.5 to 4 millimeters, about ⅛ inch long) troublemakers also suck blood. They live near mud or moist soil and marshes.

Horseflies: Largest of the biting flies, horse flies have heavy bodies, are often colorful, and live around stables. They lay eggs in lakes and ponds. Horseflies are one of the hardest flies to control and kill.

Deerflies: These medium-size flies with dark-banded wings also drink blood, transmit disease, and create painful bite wounds. They're often resistant to insecticides.

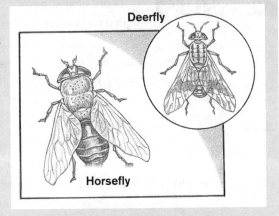

Horseflies don't bother just horses. Compared with other flies, they're as big as horses (up to an inch long). These blood-sucking predators are extremely aggressive.

Deerflies may be small (¼ to ⅜ inch long), but they're aggressive, and their bites are painful. Look for one large spot on each wing.

a day. Use a soft cloth or gauze pad soaked in water or sterile saline contact lens solution.

■ Apply antibiotic ointment in a thick layer several times a day. This not only helps prevent infection but also provides a mechanical barrier to keep the flies away. You'll need to reapply it very often because pets tend to wipe off the ointment by rubbing their sore ears against objects.

■ Use a fly-repellent gel to keep the flies off your pet. Products like Pet-Guard gel are available at pet-supply stores or your veterinarian's office. You need to apply it several times a day and slather it on pretty thickly to keep off the flies. If you don't have a fly repellent, a pet-safe flea repellent will also work. Spray the repellent on a gauze pad and wipe it onto your pet's ears, the top of his head, and around his neck. Be sure to follow package directions—some flea sprays are dangerous in combination with other insect repellents.

■ You can get rid of the problem completely just by cleaning up your yard. Stable flies lay eggs and mature in decaying material like grass clippings, seaweed along beaches, wet haystacks, and feces. The life cycle from egg to adult fly is about 2 to 3 weeks, so just picking up the dog piles frequently—daily, if necessary—will drastically reduce the pests, since flies won't be attracted to your yard.

THE BEST APPROACH

Fly Repellent

Flies are most attracted to horses, but they'll make do with your dog's ears when nothing else is available. Fly repellents designed for pets work okay for most dogs, and even petroleum jelly slathered on their ears can provide a mechanical barrier to keep off the pests. But veterinarians say that products designed to protect horses from fly bites may be an option for large dogs for a limited amount of time. They not only repel the bugs but also kill flies on contact so that they don't lay eggs and produce more biting pests.

Swat Fly Repellent Ointment comes in 6-ounce jars in either pink or clear formula and is available from pet-supply catalogs. It contains pyrethrin, a natural insecticide that's safe for pets, and repels several species of flies that can be pests to pets. You can use it sparingly on your pet's face, ears, and even around open wounds to prevent maggot (fly larvae) infestations. Don't apply it to broken skin or to the wounds themselves. Don't use it for more than 3 consecutive days or on pets who weigh less than 50 pounds. (For more information about maggots, see page 284.)

Advisors

■ Michael G. Abdella, D.V.M., is a veterinarian at Aliso Viejo Animal Hospital in Alisa Viejo, California.

■ Lorrie Bartloff, D.V.M., is a veterinarian at Three Point Veterinary Clinic in Elkhart, Indiana.

■ Mauri Karger, D.V.M., is a veterinarian at I-20 Animal Medical Center in Arlington, Texas.

Food Allergies

CALL YOUR VET: **IF NEEDED**

Food allergies can affect any dog or cat, but they aren't nearly as common as pollen or flea allergies. The pet usually reacts to a protein ingredient in his food, like milk or beef. The most typical reaction in dogs is all-over itching, while cats develop itchy faces and heads. Less often, the pet reacts with vomiting or diarrhea.

In some cases, a pet develops a more serious allergic reaction to the food he eats and breaks out in welts. The swelling usually develops within 20 to 60 minutes on the face, around the eyes and muzzle, and on the head and is extremely itchy. The pet will paw at the swelling or rub his face on the carpet or furniture. Even less often, a pet can suffer an anaphylactic reaction to food—a violent allergic reaction that happens within only a few minutes. He may have trouble breathing, vomit, have sudden diarrhea, or even collapse.

Most food allergies can be easily controlled once the protein culprit or other ingredient has been identified and avoided, and even hives can be safely treated at home. Anaphylactic reactions need immediate medical help—and first aid can save your pet's life.

🔧 DO THIS NOW

Clear the airway. If your dog or cat suffers a severe reaction, you'll usually notice breathing problems within only a few minutes. The lungs can fill up with fluid, so he will strain to breathe, and the respiration will sound bubbly, like water gurgling. Pets need immediate veterinary care, but you can help by clearing the airway.

Turn your dog or cat upside down with his head hanging toward the floor for 10 seconds. With cats and small dogs, simply grasp them by circling your hands around the abdomen in front of the pelvis. Hold larger pets around the hips.

Be prepared to perform artificial respiration or CPR. This may be necessary for vio-

You can help your pet breathe by holding her upside down with your hands around her stomach just in front of her hips.

lent food reactions. Lay your pet on his side, open his mouth, and use a dry cloth to get a good grip to extend his tongue. (This helps open the airway.) Then, close his mouth, seal his lips, and blow into his nose. Give two quick breaths immediately and watch to see if his chest rises. Continue blowing into his nostrils about 15 to 20 times a minute until he breathes on his own or until you reach veterinary help. (This technique is illustrated on page 20.)

If his heart has stopped, you'll also need to give your pet chest compressions. For cats and small dogs, cup a hand over the point of the chest just behind the elbows and squeeze firmly between your fingers and thumb, pressing in about ½ inch, about 80 to 100 times a minute. Give a breath into the nose after every five compressions until your pet revives or until you reach medical help.

Put a larger dog on his side on a firm, flat surface and put both hands on top of each other against the chest. Use both hands to compress the chest by 25 to 50%. (This technique is illustrated on page 21.) Alternate breaths and compressions as for small pets. It's best to have someone drive you and your pet to the vet while you're performing CPR.

Induce vomiting if your pet is breathing. When the reaction is confined to your pet's face or head, and as long as there is no problem with breathing, it's a good idea to induce vomiting. The reaction will continue as long as the food remains in your pet's stomach, so you'll want to get rid of it. Use a needleless syringe or turkey baster to give your pet 1 to 2 teaspoons of 3% hydrogen peroxide for every 10 pounds of body weight. If necessary, you may repeat the dosage two or three times, allowing 5 minutes between doses.

Give your pet an antihistamine. An antihistamine like Benadryl will help counteract mild allergic reactions to food, such as hives or all-over itchy skin. It also has sedative effects, which will calm your pet so that he doesn't continue to obsessively scratch the itch. The liquid usually comes in a dose of 12.5 milligrams per teaspoon; pills are 25 milligrams each. You can give 1 milligram per pound of body weight every 6 to 8 hours until the reaction subsides; this means that a 10-pound cat or dog would get about ¾ teaspoon of liquid or half a pill.

Use cool water to calm the itch. Fill up the tub and let your dog soak for 20 minutes two or three times a week. Add a soothing oatmeal bath product like Aveeno Soothing Bath Treatment for extra comfort. Oatmeal products like Aveeno have natural anti-itch properties that help keep pets comfortable.

 ## FOLLOW-UP CARE

■ A food-elimination trial helps pinpoint the exact food ingredients that cause your pet's problems. This involves having your dog or cat eat a diet that he has never eaten before. For instance, a kangaroo meat and oatmeal diet made by Iams, available from the vet, works well for the test. Once your pet's skin returns to normal, add suspect ingredients back into the diet one at a time to see which one prompts itching. Then you can read food labels and avoid chicken or lamb, for instance, if that's what caused the problem.

■ You can find essential fatty acid (EFA) food supplements at pet-supply stores or at your veterinarian's office. They contain omega-3 and omega-6 fatty acids that heal skin and help keep it healthy. EFAs also have some anti-itch prop-erties. Check with your veterinarian for the right brand and dosage for your pet.

THE BEST APPROACH

High-Tech Allergy Diets

An elimination diet can take several weeks to pinpoint all the different food ingredients that may be bugging your pet. And even when you do discover the culprits, they may be so common that it's hard to find a diet that doesn't include them. Veterinarians say that pets eat so many different foods these days that it has become nearly impossible to find "novel proteins" that they have never tasted before, and that makes it very hard to diagnose and control food allergies (pets usually react to a protein ingredient in their food).

The newest treatments for food allergies are designer diets that use proteins with a low molecular weight. The protein molecules are cut up into such tiny fragments that the pet's body no longer recognizes them and stops reacting with itchy skin. There are only a few diets available so far, like EXclude, made by DVM Pharmaceuticals, and CNM HA-formula, made by Purina. They are available by prescription from your veterinarian.

Advisors

■ Lowell Ackerman, D.V.M., is a veterinarian at Mesa Veterinary Hospital in Scottsdale, Arizona, and author of *Skin and Coat Care for Your Dog* and *Skin and Coat Care for Your Cat*.

■ Lyndon Conrad, D.V.M., is a veterinarian at Noah's Landing Pet Care Clinic in Elkhart, Indiana.

■ Susette Nygaard, D.V.M., is a veterinarian at East Lake Veterinary Hospital in Dallas.

■ Denise Petryk, D.V.M., is a veterinarian at Puget Sound Veterinary Medical Referral Center in Tacoma, Washington.

■ Raymond Russo, D.V.M., is a veterinarian at Kingston Animal Hospital in Massachusetts.

Foreign Object in Ear

CALL YOUR VET: **IF NEEDED**

MEDICINE CHEST

Length of fabric for
   muzzling
Flashlight
Blunt-tipped tweezers
   or hemostat
Sterile saline contact
   lens solution
Squeeze bottle
Soft cloth or cotton
   ball
Antibiotic ointment
   (Neosporin)
Roll gauze, panty hose,
   or cotton sock
Antihistamine (Ben-
   adryl)

Dogs' and cats' ears are pretty well protected by fur, especially in the case of floppy-eared dogs. But once in a while, a foreign object can fall down inside the ear and get stuck. Pets in certain parts of the country, especially the south-western and western states, have problems with grass awns, the barbed seeds of various grasses and grains. The awns actually work their way into the tender skin of the ear. They're very painful and can cause infection.

Even a piece of grass or bit of sand could cause problems. A pet with a foreign object in his ear will shake his head and paw and scratch at it. Eventually, he'll develop an infection. The pet will be so uncomfortable that he may need sedation before the object can be removed. But first-aid can ease the pain and, in some cases, cure the problem.

DO THIS NOW

Muzzle your pet. Before doing anything else, fashion a temporary muzzle for your pet so that you aren't bitten when you try to help him. A foreign object in the ear can be painful, and even the most loving pet may lash out when he hurts. Use a necktie or a length of panty hose and tie it in a knot on top of his nose. Then bring the ends under his chin and knot them again. Finally, bring the ends of the strip of material back behind his head and tie them in a knot or bow behind his ears. (This technique is illustrated on page 17.)

Restrain him. Have a second person restrain your pet and hold his head steady while you examine the ear. Otherwise, your pet could be hurt if he jerks or flinches away at the wrong moment. With a dog, seat him on a tabletop or on the floor. Let his neck rest in the crook of your elbow and bring your arm

FIRST ALERT

Feline Ear Tumor

Cats and dogs often develop ear infections with a soupy or crumbly discharge, and once diagnosed, these infections are pretty easy to treat. (For more information about ear infections, see page 160.)

In cats, however, when only one ear is infected—especially if it smells really awful—there's a good chance that there's a tumor growing inside the ear canal where you can't see it. Most of the time, the veterinarian needs a special instrument called an otoscope to look deep into the ear and find the tumor. The infection won't go away until the tumor is surgically removed. These growths are usually benign (not cancerous), similar to warts. Cats usually recover from the surgery and do fine. If you suspect that your cat has a tumor, call the vet immediately.

up around him, snugging his head to your chest. Bring your other arm under his chest to hold him steady. Be sure that the affected ear is facing out for easy access.

To examine a cat or small dog, grasp him by the scruff of the neck with one hand and by the hind legs with the other, then gently stretch him out on a tabletop. (These techniques are illustrated on page 18.)

Remove what's reachable. Carefully grasp the earflap with one hand and shine a flashlight or penlight inside the ear canal to see if there's anything visible. The ear canal in cats and dogs is shaped like an L, so you can only see down so far. If you can see the foreign object at the opening of the ear canal, you can try to remove it. A pair of blunt-tipped tweezers or a hemostat (a long, thin clamp available from pet-supply catalogs) will work best. If the object is

deeper in the canal, the veterinarian should remove it.

Rinse the ear with saline solution. If you are able to remove the object, rinse out the ear with warm sterile saline contact lens solution to clean the wound or irritation. Just aim the stream of liquid with the squeeze bottle. You can also make saline by dissolving 1¼ teaspoons of table salt in 1 pint of warm water. Fill up the ear canal, massage the base of the ear, then wipe out the fluid with a cotton ball or soft cloth.

Apply an antibiotic ointment. If you've been able to remove the foreign object, it's a good idea to medicate the ear with antibiotic ointment like Neosporin. Squeeze a little ointment into the ear canal and massage the base of the ear to spread the medicine evenly. This will help fight infection and soothe the irritation.

SPECIAL SITUATION

If the object is out of reach: If you can't reach or see the foreign object, it's best to keep your pet as quiet as possible until medical attention is available. Constant shaking of his ears can bruise the earflap and cause an aural hematoma, in which blood collects and the skin swells and which needs surgery to correct. So to prevent further damage, fold the ear inside out against the top of your pet's head and secure it in place. You can use roll gauze or a length of panty hose, or cut the toe off an athletic sock and slip the tube of material over your dog's head to hold down the ear. Be sure that the material is not too tight and doesn't restrict your pet's breathing. (This technique is illustrated on page 26.)

You can also give your pet an over-the-counter antihistamine like Benadryl to reduce the irritation and swelling until the foreign body is removed. This might make him feel more comfortable even if the ear has become infected. The liquid usually comes in a dose of 12.5 milligrams per teaspoon; pills are usually 25 milligrams each. Pets will need 1 milligram per pound of body weight every 6 to 8 hours. That means a 10-pound cat or dog should get about ¾ teaspoon of liquid or half a pill.

 ## FOLLOW-UP CARE

■ If a foreign body like a grass awn has been removed from your pet's ear, your vet may prescribe antibiotics. Several days of oral antibiotics will help prevent the sore from becoming infected or speed recovery from an existing infection. For dogs, you can try hiding pills in tasty treats like cheese. Or gently grasp the top of your dog's muzzle, press your fingers against his gums right behind the large, pointed canine teeth, and when he opens wide, drop the pill onto the back of his tongue, close his mouth, and gently stroke his throat until he swallows. The same technique works for cats, but be ready with a bribe once you get the pill in your cat's mouth so that he'll swallow the treat and forget to spit out the pill. (This technique is illustrated on page 30.)

Advisors
■ Karen Hoffman, V.M.D., is a veterinarian at Delaware Valley Animal Hospital in Fairless Hills, Pennsylvania.
■ Doug McConkey, D.V.M., is a veterinarian at Canyon Creek Pet Hospital in Sherman, Texas.
■ Laura Solien, D.V.M., is a veterinarian at Maplecrest Animal Hospital in Goshen, Indiana.

Foreign Object in Eye

CALL YOUR VET: **SAME DAY**

It's common for pets to get things in their eyes, especially dogs and cats with prominent eyes like Pekingese and Persians. The fur on furry-faced breeds like Old English sheepdogs is designed to protect the eyes, but all dogs and cats have another form of protection. The nictitating membrane, also called the haw or the third eyelid, gives pets extra protection from foreign objects because it acts like a windshield wiper that sweeps from the inside corner of the eye across the eyeball. But the third eyelid can cause problems, too, because material that gets trapped under the membrane can be hard to remove.

When something is in your pet's eye, the eye can turn red and weepy, and he'll blink a lot, squint with pain, or paw at the eye. Material left in the eye for too long can lead to sores or infections.

In many cases, you'll be able to remove the irritant yourself at home with simple first aid. But if material gets stuck beneath the eyelids or is embedded in the eye, your veterinarian will need to anesthetize the eyeball to remove it. Even if you're able to remove the material, you should have the eye checked and treated the same day. Grass, dirt, and seeds often carry bacteria or fungi that can infect the eye. If your pet's eye is red, painful, or irritated but you don't see anything that you can identify as a foreign object that can be easily removed, take him to the vet right away.

DO THIS NOW

Gently restrain your pet. Any wiggling could cause more injury when you treat the eye. It's best to have a second pair of hands to help you do this. Place a small dog or cat on a table or counter and wrap him in a towel or pillowcase with only his head exposed. Hold short-muzzled pets by the scruff and beneath the jaw and long-nosed dogs by the scruff and nose to steady the head.

✚ FIRST ALERT

Eye Ulcers

An object in your pet's eye that isn't washed out with tears or removed by you or your veterinarian can scratch the surface of the eye. Grass seeds like foxtails often get stuck underneath the eyelids. Then, every time your pet blinks, the seed digs deeper and makes the sore worse, and an ulcer can develop.

Without treatment, ulcers can work their way through the surface of the eye, become infected and produce a yellow or green discharge, and eventually affect your pet's vision. Ulcers are also extremely painful. If you notice any of these symptoms, or if your pet's eye is red and painful with no discernible cause, have him checked out by your vet as soon as possible. Many times, it's hard to see an ulcer without specialized stains like fluorescein that will cause the sore to glow in the dark when your vet shines a black light on it. Once the ulcer is diagnosed, medication usually can cure the problem.

For a larger dog, loop one arm around his neck and the other arm under and around his chest and hug him to your chest. Or you can kneel on the floor with the dog facing out between your legs, with one hand wrapped around his chest and the other grasping his muzzle to steady his head. (These techniques are illustrated on page 18.)

Hold open the eyelids with your thumb and forefinger. Then try to locate the foreign object. If it's something like a blade of grass that can be easily reached, use your fingers to grab it and gently pull it out.

Use a cotton ball and saline. If the material can't be grasped with your fingers, it can be dangerous to use tweezers or swabs that could poke the eye if your pet wiggles. Moisten a cotton ball or clean cloth with sterile saline contact lens solution, twist the end into a soft point, and touch it to the object. Often, the object will cling to the cotton and can be drawn out of the eye.

Float debris out of the eye. Use an eyewash solution like Opticlear Eye Wash, available from pet-supply stores or catalogs, or sterile saline solution. First, soak a cotton ball or cloth and squeeze the liquid into the eye repeatedly. If that doesn't work, use a direct stream of saline from a squeeze bottle, and aim it at the material. (Be sure that you use saline solution and not any other contact lens cleaning solutions that may contain harsher ingredients.) It's a good idea to continue to flush the area for a minute or so even after the material is out to help prevent infection.

Treat with an antibiotic. Using an antibiotic designed for pets' eyes, like Terramycin Antibiotic Ophthalmic Ointment, is a good idea if you get the material out easily and the eye does not become red or irritated. It will help prevent infection and also soothe and protect the eye from further irritation in case some material is still in there. Pull down the lower eyelid and squeeze a small amount of ointment into the cupped tissue. If the eye remains red and your pet appears to be experiencing discomfort or pain, see your vet right away.

Use a collar restraint. Make sure that your pet doesn't make the problem worse by scratching at his eye. The only good way to do this is by having him wear a cone-shaped collar restraint called an Elizabethan collar. Or sit with him and make sure that he doesn't scratch at his eyes while someone drives both of you to the vet.

To administer eye medication, pull down your pet's lower eyelid and squeeze a small amount into the cupped tissue. You don't have to spread it around. When your pet blinks, the medicine will flow over the surface of his eye.

 ## FOLLOW-UP CARE

■ Veterinarians will almost always send you home with antibiotic drops or ointment to put in your pet's eye, and sometimes they'll prescribe pain medication as well. Usually, you'll need to medicate your pet two or three times a day. Artificial tears like Hypo Tears may also help soothe minor irritation. As long as your dog or cat holds the eye wide open and doesn't squint (a sign of pain), he's on the road to recovery. If you see squinting, or if the redness isn't going away, have your pet rechecked by your veterinarian.

Advisors
■ Grace F. Bransford, D.V.M., is a veterinarian in Corte Madera, California
■ Dennis Hacker, D.V.M., is a veterinary ophthalmologist in El Cerrito, California.
■ Albert Mughannam, D.V.M., is a veterinary ophthalmologist at Veterinary Vision in San Mateo, California.

Foreign Object in Mouth

CALL YOUR VET: **IF NEEDED**

Dogs often get objects stuck in their mouths because they love to chew and play with anything they can pick up. The most common items are broken sticks or pieces of bone. Cats are less likely to have these problems, but like dogs, they can get parts of toys stuck in their teeth, string wrapped around the bases of their tongues, or grass seeds penetrating their tongues or gums. Pets with longer fur may get painful burrs stuck in their mouths when they nibble out the foreign material that gets caught in their toes or coats.

A pet with something caught in his mouth acts frantic. He shakes his head, paws at his mouth, drools, cries, and races around. When the object cuts tissue, the saliva may be blood-tinged. Sometimes, the pet further injures himself by biting his tongue while trying to get rid of the object. Sometimes, though, the only signs will be a reluctance to eat and bad breath.

A foreign object in the mouth isn't dangerous unless it blocks breathing, but it can be painful and scary. If it's left in place for longer than a day, it can cause infection. Some pets become so hysterical that they must be sedated before the object can be removed. Objects embedded in tissue need medical treatment.

You also need to call your vet if you can't remove the object yourself or your pet won't let you look in his mouth; your pet has injured his teeth, lips, tongue, or the inside of his mouth; or there is a string or stringlike material caught or wrapped around the base of his tongue.

If it appears that the object has been there for a while (your pet may have a poor appetite or worse breath than usual), the item may be embedded, and the vet may have to surgically remove it. But often, first aid is all that's needed to get rid of a foreign object in the mouth.

DO THIS NOW

Restrain your pet. A pet with something caught in his mouth will be understandably upset and may not hold still for you to help. You'll need to carefully restrain him. Otherwise, you may hurt him while trying to remove the object, and he may bite you.

For a cat or small dog, grasp him with one hand by the loose skin of the neck and shoulders and gather the rear paws with your other hand. Gently stretch him out on one side on a table or countertop. Then a second person can carefully open her mouth to look inside.

For a larger dog, kneel on the floor beside him and hug him to your chest with one arm reaching around his neck. Put your other arm under and around his chest. Have a second person examine his mouth. (Both of these techniques are illustrated on page 18.)

Open his mouth. To open your pet's mouth, place one hand over his head and circle his muzzle with your thumb and middle fingers so the fingertips press his lips against his teeth just behind the long canine teeth. This will prompt your pet to open his mouth. Use your other hand to gently press down on the jaw and open his mouth wider. Never put your fingers between your dog's teeth to force him to open up.

 ## FIRST ALERT

Choking

When a foreign object gets caught in the back of a pet's mouth or throat, he will gag, retch, and cough, then become frantic when his air supply is cut off. Choking is a life-threatening emergency that needs immediate first aid. (For more information about choking, see page 131.)

It can be nearly impossible to reach and grip objects stuck in a pet's throat. But you can use a modified Heimlich maneuver to try to pop the blockage out of the airway. Hold a cat or small dog like a human baby, with his head up, his hind legs swinging down, and his back against your stomach. Place your fist in the dip below the rib cage and use it to pull sharply inward and upward toward your chin. Repeat two or three times quickly, then check to see if the object has been dislodged and remove it if it has. If it hasn't moved, you can continue the maneuver in the car as someone else drives you to the animal hospital.

For a bigger pet, lay him on his side as you kneel behind him with your knees against his backbone. As you lean over him, place your fist in the dip below the rib cage and push sharply up and in toward the dog's head and your knees. Repeat two or three times quickly, check to see if the object has come up, and if so, remove it. If not, continue the maneuver in the car as someone else drives you to the vet. (These techniques are illustrated on page 22.)

Use tweezers. You can sometimes remove a piece of feather or piece of a toy with your fingers. If you can't reach it, try using blunt-tipped tweezers. You'll probably need something stronger like needle-nose pliers for bones or other larger objects.

 ## SPECIAL SITUATIONS

For sticks or bones: Dogs who play with sticks or chew long bones typically get sections wedged horizontally across the roof of the mouth between the upper molars. Or sometimes, a stick or bone gets caught vertically and levers the mouth wide open so that your pet can't shut his jaws. You can use a dull butter knife or the handle of a spoon to pry the object off his teeth or the roof of his mouth.

For string or ribbon: For ribbon, tinsel, or other string-type material, check to see if any part of it has been swallowed, and if so, leave it for your veterinarian to remove. Pulling string out of the throat could cut tissue deep inside and even kill a pet. But if the material is loose in the mouth, remove it slowly and carefully. Stop if you feel any resistance and get to the vet's office right away.

 ## FOLLOW-UP CARE

■ For any kind of injury to the mouth, the vet will prescribe antibiotics for 7 to 10 days. For dogs, you can usually hide the medicine in their food. Cats tend to take liquid antibiotics more easily than pills. Tilt your cat's head back, fit a needleless syringe or eyedropper into her cheek at the corner of her mouth, and dribble in the medicine. Hold her mouth closed until you see her swallow, then immediately offer her a tasty treat that she won't refuse, like a bit of meat baby food. Often, the cat forgets to try to spit out medicine while enjoying the treat. (This technique is illustrated on page 30.)

■ If the inside of your pet's mouth has been scraped, or if he has bitten his tongue or cheeks, he may need stitches inside his mouth. Usually, the veterinarian will use absorbable sutures that won't need to be removed, but the mouth can be so sore that it will hurt your pet to eat his regular diet. Pets should be fed a soft diet for several days, until the worst of the cuts have healed. Use your pet's regular food and mix it with low-fat, no-salt chicken broth in the blender to make a watery gruel that's easy to lap up.

Advisors
■ James M. Harris, D.V.M., is a veterinarian at Montclair Veterinary Hospital in Oakland, California.
■ Peter Levin, V.M.D., is a veterinarian at Ludwig's Corner Veterinary Hospital in Chester Springs, Pennsylvania.
■ Billy D. Martindale, D.V.M., is a veterinarian at the Animal Hospital of Denison, Texas, and chairman of the board of directors of the Texas Veterinary Medical Association.
■ Kevin Wallace, D.V.M., is an instructor in the department of clinical sciences at Cornell University College of Veterinary Medicine in Ithaca, New York.

Foreign Object in Nose

CALL YOUR VET: **IF NEEDED**

Dogs who spend time outside often get foreign objects jammed up their noses. This is especially true of the hunting breeds, who have longer muzzles and keep their noses to the ground. Cats have problems with foreign bodies in the nose much less frequently. They sometimes swallow blades of grass that get stuck partway down the throat, then are snorted up and out the nose backward.

A foreign body in the nose causes sudden harsh sneezing or snorting that goes on and on. The pet paws at his nose and may bang his head around as he shakes it, trying to get rid of the object. The nose is one of the most sensitive parts of a pet's body, and most pets won't allow you to remove a foreign object while they're awake.

DO THIS NOW

Muzzle your pet. Before doing anything else, it's a good idea to muzzle your pet so that you aren't accidentally bitten while you try to help him. Use a length of panty hose or strip of material to hold his mouth closed. Tie it around your dog's nose and knot it on top of his muzzle, then draw the ends beneath his chin and knot again, and finally, bring the ends behind his head and tie them in a knot or bow behind his ears. (This technique is illustrated on page 17.) Do not muzzle your pet if he is having trouble breathing. You can wrap a cat or short-nosed dog like a pug in a towel or pillowcase with his head exposed, or try the following restraint technique.

Hold his head. One person should gently hold your pet's head. If you're the one holding his head, bring your arm up around his neck and hug him to your chest, while your other arm crosses under and around his chest. (This technique is illustrated on page 18.) Talk to him in a soothing voice to keep him calm. If you can't successfully hold your cat or short-nosed dog

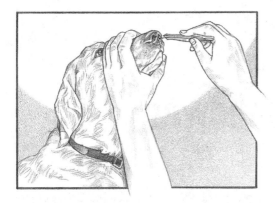

Steady your dog's head so it's easy to grasp the foreign object in his nose and extract it.

this way, don't struggle. Your veterinarian will have to remove the object.

Remove the object. When you can see the object, use your fingers or blunt-tipped tweezers to carefully reach into the nostril and pull it out. Steady your dog's head with one hand while you use the tweezers with the other.

Clean the nostril. After removing the object, gently clean the nostril with a cotton ball or gauze pad soaked with sterile saline contact lens solution.

Apply antibiotic ointment. If there's any abrasion or soreness that you can see and easily reach, apply a bit of antibiotic ointment like Neosporin to the area. Wait for a minute until the ointment soaks in before releasing your pet, because he will immediately lick his nose and clean off the medicine.

 SPECIAL SITUATION

For nosebleeds: If your pet has a bloody nose, keep him quiet so that he doesn't sneeze blood all over the carpet. Don't use a muzzle if your pet has a nosebleed, or he could choke. Instead, put a cold compress on the bridge of your pet's nose between his eyes and nostrils—a bag of frozen peas works well because it molds to the shape of the nose. Place a cold, wet washcloth on his nose, then apply the cold pack or bag of peas. The cold helps slow down the bleeding. If the bleeding doesn't stop within 5 to 10 minutes, seek immediate veterinary care. (For more information about nosebleeds, see page 303.)

FOLLOW-UP CARE

■ Watch your pet for sneezing or nasal discharge, which may indicate that there's still something stuck inside the nasal cavity or that an infection has developed.

Advisors
■ Karen Hoffman, V.M.D., is a veterinarian at Delaware Valley Animal Hospital in Fairless Hills, Pennsylvania.
■ Doug McConkey, D.V.M., is a veterinarian at Canyon Creek Pet Hospital in Sherman, Texas.
■ Laura Solien, D.V.M., is a veterinarian at Maplecrest Animal Hospital in Goshen, Indiana.

Foreign Object Swallowed

CALL YOUR VET: **IF NEEDED**

Dogs and cats sometimes swallow things that they shouldn't. Some objects go down by accident. Dogs play with bones and toys and may swallow them when pieces break off. Puppies and kittens are notorious for mouthing and swallowing dangerous items. Other objects, like milk-stained baby-bottle nipples, used tampons, and gravy-splattered aluminum foil, smell so good that pets swallow them on purpose.

As long as the object is small enough, it usually passes out of the pet's system with a bowel movement. But sharp objects like screws or broken bones can cut or stab your pet from the inside and get caught, while some objects, like tampons, swell inside the stomach and intestines once moisture hits them.

Some objects must be surgically removed. For instance, string-type objects like thread, tinsel, ribbon, Easter grass, and tape from a cassette are particularly dangerous and can cut the intestines if you try to pull them out. (Cats are particularly prone to swallowing string and must see a veterinarian immediately.) But you can help other swallowed objects pass naturally out of your pet's system with simple first aid.

DO THIS NOW

Induce vomiting if the object isn't sharp. If you see your pet swallow something that doesn't have any sharp edges—a baby-bottle nipple, soft pieces of a toy, or pea-gravel—the best thing to do is get him to vomit the object back up. The stomach empties within about 2 hours, so after that time period, if the object is small, it will have passed into the intestines, and vomiting won't help. Feed your pet a small meal, then use 3% hydrogen peroxide to make him empty his tummy. A needleless syringe, eyedropper, or turkey baster works well as an applicator to squirt the liquid to the back of his mouth. Hydrogen peroxide bubbles and tastes

FIRST ALERT

Bowel Obstruction

Any swallowed object has the potential to turn into an obstruction once it enters the digestive tract. Objects bigger than the exit from the stomach, or those that catch farther down once they've entered the intestines, can clog up the digestive tract and cause bowel obstruction. Sometimes, the object moves within the system and causes only a partial or intermittent blockage. The pet feels fine one day, then acts sick the next. As long as some bowel movement continues and he feels like eating, first aid may help move the blockage along. But a complete obstruction is a medical emergency that requires immediate veterinary help and possibly surgery.

Once the digestive tract becomes blocked, the stomach builds up gas and fluid from food and digestive juices that can't pass. Pets refuse to eat or drink and act sick or depressed. As the stomach swells, the stretch receptors reach their limit and signal the pet to vomit—this usually happens within 72 hours or so. Vomiting can also start sooner than this, even within hours of the object being ingested, as it begins to irritate the intestinal wall. Vomiting won't help if the object is stuck farther down in the intestines. (For more information about bowel obstruction, see page 103.)

nasty. It makes most dogs and cats throw up after the first or second application. It also works better with some food in the stomach, so feeding your pet first will increase the chance of success. Give 1 to 2 teaspoons of peroxide for every 10 pounds that your pet weighs. Repeat two or three times if necessary, waiting 5 minutes between doses. If he still doesn't vomit, take him to the veterinarian immediately.

Go straight to the vet for sharp objects swallowed. Pins, tacks, shards of plastic toys, screws, needles, or anything else that's sharp could hurt your pet coming back up just as much as when it went down. *Do not* induce

vomiting if your pet has swallowed an object like these. The safest course of action is to take him to your veterinarian immediately to have it removed. He may be able to remove it with a procedure called endoscopy, which is used to view internal body structures with a thin light tube inserted down the windpipe. This procedure is most effective when the pet has an empty stomach, so refrain from feeding him before you go to the vet.

Watch for signs. If you've seen your pet eat bones, wads of rawhide chew toys, pieces of leather shoes, or similar digestible objects, and he's vomiting, retching unproductively, is unwilling to eat, looks distressed, or behaves as if

Metal Toxicity

A copper penny looks anything but dangerous, and pennies and nickels are small enough that you'd think the best choice would be to let swallowed change pass through your pet's system naturally.

But your pocket change can be deadly, especially to cats and small dogs, because zinc is used to process pennies and nickels, and it can poison your pet. Copper is also toxic once it is digested and enters the pet's system. Dogs big enough to swallow batteries can develop lead poisoning from the heavy metals used to make them. The poisons can be more dangerous to your pet than the chance of obstruction.

Signs of zinc poisoning include pale gums, blood in the urine, refusal to eat, vomiting, diarrhea, and jaundice—a yellow tinge to the whites of the eyes or ears that means the liver is in trouble. Copper poisoning has similar signs, plus a swollen tummy. Lead poisoning causes loss of appetite and vomiting, but the pet also grinds his teeth and may have stomach pain, constipation, seizures, and hyperactivity.

If you suspect that your pet has eaten something that could cause metal toxicity, he needs immediate medical attention—*do not* wait for the object to pass. The battery, coins, or other metal items must be surgically removed. Your pet may also need chelating drugs (to help remove the poison from his body) as well as blood transfusions.

something is wrong, he may have an object caught in his esophagus. This frequently happens with dogs. Take your pet to the veterinarian right away. If the object isn't removed immediately, it can perforate the esophagus. (For more information on foreign bodies in the throat, see page 209.)

If you've seen your pet eat these things but he doesn't have any symptoms, the object has probably passed into the stomach without incident. Give the stomach acid a chance to dissolve or at least soften the material. The longer the object stays in the dog's or cat's stomach, the better. Digestion wears off the sharp edges of some objects, softens hard objects, digests some

objects completely, and allows some to pass more easily without getting stuck.

To promote digestion, feed your dog or cat a bulky meal of dry food to delay the passage of the object. This also switches on the digestive juices, gives the natural acids something to work on, cushions any sharp edges, and expands the stomach cavity so that the object "floats" in the middle instead of poking the sides of the collapsed and empty stomach.

Feed bulky meals for swallowed rocks. Pea-gravel and small rocks generally move out of the digestive system fairly well, but larger rocks are so heavy that they may not leave the

Feline Eating Disorders

Some cats, especially those with Oriental-breed heritage, develop a compulsive eating disorder in which they chew up and swallow multiple inedible objects like fabric and string. It's not uncommon for them to swallow 12 to 15 small objects at a time—ponytail ties are typical targets. A cat with this syndrome may not even feel particularly bad until his tummy becomes so stuffed that there's no room for food, and then the foreign objects must be surgically removed. Get immediate veterinary care if you suspect that your cat has swallowed any amount of these objects.

Veterinarians speculate that the condition may be related to another compulsive eating disorder, called wool sucking, which typically affects Siamese cats. These cats relish fine, soft fabrics like wool, so they nibble and eat holes in sweaters, Afghan throws, and similar materials. The wool-sucking habit can sometimes be stemmed by offering your cat a high-fiber diet, so try adding canned pumpkin or raw shredded lettuce to his meals. Mix 1 to 2 teaspoons of either into his food. You can also offer him lettuce to nibble on during the day instead of giving it to him at mealtime. And keep string, ponytail ties, and similar objects safely out of your kitty's reach.

stomach at all. Even if they do move, the transit time for heavy objects is much slower—rather than 2 hours in the stomach, rocks may take a day or longer to move into the intestines and another couple of days to exit the body. Feed your pet a bulky meal to help cushion the object and encourage movement, then call your vet. Pets tend to develop chronic vomiting, diarrhea, and abdominal pain in these cases and need medical attention right away.

Monitor bowel movements. If your pet is unable to vomit up the object, you'll need to monitor his bowel movements to be sure that it has safely passed. Usually, foreign objects end up in the bowel movement within 24 to 72 hours. It takes longer for very heavy or large objects. You must be very vigilant about examining the feces. Pull on disposable medical gloves (available at drugstores) and use an ice-pop stick or disposable plastic knife to slice up the deposit to look for the object. Get medical help immediately if your pet develops vomiting or diarrhea, if he hunches up and tucks his tummy in pain, or if it has been longer than 72 hours and the suspect object has not passed.

 FOLLOW-UP CARE

■ If your pet needed to have an object surgically removed, he'll have stitches, which you'll need to keep clean. Dampen a cotton ball with warm water and wipe away any drainage.

■ If he pulls at the stitches, fit your pet with a cone-shaped collar restraint called an Elizabethan collar to keep him from bothering them. He won't be able to eat while wearing the collar, though, so be sure to remove it during feedings.

■ If your pet has had surgery and has an incision in the stomach, your veterinarian may prescribe a special diet, or you can cook a soft, bland diet at home (with your vet's okay). Follow the feeding schedule that your veterinarian recommends for your pet.

Here's how to make a soft, bland diet: Boil a boneless, skinless chicken or turkey breast and mix it 50/50 with cooked and drained white rice. Or you can brown lean ground beef, drain it, and mix it 50/50 with rice. Don't add any seasoning—you want the food to be very bland. Feed the homemade diet for 2 to 3 days, then mix it 50/50 with your pet's regular food for 2 to 3 days, then gradually change back to the regular diet.

■ Puppies and kittens may grow out of the habit, but adult pets who swallow objects probably will repeat the offense if given the chance. Be vigilant in keeping all potential targets out of reach. Keep sewing supplies and spare change locked up, keep garbage and bones in sealed containers, and pet-proof toys so that there are no loose pieces.

Advisors

■ Patricia Hague, D.V.M., is a veterinarian at the Cat Hospital of Las Colinas in Irving, Texas.

■ Janie Hodges, D.V.M., is a veterinarian at Valley View Pet Health Center in Farmers Branch, Texas.

■ Chris Johnson, D.V.M., is a veterinarian at Westside Animal Emergency Clinic in Atlanta.

■ Barry N. Kellogg, V.M.D., is a veterinarian at the Center for Veterinary Care in Great Barrington, Massachusetts, and the head of VMAT 1 (Veterinary Medical Assistance Team), the national disaster team for veterinary medicine.

■ Susan Little, D.V.M., is a veterinarian at Bytown Cat Hospital in Ottawa, Ontario, Canada.

■ Mike McFarland, D.V.M., is a veterinarian at the Emergency Animal Clinic in Dallas.

Foreign Object in Throat

CALL YOUR VET: **IF NEEDED**

Pets cough, gag, have noisy breathing, or hold their mouths open in a strange way when they have objects caught in their throats or windpipes. Cats often have problems with string-type objects (as well as the attached needles in the case of swallowed thread) and need immediate medical attention. *Never* pull string out of your pet's mouth; often, it's attached somewhere deep inside his body, and you could kill him. Your vet will have to remove it. You can remove the string yourself only if you've just seen your pet eat and swallow it, you can still see the string, and you're sure that there isn't a sharp object on the end of it. Dogs love to chew and often get sticks, bones, or toys (or chewed-off pieces of them) stuck in their throats or windpipes.

DO THIS NOW

Get two people to help you. You'll need as many as two other people to help you so that you don't get bitten. One person should restrain your pet by wrapping him in a towel or pillowcase or hugging him to his chest. If your pet won't hold his mouth open on his own, another person must hold it open while you recover the object. Have the helper place the palm of one hand over the bridge of your pet's muzzle, with the thumb and middle fingers gently pressing against the teeth just behind the canines (the long fangs). The other hand should grip his lower jaw, with the thumb and middle fingers pressing gently against the teeth. The pressure will prompt him to open wide.

Sweep back into his mouth with your fingers to dislodge the object. It should come free quickly with a finger sweep if it's going to, so don't waste time repeating the maneuver more than twice.

Attempt to remove the object. You can try to remove the object by yourself if your pet will allow you to open his mouth and look into it. If you have a large dog, back him into a corner and hold him between your knees. For a cat or small dog, place him on your lap or on a table, then tuck him under your arm. Use one hand to hold the top jaw open and look for the object. You can use needle-nose pliers to attempt to dislodge it, but don't use your fingers unless your pet is unconscious. If you can't get it out after one or two tries, get to the veterinarian immediately.

Do a modified Heimlich maneuver. If the object stops respiration, pets often lose consciousness very quickly. Use a modified Heimlich maneuver to try to dislodge the ob-

For a larger dog, lay the dog on her side on the floor and kneel behind her so that her head points to your left. Fit your right fist just below her rib cage and press sharply upward and inward toward her head. Repeat two or three times, then check to see if you can pull out the object.

ject so that your pet can breathe again. The technique varies depending on the size of your pet.

For a cat or small dog, hold his back against your stomach with his head up and his feet hanging down. Put your fist just underneath the rib cage—you can feel the soft, hollow place easily—and push inward toward your belly and upward toward your chin at the same time. Use a strong thrusting action to help dislodge the object.

Lay a larger dog on his side and kneel behind him so that his backbone is against your knees, with his head pointing to your left. Lean over him in a crouched position and put your right fist just below his rib cage. Use your fist to push sharply upward and inward toward your knees and his head. The diaphragm will be directly below your fist, and it will help push air from

To use the Heimlich maneuver on a cat or small dog, hold his back against your stomach with his head up and his feet hanging down. Put your fist just underneath the rib cage and push inward toward your belly and upward toward your chin at the same time. Use a strong thrusting action to help dislodge the object.

the lungs up through the throat to dislodge the object. Repeat the maneuver two or three times, checking after each try to see if the object has come loose in his mouth.

Give a thrust to the back. If the Heimlich maneuver doesn't work after a few attempts, try a thrust with an open cupped hand on your pet's back—clap him on the back three or four times in a row. Be sure that his neck stays in a straight line with his back so that there are no kinks in his throat to get in the way. If this technique still doesn't dislodge the object, continue trying this and the Heimlich maneuver in the car while someone drives you to the animal hospital as soon as possible.

Restart breathing. Once the throat is clear, make sure that your pet starts breathing. If he doesn't, you may need to give artificial respiration. Wrap one hand around your pet's muzzle to close his mouth, place your other hand on his chest to monitor its rise and fall, cover his nose with your mouth, and blow two quick puffs into his nose. His chest should move with the air. Continue giving 15 to 20 breaths a minute until he starts breathing on his own or until you reach medical help. (This technique is illustrated on page 20.) If you don't feel his chest move with your breaths, there's still a blockage.

 # SPECIAL SITUATIONS

For sticks in a dog's mouth: Dogs who chew sticks will often get a broken piece wedged between their back teeth. Use a butter knife to gently pry under the stick until it comes loose. If it doesn't come loose after one or two tries, take the dog to the vet as soon as you can.

For grass in a cat's nose: Cats often eat grass to make themselves vomit, but sometimes a grass blade comes back up the nasal passage instead of out of the mouth. Part of it hangs down the back of the throat, making the cat gag and cough, while the other end sticks out the nose. You can gently pull the grass blade through the nose, but if it breaks off, get to the veterinarian as soon as possible since the cat will need to be sedated to retrieve the rest of it.

 # FOLLOW-UP CARE

■ Your pet's throat needs several days to heal, and the soreness may make it hard for him to eat regular food. Feed him a diet of soft food for at least a week after the injury. You can make a watery gruel by mixing his food in the blender with water or low-fat, no-salt chicken broth until the mixture is the consistency of Cream of Wheat.

Advisors

■ James M. Harris, D.V.M., is a veterinarian at Montclair Veterinary Hospital in Oakland, California.

■ Billy D. Martindale, D.V.M., is a veterinarian at the Animal Hospital of Denison, Texas, and chairman of the board of directors of the Texas Veterinary Medical Association.

■ Kevin Wallace, D.V.M., is an instructor in the department of clinical sciences at Cornell University College of Veterinary Medicine in Ithaca, New York.

Fractures

CALL YOUR VET: **SAME DAY**

MEDICINE CHEST

Blanket
Karo syrup or honey
Length of fabric or pil-
    lowcase for muz-
    zling
Sterile gauze pads or
    nonstick absorbent
    pads (Telfa pads)
Sterile saline contact
    lens solution
Clean absorbent
    cloth or sanitary
    napkin
Elastic bandage (Ace
    bandage), panty
    hose, or tape
Pet carrier or other
    rigid object
Heavy tape
Towel
Rolled-up newspaper
    or magazine
Plastic wrap (Saran
    Wrap) or garbage
    bag
House-training pads
Buffered aspirin
    (Bufferin)
Antiseptic liquid soap
    (Betadine Skin
    Cleanser)
Elizabethan collar
Bubble wrap

Dogs have about 319 bones, and cats have 244—and every single bone, from the jaw to the tail tip, can be broken. Fractures usually happen because of trauma, like being hit by a car or falling out of a window. Fractures don't kill pets, but they are always extremely painful. And the injury that caused the fracture has the potential to harm other important organs and cause life-threatening problems.

Pets in pain usually breathe faster, and a broken rib could make breathing difficult if it punctures a lung. Pets will often favor the injured part of the body. For instance, a fractured pelvis or leg makes a pet refuse to (or be unable to) stand up, while a broken jaw bleeds, and the animal will drop food or refuse to eat.

With a closed fracture, the bone remains inside the tissue. You'll still know that there's a problem if your pet holds his leg at an odd angle or if it dangles in a strange way. An open fracture, however, punches through the skin—the bone may show, or the wound may bleed, and that can result in serious blood loss and dangerous infection.

Pets with fractures need immediate medical care. Prompt first aid will help prevent further damage and ease your pet's pain and distress; in some cases, it may even save his life.

🩹 DO THIS NOW

For All Fractures

Watch for shock. Dogs and cats can suffer shock from the trauma of a fracture. With shock, the circulation shuts down and your pet will act dizzy, seem unaware of her surroundings, and have pale gums. Shock happens very quickly, and pets need medical attention within 10 to 20 minutes to save their lives. Wrap your dog or cat in a blanket to keep her warm—this can help slow down the process and give you a few extra minutes to get help. You can also put a drop or two of Karo syrup or honey on your pet's gums to help keep her conscious. (For more information about shock, see page 333.)

Restart breathing. A pet in shock can stop breathing. Artificial respiration can keep them alive until you reach medical help. Hold her mouth shut with your hands, cover her nose with your mouth, and blow into her nostrils with two quick breaths, just hard enough to expand the chest. Then stop and let the air escape. Continue giving 15 to 20 breaths per minute until your pet breathes on her own again or until you reach the animal hospital. (This technique is illustrated on page 20.)

Perform CPR. If your pet's heart has stopped beating, you will have to administer CPR. Determine if your pet's heart has stopped by taking her pulse. You won't be able to feel a pulse in the carotid artery in the neck as you can with people. Instead, press the fingertips of your index, middle, and ring fingers into the crease where the inside of her thigh meets the body and feel for the pulse in the femoral artery, which is very big and near the surface. (This technique is illustrated on page 13.) If you can't feel it, try listening or feeling for the heartbeat. Put your ear or hand flat against your pet's left side directly behind the elbow.

If you don't detect a heartbeat, you will have to begin chest compressions. For cats or small dogs, cup your hand over the point of the chest just behind the elbows. Squeeze firmly, pressing in about ½ inch, with your thumb on one side and fingers on the other. This action not only pumps the heart, it also makes the pressure inside the chest (and against the heart) rapidly increase and decrease and helps move the blood. Ideally, one person gives chest compressions while a second performs artificial respiration. Alternate one breath for every 5 compressions. The goal is 80 to 100 compressions and 15 to 20 breaths per minute until your pet revives or until you reach medical help.

Put a medium-size or large dog on a flat surface. You can lay him on either side. Put one hand on his chest and put your other hand on top of the first. Use both hands to thrust down firmly, compressing the chest by 25 to 50%. (This technique is illustrated on page 21.)

Pressing over the heart won't help dogs who weigh more than 30 pounds because their ribs are so rigid that even strong thrusts won't affect the heart. Instead, use both hands to thrust down firmly on the highest part of the chest. This will change the pressure inside the body, and this in turn will move the blood.

Fracture Facts

There are several categories of fractures. Fatigue fractures, which are uncommon in pets, happen with repetitive stressful movement. Pathological fractures are caused when bones become weak from disease, like cancer or hyperparathyroidism. Greenstick fractures are splits or cracks, and they happen most often in growing puppies or kittens. Traumatic fractures, the most common kind, happen as a result of falling or being struck by cars. Every bone can potentially be fractured, but some are broken more often than others.

Pelvic fractures happen most often in dogs, with the femur (thighbone) the next most common site. Small dogs sometimes break front legs when they fall or leap from their owners' arms.

In cats, the femur accounts for 30 percent of all fractures seen, and 22 percent are pelvic fractures. Cats often break their jaws, splitting their chin bones in half when their heads crack against the floor or ground after leaps or falls from high places. Unlike people, pets almost never break their necks.

Muzzle if necessary. Even the friendliest dog or cat may lash out when she is in pain, and you can't help her if she wants to bite you. As long as she is breathing normally and the injury doesn't involve the jaw, you can muzzle long-nosed dogs with a necktie, panty hose, or some other long strip of material. Just make a loop, slip it gently over her nose, and tie a half-knot. Loop the ends beneath your dog's chin and make another knot. Then take the ends back over the neck and tie them in a knot or bow firmly behind the ears. This will keep her mouth from opening. (This technique is illustrated on page 17.)

A cat or short-nosed dog like a pug is hard to muzzle. Put a pillowcase over her head so that she has something to bite on before she can get to you. Don't use a pillowcase or muzzle if your pet is having any trouble breathing.

Don't move exposed bones. Broken bones sometimes cut an artery—look for blood-clotted fur where an open fracture has punched through the skin. If the bone is outside the skin, *leave it alone,* and do not try to pull it back into place, or you could cause even more damage to the tissue. Exposed bone is very susceptible to infection. Use a sterile gauze pad or a nonstick absorbent pad like a Telfa pad if you have it, or a clean cloth. The pad or cloth should be large enough to cover the area completely to keep the dirt out and heavy enough so that it won't fall off. Soak the material in sterile saline contact lens solution and then gently cover the bone and open wound with it. The saline solution will help keep the tissue moist and the bone healthy.

Stop the bleeding. If there is bleeding from a wound but no exposed bones, apply direct pressure. Use a sterile gauze pad, a clean absorbent cloth, or even a sanitary napkin. Put it on top of the wound and press with your hand or fingers—most bleeding stops in about 5 minutes. Don't lift up the pad or it could disturb the clot. Just put a second pad on top of the first if the blood soaks through. You can use an elastic bandage like an Ace bandage, panty hose, or tape to hold the pad in place. (For more information about bleeding, see page 95.)

For Back Fractures

Take your pet to the veterinarian immediately. Transport her carefully, with as little movement of the injury as possible. Every bump not only hurts but can also make the broken bones cut into the tissue or arteries and cause more damage. This is especially important with back fractures, which could injure the spinal cord and cause paralysis.

A pet with a back injury should be transported to the animal hospital on a rigid, flat object, if possible. For a small pet, you can use a pet carrier, an oversize book, a cutting board, or even a sturdy trash-can lid. A bigger dog may fit on a large board or an ironing board.

Set the rigid surface next to the injured pet and gently slide a sheet or towel under her. Use the fabric to gently pull her horizontally onto the surface. For a big pet, two or more people may be needed to shift her. One person should lift her by the shoulders and neck while the other lifts her at the hips (at the same time) to place her on the carrier. Or gently slide a sheet or towel under your pet, then both of you use the fabric to slide her onto the rigid surface. Once the pet is on the carrier, each person should pick up one end to carry her to the car.

If you don't have a rigid object to use for transport, put your pet in the middle of a blanket and use it like a stretcher. Have two people lift the blanket by the corners.

You need to avoid jostling your pet as much as possible. Cover her with a towel or blanket, then tape her to the surface. Use strips of duct tape or other heavy tape over her body behind her front legs and in front of her rear legs. (This technique is illustrated on page 29.) Do not tape her legs, tail, or neck because your pet could further injure herself if she struggles against the restraint. You can put a larger dog in the backseat or cargo area of a car after stabilizing her on the rigid surface. One person should sit with your pet to try to keep her calm and still on the ride.

For Leg Fractures

Check for stopped breathing. If your pet is in shock and not breathing, follow the instructions for administering artificial respiration as described on page 213. Forgo a splint and get to the veterinarian as soon as possible, continuing artificial respiration in the car if necessary. Attempt to stop any bleeding on the way.

Splint broken legs. When you are more than 30 minutes away from veterinary care, it's helpful to put splints on broken legs. This keeps the bones from moving, reduces pain, and pre-

Treatment and Care Options

When a person breaks a bone, there are all kinds of ways to fix the break, from a cast to surgery. Pets are no different. Each technique helps healing in a different way and may require special care at home.

The simplest fix is a splint called a Robert Jones Splint-Bandage. Cotton sheets are wrapped around the entire leg, then covered with gauze bandage that puts pressure on the leg to prevent the joint from moving. It works fine for fractures that are fairly stable. You need to watch to be sure that the toes don't swell; if they do, the wrap is too tight and needs to be changed.

Intermedullary pins (I.M. pins) surgically "thread" the pieces of bone back together. Vets position them together with wire, which holds smaller pieces of bone in place. The pin stays in place until the bone heals, while the wire remains permanently. With this surgery, there's a small entry wound for the pin, which you need to keep clean and monitor for infection.

A bone plate surgically fixes fractures by attaching all the broken pieces to one solid piece of metal, using screws for the attachment. It works well for very active pets because they can get up and walk on the broken leg the very next day. Bone plates usually stay in place permanently. Usually, there is a long incision, which you'll need to monitor for infection and keep clean.

External fixators are metal contraptions that fit against the outside of a pet's body and screw into the bone through the skin and flesh to stabilize it. External fixators work well for some fractures, but the contraption can be unwieldy and can get caught on furniture.

vents additional damage or bleeding under the skin. Always immobilize the joint above and below the break.

A fracture in the femur (the large upper bone in the rear leg) or humerus (the corresponding bone in the front leg), both of which are attached directly to the body, has no joint that's easy to immobilize. For these fractures, it's best to not even try to splint them unless there's exposed bone. In that case, cover the open wound with a nonstick absorbent covering like a Telfa pad or clean cloth, then wrap the limb in a towel to pad the wound.

Splint correctly. For fractures in the lower leg, make sure that the splint reaches all the way up the leg. Wrap a soft towel or cotton wrap around the leg, then use a rolled-up newspaper or magazine or split open the cardboard core from a roll of paper towels and position the leg inside. Don't try to straighten or reposition the fracture, though; you just want to pad the leg and use the rigid items to lend stability. Wrap the leg with an elastic bandage like an Ace bandage, panty hose, or plastic wrap like Saran Wrap to hold the splint together. Start wrapping from the foot, leaving the toes exposed, and move up until you've covered the whole leg.

Watch for swelling. Once the bandaged splint is in place, hold a piece of paper against the foot and mark the distance between the two center toenails. You can use the marks on the paper to monitor whether the foot swells from a bandage that's too tight—the toenails will start to separate and turn cold. If the swelling doubles the space between the nails in 10 to 15 minutes, loosen the bandage and reapply it.

SPECIAL SITUATIONS

For pelvic fractures: Pets with pelvic fractures that have not been repaired surgically shouldn't walk because that makes the broken bones move and keeps them from healing. Confine your pet to a kennel, cage, or very small room and carry her outside or to the litter box as needed. If the fracture has been surgically repaired, follow your veterinarian's advice regarding exercise and movement.

You can make cleanup inside easier with absorbent material like Piddle Pads, which are used for house-training. The pads contain an antibacterial treatment that reduces odor, and they have a leak-proof plastic backing. Simply spread them in the confinement area and let your pet rest on top of them. You can get them from pet-supply stores and catalogs.

For orthopedic surgery: Pets who go through orthopedic surgery to fix their fractures may not be sent home with antibiotics because the procedure is so sterile. Watch the stitches or other wounds closely—a red-tinged watery discharge, a bit of redness, or some soreness is okay. But if the discharge becomes thick and white or green, smells bad, or feels hot to the back of your hand, your pet may need antibiotics after all, so see your veterinarian.

For broken jaws: Pets with broken jaws need soft foods for up to 4 weeks, until the wire stabilization is removed. Regular canned food works for some pets, while others need to have it pureed with low-fat, no-salt chicken broth in the blender to make a gruel that they can lap up.

FOLLOW-UP CARE

■ It takes most fractures about 6 to 8 weeks to become stable and up to 18 weeks to completely heal. For at least the first month, your pet must rest and avoid using the injured part as much as possible. She shouldn't be allowed to climb stairs, run, or jump.

■ Contamination of an open fracture wound can cause infection, and the vet will prescribe antibiotics. For closed fractures, antibiotics probably won't be prescribed unless there are also cuts and scrapes on other parts of the body. To give pills, place your hand around your pet's muzzle and gently press your fingers against the sides of her lips so that they rub against her teeth. This will prompt her to open wide, and when she does, you can push the pill to the back of her tongue, close her mouth, and stroke her throat so that she'll swallow. (This technique is illustrated on page 30.) Some dogs will take pills that are hidden in treats, like cheese or a piece of hot dog.

■ To treat pain in dogs, your vet may prescribe drugs like carprofen (Rimadyl). Or you could give buffered aspirin like Bufferin. The usual dose is 10 to 25 milligrams per 2.2 pounds of body weight two or three times a day. Do not give aspirin to cats.

Your vet will prescribe appropriate drugs to ensure that your pet is comfortable and pain-free. If you think that she is still in pain after she takes the medication, call your veterinarian for further advice.

■ Keep any surface wound clean with a mild antiseptic liquid soap like Betadine Skin Cleanser.

■ Continue to watch for swollen toes, which can mean that the bandage or splint is too tight and needs to be reapplied.

■ Splints and bandages need to stay dry, or they'll rub the pet's skin, causing sores or infection. To protect the bandage, tape a plastic garbage bag or plastic wrap over it when your pet must go outdoors.

■ Dogs and some cats nibble at bandages, splints, or sutures. Put an Elizabethan collar (a cone-shaped restraint) on your pet. It will keep her from damaging the bandage, which could interfere with healing. She won't be able to eat while wearing the collar, though, so be sure to remove it during feedings.

THE BEST APPROACH

Bubble Wrap

To splint a fractured leg, you need material that not only cushions the leg but also keeps it padded and stationary. Bubble wrap does all three things beautifully. Cut the sheet of bubble wrap to fit the curve of your pet's resting limb, lay the leg on the plastic, and wrap it around. Secure it with tape.

Advisors
■ Dale C. Butler, D.V.M., is a veterinarian at Best Friends Animal Hospital in Denison, Texas.
■ Charles DeVinne, D.V.M., is a veterinarian at Animal Care Clinic in Peterborough, New Hampshire.
■ Thomas Munschauer, D.V.M., is a veterinarian at Middlebury Animal Hospital in Vermont and past president of the Vermont Veterinary Medical Association.
■ Kevin Wallace, D.V.M., is an instructor in the department of clinical sciences at Cornell University College of Veterinary Medicine in Ithaca, New York.
■ David Wirth-Schneider, D.V.M., is a veterinarian at the Emergency Clinic for Animals in Madison, Wisconsin.

Frostbite

CALL YOUR VET: **SAME DAY**

Ice cubes often overflow their trays because water expands as it freezes. The same thing happens when dogs and cats get frostbite. Water in the body's cells freezes and expands, causing cells to rupture. Frostbite usually occurs in the extremities, such as the ear tips, tail, and toes, because the body responds to extreme cold by diverting blood into the torso. Parts away from the center of the body get less blood, which causes them to freeze more easily.

Frostbite can be hard to recognize because the characteristic pale white, gray, or blue color of frozen skin may be invisible beneath the pet's fur. Pets with frostbitten toes will limp, and frozen ear tips will often droop. The affected skin will be hard and nonpliable, and it will be extremely cold. Days afterward, there may be redness, blisters, and possibly a serious infection. All cases of frostbite should be seen by a veterinarian immediately after first aid at home.

DO THIS NOW

Check your pet's temperature. First, take her inside right away. Pets with frostbite often have hypothermia as well, so use a rectal thermometer lubricated with petroleum jelly to take her temperature. (This technique is illustrated on page 9.) If her temperature is below 99°F, begin treatment for hypothermia right away. (For more on hypothermia, see page 248.)

Thaw the frostbitten areas. Try to thaw the affected areas by dunking them in lukewarm water for about 20 minutes. Small areas of skin that are not deeply frozen are often very red immediately after rewarming. The skin will become softer, warmer, and more pliable. One dunking should be enough, so repeat only if necessary.

Dunking isn't easy when the frostbite has occurred on the ear tips or scrotum. You can warm these areas by wetting a cloth or paper towel with lukewarm water, leaving it dripping wet, and holding it against the affected skin for 20 minutes. Don't rub the area; just hold the towel gently against the skin. Exchange the cloth for a fresh warm one every couple of minutes. Use this procedure to warm any affected areas if your pet has hypothermia in addition to frostbite—since water evaporation removes heat, you don't want him to get too wet. Put the wet cloth only on the frostbitten areas.

 ## FOLLOW-UP CARE

■ For mild frostbite, your veterinarian may advise you to apply an antibiotic ointment like Neosporin. Or he may recommend using a protective ointment containing zinc, like Desitin, which can help skin damage heal more quickly. Follow your vet's instructions for application.

■ Dogs and cats with sore skin will often lick it so much that healing is very slow. Your veterinarian may recommend using an Elizabethan collar, a cone-shaped collar that fits around the neck and face and stops pets from licking. Be sure to remove it during feedings.

■ Veterinarians usually apply bandages to areas with serious frostbite. You'll need to keep them dry to prevent further skin damage or infections. You can protect bandages on your pet's legs by wrapping them with plastic wrap like Saran Wrap or a bread wrapper or garbage bag and taping the plastic in place. Use the wrapping only when your pet goes outside. Inside, removing the plastic will allow the bandages to breathe. Check with your vet for instructions on how often the bandages should be changed.

■ Your pet may need prescription antibiotics when he comes home. Follow your veterinarian's instructions for dosage. For dogs, you can hide pills in a hunk of cheese or other treat. Cats may not be fooled as easily, though, so use a pill syringe and give your cat a treat afterward as a reward. (This technique is illustrated on page 31.)

Advisors

■ Shane Bateman, D.V.M., D.V.Sc., is a veterinarian board certified in the American College of Emergency and Critical Care Medicine and assistant professor of emergency and critical care medicine at Ohio State University College of Veterinary Medicine in Columbus.

■ Sandra Sawchuk, D.V.M., is clinical instructor at the University of Wisconsin School of Veterinary Medicine in Madison.

Fur Contamination

CALL YOUR VET: **IF NEEDED**

Dogs and cats often walk through or brush against fresh paint or tar. Motor oil, wax, and chewing gum are other common fur contaminants. Most petroleum products are absorbed through the skin, so in addition to being unsightly, fur contamination can cause dangerous toxicity, especially if the pet swallows the substance when he tries to clean it off. (For more information about poisoning, see page 311.)

Other fur contaminants, like tar, wax, or the oil from decorative lamps, can cause painful burns. (For more information about chemical burns, see page 106.) In most cases, however, you can safely remove the foreign material from your pet's fur at home.

 DO THIS NOW

Wear gloves. Substances that are potentially toxic to your pet can also be dangerous to you. To keep from contaminating your own skin, wear rubber gloves when trying to remove anything from your pet's fur. Thin, disposable medical gloves won't work because most paints and solvents dissolve the material and go right through the gloves. Heavy rubber gloves like Playtex dishwashing gloves are best.

Use turpentine for oil-based paint. For oil-based paint that has dried, about the only thing that will remove it is a solvent—turpentine is best. Put a small amount on a clean rag and hold it against the paint to soften and remove it. Keep your pet from licking the area, and once the paint has been removed, immediately wash off the turpentine with soap and water.

Use flour and vegetable oil for big messes. You can remove oil-based paint and motor oil with vegetable oil or mineral oil, but it takes time. First, rub in a large amount of oil, then blot with paper towels. Repeat several times to remove as much of the contaminant as possible. If there's a lot of contamination, once you've used the oil, you can rub flour or powdered starch into the fur to help absorb the substance. Use a wide-toothed comb to remove the mixture, then bathe the fur with diluted dishwashing liquid such as Dawn and rinse thoroughly to get rid of the remaining oil and powder.

Soften tar. Tar can be difficult to remove from fur, but a great deal of it can be softened and removed by rubbing petroleum jelly, Crisco, or even peanut butter into the mess. Wipe off the softened tar with paper towels. Repeat several times—you may need to let it soak for several minutes to get the best effect. Afterward, wash your pet thoroughly with soap and water.

Trim out sticky substances. Sticky candy, glue, or chewing gum in pet fur isn't dangerous, but it is annoying. Most sugar-based substances wash out with plain water. But gum and glue often must be trimmed out. Trimming is also a good option when you can't get out all of the

It's easy to accidentally cut your pet's skin with scissors, so don't use them to remove a sticky mat unless you can work a comb between it and your pet's skin. And use only blunt scissors.

contaminant with other methods. Apply an ice cube to the substance to harden it, then use electric clippers to safely trim away the mat. If you don't have clippers, use blunt scissors, and thread a comb through the fur first to protect the skin.

You can dissolve and remove a small amount of chewing gum with a bit of nail polish remover on a cotton ball. Be sure to thoroughly wash out the acetone with soap and water afterward, though, because it can be very irritating to the pet's skin or dangerous if he licks it.

Apply ice for wax or latex paint. Ice makes the wax or paint brittle so you can peel most of it off with your fingers or a comb. Then wash the rest out with soap and water.

 **FOLLOW-UP CARE**

■ If your pet swallowed some of whatever got on his fur, he'll probably have an upset stomach.

Dealing with Hair Mats

Thickly furred dog breeds like Chows and collies and longhaired cats like Persians are prone to hair mats. Any matted fur is unsightly, but mats in the armpits and groin are painful. Mats can cause bruises and sometimes raw sores. A pet with matted fur may be reluctant to move because it hurts to walk, and she may flinch or snap if you touch her. With the proper tools and care, however, mats are easy to remove at home.

Have someone gently restrain your pet so that you can use both hands. First, work powdered cornstarch into the wad of dry fur to help separate the hairs and make the mat easier to comb out. Hold the fur to avoid pulling it and use a wide-toothed comb or slicker brush to work on the tangle. If your pet won't tolerate this, shave out the mat with electric clippers, a mustache trimmer, or a razor. If all you have is blunt scissors, thread a comb under the mat before cutting.

Once the mat has been removed, you can relieve swelling or discomfort by applying ice wrapped in a wet washcloth for 10 to 15 minutes twice a day for 2 days. If you shaved the mat, you can use witch hazel, a soothing herbal solution that's available in drugstores, to relieve irritation from the clipper blades. Or you can apply a hydrocortisone cream such as Cortaid to the hairless areas. To prevent new mats, groom your pet regularly.

Feed him bland food for a day or two. Boil rice until it's very soft and flavor it with low-fat, no-salt chicken broth, plain yogurt, or low-fat cottage cheese. If you're not sure that what your pet swallowed is nontoxic, call the vet or poison-control center immediately.

THE BEST APPROACH

Dishwashing Liquid

To break up oily or greasy fur contaminants such as heavy oils, petroleum products, and some waxy products, nothing beats Dawn dishwashing liquid.

With heavy contamination, you may need to dissolve or dilute the substance with something like Crisco first. Then lather your pet with Dawn, let the suds soak for 5 to 10 minutes, and rinse. Repeat this process several times, then rinse off all the soapsuds, because Dawn can be drying and irritating to the skin.

It's a good idea to follow the Dawn bath with a soak in Aveeno Soothing Bath Treatment or other oatmeal product to soothe irritated skin.

Advisors

- E. Murl Bailey Jr., D.V.M., Ph.D., is professor of toxicology at Texas A&M University College of Veterinary Medicine in College Station.
- Nina Beyer, V.M.D., is a veterinarian at Greenfield Veterinary Associates in Mantua, New Jersey.
- Tam Garland, D.V.M., Ph.D., is a veterinarian at Texas A&M University College of Veterinary Medicine.
- Tracy Ridgeway, D.V.M., is a veterinarian at Riverview Animal Clinic in Clarkston, Washington.

Gunshot Wounds

CALL YOUR VET: **IMMEDIATELY**

Pets get shot more frequently in rural communities, particularly during hunting season. But more often, dogs and cats injured by guns are shot intentionally, either because the pet trespassed and threatened livestock or simply out of malice.

The seriousness of the wound depends on the speed (velocity) of the bullet and how close the pet was to the gun when it was fired. The faster the bullet and the greater the pet's proximity to the gun, the greater the damage, because the bullet causes a shock wave that pushes energy and tissue ahead of it. Bullet speed varies from about 600 feet per second to more than 3,000 feet per second, depending on the kind of gun. And the larger the caliber, the greater the damage—a .22 may leave behind a tiny hole, while a .45 destroys tissue both going in and coming out.

When a bullet passes through the body, the exit wound typically is much larger than the entry wound, so you'll see some bleeding. But in most cases, the entry wound is very small, and since it's hidden by fur, you may not notice the injury immediately. A bullet that punches through the intestines can cause peritonitis within hours. This infection, caused by feces leaking into the abdomen, is deadly and requires intensive medical treatment. The sooner it is treated, the more likely your pet will survive. A lung injury causes strained breathing, while bullets can cause limping if they fracture a bone or sever a nerve. If the bullet damages your pet's major blood vessels, heart, liver, spleen, or kidneys, massive bleeding can occur.

The most dangerous gunshot wounds target the chest and abdomen. In fact, a dog may be shot in the flank, but the bullet can travel and end up in the lung. Anytime you suspect that your pet has been shot, get him medical attention immediately. You can increase his chance of survival and speed his recovery with first aid.

🩹 DO THIS NOW

Make a muzzle. Gunshot wounds are extremely painful, and your dog or cat probably will object to your touch, even though you want to help him. As long as he's breathing normally, it's a good idea to muzzle an injured pet so that you don't get bitten. For long-nosed dogs, use panty hose, a necktie, or other long material. Make a loop and slip it over the bridge of his nose, then snug it down in a single knot. Tie the ends a second time beneath his chin. Finally, bring both ends back behind his ears and tie them. (This technique is illustrated on page 17.)

For cats and short-nosed dogs like pugs, try slipping a loose sock or pillowcase over their heads to give them something to bite besides you.

Control bleeding. Apply direct pressure with a clean cloth, gauze pad, or sanitary napkin. Place it directly on top of the wound and use your fingers or hands to press down until the bleeding slows. If the compress soaks through, don't remove it, because that could disrupt the clot that's forming. Just put a second pad on top of the first and continue the pressure.

A swelling that keeps getting larger may be a torn blood vessel under the skin. Firm, direct pressure often will completely stop the bleeding and swelling until you get to the veterinarian. (For more on bleeding, see page 95.)

Elevate the injured area. Raise the injured part unless the wound is in the chest or abdomen. It can help slow down the bleeding.

Treat shock. A gunshot wound often causes shock, a condition in which blood circulation and other body systems shut down in reaction to the injury. Pets in shock have pale gums and act weak, and they can die within 10 to 20 minutes. When your cat or dog is in shock, you can delay its progression by wrapping him in a blanket to keep him warm. You can also put a drop or two of Karo syrup or honey on your pet's gums to help keep him conscious. (For more information about shock, see page 333.)

Watch for stopped breathing. Pets who go into shock can stop breathing, so be prepared to perform artificial respiration. To breathe for your pet, close his mouth with one hand and place the other hand over his chest to monitor the rise and fall of his lungs. Cover his nose with your mouth and give two quick breaths. Watch for his chest to expand, then let the air escape. Give 15 to 20 breaths a minute until he begins breathing again on his own or until you reach veterinary help. (This technique is illustrated on page 20.)

Watch for a stopped heart. If your pet's heart stops beating, you'll need to perform CPR. It's best to have someone drive you and your pet to the animal hospital while you're performing CPR.

For cats and small dogs, cup a hand over the point of the chest just behind the elbows and squeeze firmly between your fingers and thumb, pressing in about ½ inch, about 80 to 100 times a minute. Give a breath into the nose after every five compressions until your pet revives or until you reach medical help.

Shotgun Wounds

Unless the gun is fired at very close range or penetrates the eye, injury from a shotgun is probably one of the least dangerous gunshot wounds. Unlike bullets, most shotgun pellets, when fired from a distance, penetrate only the skin and the immediate underlying tissue. You should still take your pet to the vet immediately. Often, antibiotics are needed to ward off possible infection, but usually, the pellets won't need to be surgically removed. Even though shot is made of lead, your pet won't be poisoned by lead unless the metal is swallowed. (When lead is swallowed, the hydrochloric acid in the stomach changes it into a form that can be absorbed through the intestines into the bloodstream and poison your pet.)

Put a larger dog on his side on a firm, flat surface and use both hands on top of each other to compress the chest by 25 to 50%. (This technique is illustrated on page 21.) Alternate breaths and compressions as for small pets until your pet revives or until you reach medical help.

Seal "sucking" chest wounds. A bullet that goes in one side of the chest and out the other creates a large exit hole that can turn into a sucking chest wound. You'll see bubbling and hear the air rushing into the body through the hole as your pet strains to breathe. That's because the hole lets air leak into the chest cavity, which collapses the lung. Wrap plastic wrap like Saran Wrap over the wound and around your pet's body to seal the wound. Wrap lightly to seal the area, but not tightly enough to restrict breathing, and transport your pet with the injured side down. (For more information about chest injuries, see page 128.)

If your pet has a small sucking wound on his chest wall, put a glob of K-Y Jelly or petroleum jelly on the hole to try to seal it, then wrap it with plastic wrap. This helps keep any more bacteria from contaminating the wound.

Use padding for broken ribs. If you suspect that your pet's ribs are broken, gently pad the damaged side with a thick clean towel and carefully transport your pet with his injured side down. This will give the ribs some rigidity so that your pet can continue to breathe (broken ribs can interfere with respiration). This not only helps control bleeding and keeps the wound clean but also helps seal the hole and reduce the chance that the lung will collapse. If your pet is struggling to breathe and fights to remain sitting, however, don't struggle with him. Just seal the wound as well as you can and get him to a vet as quickly as possible.

Clean and wrap abdominal wounds. Bullet wounds in the abdomen need to be kept clean, especially if the organs are exposed. A towel or a lint-free cloth like a pillowcase works well to help contain the injury so that the intestines or other organs don't spill out of the hole. Wet the towel or pillowcase with water or sterile saline contact lens solution to keep the organs from drying out and being injured further. Make a band from plastic wrap or a clean plastic garbage bag. Place the band over the moist padding, wrap it around your pet's body, and tape it in place. Make sure that the band is not wrapped too tightly; it just needs to hold the organs in place. (For more on abdominal injuries, see page 55.)

Stabilize broken bones. A bullet often breaks a bone, and you'll need to stabilize the limb. Wrap the leg in a thick towel or bubble wrap. This will help keep your pet from moving the injured leg, which could make the fracture worse. (For more information on fractures, see page 212.)

Transport your pet carefully, especially when you suspect a back injury. You can place a cat or small dog in a box or pet carrier. Even a cookie sheet, breadboard, or a sturdy lid from a trash can keep a small pet immobile until he can be examined. Set the intended carrier directly beside your pet. Gently slide a sheet or towel under him, then use the fabric to gently pull him onto the rigid surface. The goal is to get your pet on or into the carrier with minimal jostling. You may need to wrap a towel or elastic bandage like an Ace bandage around your pet and the board to keep him secure on its surface. (This technique is illustrated on page 29.)

For larger dogs, an ironing board can work well. Or you can use a towel or blanket to fashion a stretcher. You'll need two people to grasp the corners of the fabric and carry your pet to the car. It's best to have somebody watch

Doggy Bulletproof Vests

Dogs used by the police are at particular risk for being shot in the line of duty, though they often survive with prompt medical attention. But the U.S. Police Canine Association, which represents about 2,600 K-9 officers, reported that six dogs owned by members were killed in 1998.

To protect their canine officers, many law enforcement organizations are now investing in body armor for the dogs. Police dogs in Irving, Texas, wear 3-pound vests that attach with Voloro and are designed to stop a 9-millimeter bullet. One Arlington manufacturer that makes body armor for police officers has designed dog vests for Texas police dogs and for several Florida departments. San Diego County also uses Kevlar dog vests, and police dogs in New Jersey's Monmouth County wear similar protective gear.

over your pet during the ride to the hospital to calm and quiet him and also to be alert in case he stops breathing.

SPECIAL SITUATION

For digestive tract injuries: If the bullet injures the digestive tract, a soft diet may be necessary for several days to a week or more, until the intestines and stomach heal. There are highly digestible soft diets available by prescription from your veterinarian. But in most cases, you can use your pet's regular food and mix it in the blender with an equal amount of water or low-fat, no-salt chicken broth. Feed this gruel for 5 days and gradually use less liquid until your pet is again eating his everyday diet.

 ## FOLLOW-UP CARE

■ Gunshot wounds are one of the dirtiest types of injuries because as the bullet penetrates the body, it drags skin, fur, and dirt the length of the wound. For that reason, most of the time, your vet will leave the hole open to drain rather than stitch it. You'll need to keep the wound clean. Use a gauze pad dampened with warm water or sterile saline solution to gently clean away any discharge.

■ Most pets will receive intravenous antibiotics to fight infection while they are in the hospital, and they'll go home with antibiotic pills as well.

You can hide pills in tasty treats—most dogs are happy to take medicine this way, but cats tend to eat around the pill. A pill syringe, available from most pet-supply stores, is a great way to give medication to cats. Load the syringe with the pill or capsule, then place one hand on top of your cat's head and circle his muzzle with your thumb and middle fingers so that the fingertips press against his teeth just behind the canine teeth. This will prompt your pet to open wide. When he does, lay the pill syringe on his tongue so that the exit end points at the back of his throat but doesn't quite touch. Quickly depress the plunger to deposit the pill on the back of his tongue, then remove the syringe and close your cat's mouth. Stroke his throat until you see him swallow and have a treat ready to give him so that he'll swallow the treat and forget about trying to spit out the pill. (This technique is illustrated on page 31.)

Advisors

■ Patricia Hague, D.V.M., is a veterinarian at the Cat Hospital of Las Colinas in Irving, Texas.

■ Barry N. Kellogg, V.M.D., is a veterinarian at the Center for Veterinary Care in Great Barrington, Massachusetts, and the head of VMAT 1 (Veterinary Medical Assistance Team), the national disaster team for veterinary medicine.

■ Mike McFarland, D.V.M., is a veterinarian at the Emergency Animal Clinic in Dallas.

■ Lenny Southam, D.V.M., is a house-call veterinarian at Targwood Animal Health Care in West Chester, Pennsylvania; manager of CompuServe's Vet Care Forum; and coauthor of *The Pill Book Guide to Medication for your Dog and Cat*.

Head Entrapment

CALL YOUR VET: **IF NEEDED**

Cats and kittens have small, round heads that easily slip back out of nooks and crannies as they investigate them. But dogs, especially puppies, can get their heads stuck in the oddest places because a change in position can make the head too big for the opening. Also, youngsters may not have the patience or sense to duplicate the original position that got them there in the first place. They may stick their heads through chair slats, stairway banisters, or wire fences, or even inside glass jars to lick something tasty.

Head entrapment isn't a medical emergency unless your pet is having trouble breathing, but dogs can become hysterical and hurt themselves trying to escape. It can become like a Chinese finger puzzle, where the harder you pull, the tighter the trap becomes. But in most cases, you can rescue the pup yourself, and first aid can soothe any scraped skin or hurt feelings.

🩹 DO THIS NOW

Calm him down. First, calm the dog so that he stops struggling. Position yourself behind him and gently push his body nearer to the object he's trapped in so that he's no longer strangling himself as he tries to back up. If possible, it's a good idea to have one person stay on the tail side of the pup to control that end while you work from the front to free him.

Protect yourself. If your pet isn't having trouble breathing, it's a good idea to muzzle him or otherwise keep him from biting. The person at his head will need to grasp the nose to guide him out of the trap, and the pet may snap out of fear or discomfort.

For a long-nosed dog, use a long strip of soft cloth, like a leg from panty hose. Make a loop

229

around his muzzle and tie a single knot on top of his nose. Then bring the ends under his chin and tie another single knot. Finally, bring the ends behind his ears and tie them in a knot or bow. (This technique is illustrated on page 17.) For short-faced dogs like pugs, you can fit a pillowcase over their heads to give them something else to use their teeth on.

Use a lubricant to help him slide out.
While the dog is relaxed and not pulling against the trap, use a lubricant like K-Y Jelly or petroleum jelly to grease the fur of his neck and especially the crest of his skull (this is the thickest part of the head and is usually what holds up

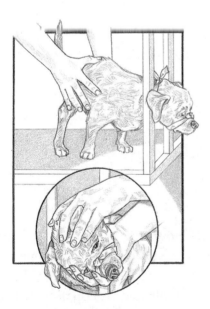

A dog's head is narrower from top to bottom than it is from side to side, so you can often free a trapped dog by gently turning his head sideways. A muzzle will keep you from being bitten as you free him, and greasing the dog's head and neck may help him slip free more easily.

the rescue). This will also keep the fence rail or other object from scraping skin as the dog's head comes free.

While one person holds the back end, the second person should gently grasp the dog's muzzle and turn his head sideways. Dogs' skulls are usually flatter from top to bottom and broadest from side to side, so turning the head a bit often helps it slide out with no problem.

SPECIAL SITUATION

If your pup's head is stuck in a glass jar:
First, grease the neck of the jar and your pet's fur with K-Y Jelly or petroleum jelly. Then, wrap the glass in a towel for a good grip and gently pull. Try to extend your pet's head so that it's in a straight line with his neck; that is, a typical sniffing position. Usually, the jar isn't stuck past the ears, and it will easily slip off. Try only one or two times to remove the jar. If it doesn't work quickly because it's too tightly stuck or your pet is too agitated, get to the animal hospital so that your pet can be sedated and the jar can be removed more easily.

If you do try to remove a stubborn jar, have a second person hold your dog so that he can't move around. If you can, put some kind of padding, like tissues or a small towel, inside the jar to protect the dog's face and eyes. Then, wearing heavy gloves, use a heavy, blunt object to gently break the glass at the large end of the jar. If the jar breaks but leaves a ring of glass around your pet's neck, you'll need to break it to remove it the rest of the way. You should protect

If your puppy sticks his head in a glass jar and can't pull it out again, have a second person hold him so that he can't move around. Then, wearing heavy gloves, gently break the glass at the large end of the jar so that you can reach the puppy's face. Wrap his head in plastic wrap to protect his eyes and insert cloth between the rim of the jar and the pup's neck so that he can't get cut. Insert a spoon, bowl side down, between the cloth and the glass rim. To break the rim, tap it sharply with a soup ladle over the spot where the other spoon is inserted.

yourself by wearing cloth gloves and glasses—sunglasses will work if you have nothing else.

First, cover your dog's eyes to protect them. You can use plastic wrap like Saran Wrap to cover his muzzle and eyes at the same time—it sticks to itself but will be easy to remove afterward because it won't stick to the fur. Have your helper calm and steady your dog so that he sits very still while you work with the broken jar.

Insert some padding like a folded cloth between the top of the dog's neck and the glass to keep him from getting cut. Then slip something solid, like the bowl of a metal spoon, between the padding and the glass. Finally, use the heavy metal handle of a table knife or the bowl of a metal soup ladle to hit the glass sharply right on top of where the spoon is resting. It may take two or three sharp cracks, but hitting the glass between the two pieces of metal should shatter it away from the dog's neck. Again, if this doesn't work after one or two tries, go to the vet.

FOLLOW-UP CARE

■ Cuts or scrapes should be cleaned with soap and water. You can use an antiseptic liquid soap like Betadine Skin Cleanser.

■ If there are cuts, you can use an antibiotic ointment like Neosporin four times a day to prevent infection and help speed healing. Continue applying the ointment for a week, or until the cuts and scrapes have healed or formed scabs.

Advisors
■ Lorrie Bartloff, D.V.M., is a veterinarian at Three Point Veterinary Clinic in Elkhart, Indiana.
■ Clint Chastain, D.V.M., is a veterinarian at Preston Road Animal Hospital in Dallas.
■ Laura Solien, D.V.M., is a veterinarian at Maplecrest Animal Hospital in Goshen, Indiana.

Head Injuries

CALL YOUR VET: **IMMEDIATELY**

The brain is encased in bone, surrounded by cushioning fluid, and suspended inside the skull by ligaments that act like shock absorbers. But any hard shock to the head can cause the cranial equivalent of whiplash, bouncing the brain against the side of the skull and bruising or tearing the tissue.

Head injuries aren't always visible, although there may be bleeding from the nose or ears. The symptoms are usually more subtle. Pets may stare into space or act dazed. They'll be unsteady on their feet, and their eyes may look in different directions. Or they'll simply pass out, and you may not know why.

DO THIS NOW

Wrap him in a blanket. Since a pet with a head injury often loses consciousness, you'll want to wrap him in a blanket before doing anything else. This will protect him if he should wake up and thrash around. By keeping your pet warm, you'll also help prevent shock, a life-threatening condition in which the body's organs don't work efficiently or even stop functioning altogether. Shock can kill a pet in as little as 10 to 20 minutes. (For more on shock, see page 333.)

Transport him carefully. Any jostling can increase bleeding or make brain bruises worse. If you have to move your pet, keep him as still as you can. Put a small pet in a carrier or box. You can slide a large dog onto a rigid surface, such as a piece of plywood. You can even use an ironing board in a pinch. Tape or tie him down so that he can't roll off. (This technique is illustrated on page 29.)

Watch how you position him. Keep your pet's head level with his feet unless he starts trying to cough or vomits. In that case, lower his head to allow the fluids to drain out, then return him to a level position.

Check his breathing. If your pet stops breathing, you'll need to give artificial respiration. Hold his mouth closed, cover his nose

FIRST ALERT

Seizures

Sometimes, severe brain injuries can damage tissues and cause electrical currents to go awry. Within hours of head injuries, some pets will experience seizures, ranging in severity from momentary confusion to total collapse. And they may continue having seizures off and on for the rest of their lives. This isn't as bad as it sounds, however. Most seizures last less than a minute. They can be controlled with medication, and they rarely cause serious problems. (For more information on seizures, see page 330.)

with your mouth, and give two quick breaths. Watch to see if his chest rises. Then give 15 to 20 breaths a minute until he starts breathing or you can get him to a vet. (This technique is illustrated on page 20.)

Control bleeding. Bleeding from head wounds generally looks more serious than it is, but you still need to stop it. If the bones seem intact, you can apply pressure to the head while on your way to the veterinarian. If you detect any crunching or see broken bones through the skin, do *not* apply pressure. Just get to the vet as soon as possible.

Hold a clean cloth or a gauze pad against the wound until the bleeding stops. This will usu-ally happen in 5 minutes or less. (For more information on bleeding, see page 95.)

 FOLLOW-UP CARE

■ It's not uncommon for a pet to show remarkable improvement after a head injury, then have a crisis hours later. The signs aren't always visible. Some pets simply go to sleep and never wake up. To make sure that your pet is recovering properly in the 24 hours following the injury, wake him up every 1 to 2 hours. He should wake up easily and be alert. If he doesn't wake easily or is unusually groggy, there may be swelling, bleeding, or clotting within the brain. Take him back to the veterinarian immediately.

Advisors

■ Shane Bateman, D.V.M., D.V.Sc., is a veterinarian board certified in the American College of Emergency and Critical Care Medicine and assistant professor of emergency and critical care medicine at Ohio State University College of Veterinary Medicine in Columbus.

■ Bernadine Cruz, D.V.M., is a veterinarian at Laguna Hills Animal Hospital in California.

■ Carin A. Smith, D.V.M., is a veterinarian in Leavenworth, Washington, and author of *101 Training Tips for Your Cat*.

■ David Wirth-Schneider, D.V.M., is a veterinarian at the Emergency Clinic for Animals in Madison, Wisconsin.

Head Swelling

CALL YOUR VET: **IF NEEDED**

Most head swelling results from traumatic injury, such as being hit by a car or falling from a tree. Your pet's eyes may not work together, or he may act dizzy or lose consciousness. These cases are emergencies that need immediate medical attention. (For more on head injuries, see page 232.)

At other times, head swelling is the result of an allergic reaction to an insect bite or bee sting or is caused by an abscess from a bite wound. (For more information about abscesses, see page 60; for bee stings, see page 79.) But as long as your pet acts as if he feels fine otherwise, first aid can reduce the swelling and in some instances may be all that's needed.

DO THIS NOW

For Swelling from Injury

Keep him calm. If you suspect that head swelling is due to some sort of trauma, check to see if your pet has full control of his senses. If he acts disoriented or dizzy, walks in circles, or acts like he can't see, it's best to keep him quiet and calm until you can get medical help. Wrap him in a blanket to keep him warm and restrain his legs so he doesn't move around too much. Doing this also keeps him from scratching at the swelling and injuring himself further.

Elevate his head. If your pet loses consciousness, try to keep his head elevated instead of letting it hang over the edge of the car seat or stay level with the seat or the floor. Elevation helps the blood flow better and may also relieve or reduce any increased pressure in the head that's causing the swelling. (For more information about loss of consciousness, see page 396.)

Apply a cold compress. If you're not sure if the swelling is due to an injury or an allergy, it's

FIRST ALERT

Dental Disease

A dog or cat with a swollen head or face should have his teeth examined. The roots of some teeth are directly beneath the eyes, and when a tooth is infected or the root is abscessed, the face swells. Often, the animal also drools and refuses to eat because of the pain.

Generally, the pet must be anesthetized so that the tooth can be repaired or pulled. Often, the pet will then need a round of antibiotics to get rid of the infection. And because pets with sore mouths have trouble eating, feeding a soft diet for up to a week after a dental procedure can help. Since changes in diet can cause stomach upset, the best temporary solution is to run the pet's regular food through a food processor with enough water or low-fat, no-salt chicken broth to make a gruel.

best to use an ice pack or a cold compress to help reduce swelling. First, rinse a clean washcloth in cold water and hold it against the swollen area. Then, place the cold pack on top of the washcloth and leave it on for 10 to 30 minutes several times a day. You can use a ready-made cold pack, a plastic bag filled with ice, or a bag of frozen vegetables like corn or peas, which will conform to the shape of your pet's head and face. Or wet a towel with cold water and put it in the freezer for 5 minutes, then apply the chilled cloth to the swelling.

For Swelling from Bite Allergy

Use a soothing paste. If you're sure that the swelling is due to an insect bite or sting, mix Ac'cent Flavor Enhancer with water to make a paste, then apply it to the sting. This product contains monosodium glutamate (MSG), which helps neutralize the sting by drawing out the venom. It's best to remove the fur from around the site, however, so the paste doesn't make a mess. Use blunt scissors or electric clippers to trim the fur to about 1 inch long around the bite. (This technique is illustrated on page 114.)

Give an antihistamine. For head swelling due to an allergic reaction, it's very safe to give an antihistamine like Benadryl. It can help reduce the itching and swelling until the reaction subsides or you can get medical attention. The liquid usually comes in a dose of 12.5 milligrams per teaspoon; pills are 25 milligrams each. Your pet will need 1 milligram per pound of body weight every 6 to 8 hours, which means that a 10-pound cat or dog should get about ¾ teaspoon of liquid or half a pill.

Use an Elizabethan collar. A pet with head swelling may try to rub at the sore area, either by rubbing his face against the furniture or carpet or scratching and pawing at his head. A cone-shaped collar restraint called an Elizabethan collar can help keep him from scratching or otherwise injuring his eyes.

 ## SPECIAL SITUATION

If the swelling is due to a food allergy: Rarely, your pet's head may swell after he eats something that causes an allergic reaction. If that's the case, and your pet is alert, responsive, and does not have difficulty breathing, empty his stomach by making him vomit. The best way to do this is to give 3% hydrogen peroxide. The dose is the same for dogs and cats: 1 to 2 teaspoons per 10 pounds of body weight. Use an eyedropper, needleless syringe, or a turkey baster to squirt the liquid on the back of your pet's tongue. The foaming action and the taste should prompt vomiting within 5 minutes, but if it doesn't, you can repeat one or two more times, allowing 5 minutes between doses. (For more information about food allergies, see page 190.)

 ## FOLLOW-UP CARE

■ If your pet needs an anti-inflammatory medication to keep swelling under control, the vet will prescribe it. After your pet has an initial injection at the veterinarian's, you can give him the pills hidden in a treat.

■ If it's determined that the swelling is due to a food allergy, you'll need to work with your veterinarian to figure out which food ingredient caused the reaction. Once it's identified, just feed your pet a food that doesn't contain that ingredient.

■ If your pet has scratched his eye while trying to relieve discomfort by rubbing or scratching, the vet may prescribe an eye ointment to relieve pain and prevent infection. To apply it, tip your pet's head up, gently pull down the lower eyelid, and drip or squeeze the ointment into the cupped area. Your pet's blinking will spread the medicine. (This technique is illustrated on page 32.)

Advisors
■ Dawn Crandell, D.V.M., is a veterinarian at the Veterinary Emergency Clinic of York Region in Aurora, Ontario, Canada.
■ Albert Mughannam, D.V.M., is a veterinary ophthalmologist at Veterinary Vision in San Mateo, California.
■ Denise Petryk, D.V.M., is a veterinarian at Puget Sound Veterinary Medical Referral Center in Tacoma, Washington.
■ George White, D.V.M., is a veterinarian at I-20 Animal Medical Center in Arlington, Texas.
■ Anna E. Worth, V.M.D., is a veterinarian at West Mountain Animal Hospital in Shaftsbury, Vermont.

Heatstroke

CALL YOUR VET: **IMMEDIATELY**

Heatstroke happens when the normal body mechanisms can't keep the temperature in a safe range. Dogs and cats can get overheated very easily because they don't have very efficient cooling systems.

Cats and dogs do not sweat to regulate body temperature. They fluff their fur to circulate cool air to the skin, and cats lick themselves so that the evaporation of saliva helps dissipate heat. Cats don't usually pant unless they're already overwhelmed by the heat, but dogs pant as a primary method of cooling off. The rapid exchange of cool outside air with the warm, humid air inside the lungs, plus the evaporation from the lolling tongue, helps keep a dog's temperature in normal ranges.

When the outside air temperature is equal to or higher than a pet's body temperature—that's about 99° to 102.5°F—evaporation won't help, and heatstroke can occur. A pet with moderate heatstroke—when his temperature reaches 104° to 106°F—will have a bright red tongue and gums and thick, sticky saliva, and he'll pant rapidly. Most pets will recover within an hour if you give them prompt first-aid treatment.

Body temperatures higher than 106°F can be deadly. A pet can go into shock and may develop failure of the liver, kidneys, lungs, heart, or brain. His gums may turn pale; he'll act weak and dizzy; he'll develop a bloody nose, bloody vomiting, and diarrhea; and he can fall into a coma when the brain begins to swell. At temperatures of 107°F and higher, pets develop disseminated intravascular coagulation, a condition in which the blood-clotting system fails. They'll die without immediate first aid and veterinary attention.

For Severe Heatstroke (body temperature above 106°F)

Get to the vet right away. Use a rectal thermometer lubricated with petroleum jelly to take your pet's temperature to determine what degree of heatstroke he has. (This technique is illustrated on page 9.) Pets with temperatures higher than 106°F need to see a veterinarian immediately. Rectal thermometers usually register only as high as 108°F, and a pet with heatstroke may have a body temperature that goes off the scale and reaches 110°F or higher.

If you can be at the animal hospital in 5 minutes or less, call the hospital to tell them that you're on your way and how high your pet's temperature is; that will tell your veterinarian exactly what type of emergency treatment your pet will need. Then get in the car and go immediately to the vet.

It's safest to do this with another person to either drive or take care of your pet while you drive. Make sure that the car is cool for the trip, and try to grab a bottle of rubbing alcohol and as much ice as you can on your way out the door. Position your pet in front of the air vent to achieve as much evaporation as possible. Try to cool your pet on the way by applying the ice and alcohol to his armpits and groin.

Cool him. If he's conscious or if you live farther than 5 minutes away from the animal hospital, try to lower his temperature to 106°F before rushing him to the vet. Use the garden hose or shower or get him into a tub or sink full of cold water. Check his temperature every 5 minutes to be sure that it's coming down. When your pet's temperature is above 106°F, he'll be very dizzy or nearly unconscious, so be sure to keep his head above the water.

Give him an ice pack. First, put a cold, wet washcloth on the back of your pet's neck and head. Then put an ice pack or bag of frozen peas on top of the washcloth. This not only cools him off but also helps reduce the heat in the brain and prevent brain swelling, which can kill him.

Let him drink as much cold water as he wants. Even better, offer a rehydration fluid like Pedialyte or Gatorade. That can help cool him off from the inside out and help replace important electrolytes like salt that he may have lost from dehydration. (For more information about dehydration, see page 148.)

Watch for shock. Pets with severe heatstroke are at risk for shock. Take your pet to the hospital immediately. Do not wrap him in a blanket if his temperature is above 104°F. If you have cooled him off and his temperature is less than 100°F, wrap him in a blanket for the trip to the hospital.

If your pet has gone into shock, he may have low blood sugar levels. Raising his blood sugar levels with a dose of Karo syrup or honey may help. If you have time on the way out the door to quickly grab some, rub it onto his gums on the way to the hospital—it will be absorbed through the skin. (For more information about shock, see page 333.)

Be prepared to give artificial respiration and CPR. Pets with severe heatstroke may stop breathing from shock, and sometimes, heatstroke can cause their throats to swell shut.

Hold your pet's mouth shut, put your mouth over his nose, and give two quick breaths, watching to see his chest expand with air. Continue to give 15 to 20 breaths a minute until he starts to breathe on his own or until you reach the animal hospital. (This technique is illustrated on page 20.)

If your pet's heart has stopped, you will have to administer CPR. Determine if his heart has stopped by taking his pulse. You won't be able to feel a pulse in the carotid artery in the neck as you can with people. Instead, press your fingertips into the crease where the inside of the thigh meets the body and feel for the pulse in the femoral artery, which is very big and near the surface. (This technique is illustrated on page 13.) If you can't feel a pulse, try listening or feeling for the heartbeat. Put your ear or hand against your pet's left side directly behind the elbow.

If you don't detect a heartbeat, you will have to begin chest compressions. To give compressions for a cat or small dog, cup your hand over the point of the chest just behind the elbows, with your thumb on one side and fingers on the other. Squeeze firmly, compressing by about ½ inch. This not only pumps the heart but also makes the pressure inside the chest (and against the heart) rapidly increase and decrease and helps move the blood. Ideally, one person gives chest compressions while a second performs artificial respiration. Alternate one breath for every 5 compressions. The goal is 80 to 100 compressions and 15 to 20 breaths per minute until your pet revives or you reach medical help.

Lay a larger pet on either side on a flat surface. Put one hand on top of the chest behind the elbow and your other hand on top of the

Extra-Hot Dogs

Dogs are designed to cool off by breathing in and out to exchange hot air for cool and by panting to promote evaporation from the tongue. But certain dog breeds have more difficulty staying cool than others, and they also have less protection against hot weather. Dogs with flat, pushed-in faces like English bulldogs, pugs, and Pekingese also tend to have foreshortened windpipes, so they can't breathe as efficiently as longer-nosed dogs. These dogs can suffer heatstroke just by overexercising, even on a relatively cool day, and they often have problems in weather that wouldn't bother other dogs. You'll know that your pet is at a higher risk for heatstroke if he often snores or snorts or makes a lot of respiratory noises, like whistles or wheezes.

first. Use both hands to thrust down firmly. You should compress the chest by about 25 to 50%. (This technique is illustrated on page 21.) Alternate breaths and compressions as for small pets.

Continue your attempts to cool your pet as you're administering artificial respiration and CPR on the way to the hospital. As he cools, he's more likely to begin breathing again. Again, it's safest to enlist a friend to help.

For Moderate Heatstroke (body temperature between 104° and 106°F)

Get him into a cool place. If you have taken your pet's temperature and it is between 104°

and 106°F, he has moderate heatstroke. You still need to take measures to reduce his temperature, though, so take him inside and turn up the air conditioner. If you don't have air-conditioning in your house, start your car's air conditioner and when your car is cool, sit inside with your pet. Or set him in front of a fan. Once the temperature outside his body is lower than the temperature on the inside, his panting will start to work, and he'll begin to cool off.

Monitor his temperature. Take his temperature every 10 minutes to see how serious the heatstroke is and if he's recovering. Dogs and cats who start out with a temperature of 106°F or lower usually recover quickly.

Use ice packs or cool water. Wrap your pet in cold, wet towels and place ice packs in his armpits and groin region. There are major blood vessels in these areas, so the cold will chill his blood and help him cool off more quickly as the blood cools the whole body from the inside. You can also put him in a tub of cool water or in the shower, or you can put him in the shade outside and use a garden hose to give him a cool rinse until his temperature drops.

Turn on a fan. This will increase evaporation, which will help cool him off.

Offer him some cold water to drink. Or give him an ice cube to lick.

Stop the cooling process at 103°F. Your pet will pant as long as he's too hot. Once his temperature returns to normal, he'll stop panting

and his breathing will slow down and be less frantic. Once his body temperature has dropped to 103°F, stop the cooling-off process, so he doesn't become chilled. Keep him relatively inactive and away from direct heat or sunlight.

 SPECIAL SITUATIONS

For pets with long, heavy fur: These animals tend to shed most of their undercoats by the time hot weather rolls around. A pet's coat actually helps insulate him from extreme heat while letting air currents in to cool him off. But if the fur gets tangled and matted, it holds the heat close to the body and prevents air circulation from reaching the skin and cooling it. So keep your pet brushed to help prevent heatstroke, or trim the long fur to a more manageable length.

To prevent problems with blow dryers and carriers: Pets who are left under hot blow dryers after baths can suffer heatstroke at any time of the year, and pet carriers that have poor ventilation can become deathtraps. If you need to confine your pet in a carrier or cage, make sure that there's plenty of ventilation. People with show dogs and cats often use small fans that attach to the cage to keep their pets cool in hot weather. You can find battery-powered crate fans in pet-supply catalogs.

For old or overweight pets or those with breathing problems: These animals are at highest risk for heatstroke because even their normal cooling systems lose effectiveness. Keep these pets inside in air-conditioning during hot weather, and don't let them exercise in the heat.

FOLLOW-UP CARE

■ Pets who recover from moderate heatstroke probably won't have ongoing health problems, but severe heatstroke can damage the organs, especially the kidneys. Watch for blood in the urine. If your veterinarian has already found some damage, he may prescribe a special diet like Hill's Prescription k/d (kidney diet). Therapeutic diets like k/d are formulated to put less strain on damaged kidneys by reducing the amount of waste products from digestion. Try mixing the food 50/50 with his old diet for the first few days to ease him into the new routine, then gradually decrease the amount of the old food until he's eating only the new one.

■ Pets who have heatstroke once have an increased risk of getting it again unless steps are taken to help keep them cool in hot weather. Most heatstroke victims have been left in a car during hot weather or confined in a yard or concrete run without shade. Whenever the temperature gets above 80°F, make sure that your pet has access to shade.

■ Dogs and cats always need fresh water to keep themselves cool, but despite our best efforts, they can run out of water, or it can spill and leave them thirsty. Pet-supply stores and catalogs carry different types and sizes of water dispensers that provide a nonstop, nonspillable water supply for pets. Some, like the Lixit Dog Waterer or the Automatic Dog Waterer, attach to an outdoor spigot.

THE BEST APPROACH

Rectal Thermometer

Dogs' and cats' temperatures are measures of their health. Too high a temperature indicates a fever, and too low indicates shock. In emergency cases like heatstroke or its opposite, hypothermia, your pet's temperature determines what type of first aid you should use.

The ear thermometers that people use probably won't be as accurate for pets because dogs' and cats' ears are more open than human ears. It's also hard to get a pet to hold a thermometer under his tongue, so rather than an oral thermometer, you should choose a rectal thermometer. The same kinds of rectal thermometers that people use also work for dogs and cats.

Standard bulb thermometers are inexpensive, and they're the veterinarians' favorite. They take a couple of minutes to register the temperature. Digital thermometers cost a little more, but they may be easier to read than bulb thermometers and register the temperature a bit faster in times of emergency. Rectal thermometers are available from drugstores and pet-supply catalogs.

Advisors

■ Charles DeVinne, D.V.M., is a veterinarian at Animal Care Clinic in Peterborough, New Hampshire.

■ Larry Edwards, D.V.M., is a veterinarian at Canyon Creek Pet Hospital in Sherman, Texas.

■ Ken Lawrence, D.V.M., is a veterinarian at the Texoma Veterinary Hospital in Sherman, Texas.

Hives

CALL YOUR VET: **IF NEEDED**

You may not even notice if your long-haired dog or cat comes down with hives, but you can feel the rash of welts beneath the fur. Short-haired pets like Dalmatians or Boxers look like checkerboard dogs when the dots of raised skin make their fur stand up in splotches. Hives can also make your pet's face swell and his eyes swell shut.

Hives are an allergic reaction. In people, allergic reactions usually cause breathing problems like asthma, but allergies in pets usually target the skin. Hives typically develop from an insect sting, but they can also be prompted by inhaled pollen or a contact allergy from something like a carpet cleaner. Vaccinations can also prompt a reaction of hives in certain pets. Usually, the reaction develops within 30 minutes to 24 hours after the exposure, and the hives can cover just part of the body or your entire pet.

Hives are more an uncomfortable nuisance than an actual danger to your dog or cat. The reaction makes them itch, and pets will rip and tear at their skin to relieve the irritation. First aid can go a long way to soothe your pet and speed his recovery.

📁 DO THIS NOW

Give an antihistamine. To reduce the allergic reaction, give your pet an antihistamine like Benadryl—it's very safe for pets. An antihistamine will not only reduce the inflammation and swelling but will also make your pet drowsy, and this sedative effect can help calm your pet's anxiety so that the itching doesn't worry him as much. The liquid form of Benadryl usually comes in a dose of 12.5 milligrams per teaspoon; pills are usually 25 milligrams each. Pets will need 1 milligram every 6 to 8 hours for each pound they weigh. That means a 10-pound cat or dog should get about ¾ teaspoon of liquid or half a pill.

FIRST ALERT

Anaphylaxis

Most reactions to insect stings or vaccinations are mild and cause only aggravating discomfort. Occasionally, however, pets can have a life-threatening reaction called anaphylaxis, which causes sudden swelling, trouble breathing, and collapse. The signs generally happen within 15 to 30 minutes, and pets can go from being normal to near death within minutes.

If you see these symptoms, give your pet an antihistamine like Benadryl as soon as possible. Pets suffering from anaphylaxis many have trouble swallowing because their throats often swell, so pills may not work as well as a liquid. The liquid form of Benadryl usually comes in a dose of 12.5 milligrams per teaspoon; pills are usually 25 milligrams each. Pets will need 1 milligram per pound of body weight every 6 to 8 hours. That means a 10-pound cat or dog should get about ¾ teaspoon of liquid or half a pill.

Draw up the liquid in an eyedropper or needleless syringe. Squirt it into your pet's cheek pocket, close his mouth, and stroke his throat until you see him swallow. (This technique is illustrated on page 30.) This can help bring down the swelling and ease his breathing, but anaphylaxis is a life-threatening emergency. Take your pet to the veterinarian right away. (For more information about anaphylaxis, see page 79.)

Soak him in cold water. The rash that comes with hives causes extreme itchiness that goes away only with time. But you can relieve some of the discomfort and make the itch temporarily bearable with a cold-water soak. Warm or hot water just makes the inflammation worse, but icy temperatures literally cool off the burn. Either fill the tub with icy water or hose your pet off outside. A children's wading pool also works well. He'll need to soak for 10 to 20 minutes at least once a day—more often, if he's willing. If the water doesn't reach high enough to cover all the itchy spots, dip water with a cup or pitcher and pour it over him until all his fur is soaked.

Soothe itchy skin with oatmeal. You can fill a cotton sock with regular oatmeal flakes and run water through the sock. Or add half a packet of a commercial oatmeal product like Aveeno to your pet's bathwater.

Add tea to the bathwater. Black and green teas contain tannins, natural compounds that can relieve itching. Brew a pot of tea and after it has cooled, add it to the bathwater. Or dab the cooled steeped tea bags on the itchiest spots.

Try a cold compress. Cats and some dogs won't willingly go into the water. Instead, you can use a cold compress and apply it directly to the affected parts of your pet's body. Commercial cold packs that you stick in the freezer remain pliable even when frozen, and they'll mold to his body. You can also use a bag of frozen corn or peas. Just be sure to place a cold, wet washcloth against his skin first, then place the cold pack on top. You can apply the cold pack for 10 to 30 minutes several times a day.

FOLLOW-UP CARE

■ In most cases, hives go away within 12 to 24 hours after the pet has been given an antihistamine. But some pets have problems with hives for up to 3 days, so one dose of antihistamine won't be enough. You can give Benadryl every 6 to 8 hours as needed, but no more than three times a day.

■ If your pet still has problems the second day, your veterinarian may want to prescribe something that's more effective, like steroids, to reduce the reaction.

■ Continue using the cold compresses or soaks for as long as your pet needs them. Do this for 10 to 30 minutes at a time several times a day for 2 to 3 days. By that time, the allergic reaction should be gone.

Advisors

■ Dale C. Butler, D.V.M., is a veterinarian at the Best Friends Animal Hospital in Denison, Texas.

■ Jeffrey Werber, D.V.M., is a veterinarian at Century Veterinary Group in Los Angeles.

■ Dennis L. Wilcox, D.V.M., is a veterinarian at Angeles Clinic for Animals in Port Angeles, Washington.

Hot Spots

CALL YOUR VET: **IF NEEDED**

Cats rarely get hot spots, but dogs, especially thickly furred breeds like golden retrievers and Chow Chows, often develop red, wet sores that make their skin look like raw hamburger. Hot spots, known technically as moist pyotraumatic dermatitis, are caused by a wide range of things. Usually, a bug bite, tiny sore, or scratch in the skin begins to itch, the dog starts licking and chewing, bacteria start to grow, and the sore spreads incredibly fast. It can go from the size of a pinprick to several inches within 30 minutes, and if left untreated, it can grow 20 times larger in a single day.

Hot spots look awful, and they may be extremely painful. But they involve only the very top layer of skin and heal quickly with first aid.

DO THIS NOW

Trim the fur. A hot spot oozes serum that mats the fur together so it's difficult to properly clean and medicate the sore. Use blunt scissors to cut away the fur around the sore. First, apply K-Y Jelly to the spot, then slip your index and second fingers through the fur and hold them against the sore. Cut the fur so it's level with your fingers, leaving a 1-inch border all around the sore. (This technique is illustrated on page 114.) Then thoroughly rinse the area with warm water. The trimmed fur sticks to the jelly and washes out. Finally, use electric clippers to shave off the fur just past the outer margins of the sore. (Hot spots are extremely sore, so if your pet isn't cooperative, you may need to have a vet or groomer cut the fur.)

Do a thorough cleaning. Once you've trimmed the fur, clean the sore. Any water-based cleanser is fine, but an antiseptic liquid soap like Betadine Skin Cleanser is best. Be sure to rinse off all the cleanser, or the irritation may become worse when the soap scum dries on the skin. After rinsing gently, pat the area dry with a clean cloth.

Use the right medication—or a tea bag. Never put ointment on hot spots, because it seals in the infection, which can then spread deeper into the skin. Alcohol is too strong for open wounds and is painful. Instead, medicate with an antibacterial spray or cream that dries up the sore, like a 5% benzoyl peroxide product such as Clean & Clear Persa-Gel 5, which you can find at drugstores and supermarkets.

If you don't have an appropriate medication handy, a tea bag will work fine. Tea (black, not herbal) contains tannic acid, which is a natural astringent that dries and heals sores more quickly. Soak a tea bag in hot water, remove it and let it cool, then apply it directly to the hot spot for 5 minutes. Use this treatment three to six times a day until the spot is dried up and healing.

🩹 FOLLOW-UP CARE

■ The most important thing is to halt the itch cycle so that your pet stops chewing or licking the hot spot, which keeps it from healing and can make the infection worse. It's usually necessary to use a cone-type collar restraint called an Elizabethan collar to keep your pet from licking.

■ An antibacterial spray called Lido-Med Spray, which is available from pet-supply catalogs, contains a topical anesthetic that cools the burn and stops the discomfort. Apply as necessary. Products that contain witch hazel are also very cooling and soothing to hot spots because witch hazel evaporates quickly. Spray witch hazel on up to three times a day.

A Lick and a Promise

In homes with multiple dogs, treating a hot spot often means facing unexpected problems. That's because even though the pet with the hot spot wears a restraining collar and can't reach the sore to lick it, his helpful housemates are more than willing to scratch his itch for him. Hot spots ooze serum, a clear, sticky fluid that has an odor and taste that must be attractive to dogs. And the more the sore is licked, the more it oozes, which prompts more licking—and on and on.

You can use a deterrent to stop pets from chewing, biting, and licking themselves or each other. Apply a thin coat of Vicks VapoRub to the fur around the hot spot. The odor will repel most dogs, and the taste is nasty, too. Apply some around the sore a couple of times a day, but don't put it directly on the sore, since it may burn.

■ After the first day or so, the hot spot won't be quite as tender, but it will still be a bit weepy until it starts to dry. Use a topical product to dry and cleanse the area. You can spray the area with Burow's Solution two or three times a day, or dab on liquid boric acid twice a day (a pharmacist can order this natural antiseptic for you). Do this for a couple of days, until the sore starts to dry up and seems less irritated.

■ Only about 10 percent of hot spots need antibiotics, but if your best efforts fail to dry up the sore or if it seems to spread, take your pet to the veterinarian. For some reason, golden retrievers seem to have the worst problems, but any pet may need both antibiotics and steroids to fight infection and inflammation. Usually, you'll need to give the pills for 7 to 14 days. (For pilling techniques, see page 30.)

THE BEST APPROACH

Electric Clippers

Once bacteria move into an itchy bite or sore, they spread like wildfire from hair follicle to hair follicle, until the hot spot covers an enormous area. But you can stop the growth in its tracks by shaving off the fur just past the outer margins of the sore.

Cutting heavy fur with scissors can be dangerous when your pet is wriggling, because you risk cutting skin as well as fur. Plus, you won't get nearly as close as you should. Electric clippers designed for professional pet grooming are the best tool for the job. Those made by Oster or Wahl are best.

Professional models can cost more than $100 and have all kinds of blade attachments available. All you really need, though, is something like the Wahl Pocket Pro Trimmer, a compact, 4-inch, miniature cordless clipper that dog and cat show professionals carry for last-minute touch-ups. It comes with two trimming attachments, a cleaning brush, oil, a blade guard, and one AA alkaline battery, and costs about $20 from pet-supply catalogs.

For very furry pets, you'll still need to clip off the fur with blunt scissors to within an inch or so of the skin, then use the trimmer to shave down to the skin and past the margins of the hot spot.

Electric clippers are not only great for treating occasional hot spots, they are also perfect for trimming fur away from the eyes to treat eye irritation, from the ears for treating ear infections, and from around the anal area to help prevent mats that can interfere with normal elimination.

Advisors

■ Lowell Ackerman, D.V.M., is a veterinarian at Mesa Veterinary Hospital in Scottsdale, Arizona, and author of *Skin and Coat Care for Your Dog* and *Skin and Coat Care for Your Cat.*

■ Karen Hoffman, V.M.D., is a veterinarian at Delaware Valley Animal Hospital in Fairless Hills, Pennsylvania.

■ Jeffrey Werber, D.V.M., is a veterinarian at Century Veterinary Group in Los Angeles.

Hypothermia

CALL YOUR VET: **SAME DAY**

Dogs and cats don't get dangerously cold very often because they have a strong shiver reflex. Shivering increases the body's metabolism and generates heat. And their fur is a great insulator. It traps warm air next to the skin, keeping pets' internal temperature in the normal range of 99° to 102.5°F. As a result, they're less likely than people to suffer from hypothermia, or low body temperature. (All of the temperature ranges given are approximate and may overlap. Because each animal is different, it's a good idea to take a baseline temperature reading for your pet and file it away in his first-aid kit. See page 9 for an illustration of taking a pet's temperature.)

Things change when there's a lot of wind or pets' fur gets wet, or when they spend more time outside than their bodies are designed to handle. As body temperature drops, so do essential functions such as breathing and heart rate. Pets with mild hypothermia, in which body temperature is between 95° and 99°F, will shiver, tremble, act sleepy, and be cold to the touch. Most pets with mild hypothermia will recover within an hour with the help of simple first aid.

Pets with moderate hypothermia have temperatures in the range of 90° to 95°F. They can be treated with first aid at home, but they may take longer to recover than those with mild hypothermia. After home therapy, a pet with moderate hypothermia needs to see a vet the same day. But if his temperature doesn't rise after first aid, he needs to go to the hospital without delay.

Severe hypothermia can be deadly. Pets stop shivering when their body temperatures drop to around 90°F, and without shivering, it's nearly impossible for them to warm up without extra help. With severe hypothermia—body temperature of about 90°F or lower for longer than 30 minutes—pets lose consciousness, their organs begin to fail, and the heartbeat and breathing nearly stop altogether. Severe hypothermia requires emergency first aid and immediate veterinary attention.

FIRST ALERT

Frostbite

Hypothermia isn't the only condition caused by extreme cold. Dogs and cats who are cold enough to get hypothermia also have a high risk of getting frostbite, especially when they've been trapped in snow or exposed to very cold winds.

Frostbite occurs when the body diverts blood from the face, ears, and limbs and routes it to the abdomen in an attempt to keep the organs warm. This shift in circulation can save a pet's life, but it leaves the extremities unprotected from the cold. Here's what to watch for.

- The skin on frostbitten areas will be discolored—it's usually pale, white, blue, or gray—and it will be extremely cold to the touch. It may become very red after thawing if the blood vessels in the area have not been badly damaged.
- Check the toes and tail for discoloration or redness because they're very vulnerable to frostbite.
- Cats often get frozen ear tips because of the thin skin and sparse fur on their ears. In addition, the ear tips are exposed to cold even when a cat curls into a protective ball.
- Male dogs, including those who have been neutered, often suffer frostbite on the thin skin of the scrotum because it's exposed to cold even when they sit or lie down.

Pets with frostbite always need immediate veterinary care, although they'll often recover when the frozen areas are warmed gently and gradually. (See page 219 for more information on frostbite.)

For Severe Hypothermia (body temperature about 90°F or less)

Get to the vet as soon as possible. Pets with severe hypothermia must see a veterinarian as soon as possible. Rectal thermometers register to only 93°F, so watch for the shiver reflex; it stops when body temperature drops to around 90°F. Dogs and cats who are so cold that they aren't shivering need emergency veterinary care.

A pet whose core body temperature has been below 90°F for longer than 30 minutes needs to be rewarmed from the inside out, using special techniques that your vet is trained to perform. Trying to rewarm him yourself in this situation can be dangerous. If your pet's temperature has probably been lower than 90°F for more than 30 minutes, *do not* apply external sources of heat. Dry your pet off if he's wet, wrap him in a blanket, put him in a heated car, and go to the vet quickly.

If your vet is more than 30 minutes away or if your pet's temperature has dropped below 90°F within the past 30 minutes, however, you should apply an external heat source like a hot-water bottle wrapped in a towel. Don't wait for his temperature to increase to 99°F to leave—just begin rewarming, then be on your way. (See "For Moderate Hypothermia," below, for rewarming instructions.) Take hot-water bottles and towels to wrap them, along with some hot water in thermoses to refill the bottles, if possible, and continue the rewarming process in the car while someone else drives you to the vet.

Rub Karo syrup on your pet's gums. Pets with severe hypothermia are at risk for shock. They may also have very low blood sugar levels. It may be helpful to try to raise them while you're on the way to the vet. The easiest way to do this is to rub a drop or two of Karo syrup or honey on his gums. The honey or Karo will be absorbed through the tissues and may raise blood sugar almost instantly. However, your pet may be too cold to have enough circulation for it to be well-absorbed. (For more information on shock, see page 333.)

For Moderate Hypothermia (body temperature between 90° and 95°F)

Warm your pet, then go to the vet. Wrap hot-water bottles in towels and apply them to your pet's groin, the sides of his neck, and his armpits. These are areas where large blood vessels are near the surface. The heat will warm the blood, which in turn warms the body from the inside out. You can substitute plastic water containers or soda bottles for the hot-water bottles, but don't apply them directly to the body. Keep two or three layers of towels between your pet and the heat source to prevent burns. You can also fill a thick sock with uncooked rice and mi-crowave it for a couple of minutes. Let it sit for at least 5 minutes so the heat is distributed evenly, and be sure to check the temperature all over the sock so it won't burn your pet.

After he is warmed up and his temperature has gone back to 99°F, your pet needs to be checked out by your veterinarian the same day. However, if his temperature does not start increasing within 30 to 45 minutes of starting the rewarming process, go to the emergency clinic immediately. Take along some hot-water bottles wrapped in thick towels and continue your rewarming efforts during the ride.

For Mild Hypothermia (body temperature between 95° and 99°F)

Warm your pet. Take your pet inside and turn up the heat. If you can't get someplace warm, try to put him inside your clothing to share your body heat. Keeping him warm will allow his body to conserve energy and begin recovering.

Take his temperature. Use a rectal thermometer every 10 to 15 minutes to see how serious the hypothermia is and whether he's recovering. Dogs and cats with mild hypothermia usually recover quickly.

Dry him off. Dry his fur thoroughly, either with towels or with a hair dryer set on low and held about 12 inches away. Keep the dryer moving around your pet's coat while you warm him—holding it motionless could burn him. Don't submerge him in warm water, because water evaporates, removing heat in the process.

Wrap your pet up. Wrap him loosely in a blanket or towel, preferably one that's been slightly warmed in the dryer. Shivering is a good sign because it means that the body is responsive and trying to warm itself. Keep him covered until the shivering stops.

Feed your pet warm liquids. Fill his water bowl with warm water or, better still, warm chicken broth. Warm liquids heat the body from the inside and also help stimulate the body's natural warming mechanism. Chicken broth provides more calories to fuel the process.

Check his temperature again. Continue the rewarming process until your pet's temperature is back to 99°F. Most cases of hypothermia, even the mild type, are the result of accidents involving cold water or are caused by exposure. If your pet's temperature has not increased within 30 to 45 minutes of starting the rewarming process, don't wait; take him to the veterinarian immediately.

🥫 SPECIAL SITUATIONS

If you suspect a stopped heart: Be prepared to perform artificial respiration if your pet stops breathing and CPR if his heart stops beating. First, determine if your pet's heart has stopped by taking his pulse and checking his reflexes. Press your fingertips into the crease where the inside of the thigh meets the body and feel for the pulse in the femoral artery, which is very big and near the surface. (This technique is illustrated on page 13.) If you can't feel a pulse, try

listening or feeling for the heartbeat. Put your ear or hand flat against your pet's left side directly behind the elbow. If you can't detect a heartbeat, check his reflexes for responsiveness. (See page 124 for more information.)

If his heart is beating but he is not breathing: In this case, you need to give artificial respiration. Close your pet's mouth with your hands to seal his lips, then put your mouth completely over his nose, give two quick breaths, and watch for his chest to expand. Give 15 to 20 breaths a minute until he starts breathing again or until you reach the animal hospital. As he warms up, he's more likely to begin breathing on his own. (This technique is illustrated on page 20.)

If your pet's heart has stopped and he's not breathing: You'll need to perform chest compressions along with artificial respiration. If you are by yourself, give five chest compressions alternating with one breath, compressing the chest by 25 to 50%. The goal is 80 to 100 compressions and 15 to 20 breaths per minute until your pet revives or until you reach medical help. If you have someone there to help, one person gives five compressions, then pauses for the other to give a breath.

To give chest compressions to cats or small dogs, cup your hand over the point of the chest just behind the elbows. Squeeze firmly in a "coughlike" manner, pressing in about $1/2$ inch, with your thumb on one side and fingers on the other. Lay a larger dog on his side, then place one hand on top of the other on his chest. Use

Some Like It Cold

If you're planning to get a dog and are interested in a breed that can withstand long winter hikes, you'll want to take a look at the northern sled dogs, such as Alaskan malamutes, Samoyeds, and Siberian huskies. These are dogs for whom icy weather and towering snowbanks are as comfortable as the beach in July.

The secret lies in their coats. They have rough, weather-resistant outer coats that shed water. Underneath are thick, woolly undercoats that provide great insulation. The woolly coats even extend between the toes and the paw pads, acting like furry snowshoes.

Despite their cold-weather advantages, sled dogs aren't perfect for all people and places. For one thing, they suffer mightily in the heat—and for sled dogs, anything over 65°F is a little warm. When these dogs are doing what they love best—running in the snow—they can eat four times more than other dogs. But even they need to be acclimated to cold temperatures. Although they'll do better than average dogs, they need to build up their endurance if they are going to be outside for long periods of time.

both hands to compress firmly. (This technique is illustrated on page 21.)

 FOLLOW-UP CARE

■ Pets who have had hypothermia once have a high risk of getting it again because damage to the body caused by extreme cold reduces its ability to stay warm. They may need a little bit of help keeping their temperatures in a safe range.

■ Dogs and cats who lived outside comfortably when they were young should be indoors during cold weather as they get older. Older pets tend to have less fat and muscle—tissues that are essential for insulation and producing internal heat.

■ Pets with short fur should wear sweaters when spending time outside.

■ If your pet normally lives indoors but will be spending a lot of time outside, veterinarians recommend giving him small tastes of cold weather before winter descends. He should start spending 2 to 3 hours a day outside, beginning in early September.

■ Dogs and cats need places where they can escape from wind and rain. Shelters should be insulated and raised off the ground, with the door facing away from the direction of prevailing winds. There should be a flexible cover over the door to block drafts. Small shelters are better than big ones because dogs and cats prefer cozy dens and because small spaces stay warmer since they hold body heat. Cover the floor with blankets, straw, or cedar chips. These allow your pet to burrow into the bedding and make a cocoon-like nest that can be more easily warmed by their bodies. Check the shelter's temperature periodically—it shouldn't dip below 40°F.

■ Pets always need fresh water to generate internal body heat. Eating snow isn't a good substitute because it chills the body. Some pet-supply stores sell heated water bowls with automatic thermostats, which ensure that the water won't freeze.

■ Dogs and cats need more calories in winter because their metabolisms run a lot faster to keep them warm. They need about 7½ percent more food for each 10-degree drop in temperature. That means that pets who spend a lot of time outside need about 30 percent more calories during the coldest months. One way to increase calories is to add about a tablespoon of fat or vegetable oil to each cup of dry food. Or give your pet puppy or kitten foods, which are very high in calories, until the weather starts to warm.

THE BEST APPROACH

Safe Heating Pad

Heat is nature's great healer. Heating pads and heat lamps are effective, but they require close supervision. In fact, veterinarians don't usually recommend using electrical sources of heat because they can burn your pet's skin quickly. This is especially true for pets with hypothermia because they burn very easily. Veterinarians prefer other, gentler sources of heat, like hot-water bottles. But even hot-water bottles can burn your pet if the water in them is too hot. Test the temperature before using a hot-water bottle on your pet by holding it against your skin—it should feel comfortably warm. Wrap it in thick towels before applying.

One product you can try is the Lectro-Kennel. Designed for keeping newborns warm and also for postsurgical recovery, this is an all-purpose, low-temperature heating pad that comes in small, medium, and large sizes. Wrap the pad in thick towels, then apply to pets with mild hypothermia. It's also good for warming pet beds and shelters.

Advisors

■ Shane Bateman, D.V.M., D.V.Sc., is a veterinarian board certified in the American College of Emergency and Critical Care Medicine and assistant professor of emergency and critical care medicine at Ohio State University College of Veterinary Medicine in Columbus.

■ Sandra Sawchuk, D.V.M., is clinical instructor at the University of Wisconsin School of Veterinary Medicine in Madison.

Impetigo

CALL YOUR VET: **IF NEEDED**

MEDICINE CHEST

2.5% benzoyl peroxide
  shampoo (Oxy 5) or
  antiseptic liquid
  soap (Betadine Skin
  Cleanser)
Warm water
Washcloth
Towel
Cup
Antibiotic ointment
  (Neosporin)
Needleless syringe or
  eyedropper
Oatmeal conditioner or
  oatmeal
Cotton sock

Also called puppy pyoderma, this skin infection usually affects dogs who are from 3 weeks to 1 year old. It's rarely dangerous, and it's considered a nuisance disease. Cats aren't affected.

Puppies with impetigo develop red pimples that may break open and turn pussy or crusty. They're usually found on the bare tummy or hairless inner thighs. The pimples differ from abscesses, which are larger, deeper in the skin, and fluid-filled, and they move when gently touched. Crowded, dirty, or stressful surroundings may make it more likely for pups to develop impetigo. Most cases of impetigo are easy to treat and cure at home with simple first aid.

DO THIS NOW

Bathe your puppy. Soap and water clear up mild cases of impetigo faster than anything else. You can use a 2.5% benzoyl peroxide shampoo like Oxy 5 or an antiseptic liquid soap like Betadine Skin Cleanser, but avoid "people shampoo" because it can dry out and irritate the skin. Shampoo your puppy three times a week. If the impetigo worsens or if your puppy isn't better after 1 to 2 weeks, see your veterinarian. Moderate to severe cases of impetigo (when the puppy has red pimples covering the majority of the affected area and is bothered by the pimples or is in pain) also require a visit to your vet.

To bathe your puppy, fill the sink or a basin with warm water about puppy temperature (101°F, which will feel comfortably warm on your wrist). Lower your puppy into the water and dip water over his body with a cup, holding his head up so that you avoid his face and don't get water in his ears or eyes. Once he's wet, lift

Keep your pup's face dry by pouring water over him with a cup.

Make sure that you rinse your pup thoroughly, especially his belly. Use lukewarm water and support him firmly.

him out onto a towel or set him in the empty "dry" side of a twin sink.

Gently soap up his body, paying particular attention to the tummy area. Use a washcloth to clean his face. After your pup is sudsy and clean, rinse him by setting him back in the warm water and using the cup to dip and pour clean water over his body. It's very important to get off all the soap. When you're sure that he's squeaky clean, rinse him once more with warm water from the faucet. Be sure to check the temperature on your wrist before the second rinse.

Wrap your wet pup in a towel and blot off as much water as possible. Puppies have trouble regulating their body temperatures and can easily become chilled, so it's important to keep him in a warm room, away from drafts, until he's dry.

Launder your puppy's bed. Wash your puppy's bedding in hot water to get rid of infectious material that might cause reinfection.

Apply an ointment. Put an antibiotic ointment like Neosporin on the sores on your puppy's tummy twice a day. Play with him for a few minutes after the application to be sure that it is absorbed before he tries to lick it off. If he does lick it, don't panic—it won't hurt him. Just reapply the medicine.

FOLLOW-UP CARE

■ If you bathe your puppy every day for 5 days in a row, a mild case of impetigo should go away. Use either 2.5% benzoyl peroxide shampoo, which cleans deep in the hair follicles, or an antiseptic liquid soap.

■ Apply antibiotic ointment to the skin sores on your puppy's belly after each bath.

■ Change your puppy's bedding every day or wash it after each use. Bacteria from open sores can easily contaminate the fabric and reinfect the skin.

■ Several kinds of bacteria may cause impetigo, and if bathing doesn't cure the problem, medical tests can determine the best antibiotic to use to clear it up. Usually, a 2-week course of antibiotics prescribed by the vet will cure the infection. With small puppies, a liquid medicine usually works best. Use a needleless syringe or eyedropper and squirt the medicine into his cheek. Then hold his mouth closed until you see him swallow. (This technique is illustrated on page 30.)

THE BEST APPROACH

Oatmeal Fur Conditioners

Bathing your puppy to keep him clean is the most important step in healing skin infections like impetigo. But repeated shampooing can also dry out tender puppy skin, and the inflammation can lead to other skin problems.

Groomers recommend following baths with a skin and coat conditioner, such as Francodex Oatmeal Creme Rinse, to counteract the drying effect of the soap. One of the best ingredients to look for is oatmeal, a natural substance known to soothe skin problems. But if you don't have a commercial oatmeal conditioner, you can also help your puppy by putting oatmeal in the final rinse water. Just fill a cotton sock with the dry cereal, run the water through the sock, then use the oatmeal water.

Advisors

■ Nina Deyer, V.M.D., is a veterinarian at Greenfield Veterinary Associates in Mantua, New Jersey.
■ Emily King, D.V.M., is a veterinarian at Kryder Veterinary Clinic in Granger, Indiana.

Incontinence

CALL YOUR VET: **IF NEEDED**

Pets may urinate in the house to get your attention if they are upset, the litter box is dirty, or they aren't walked often enough, but these are behavior problems and are not related to incontinence. Urinary incontinence is caused by a physical problem. It is common in older spayed dogs because the decline in the hormone estrogen causes a decrease in control of the sphincter muscle that gives them bladder control.

Incontinence happens when the pet is relaxed, tired, or sleeping: She dribbles urine and doesn't know it. Any pet can develop the problem, but large and giant-breed dogs, obese dogs, and dogs with docked tails, especially Old English sheepdogs, Rottweilers, Dobermans, and weimaraners, have the highest incidence.

Other causes of incontinence, especially in cats, are urinary tract infections or blockages. (For more information about urinary blockage, see page 402.) Intact male dogs can develop problems as a result of prostate disease, and neutering usually cures these cases. Incontinence can also be a sign of metabolic disease. Medical attention is necessary to determine the cause and best treatment for the problem, but first aid can relieve some of the symptoms.

DO THIS NOW

Limit her water. In many cases, incontinence isn't a problem of control but of capacity. It happens when your pet drinks too much water before bedtime and can't contain herself until her morning bathroom trip. You can often reduce or eliminate nighttime leakage or dribbling simply by picking up the water bowl 2 hours before bedtime and making sure that your pet goes outside right before you turn in for the night.

FIRST ALERT

Kidney Failure

One of the earliest signs of kidney failure in cats and dogs is incontinence, when the kidneys lose their ability to concentrate the urine effectively and recapture as much water as they normally would, which results in an increased volume of urine to eliminate. It's estimated that about 10 percent of dogs and up to 30 percent of cats over the age of 15 suffer from chronic kidney disease. Unfortunately, you probably won't see signs of chronic disease, such as increased urination and thirst, until the kidneys have lost up to 70 percent of their function.

The signs of acute kidney disease come on suddenly and are severe. In addition to increasing her intake and output of water, the pet becomes weak and depressed, loses weight, and can develop mouth sores and ammonia-scented breath. Signs of chronic kidney disease (which are the same as signs for acute kidney disease), on the other hand, come on very gradually. Drugs, supportive care like fluid therapy, therapeutic diets, and sometimes kidney transplants are treatment options. In either case, take your pet to the vet right away.

Keep her clean. Dogs who suffer from incontinence are usually elderly and may also be arthritic. Older pets aren't always flexible enough to be able to keep themselves clean or to move away from their "accidents," so their skin may be irritated by prolonged contact with urine. This problem, called urine scald, is a kind of canine diaper rash that causes red, irritated skin around the vulva, penis, or flanks that looks like a burn. The best way to prevent it is to keep your pet clean by swabbing off any urine with a clean, wet cloth. Usually, your dog will need to be washed off first thing in the morning.

Set up a barrier. To protect the skin from urine scald and soothe inflamed skin, after cleaning the area, smooth on a protective cream like Desitin.

Try an antibiotic ointment. When urine scald is already a problem, after you've cleaned the area, apply an antibiotic ointment like Neosporin. It will soothe the skin and also help prevent secondary infections.

Eliminate parasites. Incontinent pets can develop sores from urine scald that attract flies during the summer months. The flies lay eggs in the sores, and the eggs hatch into maggots. If you see these white worms infesting your pet, you'll need to clean out the wound and get rid of the maggots. The easiest way is to submerge the affected area in warm, soapy water. When the maggots come to the surface to keep from drowning, you can pick them out. (For more information about maggots, see page 284.) Then rinse your pet and dry her thoroughly.

Use plastic and pads. Incontinence is often a problem of older pets, and the best you can do is provide protection for your pet and for your carpet or floor. Put down a sheet of plastic, then spread disposable diapers on the plastic. Products like Depend Undergarments work well to catch urine. They not only absorb the liquid, they also pull it away from your pet, reducing the chance of urine scald.

FOLLOW-UP CARE

■ Your vet may prescribe phenylpropanolamine, or PPA (Propagest), which you'll have to give your pet a few times a day to increase the strength of the sphincter in the urethra and help promote urine control.

■ Estrogen treatment helps some female dogs, who need to take the medicine for the rest of their lives. Diethylstilbestrol (DES) or Premarin is given in tiny doses in a specific regimen prescribed by your vet. Since DES can have some serious side effects, it must be regulated by your veterinarian.

■ When the cause of the incontinence is a bladder or urinary tract infection, you'll probably need to give your pet antibiotics for up to 3 weeks. The type of antibiotic depends on the bacteria that caused the infection; usually it's dogs more often than cats who have cystitis caused by bacteria.

■ Keep your pet and her resting area clean by using absorbent pads.

■ Continue to monitor your pet's urinary habits and rinse off any urine as needed. It's a good idea to check your pet at least twice a day, especially in the morning when she first wakes up. Use an antibiotic ointment or a protective cream as needed on any inflamed areas of skin.

THE BEST APPROACH

Doggy Diapers

Incontinence in older spayed dogs tends to be a management problem—keeping your pet clean and comfortable and protecting your carpet and furniture. Doggy diapers are an excellent way to minimize the mess. Canine sanitary pads and protective pants like Pet Bloomers, which are often used for females in heat to protect against soiling, can also be useful for incontinence. Pet Bloomers fit over the dog's tail and fasten with Velcro; they are machine washable and are available at pet-supply stores. The cost varies depending on the size of the dog, with medium to large sizes running around $20.

Advisors

■ Tracy Ridgeway, D.V.M., is a veterinarian at Riverview Animal Clinic in Clarkston, Washington.

■ Anna E. Worth, V.M.D., is a veterinarian at West Mountain Animal Hospital in Shaftsbury, Vermont.

■ Sophia Yin, D.V.M., is a veterinarian in Davis, California, and author of *The Small Animal Veterinary Nerdbook*.

Ingrown Nails

CALL YOUR VET: **IF NEEDED**

The toenails of many dogs and cats are naturally curved, and they grow all the time. Outdoor cats and dogs may wear down their nails, but pets who spend most or all of their time indoors don't walk and run enough to wear off the excess. If nails aren't kept trimmed, the growing nail can be damaged and split. (For more information about nail damage, see page 298.) And sometimes, the nail just curves around and grows into the flesh.

Any toenail can become ingrown, but often, the ingrown nail is the dewclaw—the "thumb" toe that's high on the side of the pet's leg. That's because it doesn't touch the ground, so it has no normal wear. Also, the long fur of some pets can hide the overlong nail until it becomes a problem. The problem is more common in toy breed dogs like Chihuahuas and in longhaired older cats because their toenails tend to thicken and grow faster.

A pet with an ingrown toenail often limps on the affected paw, holds it up, and licks it a lot, or even leaves bloody paw prints. Ingrown nails are very painful, and in severe cases, your pet may need to be sedated by your veterinarian before the problem can be treated. But often, first aid can take care of the nail.

DO THIS NOW

Restrain your pet. Ingrown nails are very painful, and your pet probably won't want you to touch the injured foot. You'll need somebody to help restrain him while you take care of the problem. It's easiest to work on small dogs and cats on a tabletop. You can gently grasp the loose skin at the back of the neck with one hand, capture the hind feet with the other hand, and stretch your pet out on his side.

For a larger dog, kneel on the floor next to him with one arm under and around the dog's neck and the other under and around his chest so that you're hugging him to your chest. (These techniques are illustrated on page 18.)

Consider muzzling. Some pets may need to be muzzled if you don't have an extra pair of hands to help restrain them. With long-nosed dogs, a length of fabric—like a necktie or scarf—will work in a pinch. Make a loop, slip it over your dog's nose, and tighten the knot. Loop the ends beneath your dog's chin and make another knot. Then bring the two ends back over the neck and tie them in a knot or bow behind his ears. (This technique is illustrated on page 17.) A small pet can be contained by a towel or pillowcase, with just the affected foot exposed.

Use pet nail trimmers. The scissors-type nail trimmers like the Millers Forge brand are the best choice to treat ingrown toenails. You can get them from pet-supply stores or catalogs. (These clippers are illustrated on page 297.) Otherwise, very sharp, blunt-tipped scissors or human nail clippers may be all right for small pets. But don't use human clippers on larger dogs; they won't do the job correctly.

Cut the claw just above where it jabs into the pad. (Be careful not to cut the quick; its location is described under "Follow-up Care.") Be prepared for your pet to flinch, because the movement of the nail will hurt. Leave enough to be able to grasp it.

Be gentle. Grasp the cut-off piece of exposed nail that's protruding from the pad. You may be able to use your fingers. If not, try blunt-tipped tweezers or needle-nose pliers. Pull out the part that's stuck in the pad with a slow, gentle motion.

Clean bleeding paws. Don't be surprised if the pad bleeds. This will actually help clean out the wound, so a small amount of bleeding is fine. Wash the paw with mild antiseptic liquid soap like Betadine Skin Cleanser and warm water to keep the wound clean and help prevent infection.

✏ FOLLOW-UP CARE

■ Trim back the rest of the overlong nail. Trim it a little at a time every few days, cutting just the very tip. If you cut too high the first time, you'll hit the quick, which looks like a pink or reddish pink miniature claw inside transparent or pink nails. The quick contains blood vessels, and cutting into it will make the nail bleed. This is extremely painful, and you will never get near that foot again, which is why it's best to trim less nail more often. The quick will recede as the nail is trimmed. Especially in black nails, since you can't see the quick, it's best to just take a little bit off the end of the nail, about ⅛ inch, once or twice a week. Once you get the nails to

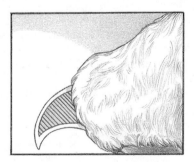

It's easy to see the dark line of the quick in a light-colored nail. The quick is the part with blood vessels, so make sure that you don't cut into it when you're trimming your pet's claws, or they'll bleed.

a reasonable length, be sure to routinely trim them every couple of weeks to prevent a repeat of the problem.

■ Often, an ingrown nail causes swelling and inflammation in the pad. Soak the affected foot in warm water to which you've added a couple of tablespoons of Betadine Solution or Epsom salts. This not only keeps it clean but also soothes the pain and can help prevent infections or help an existing infection heal. Purchase Betadine Solution from the vet or from pet-supply stores in a strength of 0.01 to 0.1%. If you purchase higher-strength Betadine, dilute it with distilled water until it's the color of weak tea, or call your vet for complete dilution instructions. If you're using Epsom salts, dilute them by adding 1 cup of the salts to 2 gallons of water. Soak the foot two or three times a day for 10 minutes, or as long as your pet will hold still.

■ Watch for swelling and continued limping, along with a fever and discharge of pus, which could indicate infection. See the veterinarian if you suspect infection. Your pet will probably need oral antibiotics. Usually, you'll need to give pills at least once a day for 7 to 10 days, depending on the type of medicine and the severity of the infection. To give your pet a pill, encircle his nose with your fingers and press your fingertips against his gums, right behind the long canine teeth. This will prompt him to open his mouth, and when he does, place the pill on the back of his tongue. Close his mouth and stroke his throat until he swallows. (This technique is illustrated on page 30.)

■ Dogs especially may be bothered by the injured pad as it heals, and they often lick and chew at the place until their attentions make it worse. Put a collar restraint called an Elizabethan collar on your pet until the pad has begun to heal—usually, 2 to 3 days is enough.

Advisors

■ Bernadine Cruz, D.V.M., is a veterinarian at Laguna Hills Animal Hospital in California.

■ Jean C. Hofve, D.V.M., is a veterinarian and Companion Animal Program coordinator for the Animal Protection Institute in Sacramento.

■ Jeffrey Werber, D.V.M., is a veterinarian at Century Veterinary Group in Los Angeles.

Jaw Entrapment

CALL YOUR VET: **IF NEEDED**

It doesn't happen often, but dogs can get their lower jaws stuck when they chew on bones or other objects. Most often, young pets who don't know any better try to chew metal fencing to get out of a kennel and get their teeth and lower jaws trapped. At other times, they'll manage to thread the hollow part of a marrow bone over the lower jaw, where their lower eyeteeth prevent it from coming back off.

Jaw entrapment isn't a medical emergency, but it's upsetting for dogs. They may become frantic, and they can hurt themselves trying to get free. If a dog is very upset, the veterinarian needs to make a house call, since the dog may need sedation before she can be helped. But often, first aid will take care of the problem.

DO THIS NOW

Calm your pet. Speak softly and stroke your dog to calm her down. With her jaw trapped, it will be difficult for your dog to bite you, but use her behavior as a guide and don't make any sudden movements. As long as she's agitated and struggling, there's nothing you can do to help her. And an upset pet will not only make any injury worse but could also hurt you.

Lubricate her chin. Try greasing up your dog's chin with globs of a lubricant like petroleum jelly or K-Y Jelly. If you don't have them, try margarine or cooking oil to lubricate the area. This can not only help make the jaw slippery so that it slides out of the fencing or bone more easily but also helps protect the skin from scrapes. And it's nontoxic, in case the dog gets any in her mouth.

FIRST ALERT

Tooth Damage

Dogs who chew fences, rocks, or hard bones are prone to wearing down or breaking their teeth. Most of the time, if the fracture affects only the tooth enamel, there's no treatment necessary. But if the break reaches down into the dental pulp—the part that contains the living blood vessels—the tooth damage will be painful for your dog, and you'll need to take her to the vet. She may develop a swollen jaw on the affected side if the root becomes abscessed. And often, she'll drool and refuse to eat. The tooth will need to either have a root canal or be pulled. (For more information about tooth damage, see page 393.)

Use pliers if necessary. If you aren't able to slip off the object with your fingers, you may be able to pry it off with pliers.

 SPECIAL SITUATIONS

If your pet is trapped by a fence: If your dog's jaws are stuck in a wire or chain-link fence, use pliers to pry the opening wider apart. If that doesn't work, you may need to cut the metal with wire clippers to get your dog out. Cut a wire that is close to, but not against, your dog's jaw so that you can free her.

If a bone is wedged on the jaw: Most of the time, a bone will be caught so snugly on the jaw that it won't easily slip off and must be cut apart. Bones can get wedged in a number of places, but most commonly, a round, narrow bone slips over the lower jaw and becomes stuck behind the lower teeth. Wire cutters work on small bones, but you'll need much larger cable cutters for big bones. A wedged bone is usually not life-threatening unless it's obstructing breathing by making the jaw swell. If you can't remove the bone after one or two attempts, take your pet to the vet.

Have a second person restrain your pet before you begin so that she won't hurt herself if she starts to move as you begin to cut the bone. Fit the cutters to the narrowest edge of the bone. You don't have to try to cut through the whole thing at once—cutting just a small amount at a time may be enough to shatter one side so that it will slide off your dog's jaw. Be sure to snip quickly, and don't prolong the effort.

 FOLLOW-UP CARE

■ For scrapes on the inside of the mouth, dilute an antiseptic solution like Betadine Solution with distilled water until it's the color of weak tea, then flush the area. You can use a turkey baster, needleless syringe, or even a squirt gun to direct the liquid against the sore place in the mouth. It's best to have your dog lie on her side so that the liquid runs back out the other side of her mouth and she doesn't swallow it. One thorough rinse will probably be enough—dog saliva actually has some antibacterial properties, so unless the bone was stuck there for days, infection probably won't be a problem.

■ Clean scrapes or sores on the outside of the jaw with soap and water. You can use an antiseptic liquid soap like Nolvasan or Betadine Skin Cleanser on the outside. If you don't have either, plain hand soap works fine. Just be sure to rinse off all the soap, then gently pat dry.

■ Apply an antibacterial ointment like Neosporin four times a day. Since dogs often lick off the medicine pretty rapidly, and since the ointment is safe to ingest, more is better. Use the ointment until the sore has completely healed, usually in about a week.

■ Watch the area for any swelling or for worsening of the sores. Give your vet a call for advice—he may tell you to bring your pet in for a checkup.

■ If a piece of bone or metal fence caused more than a scrape or shallow cut—a stabbing wound, for instance—your dog may need stitches. After visiting the vet, keep the suture site clean by dabbing it with a bit of sterile saline contact lens solution on a gauze pad.

■ Deeper wounds will need oral antibiotics from the vet to prevent infection or speed the healing of existing infection. You may need to give a liquid medicine if your dog's mouth is very sore. Tip your dog's head up, insert a needleless syringe or eyedropper into her cheek, squirt in the medicine, and hold her mouth closed until she swallows. (This technique is illustrated on page 30.)

■ If your dog's mouth is very sore, she may need to eat a soft diet at first. You can make a gruel out of her normal food by mixing it in the blender with some low-fat, no-salt chicken broth. Usually, the gruel diet is necessary for only 2 to 3 days.

Advisors

■ Lorrie Bartloff, D.V.M., is a veterinarian at Three Point Veterinary Clinic in Elkhart, Indiana.

■ Clint Chastain, D.V.M., is a veterinarian at Preston Road Animal Hospital in Dallas.

■ Laura Solien, D.V.M., is a veterinarian at Maplecrest Animal Hospital in Goshen, Indiana.

Jaw Swelling

CALL YOUR VET: **SAME DAY**

The number one cause of jaw swelling is trauma, when a dog or cat bangs his jaw by falling from a tree, running into something, or perhaps being hit by a car. The swelling could be simply a bruise, or it could be something as serious as a fracture. (For more information about fractures, see page 212.)

The second most common cause of jaw swelling is an abscess, caused by anything from a bite wound to tooth disease. But a pet's jaw can also swell from allergic reactions to insect stings or even from poisonous snakebites. (For more information about snakebites, see page 350.)

When your pet also acts depressed and lethargic, refuses to eat, and is in pain, he'll need medical attention as soon as possible. Dogs or cats who act normal otherwise should be seen within a day or so if the swelling doesn't go away. First aid may be all that's necessary for bruises or minor allergic reactions.

DO THIS NOW

Cool it. If your pet has sudden swelling as a result of trauma, apply a cold pack or cold compress to relieve the pain and help bring down the swelling. First, place a cold, wet washcloth on the swollen area. Then, apply a commercial cold pack, a plastic bag of ice, or even a bag of frozen peas or corn, which will conform most easily to the shape of your pet's jaw. Apply the cold pack or ice for 10 to 30 minutes several times a day until the swelling goes away.

Examine your pet's facial area. Look for punctures or wounds, which often cause swelling from an abscess. If the swelling feels hot or is infected, take your pet to the veterinarian.

Feed him soft food. Pets with swollen jaws have trouble eating regular food. Feed a soft diet like a canned commercial food or meat baby food until the problem can be treated. You can turn a dry diet into a soft one by mixing the food in the blender with low-fat, no-salt broth.

FIRST ALERT

Mandibular Osteopathy

Young terrier dogs, especially West Highland white terriers, Scottish terriers, Cairn terriers, and Boston terriers, can inherit a tendency to develop painful swollen jaws that make it hard for them to open their mouths. Some Labrador retrievers, Great Danes, and Doberman pinschers also seem prone to mandibular osteopathy, in which excess bone material is deposited in the joints of the lower jaw. The first signs are drooling and reluctance to eat. When you try to open your dog's mouth, he'll cry out in pain.

Treatment includes several months of steroid medication. It's important to start treatment as soon as you notice a problem. If your dog is reluctant to eat, drools, and is in pain when he tries to open his mouth, take him to the veterinarian immediately. In extreme cases, your dog also may act very depressed and have a high fever (over 104°F). The vet will probably take x-rays to confirm that it is mandibular osteopathy, and then begin treatment.

 SPECIAL SITUATIONS

If your dog snaps at a bee or your cat is stung by a wasp: Stings can cause the jaw to swell. You can give an over-the-counter antihistamine like Benadryl to lessen the allergic reaction. Liquid Benadryl usually comes in a dose of 12.5 milligrams per teaspoon; pills are usually 25 milligrams each. Pets will need 1 milligram per pound of body weight every 6 to 8 hours. That means a 10-pound cat or dog should get about ¾ teaspoon of liquid or half a pill. This will help reduce the swelling, and it also tends to make pets sleepy so that they aren't as bothered by the painful reaction. (For more information about bee and wasp stings, see page 79.)

For acnelike skin infections in cats: Cats often get these infections on their chins, which can cause swelling. Clean the area once a day with warm water or 3% hydrogen peroxide on a cloth or cotton ball. You can also use a product that contains 1 or 1.5% benzoyl peroxide (available from the veterinarian), which works well to flush out the stopped-up hair follicles. This type of medication is best for long-term treatment because over-the-counter preparations usually are 5% or stronger and can cause more irritation of the cat's sensitive skin. Be sure to rinse off the medicated wash, or it can be very drying and increase the inflammation.

 FOLLOW-UP CARE

■ Whenever infection is diagnosed, as in tooth abscess, skin abscess, or jaw infection, the vet will prescribe antibiotics. It can be painful, though,

Feline Fat Chin

Cats can develop swelling at the point of the chin. The tissue swells with fluid to enormous proportions. It's usually bright red and looks like the cat has hurt himself. In fact, it's a skin irritation or inflammation that may be related to the eosinophilic granuloma complex, a group of mysterious skin diseases that affect some cats.

Veterinarians aren't sure what causes fat chin. Unlike other types of swelling, this swelling probably can't be reduced by using a cold compress. It usually can be treated fairly easily by the vet, however, with cortisone injections.

to lever your cat's or dog's sore jaw open to give pills, so liquid medicine is often prescribed. You can gently insert a needleless syringe or eye-dropper into your pet's cheek, even without opening his mouth, and squirt in the medicine. (This technique is illustrated on page 30.)

■ Pets with sore jaws won't want to eat, but they do best when given soft or liquid diets that are easy to lap up and don't require chewing. If the jaw was broken, your pet has probably had surgery to repair it. (Signs of a broken jaw include holding the mouth open, presence of blood in the mouth, an asymmetrical face, and pain when opening the mouth.) Your veterinarian will give you instructions on how to feed your pet while his jaw heals.

Advisors

■ Dawn Crandell, D.V.M., is a veterinarian at the Veterinary Emergency Clinic of York Region in Aurora, Ontario, Canada.

■ Emily King, D.V.M., is a veterinarian at Kryder Veterinary Clinic in Granger, Indiana.

■ Denise Petryk, D.V.M., is a veterinarian at Puget Sound Veterinary Medical Referral Center in Tacoma, Washington.

■ Drew Weigner, D.V.M., is a veterinarian at The Cat Doctor in Atlanta.

Jellyfish Stings

CALL YOUR VET: **IF NEEDED**

MEDICINE CHEST

Petroleum jelly
Rubber gloves
Rubbing alcohol
Sticky tape
Sand
Towel
Antihistamine (Benadryl)
Baking soda
Cool water
Cold, wet washcloth
Cold pack or compress
Towel
Hot pack or compress

The warm, salty waters of the East, West, and Gulf Coasts and the Tidewater areas like the Chesapeake Bay are home to a variety of boneless sea creatures collectively referred to as jellyfish. They can travel singly or in schools, and the "bell" of the body—called the medusa—sprouts multiple tentacles that contain millions of microscopic stinging cells, called nematocysts. These stinging cells inject toxins, which paralyze prey so that the jellyfish can capture it in its tentacles. These cells are not controlled by the jellyfish but simply react whenever contact is made with any solid object, even a swimming human or dog.

Dogs who swim in jellyfish-inhabited waters need some protection. Spread petroleum jelly on any exposed skin, including the footpads, nose leather, tummy, testicles, and eye rims, to keep the venom from penetrating to the skin.

Most jellyfish stings are more a nuisance than a danger, but they are painful around the eyes, nose, mouth, feet, or hairless tummy. The skin can turn red and swell or develop hives. (For more information about hives, see page 242.) Despite the discomfort, most jellyfish stings can be treated with first aid.

DO THIS NOW

Wear rubber gloves. If you touch the tentacles of the jellyfish with your bare hands, you could also be stung. If you disturb even bits and pieces of the tentacles, they can release more stinging nematocysts.

Use rubbing alcohol. When the tentacle pieces remain in contact with your pet's skin, brushing them away with a towel or even rinsing them away with water will protect you from stings, but it can prompt a release of even more stinging cells, which can sting your dog many more times. Instead, pour plain rubbing alcohol (70% or more) on the tentacles—this will stabilize the nematocysts and prevent them from triggering more stings.

Try tape. You can also try using sticky tape to remove jellyfish pieces from your dog's fur. Apply the sticky side to the tentacle and when it sticks, lift it off.

Remove remains. If the jellyfish remains are just stuck in the fur and aren't touching skin, pour some sand over them. Or you can use a towel to remove them or pour seawater over them. Don't use fresh water, which releases more toxins.

Give him Benadryl. An over-the-counter antihistamine like Benadryl will help take the edge off the allergic reaction and calm down the swelling in the skin. The liquid form of Benadryl usually comes in a dose of 12.5 milligrams per teaspoon; pills are usually 25 milligrams each. Pets will need 1 milligram per pound of body weight every 6 to 8 hours. That means a 10-pound dog should get about ¾ teaspoon of liquid or half a pill.

Make a baking soda paste. Pack the sting sites with a paste made from baking soda and water to soothe the sting. If your dog suffered multiple stings, add baking soda to cool water and bathe him in the solution, letting him soak for 10 minutes (or as long as he'll hold still).

Alternate cold and heat. Cold compresses— ice wrapped in a cold, wet washcloth—help numb the sting and reduce swelling. Apply them for 10 to 30 minutes. Then, alternate with a towel-covered hot compress—5 minutes on, 5 minutes off until it cools—to bring healing blood back into the area and flush out the poison. Alternate cold and hot packs for 20 minutes.

FOLLOW-UP CARE

■ Once you've taken the steps recommended above, no follow-up care should be necessary. If you're at all unsure, though, check with the vet.

THE BEST APPROACH

Papaya

Jellyfish venom is made of protein and is destroyed by anything that digests or breaks down protein. This principle is what makes meat tenderizer so effective as a home remedy for beestings, since its active ingredient, papain, digests protein. (Meat tenderizer also works for jellyfish stings; you can add a bit of water to make a paste and apply it to the inflamed area.) Papain is derived from papaya, and many people are now using fresh papaya as a more effective remedy for jellyfish stings. Applying a slice of the fresh fruit to a sting relieves the pain instantly. This is especially helpful for dogs who have been stung in the mouth, where a paste or a dab of ammonia won't work.

Advisors

■ E. Murl Bailey Jr., D.V.M., Ph.D., is professor of toxicology at Texas A&M University College of Veterinary Medicine in College Station.

■ Tam Garland, D.V.M., Ph.D., is a veterinarian at Texas A&M University College of Veterinary Medicine in College Station.

■ Grady Hester, D.V.M., is a veterinarian at All Creatures Animal Clinic in Rolesville, North Carolina.

Kneecap Slipping

CALL YOUR VET: **IF NEEDED**

Toy dog breeds often have problems with the kneecap bone slipping out of place because of the way their straight, short legs are designed. Typically, a small dog will run, then hesitate and almost skip, then limp, and then try to stretch the leg backward to relieve the pain. With small dogs, the problem may come and go as the kneecap slips in and out of position.

Larger dogs are not as prone to slipped kneecaps. Instead, they generally have a sudden onset of lameness, which may actually indicate a torn cruciate ligament. These ligaments form an X inside the knee joint and connect the femur (thighbone) with the tibia (the bone below the knee). In fact, large, athletic dogs—such as racing dogs, field dogs, or other dogs who run or exercise daily—can tear the cruciate ligament in the same way that human athletes hurt themselves. This condition also occurs in overweight dogs.

The problem may get worse as the dog ages, and some dogs may need surgery to correct the problem. But many can be managed with home care, and first aid often is all that's needed. You should mention any episodes of slipped kneecap that correct on their own to your vet during your next visit. If your dog, especially if he's large, has any sudden lameness, call your veterinarian right away.

DO THIS NOW

Pop the knee in. Dogs can usually pop the knee back into position if it slips out of place, but sometimes it locks. That's painful, and it prevents normal flexing of the joint. If it happens, you must help return the kneecap to a normal position.

It's best to have a second person pet and talk to your dog and help him relax while you treat the knee. The other person should hold your pet gently but with firm restraint by putting one arm around his neck and the other around his chest. If your dog is in pain or seems agitated,

If your dog's kneecap has popped out of place, have another person restrain your pet while you straighten his leg, place your fingers flat on his kneecap, and push it back into place.

you may want to muzzle him as well. Loop a necktie or panty hose around his nose and knot it on top. Bring the ends under his jaw and tie them again, then tie them behind his head. (This technique is illustrated on page 17.)

To reposition the kneecap, slowly extend the leg out straight, place your fingers on the kneecap, and push it back into place. If your pet has any swelling or pain after you have popped the kneecap back into place, contact the vet.

🩹 FOLLOW-UP CARE

■ For pain, you can give your dog buffered aspirin such as Bufferin at a dose of 10 to 25 milligrams per 2.2 pounds of body weight two or three times a day. For dogs who weigh less than 20 pounds, the vet may prescribe pain medication like carprofen (Rimadyl).

■ When a large dog suffers from a slipped kneecap, chances are that ligaments will eventually tear, and your dog will need surgery. If your dog has had knee surgery for a slipped kneecap or ligament tear, rehabilitation will be necessary at home over a period of 4 weeks to 3 months.

Confine your dog when you bring him home after surgery, and prevent him from running, jumping, or going up or down stairs for the first 2 weeks. If your dog is calm and you don't leave him alone in the house, you may confine him to one floor of your house. But if your dog is very active or will be left alone, it would be best to confine him to a crate. Walk him on a leash so that you can control his movement—if he overdoes it, he could reinjure his knee. Start with short trips to the backyard for the first week. Gentle exercise, like a walk for a block at a time, for the second week will keep the knee flexible as it heals. During the third week, your dog can start walking uphill or swimming to build strength. Gradually increase his activity during the fourth to eighth weeks, until he's back to a full range of exercise. If your dog is obese, your veterinarian will probably put him on a weight-loss plan.

Advisors
■ Peter Davis, D.V.M., is a veterinarian at Pine Tree Veterinary Hospital in Augusta, Maine.
■ Terry Kaeser, D.V.M., is a veterinarian at Goshen Animal Clinic in Goshen, Indiana.
■ Margaret J. Rucker, D.V.M., is a veterinarian at Southwest Virginia Veterinary Services in Lebanon, Virginia.

Leg Swelling

CALL YOUR VET: **IF NEEDED**

MEDICINE CHEST

Cold, wet washcloth
Cold pack or compress
Buffered aspirin
  (Bufferin)
Hot pack or compress
Towels
Bucket
Warm water
Epsom salts
Antihistamine (Ben-
  adryl)

A cat often develops a swollen leg when he's bitten by another cat and the injury becomes infected. Athletic dogs who roam unattended outside, hunting dogs, and performance dogs may strain or sprain a muscle or tendon or develop a hematoma—a collection of blood caused by a broken blood vessel—when a leg is bruised. Dogs also can develop abscesses or cellulitis—an inflammation of the tissue—that makes the leg swell. Often it's caused by being jabbed with a stick that leaves huge splinters in the tissue. Occasionally, a beesting or snakebite will cause leg swelling. And of course, a fractured leg also results in swelling. (For more information about abscesses, see page 60; for beestings, see page 79; for fractures, see page 212; and for snakebites, see page 350.)

Leg swelling can be caused by so many things—even metabolic problems like diabetes—that it's always a good idea to get medical attention. Giant-breed dogs like Great Danes are prone to bone cancers on the legs that swell and are painful. But usually, a sudden swelling of a leg from a bruise, sprain, or minor infection can be easily treated with first aid.

DO THIS NOW

Watch for serious symptoms. You should take your pet to the vet if he won't put any weight on one of his legs, if he's depressed or not acting normally, if he's not eating or drinking well, or if his limp on the swollen leg hasn't improved in 48 hours. He may have a broken leg. He also needs veterinary attention if he has fever along with these symptoms and

no decrease in the swelling in 24 hours. The vet will probably prescribe antibiotics.

Apply a cold compress. A swollen leg and no symptoms other than a slight limp may mean that he has sprained, strained, or bruised the leg, and putting a cold compress on the sore spot may help. That stops the body from releasing

273

FIRST ALERT

Metabolic Disease

When a pet's heart begins to fail, the body isn't able to maintain circulation, and fluid begins to collect in the body. Leg swelling is a common sign of heart failure in dogs, and the swelling can also happen with liver disease. Fluid collects in the lower legs and doesn't circulate back out, causing edema, or swelling in the tissues.

Edema from metabolic disease can develop in only one or two legs, but more often, it affects all four. You can tell that it's edema and not infection simply by pushing your thumb against the swollen tissue—you'll leave a dent in the tissue if it's edema. With longhaired pets, you'll be able to feel rather than see the dent left behind if you continue to gently run your finger over the area.

Leg swelling is just one sign of serious disease. Immediate medical attention is necessary to determine the exact cause before treatment can begin. Your veterinarian may prescribe drugs like furosemide (Lasix) to get rid of the fluid retention and help breathing, as well as medication to help regulate a failing liver, if that's what is causing the problem.

pain-causing chemicals that prompt the swelling and inflammation. Rinse a clean washcloth in cold water and hold it against the injury, then place a cold pack or plastic bag of ice on top of the wet cloth. Do this for 10 to 30 minutes several times a day. A bag of frozen peas or corn works well as a cold pack to mold to the body contours. This also helps numb the sore area.

SPECIAL SITUATIONS

If your dog has arthritis: After you've checked with your vet, you can give buffered aspirin like Bufferin to dogs on a temporary basis to help take the edge off a painful bruise or swollen, painful joints due to arthritis. It's best to give a buffered aspirin product that's less harsh on the stomach, and be sure to give it with food. The usual dose is 10 to 25 milligrams per 2.2 pounds of body weight two or three times a day. Aspirin is also an anti-inflammatory, so it can help bring down the swelling. Do not give aspirin to cats.

If swelling is from an abscess: Leg swellings from abscesses feel hot, and your pet may have a fever. Instead of a cold compress, apply a hot compress to pull blood circulation to the area and help speed healing by bringing the infection to a head. Soak a clean cloth with water as hot as you can stand it, and wring it out. Or use a premade hot pack or hot-water bottle wrapped in a towel. Apply it to the swollen area two to five times a day, 5 minutes on, 5 minutes off until it cools. Do not put a hot pack in the armpits or groin area.

Shifting Fluid

Pets who are dehydrated are often given fluid therapy beneath the skin of the shoulders. Within a short time, the liquid migrates downward and often looks like "water wings"—balloons of liquid on both sides of the body. Sometimes, however, it migrates even farther and can make the legs look swollen. The fluid will be absorbed over the period of an hour or so, and the swelling will go away on its own.

For infections or splinters: When the swelling is on the lower leg and you know it's caused by an infection or a splinter and not trauma, you can fill a bucket with warm water, add Epsom salts, and soak the area. Dissolve 1 cup of the salts in 2 gallons of warm water and have your pet stand in the water for 10 minutes at a time. This helps draw out the infection and is especially helpful to prompt the body to expel splinters that may have caused the swelling.

For allergic reactions: Sometimes a leg will swell from an allergic response to an insect bite or sting, a contact allergy, or food sensitivity. You can give an antihistamine like Benadryl to help counter the inflammation and swelling.

The liquid form of Benadryl usually comes in a dose of 12.5 milligrams per teaspoon; pills are usually 25 milligrams each. Pets will need 1 milligram per pound of body weight every 6 to 8 hours. That means a 10-pound cat or dog should get about ¾ teaspoon of liquid or half a pill. If you're not sure what caused the swelling, a trip to the vet will help sort it out. (For more information on food allergies, see page 190.)

 FOLLOW-UP CARE

■ Leg swelling from any kind of trauma will benefit from cold packs for 10 to 30 minutes several times a day for 2 to 3 days. But after that period, when the swelling has started to go down, switch to warm compresses. You can use a hot-water bottle wrapped in a towel and apply it for up to 20 minutes at a time two or three times a day. The warmth improves circulation, helps heal the damage, and also loosens up tight muscles.

■ Hot packs also work wonders for infections and abscesses. Moist heat, though, is the best choice to help bring the sore to a head and keep the wound draining. You can wrap the swollen leg in a warm, damp towel—5 minutes on, 5 minutes off until it cools—two to five times a day.

Advisors
■ Alvin C. Dufour, D.V.M., is a veterinarian at Dufour Animal Hospital in Elkhart, Indiana.
■ Margaret J. Rucker, D.V.M., is a veterinarian at Southwest Virginia Veterinary Services in Lebanon, Virginia.
■ Drew Weigner, D.V.M., is a veterinarian at The Cat Doctor in Atlanta.
■ Anna E. Worth, V.M.D., is a veterinarian at West Mountain Animal Hospital in Shaftsbury, Vermont.

Lick Sores

CALL YOUR VET: **SAME DAY**

Lick sores—technically called lick granulomas—aren't emergencies, but they're certainly a serious aggravation for dogs. Nearly anything, from a bug bite to a foreign body, or even an allergy or fracture, can cause a lick sore when the discomfort triggers a dog to start the lick cycle. Or a dog may get bored and lick to relieve tension, and it becomes a habit like nail biting in people.

Licking works the same way that scratching does in people—it feels good because it causes the body to release endorphins, natural painkillers made by the brain. It feels so good, in fact, that the dog feels rewarded for licking and won't stop, even when it creates a sore. Lick sores are almost always on the lower leg, which is easy for a dog to reach. It is most common in middle-aged, less active dogs, especially Labrador retrievers, Great Danes, Doberman pinschers, and other large, short-furred breeds. The sores at first look red and shiny, but eventually, the skin becomes thick, hard, and raised.

Lick sores always need medical attention to be properly diagnosed and treated. But first aid can temporarily relieve the discomfort until help is available.

🩹 DO THIS NOW

Muzzle your pet. Do this before anything else, because lick sores can be painful, and your dog could lash out at you when you try to treat him. Tie a loop in a necktie or a length of panty hose, slip it around his muzzle, and tighten the knot. Then bring the ends down under his chin and knot them again. Finally, bring the ends of the fabric behind your dog's ears and tie them. (This technique is illustrated on page 17.) You can control a short-nosed dog like a pug by wrapping him in a towel or pillowcase.

Trim the area. Usually, your dog will have worn off most of the fur around the area by licking. If there's any left near the sore, remove it with a mustache trimmer, electric shaver, blunt scissors, or electric clippers. (This technique is illustrated on page 114.)

Soak and clean the area thoroughly. Sometimes, lick sores are infected or highly susceptible to becoming infected. Use plain soap and water if that's all you have, but an antiseptic liquid soap like Betadine Skin Cleanser is even better. Be sure to rinse thoroughly, then gently pat dry with a soft cloth. It's best to use cool water because that also helps relieve the itching.

Use a cortisone cream. An over-the-counter cream like Cortaid will calm itching and inflammation. You can use it two or three times a day for temporary relief until you see the vet.

Try an antihistamine. An over-the-counter antihistamine like Benadryl may help the itching, but even if it doesn't, it may make your dog sleepy and help keep him from licking the sore so much. Liquid Benadryl usually comes in a dose of 12.5 milligrams per teaspoon; pills are usually 25 milligrams each. Pets will need 1 milligram per pound of body weight every 6 to 8 hours. That means a 10-pound dog should get about ¾ teaspoon of liquid or half a pill.

Collar him. In many cases, the only way to break the lick cycle is to physically restrain your dog from bothering the sore. You can use a cone-shaped Elizabethan collar restraint to keep him from it. Or you can use a cloth wrap, which lets the sore breathe but prevents his tongue from reaching it. A cotton sock works well for lick sores on legs. Slip the sock on and tape it to the fur with adhesive tape or an elastic adhesive bandage like Elastoplast to keep your dog from removing it.

 FOLLOW-UP CARE

■ In many cases, your veterinarian will prescribe medication called synotic-banamine, a combination analgesic and anti-inflammatory that kills the itch and pain and helps break the cycle. Keep your dog from licking until it's absorbed. You can try feeding him a treat or offering a chew toy to keep his mouth busy.

■ If the sore has become infected, you'll probably need to give your dog oral antibiotics for at least 7 days, and possibly for 2 weeks. A dog is pretty easy to pill—just grasp the top of his muzzle and gently press his lips against his teeth on each side, behind the long canine teeth, to prompt him to open. Then pop the pill onto the back of his tongue, close his mouth, and stroke his throat until he swallows. (This technique is illustrated on page 30.)

Advisors
■ Doug McConkey, D.V.M., is a veterinarian at Canyon Creek Pet Hospital in Sherman, Texas.
■ Laura Solien, D.V.M., is a veterinarian at Maplecrest Animal Hospital in Goshen, Indiana.
■ Jeffrey Werber, D.V.M., is a veterinarian at Century Veterinary Group in Los Angeles.

Limping

CALL YOUR VET: **IF NEEDED**

MEDICINE CHEST

Length of fabric or pil-
  lowcase for muz-
  zling
Cold, wet washcloth
Cold pack or
  compress
Buffered aspirin
  (Bufferin)
Hot pack or compress

Limping can indicate a serious injury, such as a leg fracture or dislocation, which occurs when a bone pops out of the joint. (For more information about dislocation, see page 271.) But more often, dogs and cats limp after they sprain or strain their muscles when they overdo exercise, or after they bruise themselves by banging into something. An overweight dog can hurt himself and develop a limp from just walking up the stairs. Even a thorn, nail, splinter, or other object stuck in your pet's paw can cause him to limp.

Limping in cats is most often caused by abscesses from bite wounds, and large-breed dogs can develop limps from hip dysplasia, a condition in which the hip joints don't fit together normally. Older dogs and cats who develop arthritis and painful joints may also limp.

It can be hard to tell where the pain is when a dog or cat limps. The pet will usually hold up or take the weight off the affected leg when standing, and when moving, he will take shorter steps on the sore leg. His head may bob or nod when he attempts to put weight on the sore leg. Fractures, dislocations, and any limp that lasts longer than 24 hours need medical attention. But first aid can relieve the pain of sprains and some joint problems.

🩹 DO THIS NOW

Hold him still. Before doing anything else, have a second person restrain your pet so that you aren't accidentally bitten while you try to treat the sore leg. If you don't have a helper, you can make a homemade muzzle for a long-nosed dog from panty hose or a necktie. Loop the fabric around the dog's nose and tie it on top. Then bring the ends down and tie them beneath the chin. Finally, bring the ends behind the dog's neck and tie them behind his ears. (This technique is illustrated on page 17.) For a cat or flat-faced dog, try putting a pillowcase

Diagnosing a Limp

There are many reasons why your pet may limp. Here are the most common, and how to tell them apart by their symptoms.

Dislocations and fractures cause severe pain, and your pet will refuse to put any weight on the affected leg. The flesh may be bruised and discolored, and the leg may look odd or deformed.

Spinal cord and nerve injuries occur gradually with degeneration or suddenly from trauma, but there is no pain.

Infected areas are very tender and red. They feel hot and often have breaks in the skin from teeth or claws. Your pet's limping grows worse and worse over time, and he'll often have a fever from the infection.

Sprains and strains come on suddenly and often gradually improve even without treatment. Pain is mild, and your pet may still use the leg in a limited way.

Rickettsial diseases can also cause limping. These conditions are transmitted by tick bites.

Lyme disease causes joints to swell, often in more than one leg, and the swelling occurs gradually. Lameness may come and go, but it won't be cured without long-term antibiotic treatment.

Arthritis and other degenerative joint problems develop very gradually, usually with only mild pain and stiffness. The limp may subside once your pet warms up the joint through use.

over his head to give him something else to engage his teeth. Don't muzzle your pet or use a pillowcase if he is having any trouble breathing.

Treat it with a cold compress. If a soft-tissue injury like a sprain or strain happened within the past few hours, apply a cold compress to help reduce the swelling, soothe the pain, and prevent damage to the tissues. Rinse a clean washcloth in cold water, place it on the sore area, then place a plastic bag filled with ice on top. A bag of frozen peas or corn also works well, since it molds to the body. Apply compresses for 10 to 30 minutes several times a day for 3 days, after which your pet may benefit from hot packs (see "Follow-Up Care" on page 280).

Ask the vet about aspirin. To reduce some of the inflammation, swelling, and pain, you can give a limping dog buffered aspirin such as Bufferin for 1 day. The usual dose is 10 to 25 milligrams per 2.2 pounds of body weight two or three times a day. Do not give aspirin to cats.

Use hot compresses for an abscess. If the limp is caused by an abscess, see your veterinarian. Often, he will recommend applying hot compresses. Heat helps increase the blood circulation to the sore area and can bring the infection to a head so that it will drain. Soak a washcloth with water as hot as you can stand, wring it out, and put it on the sore area two to five times a day, for 5 minutes on, 5 minutes off until the cloth cools. Do not put hot compresses in the armpits or groin area. (For more on abscesses, see page 60.)

FOLLOW-UP CARE

■ After you've applied cold packs to a fresh injury for 3 days, you can switch to hot packs or compresses to bring healing blood to the area. You can use a commercial hot pack or a hot-water bottle wrapped in a towel and apply it two to five times a day, 5 minutes on, 5 minutes off until it cools. Do not put hot compresses in the armpits or groin area.

■ Dogs and cats who limp from minor sprains or strains often heal with simple rest. Confine your pet and keep him from running, jumping, or climbing until the limp subsides. It's best to continue resting your pet's leg for at least 24 hours after the limp is gone.

■ Cats who have abscesses often need antibiotics, and dogs and cats who limp from arthritis may be given medication to help with the pain.

There are various forms of pain medication for dogs and cats that are safe for long-term use. Your veterinarian will prescribe the one that is best for your pet. Dogs may be given an arthritis medicine like carprofen (Rimadyl) that doesn't have the side effects of long-term aspirin use. If your pet seems to be having side effects from any drug, consult your veterinarian.

To give a dog a pill, circle the top of his nose with your hand and press the gum line on both sides of his jaw, just behind the large, pointed canine teeth. Push the pill over the hill of his tongue, close his mouth, and gently stroke his throat until he swallows. (This technique is illustrated on page 30.) To pill your cat, grasp the loose fur at the scruff of his neck and tilt his head back so his nose points upward. His mouth will automatically drop open, so you can pull down his jaw with one finger and drop the pill onto the back of his tongue (aim for the V-shape in the center of the tongue). It helps to put some butter or margarine on the pill to help it slide down. Then close his mouth and watch for him to swallow. Cats usually lick their noses after swallowing a pill.

Advisors

■ Peter Davis, D.V.M., is a veterinarian at Pine Tree Veterinary Hospital in Augusta, Maine.

■ Alvin C. Dufour, D.V.M., is a veterinarian at Dufour Animal Hospital in Elkhart, Indiana.

■ Margaret J. Rucker, D.V.M., is a veterinarian at Southwest Virginia Veterinary Services in Lebanon, Virginia.

■ Raymond Russo, D.V.M., is a veterinarian at Kingston Animal Hospital in Massachusetts.

■ George White, D.V.M., is a veterinarian at I-20 Animal Medical Center in Arlington, Texas.

■ Anna E. Worth, V.M.D., is a veterinarian at West Mountain Animal Hospital in Shaftsbury, Vermont.

Low Blood Sugar

CALL YOUR VET: **IMMEDIATELY**

Low blood sugar, technically called hypoglycemia, can develop if your pet's pancreas malfunctions. The pancreas makes insulin, which moves sugar (glucose) into the body's cells for energy, and when there's too much insulin, the pet develops hypoglycemia. Diabetic pets who receive too much insulin will suffer from hypoglycemia, and too little insulin can cause a diabetic coma that looks very similar.

Liver disease or even a heavy load of intestinal parasites that interfere with digestion can also cause hypoglycemia. Young toy-breed dogs, like affenpinschers or Chihuahuas, often develop hypoglycemia even though they're perfectly healthy. They don't have a lot of fat stores to begin with, which the body needs for energy, and their immature livers can't manufacture the sugar they need.

As their heartbeats and breathing slow down, pets with low blood sugar become weak, sleepy, disoriented, wobbly, and glassy-eyed–they act as though they're drunk. They may start to twitch or shake, tilt their heads, develop seizures, and in the worst case, lose consciousness and fall into a coma. Pets can die without quick first aid and will need medical attention if they have diabetes.

Generally, as long as you recognize the signs in time, low blood sugar is easy to treat, but if your pet does not respond within the first 5 to 10 minutes of administering first aid, get her to the vet's office right away. Even if your pet does respond, any episode of hypoglycemia means that she will need to be examined by your vet the same day.

🩺 DO THIS NOW

Offer food for wooziness. When your pet is just starting to get woozy, give her something to eat. A couple of tablespoons of canned food usually does the trick.

Give your pet sugar. The quickest way to return your pet to normal while she can still swallow is to give her a sugar source like Karo syrup, pancake syrup, or honey. Use 1 teaspoon for pets under 50 pounds. Give a large dog (50 to 80 pounds) 2 teaspoons, an extra-large dog (over 80 pounds) 2½ teaspoons, and a giant breed (over 120 pounds) 3 teaspoons. Just let her lap it up. If your pet is very groggy, give her a bit of plain water first to be sure that she can swallow. If your pet won't lap up water, you may have to use a needleless syringe. First, give her water through the syringe to make sure that she can swallow, then try the honey or syrup.

If your pet has lost consciousness or can't swallow, rub the glucose source on the inside of her lips and gums, and it will be absorbed through the mucous membranes into the bloodstream. Honey works best for this. Your pet should return to normal in 5 to 15 minutes.

Treat shock. Pets with hypoglycemia lose their ability to stay warm because there's not enough sugar in their systems to burn for energy. They can very quickly go into shock if low blood sugar isn't reversed, and shock can kill a pet in as little as 10 to 20 minutes. Wrap your pet in a blanket with a hot-water bottle or hot pack to slow down shock and keep her stable until her system gets back on track. You can also put a drop or two of Karo syrup or honey on her gums to help keep her conscious until you get to the vet. (For more information about shock, see page 333.)

Watch for stopped breathing. A pet who falls into a coma from hypoglycemia may stop breathing and need artificial respiration. Wrap your hand around her muzzle to seal her mouth shut. Blow into her nostrils with two quick breaths, watching to see her chest expand. (With very small puppies or kittens, take care that you don't blow too hard). Give about 15 to 20 breaths a minute and stop after a minute or two for 30 seconds to see if she'll breathe on her own. Keep breathing for her until she starts breathing on her own or you reach medical help. (This technique is illustrated on page 20.)

Give CPR for a stopped heart. If your pet's heart stops beating, you will have to administer CPR. Determine if your pet's heart has stopped by taking her pulse. You won't be able to feel a pulse in the carotid artery in the neck as you can with people. Instead, press your fingertips into the crease where the inside of the thigh meets the body and feel for the pulse in the femoral artery, which is very big and near the surface. (This technique is illustrated on page 13.) If you can't feel it, try listening or feeling for the heart. Put your ear or hand flat against your pet's left side directly behind the elbow.

If you don't detect a heartbeat, you will have to begin chest compressions. To give compressions for a large or medium-size dog, put her on her side on a firm, flat surface and press with both hands flat on top of each other against the chest, compressing by 25 to 50%. For cats or small dogs, cup your hand over the point of the chest just behind the elbows. Squeeze firmly in a "coughlike" manner, pressing in about ½ inch, with your thumb on one side and fingers on the other. Ideally, one person should give chest compressions while a second performs artificial respiration. Alternate one breath for every 5 compressions. The goal is 80 to 100 compressions and 15 to 20 breaths per minute until your pet revives or until you reach medical help. (This technique is illustrated on page 21.)

 ## FOLLOW-UP CARE

■ If your pet is at risk, put a couple of tablespoons of Karo syrup in her drinking water so that she can sip it throughout the day. Remember to change the water every day, or the sugar water will grow bacteria.

■ Toy dogs prone to hypoglycemia should be fed two or three meals a day or have food out all the time. This will help keep their blood sugar levels on an even keel.

■ For a pet with diabetes, schedule meals and exercise periods so that you can regulate insulin doses. This is important to prevent low blood sugar.

■ Most diabetic pets need insulin replacement therapy, and the specific dose is very important—

too much or not enough can be dangerous. Your veterinarian will do tests to get it right, and he'll show you how to give the shots yourself.

To give an injection, draw the prescribed amount of liquid into the syringe. Then hold the syringe with the needle pointed upward, tap it, and gently depress the plunger to release any air bubbles. Lift the loose skin at the scruff of your pet's neck or on the shoulders, insert the needle beneath the skin, and push the plunger. After withdrawing the needle, rub the site for a minute to soothe any sting and help close the tiny entrance wound. (This technique is illustrated on page 73.)

THE BEST APPROACH

"Lite" Diets

Putting fat pets on reducing diets can cut the risk of low blood sugar by regulating diabetes. It helps because reducing diets stay longer in the digestive tract, and slower digestion evens out sugar levels and helps prevent hypoglycemia.

For pets with diabetes, veterinarians recommend high-fiber, low-carbohydrate foods, like Hill's Science Diet w/d or Eukanuba Glucose Control, which also have added chromium, a mineral that boosts the effects of insulin. These therapeutic diets are available only through your vet. Nondiabetic pets prone to low blood sugar may do well on one of the "lite" commercial products.

Advisors
■ Dale C. Butler, D.V.M., is a veterinarian at Best Friends Animal Hospital in Denison, Texas.
■ Ken Lawrence, D.V.M., is a veterinarian at the Texoma Veterinary Hospital in Sherman, Texas.
■ Julie Moews, D.V.M., is a veterinarian at Bolton Veterinary Hospital in Connecticut.

Maggots

CALL YOUR VET: **SAME DAY**

During the warm summer months, flies find sores hidden under a pet's thick fur or seek out the debris that collects in skin folds of wrinkle-skinned dogs like shar-peis. They also target rotten tumors, abscesses, healing incisions from surgeries, infected ears, and bed sore–type wounds in old or sick dogs and cats who don't groom themselves very well. The flies lay eggs in festering wounds and in feces stuck to the anus. Eggs hatch into maggots in less than 24 hours, and the wriggling white worms eat the dead tissue and drainage from the sore, which can become very large and serious very quickly.

Most wounds infested with maggots need medical attention. It's not the maggots that are dangerous, but rather whatever caused the weak or sick condition that allowed the dog or cat to attract the flies. It's a nasty job, but it's pretty easy for you to clean out the maggots.

DO THIS NOW

Restrain your pet if necessary. Maggot-infested areas on the skin can be very painful, and pets in pain often bite as a reflex. You may need to safely restrain your pet to protect yourself. Muzzle a long-nosed dog with panty hose or a necktie. Tie it around your dog's nose and knot it on top of her muzzle, then draw the ends beneath her chin and knot again. Finally, pull the ends back and tie them behind her ears. (This technique is illustrated on page 17.) For a short-faced pet like a pug or a cat, you can drape a pillowcase over his head to give him something else to use his teeth on.

Clip off the fur that surrounds the wound.
Besides getting in the way of treatment, fur traps bacteria and keeps reinfecting the wound. Use blunt scissors or electric clippers to get rid of the fur. (This technique is illustrated on page 114.)

Extract the maggots. You'll need to use a gauze pad, tissue, or blunt-tipped tweezers to mechanically pick out the maggots. It's not pleasant, but it is very effective. Wear a pair of disposable medical gloves (available in drugstores) so that you don't have to touch the worms.

Flush them out with water. If the wound is very deep, the maggots may be hard to reach. Fill the bathtub with lukewarm water or use the spray attachment to fill the wound with water to flush out the debris and parasites. Continue

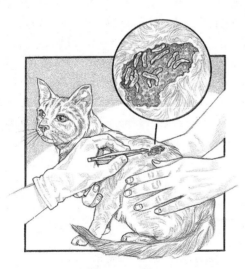

If your pet has a maggot-infested wound, muzzle him or have a second person hold him steady while you extract the white fly larvae with tweezers. You can smash them or drop them in a jar of water with some dishwashing detergent on top to drown them.

to flush the area for at least 15 minutes. The maggots will do their best to escape the wound so that they don't drown, and you can pick them off. Any worms that you miss will leave the wound on their own within 4 to 5 days to turn into pupae, the next stage before they evolve into adult flies. The water flush also gets rid of any fly eggs that haven't hatched so that there won't be a new crop of maggots.

SPECIAL SITUATION

If your pet won't groom herself: It's important to figure out what caused your pet to stop moving or grooming long enough for the flies to lay eggs. Often with older pets, the stiffness of arthritis keeps them lying too long in one place or prevents them from turning around to easily groom their nether regions. When the problem is arthritis, with your vet's okay you can give dogs buffered aspirin to relieve the pain. Ask your vet how much to give; the dosage varies based on the size of your dog. You could also apply a hot-water bottle wrapped in a thick towel to relieve pain in the affected area.

Don't give aspririn to cats. There are limited options for cats with chronic pain, but you can work with your vet to make your cat as comfortable and pain-free as possible. A hot-water bottle wrapped in a thick towel can help.

FOLLOW-UP CARE

■ In all cases, your pet will need antibiotics to help the wound heal and fight the infection that drew the maggots. With topical antibiotic ointment like Neosporin, apply a thin coating once or twice a day as directed. You may need to distract your pet with a quiet game until the ointment is absorbed so that she doesn't lick off the medicine. If your vet prescribes pills, dogs will usually accept them hidden in tasty treats like cheese. To pill your cat, put her on a tabletop, grasp the scruff of her neck, and gently arch her neck backward so her mouth automatically opens a bit. Use your other hand to pull down her chin until you can see the V-shaped indentation in the center of her tongue. Drop the pill on the V, close her mouth, and she should swallow it right down.

■ For shallow wounds, use a clean cloth dampened with sterile saline contact lens solution to clean off the area and any seepage a couple of times a day as needed.

■ Deep wounds may require saline flushes or even treatment with an antiseptic like Betadine Solution a couple of times a day. (Dilute it with distilled water until it's the color of weak tea.) This not only keeps the wound clean and prevents infection, but the steady stream of liquid also stimulates the formation of healthy granulation tissue that replaces the flesh eaten away by the maggots. You can fill a squeeze bottle and direct the stream into the wound.

■ If your pet has a history of problems with maggots and has a very thick coat that hides sores, it's a good idea to have a groomer give her an all-over trim for the summer months. Her fur should be trimmed to ¼ to ½ inch in length.

THE BEST APPROACH

Liquid Bandage

Cleaning maggots out of a wound is only the first step, and often, the tissue damage is severe. Healing takes a long time, and wound care is important to ensure that more infection doesn't develop. A product designed for horses called Dy's Liquid Bandage is the veterinarians' choice for treating invasive, massive, or slow-to-heal wounds in cats and dogs. It's a combination of soothing herbs in an olive oil and beeswax formula. Olive oil is easily absorbed into the skin and carries the medicinal herbs along with it, while the beeswax covers the wound with a waterproof barrier that repels flies but allows air to penetrate to heal the wound. The ointment works well on minor wounds, like a scrape or hot spot, too, so it's a great home remedy to keep on hand.

Advisors

■ Michael G. Abdella, D.V.M., is a veterinarian at Aliso Viejo Animal Hospital in Aliso Viejo, California.

■ Lorrie Bartloff, D.V.M., is a veterinarian at Three Point Veterinary Clinic in Elkhart, Indiana.

■ James M. Harris, D.V.M., is a veterinarian at Montclair Veterinary Hospital in Oakland, California.

■ Karen Hoffman, V.M.D., is a veterinarian at Delaware Valley Animal Hospital in Fairless Hills, Pennsylvania.

Mastitis

CALL YOUR VET: **SAME DAY**

Mother cats and dogs sometimes develop a type of infection in their breasts called mastitis. Bacteria enter the skin through scratches made by the claws and needle-sharp teeth of the babies, or germs from the mouths of the nursing puppies or kittens travel up the mother's milk ducts through the nipples. Milk-producing breasts are easily infected, and the infection increases rapidly once it starts.

Mastitis can affect a single gland or multiple breasts. Most dogs and cats have four pairs of breasts with a total of eight nipples, and the ones nearest the back legs are most prone to infection because they tend to produce more milk and are favored by the babies.

The affected glands swell and become so tender that the mother may refuse to let her babies nurse. The tissue feels hot and hard. It may turn a reddish blue color, come to a head, break open and drain, or even slough tissue. Sometimes, the milk or discharge from the nipples is filled with mucus, turns a yellowish green or bloody color, or becomes stringy. If it is a serious mastitis infection, your pet can develop a high fever, act depressed, or refuse to eat.

Pets with mastitis need antibiotics to fight the infection. But in most cases, simple first aid is a good way to relieve pain and speed the healing.

DO THIS NOW

Trim surrounding fur. Most dogs and cats lose quite a bit of fur on their tummies when they become pregnant, which prepares them for nursing. It's a good idea to trim away any remaining fur to make treating mastitis simpler. When the infection begins to drain, the discharge collects in the fur and can reinfect the breast. Use blunt scissors or electric clippers to cut the fur surrounding the infection close to the skin. If you're using scissors, slip your index and second fingers through the fur. Cut the fur level with your fingers, clipping a 1-inch border around the affected area. (This technique is illustrated on page 114.) If the skin is broken, fill the wound with water-soluble lubricant like K-Y Jelly before you clip. Then thoroughly rinse the area with warm water. The trimmed hair sticks to the jelly and washes out.

Keep the babies from nursing. Some kinds of infection in the milk could make the babies sick, too, so prevent them from nursing until after you take your pet to the vet. Puppies and kittens who are 3 weeks or older will do fine for a day or so on a soupy mix of commercial puppy or kitten food and water. Mix 2 parts canned food and 1 part water and run it through the blender. For dry food, just soak 2 parts in 1 part water until the food gets soft and mushy.

Younger babies need to be fed milk with an eyedropper or needleless syringe, but cow's milk doesn't have all the nutrients they need. There are many nutritionally complete commercial milk replacers for puppies and kittens. You can buy a nursing kit at pet-supply stores.

For a day or so, until you can get commercial bitch or queen milk, you can use a homemade formula. For puppies, combine 1 cup of whole milk, 1 teaspoon of vegetable oil, 1 drop of liquid multivitamin for human infants, and 2 egg yolks. For kittens, blend ½ cup of whole milk, 1 egg yolk, 1 drop of multivitamin, and three Tums tablets (for calcium).

Rinse away abscess drainage. When the breast abscesses and begins to drain, you can rinse off the discharge with a gentle stream of water. Because the infection makes the breast so sore, your pet may not want you to touch her,

but a gentle warm-water rinse is very helpful for healing. Then gently pat the area dry.

Apply a hot compress. Applying heat is the single best thing you can do for mastitis. The warmth increases bloodflow to the mammary glands and helps break up the infection so that it comes to a head and drains. Often, warmth will prompt the nipple to discharge the infected milk and will also help the swelling go down.

Two to five times a day, soak a washcloth or hand towel in water as hot as you can stand, wring it out, and place it on the swollen tissue. Alternate the compress 5 minutes on, then 5 minutes off until the cloth cools.

FOLLOW-UP CARE

■ The vet will prescribe antibiotics to treat the infection. For dogs, you can hide pills in a hunk of cheese or dollop of peanut butter.

To give your cat pills, place one hand on top of her head, with the thumb on one side and the middle or index finger on the other side of her lips. Gently press her lips against her teeth to prompt her to open up. With your other hand, push the pill to the back of her tongue, then close her mouth. (This technique is illustrated on page 30.) Quickly offer her a treat, like a bit of meat baby food or soft cheese. Your cat will tend to lick up the treat and swallow the pill in the process.

■ For relatively shallow infections, continue to apply hot compresses as described earlier. This will help open the infection so that it drains, and it will also help clean the wound out.

■ If the infection is mild and involves only one or two breasts, your veterinarian may recommend that you let the babies nurse on the healthy breasts while you use a method to keep them from nursing on the infected breasts. Some vets feel that as long as the mother lets her babies nurse from the uninfected breasts, it's fine for them to do so. Tainted milk tastes odd, so the babies will probably avoid the infected breasts, but to be safe, you can use an adhesive bandage to cover the affected nipple or nipples.

You can also make a tailed bandage using a rectangular piece of material—linen or cotton works best. The size of your pet will determine the size of the fabric you use. Cut several slits in opposite sides of the rectangle to make "tails" that are long enough to easily wrap around your pet's abdomen. Tie the tails over her back so that the solid fabric covers her abdomen and the infected nipples. Leave the healthy nipples uncovered. Follow your vet's instructions carefully.

■ Your veterinarian may also advise you to try to get rid of some of the contaminated milk from the breasts with mastitis. To do this, milk the glands mechanically by stimulating each nipple in turn with a warm, wet cloth. Massage and gently grasp and squeeze the base of the nipple close to the body, then gently pull the nipple away from the breast. Grasp and pull several times until you have expressed all the milk.

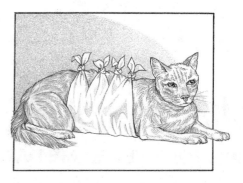

To keep babies from nursing, cut slits in the sides of a rectangle of material like T-shirt fabric or a pillowcase, then tie the "straps" over the mother's back.

■ If the infection is serious and the babies are old enough, your vet may advise you to dry up the mother's milk. Begin by withholding all food and water for 24 hours so that her body is forced to use the milk for her own nutrition. The next day, offer her one-quarter of her regular amount of food. The third day, feed her half-rations; increase to three-quarter rations the fourth day; and finally, by the fifth day, return to her regular feeding schedule. Start the babies on solid food as directed by your vet.

■ When you must feed babies who are younger than 3 weeks old for longer than a day or two, get a commercial bitch or queen milk replacement product from a pet-supply store or your vet. Feed them a commercial formula like Esbilac Milk Replacer for Puppies or KMR Milk Replacer for Kittens. Follow your veterinarian's advice about how much and how often to feed.

Advisors

■ Ann Buchanan, D.V.M., is a veterinarian at Glenwood Animal Hospital in Tyler, Texas.

■ Chris Johnson, D.V.M., is a veterinarian at Westside Animal Emergency Clinic in Atlanta.

■ Susan Little, D.V.M., is a veterinarian at Bytown Cat Hospital in Ottawa, Ontario, Canada.

Mouth Injuries

CALL YOUR VET: **SAME DAY**

Mouth injuries are much more common in dogs than in cats. A dog's love of chewing sticks, bones, and other inedible objects can result in splinters, punctures, and abrasions that can be painful. Pets also can be burned from licking caustic substances or chewing through electrical cords. Some pets slice their tongues in fights or by licking empty food cans.

Traumatic injuries—being hit by a car, falling from a tree, or getting in the way of a swinging golf club—need immediate medical attention. With any mouth injury, your pet may drool or have bloody saliva and refuse to eat. Or he may eat reluctantly or in an odd way, perhaps on one side of his mouth. Here's what to do.

DO THIS NOW

Use milk for lost teeth. If a tooth has been knocked out, as long as the root is intact and it's a healthy tooth, your vet may be able to reimplant it. Store the tooth in a glass of milk (the milk helps preserve the blood vessels), then take it and your pet to the vet right away. (For more information about tooth damage, see page 393.)

Rinse your pet's mouth. The best treatment for mouth injuries is to rinse the mouth very well. This will help speed up healing and clear out any debris that might be left behind from a stick or other foreign body. Fill a turkey baster or squirt gun with water or sterile saline contact lens solution and flush the sore for 5 to 10 minutes, or as long as your pet will let you.

Give your pet crushed ice or ice water. This will help numb the injury and also rinse it out. A sore mouth often prevents a pet from eating or drinking as much as he should, and he can become dehydrated very easily. Giving your pet ice helps prevent this. (For more information about dehydration, see page 148.)

Apply a pain reliever. For a cut or abrasion in a dog's mouth, it's best to use an over-the-counter pain reliever like Anbesol. Dab some on

FIRST ALERT

Stomatitis

A dog or cat can develop a sore mouth—stomatitis—from a variety of bacteria or viruses, but you may think that he's suffered a severe mouth injury. The pet typically drools, shakes his head, paws at his mouth, and refuses to eat. His mouth will be so sore that he won't want you to even look inside it, but when you do, the tissue will look very red, swollen, and tender. Usually, there will be a foul odor as well. If you suspect stomatitis, call your vet immediately.

a cotton swab and apply to the injury for temporary pain relief. Do not use it for cats.

Withhold food until you get to the vet. He may recommend that you not feed your pet for the first 24 hours after the injury to allow it to seal. The pain will make it hard to eat anyway.

FOLLOW-UP CARE

■ Depending on the extent of the injuries, the vet may prescribe antibiotics to prevent infection. Often, liquid medicine is prescribed when the problem is in the mouth. Tip your pet's head up and squirt the medicine into his cheek. Then gently hold his mouth closed until he swallows. (This technique is illustrated on page 30.)

■ The injury will make the mouth sore, so your pet will be reluctant to eat. Therapeutic diets like Hill's

Prescription diet a/d and Iams Maximum Calorie are available from the veterinarian. They have a puddinglike consistency that pets find very palatable. They're also extremely high-calorie, so pets don't have to eat very much. Or you can feed a soft canned diet or just mix your pet's regular dry food in the blender with some low-fat, no-salt chicken broth to make a gruel. Feed the soft or liquid diet for at least 3 days, or until the injury starts to heal.

■ Mouth injuries usually heal very quickly on their own, due in part to the antiseptic properties of pet saliva. But you can help speed up the healing process just by keeping the injury clean. After each meal, flush out your pet's mouth with clean water. You can use a turkey baster or a squirt gun to direct the flow of water all around his mouth, being careful to avoid spraying the back of the mouth near the throat so that you don't choke him.

Advisors
■ Dawn Crandell, D.V.M., is a veterinarian at Veterinary Emergency Clinic of York Region in Aurora, Ontario, Canada.
■ Terry Kaeser, D.V.M., is a veterinarian at Goshen Animal Clinic in Goshen, Indiana.
■ Margaret J. Rucker, D.V.M., is a veterinarian at Southwest Virginia Veterinary Services in Lebanon, Virginia.
■ Drew Weigner, D.V.M., is a veterinarian at The Cat Doctor in Atlanta.

Mouth Sores

CALL YOUR VET: **SAME DAY**

Mouth sores are most common in older dogs and cats who have some other illness, such as kidney disease or diabetes. Dental disease is also a common cause of painful mouth sores. Less frequently, cats get sick from upper respiratory viruses that cause mouth ulcers.

Pets who have sores in their mouths often drool and may paw at their mouths. They typically refuse to eat because it hurts too much, and they may sit in front of a full food bowl and cry. Mouth sores need medical attention to treat the underlying cause of the problem. But first aid can relieve the pain, keep your pet eating, and prevent the problem from getting worse until you can get treatment from your veterinarian.

DO THIS NOW

Give a topical treatment. Mouth sores are extremely painful. Dogs and cats often refuse to eat and can become sicker as a result. One of the best and quickest ways to relieve mouth pain for dogs is an over-the-counter pain reliever like Anbesol. Dip a cotton swab, gently open your dog's mouth, and dab it directly on the sores that you can reach. This works well for temporary pain relief, and it's perfectly safe to use to treat your dog for a day or two. Follow the package recommendations for how often to use it. *Don't* use Anbesol for cats more than one time—it could be toxic.

Ask the vet about aspirin. Buffered aspirin like Bufferin is another good short-term pain reliever, but only for dogs, only for a day or two, and only if your veterinarian recommends it. Aspirin can be dangerous for cats, as well as for dogs with kidney or liver disease and dogs who are dehydrated. It could also cause stomach upset in dogs if used for too long.

FIRST ALERT

Mouth Tumors

Mouth tumors account for about 8 percent of all cancers seen in dogs. They can become raw and very sore, then ulcerate and drain. You may not even notice the problem until your dog develops a bad mouth odor, but if you notice any abnormal swelling of his gums, lips, or tongue, take him to the vet.

Tumors are often melanomas, carcinomas, or fibrosarcomas that tend to spread throughout the body. But dogs can also develop benign (noncancerous) growths on the gums called epulides. Usually, surgery is the treatment of choice, and if the cancer is caught early, the dog can have no further problems. Sometimes, chemotherapy or other treatments can help.

The usual dose is 10 to 25 milligrams per 2.2 pounds of body weight two or three times a day. If your dog's mouth is very sore, crush the medicine and mix the powder in a bit of milk.

Give him ice. Crushed ice or ice water is a great way to offer your dog or cat some relief from mouth pain. Dogs relish licking and mouthing cold water or crushed ice, but cats may be reluctant to put anything in their mouths. You can offer an ice cube to see if your cat will lick it to cool off the pain.

Feed him liquid or soft foods. You need to keep your pet eating despite the soreness of his mouth. The best way to do that is with soft or liquid diets. Use a strong-flavored liquid like bouillon or chicken or beef broth to soften the food. Use 1 part commercial food to 2 parts liquid and mix it in the blender or food processor until it's a puddinglike consistency. Dogs often will lap up this type of liquid diet.

Give your cat baby food. Cats may refuse any kind of commercial food when their mouths are sore. Very often, though, they'll willingly eat beef or chicken baby food, especially if it's warmed to their body temperature—about 100°F—to make it more tempting. Give it to your cat for several days while his mouth heals.

FOLLOW-UP CARE

■ Bacterial infections often develop along with mouth sores, so the vet may prescribe antibiotics to prevent infections and speed the healing process. Because the mouth is so sore, the medication will usually be in liquid form so that you can squirt it into your pet's cheek for him to swallow. (This technique is illustrated on page 30.)

■ A mouth rinse of saline solution will help speed up the healing by keeping the mouth clean. A mouth rinse like Nolvadent (available from pet-supply stores and catalogs) also works

Lip Sores in Cats

Cats sometimes develop salmon-pink erosions on the upper lips or salmon-pink nodules on the point of the bottom lips that may be mistaken for spider bites. Often called rodent ulcers, the sores are actually one aspect of a group of allergic conditions called feline eosinophilic granuloma complex. The sores or plaques may also develop on the tummy or the backs of the thighs.

Although they look awful, these sores usually are not particularly painful for the cat. They range from tiny single sores that happen only once to large or multiple ulcers that return time after time. About the only thing that will help the lesions heal is cortisone injections. Make an appointment for your cat to see the veterinarian within a few days after you notice these sores.

well. It not only prevents infection but has a numbing effect and helps relieve mouth pain. You can use a turkey baster or a squirt gun to direct the flow around his mouth. (Don't direct the spray toward his throat, or you could choke him.)

■ Pets who are reluctant to eat are often tempted with therapeutic diets available from veterinarians, like Hill's Prescription Diet a/d and Iams Maximum Calorie. They are extremely high-calorie, concentrated nutrition. Their puddinglike consistency doesn't hurt sore mouths and is very tempting for sick pets. Feed it until your pet's mouth has healed enough so that he can eat his regular diet.

THE BEST APPROACH

Solarcaine

One of the quickest and most effective ways to relieve mouth pain is with an over-the-counter product that contains lidocaine, a topical anesthetic that deadens feeling. Solarcaine, a human product for sunburn relief, works well. Don't spray the medicine inside your pet's mouth, though. Instead, apply Solarcaine to a gauze pad or cotton swab and dab it on one or two mouth sores to give temporary relief. *Don't* give Solarcaine to cats more than once, because it could be toxic.

Advisors

■ Jean C. Hofve, D.V.M., is a veterinarian and Companion Animal Program coordinator for the Animal Protection Institute in Sacramento.

■ Terry Kaeser, D.V.M., is a veterinarian at Goshen Animal Clinic in Goshen, Indiana.

■ Kate Lindley, D.V.M., is a veterinarian and owner of Kitty Klinic in Lacey, Washington.

■ Margaret J. Rucker, D.V.M., is a veterinarian at Southwest Virginia Veterinary Services in Lebanon, Virginia.

■ Drew Weigner, D.V.M., is a veterinarian at The Cat Doctor in Atlanta.

Nail-Bed Infections

CALL YOUR VET: **IF NEEDED**

Dogs' and cats' feet are often exposed to bacteria and fungi in dirt and grass. A split or torn nail opens up the nail bed to germs, and fungi like ringworm eat keratin—the nonliving protein of the claw—and can weaken and infect the nail.

Infection attacks the nail root where it grows out of the toe. The skin around the claw swells, turns red and crusty, and may smell bad. In severe cases, the nail becomes brittle or powdery, deformed, or even loosens in the flesh. Pus collects in the area. Pets with nail-bed infections may limp, and they often lick the sore or itchy area.

If more than one nail bed is infected, have your vet examine your pet right away. There may be something more serious going on, and your vet may have to prescribe antibiotics or refer you to a veterinary dermatologist. But if only one nail bed is infected, you can treat it at home. If the infection does not get better after 3 to 5 days of home treatment, the vet should examine your pet. Severe cases may need oral antibiotics or an antifungal drug like griseofulvin (Fulvicin).

DO THIS NOW

Watch for sudden symptoms. It's likely to be a bacterial infection when symptoms come on suddenly (within a 2- to 3-day period) and your pet's paws and toes are very painful. If this happens, it is important to have your pet examined by your vet right away.

Soak the foot in Epsom salts. Whether bacteria or fungi cause the problem, an Epsom-salt soak will help clean out the infection and make

your pet's foot feel better. Use 1 cup per 2 gallons of lukewarm water and soak the affected foot for 10 minutes at a time. You'll want to rinse off the Epsom salts so he can't lick them off. (The salts won't hurt him, but they could give him diarrhea.) Then dry the foot thoroughly.

Clean with a soft brush. For tender toes, use a soft brush with any mild antibacterial soap to clean the crusty material and debris from the nail

295

⊕ FIRST ALERT

Immune Suppression

A nail-bed infection on a single toe or foot is usually caused by an injury. But if all four feet are in-volved, the cause more likely is a systemic illness—one that affects the whole body—and nail in-fection is just one symptom that shows on the outside.

It's common for conditions that suppress the immune system, like feline leukemia or feline im-munodeficiency, to cause nail-bed infections. Affected cats may also have a host of other vague signs, like fever that comes and goes, weight loss, and chronic skin or respiratory infections.

There's no specific treatment for either feline leukemia or feline immunodeficiency, nor is there any cure. Often, cats are infected with both viruses at the same time, but many cats live comfort-ably for many months or even years with these diseases. The key to survival is quick treatment of any infection or illness that develops, so see the vet immediately if you suspect that your cat is in-fected.

Dogs may also develop systemic immunity-related diseases that attack the tissue holding the claw in place. These serious conditions can sometimes be controlled by your vet with immune-suppressing drugs.

---

bed. A complexion brush or even a soft tooth-brush works well. Use warm water, and be sure to completely rinse off the soap and dry thor-oughly, or it could cause even more irritation.

Keep your pet still. Even when their feet aren't sore, pets often resent having their paws handled. You'll probably need two people to treat tender feet, but dogs with itchy toes may actually enjoy the treatment. Small dogs and cats can be wrapped up in a towel or pillowcase with one foot exposed at a time. If you have a larger dog, kneel beside him on the floor, with one arm around his neck and the other under and around his chest. Then just hug him to your chest. (This technique is illustrated on page 18.)

Trim damaged nails carefully. When bacte-rial infection develops from a nail injury, you must trim off the damaged part of the nail above the split or tear before the wound will heal. Do this only if the nail is broken or split and the damage has not reached the quick (the blood ves-sels inside the nail). If the nail damage includes the quick, do not attempt to cut it, because it will be very painful for your pet. Just bandage it loosely to prevent further damage and go to the vet. Use rubbing alcohol to sterilize the nail clip-pers, scissors, or even rose-pruning shears (if you have a large dog) before you trim the nail. Hold the paw securely, put the clipper in position, and make a quick, decisive cut. (For more informa-tion about nail damage, see page 298.)

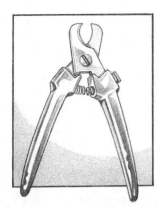

Millers Forge nail clippers work like pruners for a sharp, clean cut.

Have him wear socks. To keep your dog from licking, put a plain cotton sock over his paw. The cotton allows the area to breathe so that it will heal. Put on the sock and use adhesive tape or elastic adhesive bandage like Elastoplast to secure it to the leg.

Be sure to change the sock at least once a day to help keep the area clean and dry. It's a good idea for dogs to wear the socks when they go outside, but you should change the socks when they return. That will keep the sore nails from being reexposed to more bacteria in the yard.

Use softer litter. Cat claws will heal faster if your cat doesn't have to use them to dig in rough litter. You can try switching to a product with softer granules, like Yesterday's News Cat Litter, which is a recycled-newspaper product that won't irritate sore paws. Keep the litter boxe clean so that your cat doesn't reinfect his claws from the bacteria in his own waste.

SPECIAL SITUATION

If fungi are present: Fungi attack over a period of weeks, and your pet's toes won't be as tender, but the infection lasts longer and is harder to cure. Fungi can turn the nails brittle or make them grow in deformed, and your pet's toes will feel itchy. If your pet exhibits any of these signs, it is a good idea to have your vet examine him. Once he makes a diagnosis, he will give you a treatment plan for home care.

FOLLOW-UP CARE

■ Follow-up care is usually not needed once you've taken care of the infection.

THE BEST APPROACH

Nail Trimmers

Professional groomers, who trim hundreds of nails a day, recommend Millers Forge Quality Nail Clippers. Millers Forge clippers have stainless-steel blades that hold an edge and will easily cut through the toughest claws. In addition, they don't grab and pull on fur the way guillotine-style trimmers do.

Advisors
■ Gerald Brown, D.V.M., is a veterinarian at City Cat Doctor in Chicago.
■ Bernadine Cruz, D.V.M., is a veterinarian at Laguna Hills Animal Hospital in California.
■ Joanne Howl, D.V.M., is a veterinarian in West River, Maryland; secretary/treasurer of the American Academy on Veterinary Disaster Medicine; and past president of the Maryland Veterinary Medical Association.

Nail Damage

CALL YOUR VET: **IF NEEDED**

Pets who are active usually don't get nail damage. That's because friction (for dogs, it's the friction from walking on the ground and sidewalks; for cats, it's the friction from scratching things) wears the nails down. Nails that get too long often split or pull loose from the skin when they snag on bedding, curtains, or carpets. The dewclaw, which is the nail high on the inside of the leg, often gets damaged because it's off the ground and doesn't wear down on its own.

There are a lot of nerves and blood vessels in the toes, so nail injuries are painful and often bleed a lot. But the damage is rarely serious and can be treated with simple first aid.

 ## DO THIS NOW

Hold your pet still. A torn nail is painful, so you'll need someone to hold your pet while you perform first aid. To hold a cat or small dog, grab the loose skin at the back of the neck with one hand, capture the hind feet with the other, and stretch your pet out on her side. To hold a larger dog, put one arm under and around her neck to hug her to your chest, and the other arm around and under her chest. You may want to muzzle your dog with panty hose or a necktie just to be sure you aren't bitten. First, tie the ends on top of your dog's nose, then bring the ends under her jaw and tie them again. Finally, bring the ends behind her ears and tie them in a knot or bow. (This technique is illustrated on page 17.)

Cats can put up quite a fight, so you may need to wrap them in a towel, with only the affected foot (and the nose, so that she can breathe) sticking out.

Use pet nail clippers. To remove the damaged nail, use sharp, clean nail clippers designed for pets. If the intact portion of the nail hasn't split any further, you can just trim away the dangling part. If there is a jagged or split end that bleeds, you must cut the nail above the damaged section, which may mean cutting nearly level with the toe. Dip the clippers in alcohol first, then dry them. Grasp the pet's paw securely, position the clippers right above the damage, and cut quickly and decisively. Be prepared for a yelp and a flinch from your pet—and even more blood (the bathtub is the best place to perform this messy task). If the bleeding doesn't stop within 30 minutes, go to the vet, who will cauterize the injury.

Stop bleeding with powder. If the nail bleeds, try a styptic powder like Kwik-Stop. (Styptic pencils don't work well for pets.) The powders usually come with a sponge applicator that can be applied to the nail. If you don't have styptic powder, gently rake the cut end of the nail across a dry bar of soap or powder the cut with talcum powder, baking soda, or flour. Fill your palm with the powder and dip the nail in. Keep dipping until the bleeding stops, usually within a minute.

Wait to wash. Don't wash the paw until the bleeding has stopped entirely. Wash the affected area with a mild antiseptic liquid soap like Beta-

dine Skin Cleanser. Be very gentle around the clot so as not to dislodge it and restart bleeding. If bleeding reoccurs, stop washing, rinse the soap off, and bandage. (This technique is illustrated on page 25.) Leave the bandage on for several hours before attempting to clean the area again.

 ## FOLLOW-UP CARE

■ Damaged nails get infected easily because bacteria from the ground slip through the cracks and into the nail bed. Veterinarians sometimes give oral antibiotics just to be safe. If the nail looks intact, however, infection is much less likely, especially if you soak the foot in an antiseptic solution. Do this by diluting Betadine Solution with warm (100°F) distilled water (the solution should be the color of weak tea). Soak the foot three times a day for 5 minutes each time. Continue for 3 to 4 days. Be sure to rinse the solution off after each soak because pets will lick it off, and it's not meant to be taken internally.

Advisors

■ Joanne Howl, D.V.M., is a veterinarian in West River, Maryland; secretary/treasurer of the American Academy on Veterinary Disaster Medicine; and past president of the Maryland Veterinary Medical Association.

■ Daniel Simpson, D.V.M., is a veterinarian at West Bay Animal Hospital in West Bay, Rhode Island, and spokesperson for the Rhode Island Veterinary Medical Association.

■ Elaine Wexler-Mitchell, D.V.M., is a veterinarian at the Cat Care Clinic in Orange, California, and president of the Academy of Feline Medicine.

Neck Pain

CALL YOUR VET: **SAME DAY**

Dogs and cats can suffer neck pain from straining muscles or developing disk problems in the spine. This kind of neck pain is more common in dogs than in cats, with mastiffs, Doberman pinschers, and other large-breed dogs affected most often. They'll hold their heads stiffly and won't want to lift their faces—they may look like they're shy or depressed and cry out with pain when they move the wrong way. Neck pain often will make pets stop eating because it hurts to reach the food bowl.

There are serious diseases that can cause neck pain. An animal who has neck pain lasting more than a few hours should be taken to the veterinarian the same day. If the pain is accompanied by a fever, get to the vet right away. Neck pain from disk problems usually isn't an emergency, but it won't get better without medical attention, and it could get much worse, even causing paralysis.

Another cause of neck pain in dogs is a snakebite, since they usually get bitten on the face or neck. In cats, neck pain commonly results from wounds that become infected. While disk problems usually don't cause swelling, a traumatic neck injury, including snakebite, may swell, and infection usually also causes a fever. Elderly dogs and cats who suffer neck pain from arthritis may just refuse to move. First aid can help relieve the pain, and it may be all that's necessary to manage the signs of aging.

 ## DO THIS NOW

Remove the collar. Before doing anything else, take off your pet's collar. An injury to the neck may cause swelling until the collar chokes your pet.

Carry your pet if there's a snakebite. Snakes often bite dogs on the neck, and the bite can be extremely painful. When you suspect that your dog or cat has been bitten by a snake, keep him

FIRST ALERT

Tight Collars

Most puppies outgrow their first collars. Sometimes, the process is so gradual and the neck area is so furry that you may not notice right away. A delay in removing the collar can allow the puppy-size collar to cut into the skin, and over time, it can become embedded deep in the muscle.

The dog doesn't usually show signs of pain because the process is so gradual, but pain can develop when the area eventually becomes infected. The most noticeable sign that there's a problem is a terrible odor from the infection.

To correct the problem, the fur must be shaved away with electric clippers, the collar cut off, and the wound cleaned with an antiseptic liquid soap like Betadine Skin Cleanser. If the collar is deeply embedded, the dog needs veterinary treatment. Often, she will also need oral antibiotics until the neck wound heals. To avoid any problems, check the collar on your puppy every 2 weeks if she's a small to medium breed or every 4 weeks if she's a large or giant breed.

from walking—carry him to the car. Any type of exercise speeds up the blood circulation and can spread the poison even faster. It's hard to tell if a snakebite is poisonous or not, so immediate medical attention is always important.

Apply a cold pack. On the way to the veterinarian, apply a cold pack to the snakebite wound. This helps slow down the spread of the toxin and also helps relieve the pain. Rinse a clean washcloth in cold water and hold it against the injury, then place a cold pack, plastic bag of ice, or bag of fozen peas or corn on top of the wet cloth. (For more information about snakebite, see page 350.)

Give pain-relief medication. If you're sure that your dog hasn't injured his neck but is only in pain because of stiffness from arthritis, you can give

buffered aspirin like Bufferin on a temporary basis to relieve the pain. The usual dose is 10 to 25 milligrams per 2.2 pounds of body weight two or three times a day. Do not give aspirin to cats.

 SPECIAL SITUATIONS

For swelling on the side of a cat's neck: This is likely to be an abscess or cellulitis, usually from a bite wound. With cellulitis (a tissue inflammation), there may be little swelling but quite a bit of pain. (For more information about abscesses, see page 60.) A hot, wet compress on the painful area can help relieve the discomfort. Soak a clean washcloth with water as hot as you can stand it and apply it to the sore area.

If neck pain is from a muscle strain or disk disease: There won't be any visible swelling with these conditions. Take your pet to the veterinarian for diagnosis; he may prescribe cold packs. Apply them as described on page 301 for 10 to 30 minutes several times a day for 2 to 3 days. Then you can apply hot packs as described above or as directed by your veterinarian.

 ## FOLLOW-UP CARE

■ Any time the spine is involved in neck pain, rest is a key factor. You'll need to confine your pet for up to 6 weeks and keep him from jumping, running, or climbing until the problem area has fully healed.

■ When you take your dog out on a leash, use a harness that fits around his chest instead of a collar. When your dog tugs against a collar as he's walked on a leash, it can cause more pain to his healing neck.

Keep pets who have neck pain caused by disk disease or strained muscles from jumping around, climbing up and down stairs, or leaping off countertops. These activities could make a minor neck injury worse and even lead to paralysis. Move your cat's food bowls, toys, litter box, and other possessions to floor level.

■ Neck pain in dogs is often relieved with prescription anti-inflammatory medications. You can hide the pills in a treat like peanut butter to make sure that your dog eats it.

■ A cat with neck pain is more likely to get a prescription drug like butorphanol tartrate (Torbugesic) or even a skin patch with a drug like fentanyl (Duragesic) that's absorbed through the skin. The patch is applied to a shaved area of the cat's chest and can relieve pain for up to 3 days.

■ Bites from poisonous snakes often cause deep wounds when the area becomes infected or the poison literally digests the flesh. Deep abscesses also cause slow-to-heal wounds. In either case, you'll need to keep the wound clean by flushing it with a steady stream of water from a handheld showerhead. This water therapy also helps stimulate the flesh to regenerate and speeds up the healing process.

Advisors

■ Peter Davis, D.V.M., is a veterinarian at Pine Tree Veterinary Hospital in Augusta, Maine.

■ Kenneth J. Drobatz, D.V.M., is a veterinarian and associate professor of critical care emergency service at the Veterinary Hospital of the University of Pennsylvania in Philadelphia.

■ Raymond Russo, D.V.M., is a veterinarian at Kingston Animal Hospital in Massachusetts.

■ Sophia Yin, D.V.M., is a veterinarian in Davis, California, and author of *The Small Animal Veterinary Nerdbook.*

Nosebleeds

CALL YOUR VET: **IF NEEDED**

Nosebleeds in cats and dogs aren't common, but when they do happen, they're usually a result of some type of blunt trauma, like being struck by a car. Some kinds of poisons, cancer, and foreign objects can also cause bleeding and need immediate medical attention. (For more information about foreign objects in the nose, see page 202; for poisoning, see page 311.)

When your dog bumps his nose running into a fence in pursuit of a Frisbee, first aid will generally take care of the problem. A nosebleed should stop in 15 to 20 minutes with appropriate care. If it doesn't, your pet needs medical attention.

DO THIS NOW

Keep your pet calm and confined. In most cases, a bloody nose won't bother your dog at all. But you can end up with a real mess if she runs around and shakes her head, spraying blood over your carpet and walls in the process. The best thing to do is confine her in a small, easily cleaned room like a bathroom with a tile or linoleum floor. Speak softly to her and try to keep her calm. If you can keep her quiet for a while, you'll give a clot the chance to form more quickly, which will stop the bleeding.

Apply a cold compress. When your dog has bumped her nose and you know that the bleeding is not caused by something more serious, like being hit by a car, you can speed the clotting process by applying a cold compress. Applying ice directly to the nose could freeze the fragile tissues, so first apply a cold, wet washcloth to her nose. Then, put a cold pack, a plastic bag filled with ice, or a bag of frozen peas or corn on top of the cloth. You can use the compress for 10 to 30 minutes at a time several times a day.

FIRST ALERT

Canine Ehrlichiosis

Anything from a bump on the nose to cancer or even rat poison may cause a bloody nose. But dogs are also at risk for a bacterial disease called ehrlichiosis that's transmitted by ticks. This disease frequently causes a spontaneous bloody nose.

The bacteria develop inside the body of the tick and pass into the dog in the tick's saliva when it takes a blood meal. The disease is found primarily in the Gulf Coast region and southern states, but it has been documented wherever the brown dog tick is found. The organism infects the white blood cells. It causes a wide range of symptoms, including fever, eye and nose discharge, loss of appetite, swollen legs and lameness, muscle twitches, bleeding disorders, and depression—your pet is withdrawn and not interested in taking part in his daily activities. If your pet shows any or all of these symptoms, call your vet.

The disease is diagnosed with blood tests, and antibiotic therapy for 6 weeks or longer can cure your dog when begun promptly. Preventing exposure to ticks is the best way to keep your dog from contracting ehrlichiosis. (For more information about ticks, see page 380.)

Help a clot form. The best way to encourage a clot to form is by holding an absorbent pad or a washcloth over the affected nostril. A sanitary napkin works extremely well for this, since it's super-absorbent, but be sure to cover only one nostril, so you don't interfere with your pet's breathing.

 FOLLOW-UP CARE

■ If your pet's nosebleed was caused by a car accident or other serious incident, the vet will tell you how to treat the wounds when you return home. Otherwise, no follow-up care is required once the bleeding has stopped.

Advisors

■ Mauri Karger, D.V.M., is a veterinarian at I-20 Animal Medical Center in Arlington, Texas.
■ A. Michelle Miller, D.V.M., is a veterinarian at Animal Aid Clinic South in Elkhart, Indiana.
■ Laura Solien, D.V.M., is a veterinarian at Maplecrest Animal Hospital in Goshen, Indiana.

Pad Burns

CALL YOUR VET: **IF NEEDED**

MEDICINE CHEST

Cold water
Washcloth
Cold pack or compress
Peanut butter
Pillowcase
Antiseptic liquid soap
  (Betadine Skin
  Cleanser)
Antibiotic ointment
  (Neosporin)
Cotton sock
Tape
Roll gauze
Sterile saline contact
  lens solution
Wet-to-dry bandages
Nonstick absorbent
  pads (Telfa pads) or
  gauze pads
Plastic bag

On summer days, asphalt roads can get as hot as 140°F or more. That's plenty hot enough to fry an egg—and burn a pet's paw pads. This happens all the time with dogs. Cats are less likely to get burned on roads, but they do burn their feet on stovetops and candle flames, mainly because they pat things to investigate them.

Dogs rarely get serious burns because their footpads are very thick and tough. Burns that take off the top layer or two of skin can be treated at home, but deeper burns need veterinary care. If you see pink tissue or blisters on your pet's paw pads, your vet should examine him. Cats' paws are more delicate, and burns can take a long time to heal. A cat or dog whose foot doesn't get better in 2 days or who has burned more than one foot should be treated by a veterinarian.

DO THIS NOW

Put your pet's feet in cold water immediately. The quicker you douse burns with water, the less tissue damage there will be. They should be sprayed or soaked with cold water for at least 5 to 10 minutes. If your dog won't climb in the bathtub, fill a roasting pan with cold water and have him stand in that. If your cat won't tolerate any water, you'll have to use a compress: Use a commercial cold pack or fill a washcloth with ice and hold it on the burned pad for 10 minutes.

Coat tar burns with peanut butter. Burns from fresh tar or asphalt are among the most se-

Keeping Bandages in Place

It's hard to keep paws bandaged. Friction takes a toll, and most pets—especially cats—will lick, bite, and worry at a bandage until it comes off. The only way to keep the bandage in place is to wrap it the way veterinarians do. Here's how.

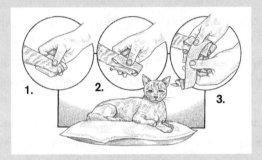

1. Put a clean pad over the burn.
2. Using roll gauze folded in half, extend a strip from the front of the foot down over the paw and under the toes.
3. Wrap a single strip of gauze around the paw, starting at the toes and moving upward until it covers the first strip of gauze.

The bandage needs to breathe, so secure only the top, using a strip of tape. After that, put a clean white cotton sock over the foot and tape it at the top. The wrapping should be firm but not too tight. You've done it right if you can slip a pencil between the foot and the wrapping without having to work too hard.

rious, not only because the temperatures can reach 325°F but also because tar sticks to the feet and keeps burning. After rinsing the paw with water, quickly slather it with peanut butter. The oil in peanut butter is a natural solvent that removes tar and asphalt.

Flood chemical burns with water. When the pads have been burned by chemicals such as road salt, a quick washing isn't enough. You'll need to flood them with cool to lukewarm water for at least 20 minutes. (Water that is too hot may speed up the absorption of the chemical through the skin. Water that is too cold may cause hypothermia.)

If your cat won't tolerate water, you'll have to wrap him in a pillowcase with the affected foot exposed and then flood the foot with water. In a pinch, you could use a bottle of sterile saline contact lens solution to flush the affected paw pads. Try to direct the stream of liquid away from the rest of the body to keep from spreading the chemical. Don't use antibiotics or other ointments because they'll trap residues of the chemical next to the skin. And make sure that your pet doesn't lick his paws. Chemicals that burn on the outside will burn on the inside, too. (See page 106 for more information about chemical burns.)

Wash the pad. Burns get infected easily, so wash the area with soap and water. An antiseptic liquid soap like Betadine Skin Cleanser is better than plain bath soap. Pat the paw dry.

Apply an antibiotic ointment. Some over-the-counter ointments contain hydrocortisone. Don't use them. Hydrocortisone has no effect on bacteria, and, as with all steroids, it can substantially slow healing time. An ointment like Neosporin works well.

Cover the paw. To protect the burn, bandage it as shown on the opposite page, slipping a clean white cotton sock over the bandage to keep dirt out of the burn and prevent your pet from licking it.

 FOLLOW-UP CARE

■ Burns usually heal from the inside out, so you don't want to seal them too completely because that promotes infection. For serious burns, veterinarians recommend bandages called wet-to-dry. They're applied wet, then allowed to dry in place, forming a surface that's similar to skin. They protect the burn and also prevent it from crusting over, which can interfere with healing. To make a wet-to-dry bandage, soak a piece of gauze in sterile saline contact lens solution, apply it to the burn, and cover it with a larger, dry gauze pad, using bandaging tape to hold everything in place. This type of bandage controls bacteria by allowing air to circulate. It should be changed twice a day for the first few days. If your pet requires a wet-to-dry bandage change on the wound, your vet will show you how to do it.

■ You don't need a wet-to-dry bandage for most burns. A good choice for a weepy wound is an absorbent, nonstick pad like a Telfa pad, which keeps burns clean but doesn't stick to the wound. In addition, Telfa pads absorb liquids and pull them away from the burn, allowing it to dry and heal more quickly. Burns that aren't weepy can be dressed with a plain gauze pad. Ask your vet which bandage will be best for your pet.

■ Apply a thin film of antibiotic or silver sulfadiazine (available from your vet) ointment on the burn every time you change the Telfa pad or bandage. Plan on changing bandages every 1 to 2 days as long as the bandage stays clean. One way to keep bandages clean and dry is to slip your pet's paw into a plastic bag when he goes outside. Be sure to remove it when he comes in.

Advisors

■ Shane Bateman, D.V.M., D.V.Sc., is a veterinarian board certified in the American College of Emergency and Critical Care Medicine and assistant professor of emergency and critical care medicine at Ohio State University College of Veterinary Medicine in Columbus.

■ Grace F. Bransford, D.V.M., is a veterinarian in Corte Madera, California.

■ Joanne Howl, D.V.M., is a veterinarian in West River, Maryland; secretary/treasurer of the American Academy on Veterinary Disaster Medicine; and past president of the Maryland Veterinary Medical Association.

■ Elaine Wexler-Mitchell, D.V.M., is a veterinarian at the Cat Care Clinic in Orange, California, and president of the Academy of Feline Medicine.

■ H. Ellen Whiteley, D.V.M, is a veterinarian in Guadalupita, New Mexico, and author of *Understanding and Training Your Cat or Kitten* and *Understanding and Training Your Dog or Puppy*.

Paw Damage

CALL YOUR VET: **IF NEEDED**

MEDICINE CHEST

Clean cloth or gauze
    pad
Cotton sock or condom
Cool water
Antiseptic liquid soap
    (Betadine Skin
    Cleanser)
3% hydrogen peroxide
Petroleum jelly
Epsom salts
Warm water
Elastic adhesive ban-
    dage (Elastoplast)
Plastic bag
Antibiotic ointment
    (Neosporin)
Elizabethan collar
Antiseptic solution
    (Betadine Solution)

Pets injure their paws in all kinds of ways. Paws can have toenails torn or pads punctured with fishhooks or cut with glass. They can be burned with flames or chemicals, and the flesh can be ground away if a pet is improperly leashed and dragged from a vehicle.

Dogs who are bored may develop a habit of licking their paws until they wear away the fur and cause sores on their toes and feet. Dogs with damaged paws usually limp or hold the paws up, while cats may just stop walking around and hide instead. Or in private, they may groom the area excessively.

Deep injuries need medical attention. For instance, if more than a quarter of the pad is cut through and you can see pink flesh, your pet will need stitches within 2 to 3 hours of the injury for it to heal properly. But you can prevent infection and soothe discomfort with first aid, and that may be all that's needed for minor damage.

 DO THIS NOW

Keep him still. It can be hard to examine the damage by yourself, so it's helpful to have a second person restrain your pet. Set a small pet on a countertop; kneel on the floor beside a large dog. If you're doing the restraining, bring one arm up around your pet's neck and the other under and around his chest and hug him to you. (This technique is illustrated on page 18.) Remember to keep the damaged paw on the side away from your body. Use the hand that's under his chest to extend that front paw and keep him from pulling it away. On the rear leg, grasp the knee to straighten his leg and extend the paw. Damage to paws is painful, so if he fights too much, it's better to take him to the vet's office to be sedated and treated.

Control bleeding. Paw injuries tend to bleed a lot, even if they aren't serious. Apply pressure directly on the wound with a clean cloth or gauze pad to stop the bleeding. Usually, it will stop within 5 minutes. If the first pad soaks through, don't remove it or you could disturb the clot that's forming. Just put a second pad on top of the first one. (For more information on bleeding, see page 95.)

Use a pressure bandage for prolonged bleeding. If the bleeding continues for longer than 5 minutes, put another pad on top of the first, slip a cotton sock over the pad, and wrap the sock with tape to make a temporary pressure bandage until you can get to the vet. If you don't have tape, a condom works well to hold the bandage in place. It prevents bloody paw prints on carpets and upholstery.

Give a cool-water rinse. If the damaged paw isn't bleeding heavily, clean it with cool water. Rinsing the area under a stream of water helps flush out any debris and can wash away chemicals that may have burned the paw as well as ease the pain of thermal burns. For burns, you'll need to rinse with cool water for at least 20 minutes. (For more information about pad burns, see page 305.)

Wash the damaged area. Plain soap is better than nothing, but an antiseptic liquid soap like Betadine Skin Cleanser is better and helps prevent infection from getting a foothold. You can use 3% hydrogen peroxide to help cleanse the area surrounding the wound, but don't put it directly on the wound.

See the vet for deep cuts. Any deep damage needs to be seen by a vet. Shallow cuts that don't bleed can get by with a thin layer of petroleum jelly to protect them. See below for bandaging information.

 ## SPECIAL SITUATION

For burns or abrasions: Paws that have lost a lot of skin, either from burns or abrasions, may require special bandages called wet-to-dry bandages. They keep the wound moist to help tissue rebuild, and they also help remove debris when they are removed. Usually, your veterinarian will apply and remove wet-to-dry bandages, but you'll need to watch your pet to make sure that he doesn't remove them.

 ## FOLLOW-UP CARE

■ For a puncture, soak the paw in 1 cup of Epsom salts dissolved in 2 gallons of warm water for 10 minutes two or three times a day. This helps keep the paw clean and brings any infection to a head.

■ If you can see pink flesh, the paw needs protection in order to heal. The only way to keep a paw bandage on is to tape it to the fur. A baby bootie or sock works well for cats and small dogs, and a regular cotton sock is fine for bigger dogs. Slip the sock over the damaged paw, then place an elastic adhesive bandage like Elasto-plast at the top directly on the fur. The cloth allows the wound to breathe and heal. There are sweat glands in the pads of the foot that make the paw moist when it can't breathe, and that's a perfect breeding ground for infection. You'll need to change the bandage daily for the first 2 to 3 days and then at least every 2 days, or anytime it gets dirty or wet.

■ Keep bandages clean by placing a clean plastic bag over the foot when your pet must go outside. Pets often lick and chew at bandages that are too tight or get wet and start to cause discomfort, so keeping them dry with the plastic makes good sense. Be sure to remove the bag when your pet comes back inside.

■ If the wound is stitched, you'll need to keep the sutures clean. Use an antiseptic liquid soap like Betadine Skin Cleanser twice a day to remove any drainage. After you dry the damaged area, put on a thin layer of antibiotic ointment like Neosporin.

■ If your pet tries to bother the paw or bandage, a cone-shaped collar restraint called an Elizabethan collar is the best way to keep him from causing more damage. He won't be able to eat while wearing the collar, though, so be sure to remove it during feedings.

■ If the paw damage gets any worse—if it becomes red, swells, or starts to smell—it could mean that there's an infection. Have it checked by your veterinarian, who may prescribe antibiotics. It can also help to soak the affected paw for 5 minutes three times a day until it heals. Use an antiseptic solution like Betadine Solution to help speed the healing and stop the infection in its tracks. Dilute the Betadine in comfortably warm distilled water until it's the color of weak tea.

Advisors

■ Gerald Brown, D.V.M., is a veterinarian at City Cat Doctor in Chicago.

■ Bernadine Cruz, D.V.M., is a veterinarian at Laguna Hills Animal Hospital in California.

■ Kenneth J. Drobatz, D.V.M., is a veterinarian and associate professor of critical care emergency service at the Veterinary Hospital of the University of Pennsylvania in Philadelphia.

■ Kate Lindley, D.V.M., is a veterinarian and owner of Kitty Klinic in Lacey, Washington.

■ Jeffrey Werber, D.V.M., is a veterinarian at Century Veterinary Group in Los Angeles.

Poisoning

CALL YOUR VET: **IMMEDIATELY**

Pets can poison themselves by swallowing something that tastes good to them, like chocolate candy, rat bait, antifreeze (which has a sweet flavor), or poisonous houseplants. Dogs are notorious for eating whole bottles of candy-coated human pills, like ibuprofen—and a childproof lid is no match for canine teeth.

Cats more typically are exposed when they walk through something or scratch a toxic plant and then swallow the poison when they clean themselves. Flea products designed for dogs often are too strong for cats, and insecticides that are safe when used alone can turn deadly if you combine them—for instance, a flea and tick collar along with a spot-on treatment (a liquid insecticide that is applied to your pet's coat) can build up toxicity on a cumulative basis. Pets can also be poisoned by having something spilled on their fur, like gasoline, motor oil, or other coal-tar toxins, or by being exposed to phenol-containing products like Lysol.

Poisons cause a huge range of symptoms that can develop within minutes or not until days later. The signs depend on the kind of poison, the amount of exposure, and the individual pet. For instance, the acronym SLUDD stands for flea-product toxicity: salivation, lacrimation (watering eyes), urination, defecation, and dyspnea (labored breathing). These symptoms generally develop within about 20 minutes. Other poisons, like warfarin—rat bait—often contain anticoagulant ingredients that make the poisoned pet bleed internally, and even after the pet has been treated, signs can continue for up to 6 weeks. Antifreeze affects the central nervous system within a couple of hours. An antifreeze-poisoned pet acts drunk at first but then returns to normal before ultimately suffering kidney failure, coma, and death. Poisoned pets also can have seizures.

Poisoning is an emergency and needs immediate medical attention. But you can save your pet's life with first aid by either getting rid of the poison, neutralizing it, or diluting it to give you time to seek help.

🩹 DO THIS NOW

Make your pet vomit. The very best way to treat most swallowed poisons is to make your pet vomit immediately—but only if he is fully conscious and in complete control. A woozy pet can inhale the vomited material on the way up and suffocate. As long as your dog or cat knows what's going on, you can induce vomiting up to an hour after he has swallowed the toxin, but the sooner the better. There are several ways to do this, and some work better in certain pets than others. (*Caution:* See "Special Situations" on page 313 before you start.)

First, feed your pet a small meal. If he won't eat it, offer any favorite treat that he'll willingly swallow. Food in the stomach not only helps dilute the poison and delay its absorption, but having something in the stomach makes it much easier to induce vomiting.

You can give 3% hydrogen peroxide—about 1 to 2 teaspoons for every 10 pounds your pet weighs—to make him vomit. It usually works better in dogs than in cats. Use an eyedropper, needleless syringe, or a turkey baster to squirt the liquid to the back of your pet's tongue. The foaming action and taste should prompt vomiting within 5 minutes. If necessary, repeat two or three times, allowing 5 minutes between doses.

For dogs, you can use syrup of Ipecac instead of hydrogen peroxide. It can be irritating to cats, though. Dosage is 1 teaspoon for dogs up to 35 pounds, and up to 1 tablespoon for larger dogs. Ipecac syrup may take a little longer to work, but

the dosage should not be repeated. Administer it the same way as the hydrogen peroxide.

Give the bottle to the vet. Many poisons have very specific antidotes, so it's important to identify the toxin. Take the bottle or package along with you to the veterinarian's office. And if your pet vomits, be sure to take a sample of the vomited material for analysis.

🥤 SPECIAL SITUATIONS

If your pet stops breathing: Be prepared to give artificial respiration if your pet stops

Poison-Control Centers

The National Animal Poison-Control Center (NAPCC), administered by the American Association for the Prevention of Cruelty to Animals, is available for telephone consultations in cases of poisoning emergency. There is a charge for this service. If you wish to charge the consultation fee to a major credit card, call (800) 548-2423. If you don't have a major credit card, call (900) 680-0000, and the fee will be charged to your phone bill.

Almost every major city has a human poison-control center whose services are free, paid for by your tax dollars, and they often have cat and dog information, too. They can tell you if something is dangerous for your pet or if it's harmless, so you'll know whether a trip to the vet is needed.

breathing. Be sure to wear disposable medical gloves (available in drugstores) when handling your pet. Form one hand into a cylinder and place the pinky end over your dog's nostrils. Put your mouth over the other end of your hand and seal his lips with your other hand so that air doesn't leak out. Blow into his lungs through his nose with two quick breaths, watching for his chest to rise (blow as though filling a paper bag—just hard enough to see his chest expand). Give 15 to 20 breaths per minute. Between breaths, let the air escape back out through his nose. Continue rescue breathing until he starts breathing again on his own or you reach medical help. If you don't have gloves, you should administer artificial respiration only through a barrier like a piece of plastic wrap (Saran Wrap) so that you don't come in contact with the poison yourself. Cut a small hole in the material and place it over your pet's nostrils before starting rescue breathing.

If your pet's heart has stopped: You'll need to perform CPR. It's best to have someone drive you and your pet to the animal hospital while you're performing CPR.

For cats and small dogs, cup a hand over the point of the chest just behind the elbows and squeeze firmly between your fingers and thumb, pressing in about ½ inch, about 80 to 100 times a minute. Give a breath into the nose after every five compressions until your pet revives or until you reach medical help.

Put a larger dog on his side on a firm, flat surface and put both hands flat on top of each

Truffle Poisoning

Dogs and cats can be poisoned by eating chocolate because the theobromine in the candy is a stimulant that affects the heart. Milk chocolate usually isn't a problem—it would take about 2 pounds of milk chocolate to poison a 7-pound pet. But baker's chocolate contains 10 times as much theobromine as milk chocolate, so the same pet could get sick from eating just 2 ounces.

Veterinarians say that most chocolate problems caused by raiding the Halloween candy just cause an upset tummy and some diarrhea. But when truffles appear around Christmas or Easter time, the very rich, dark chocolate treats can launch a full-scale poisoning episode, with vomiting, diarrhea, hyperactivity, seizures, coma, and even death. If your pet gets into the truffles, licks the chocolate frosting off a cake, or dips into the cocoa mix, induce vomiting as soon as you can, then call the veterinarian.

other against the chest. Use both hands to compress the chest by 25 to 50%. Alternate breaths and compressions as for small pets. (This technique is illustrated on page 21.)

If your pet has swallowed a caustic poison: Some caustic poisons like bleach and ammonia burn while going down the throat and cause just as much damage coming back up, while petroleum products like kerosene and

(continued on page 317)

Common Household Poisons

If you suspect that your pet has been poisoned by a toxic substance, call your vet or a poison-control center right away. Use this chart and "Common Plant Poisons" on page 316 to help you identify the source of poisoning to your vet or the poison control experts.

Poison Source	Symptoms
Acids (bleach, drain cleaners)	Swallowed: drooling, pawing at mouth, abdominal pain. On skin: crying, rolling, licking
Alkalis (ammonia, laundry detergent)	Swallowed: drooling, pawing at mouth, abdominal pain On skin: crying, rolling, licking
Antifreeze	Drunken behavior, increased thirst and urination, diarrhea, vomiting, seizures, panting, appetite loss
Baker's chocolate	Drooling, vomiting, diarrhea, excess urination, hyperactivity, muscle tremors, seizures, coma
Coal-tar products (phenol disinfectants, like Lysol; treated wood; fungicides; tar paper; photographic developer)	Depression, weakness, lack of coordination, coma, death
Flea products (Carbaryl, Sevin, Propoxur, Frontline, Advantage, Program, Fenthion, Parathion, Ronnel, Trichlorofon) *Antidote available from vet*	Variety of signs include apprehension, muscle twitches, shivering, seizures, drooling, diarrhea, hyperactivity, depression.
Lead (paint, ceramics, linoleum, golf balls) *Antidote available from vet*	Abdominal pain, vomiting, seizures, lack of coordination, excitement and hysteria (i.e., excess barking), weakness, blindness, chewing fits.
Pain medicine (aspirin, acetaminophen, ibuprofen)	Blood in vomit, appetite loss, drooling, drunk behavior. For acetaminophen (cats): blue gums, difficulty breathing
Other medicine	Various signs; if you know your pet has ingested a particular medicine, call the vet or poison control center right away
Pest baits (strychnine, vitamin D, warfarin, arsenic, bromethalin, cholecalciferol, metaldehyde, phosphorus, sodium fluoroacetate, zinc phosphide) *Antidote available from vet*	Range of signs include bloody urine and diarrhea, bleeding from body openings, thirst, staggering, abdominal pain and cramps, paralysis, seizures, strong garlic breath, coma, depression.
Petroleum products (motor oil, gas, turpentine, paint, paint thinner, paint remover, lighter fluid, kerosene)	Vomiting, difficulty breathing, tremors, seizures, coma, respiratory failure, death

Induce Vomiting	Give Charcoal	Give Oil and Bread	Bathe
NO	NO	YES	YES. If ingested, rinse mouth with milk or water. If topical, rinse thoroughly with cool water.
NO	NO	YES	YES. If ingested, rinse mouth with milk or water. If topical, rinse thoroughly with cool water.
YES	YES	NO	N/A
YES	YES	NO	N/A
YES	YES	NO	YES. If the poison is on your pet's skin or coat, first, rinse thoroughly with cool water. Bathe with a mild dishwashing liquid, then rinse again with cool water.
YES, if swallowed	YES, if swallowed	NO	YES. If the poison is a powder, brush coat first, rinse thoroughly with cool water, bathe with a mild dishwashing liquid, then rinse again thoroughly with cool water.
YES	YES	NO	N/A
YES	YES	NO	N/A
YES	YES	NO	N/A
YES	YES	NO	N/A
NO	NO	YES	YES. If the poison is on coat, rinse thoroughly with water, bathe with a mild dishwashing liquid, then rinse again.

Common Plant Poisons

Many common houseplants and landscape plants are poisonous. Review this list and give poisonous houseplants to friends and neighbors who don't have pets. If your pet chews on outdoor plants, dig up the poisonous ones or make sure that they're off-limits. Here are the worst offenders.

Poison source	Symptoms	First Aid
Azalea	Salivation, vomiting, diarrhea, muscle weakness, seizures, coma, death	Give lots of water to wash stomach; give activated charcoal
Belladona, datura, henbane, jessamine, jimsonweed	Dry, red skin; fever; seizures; excess thirst; dilated pupils	Induce vomiting
Caladium, dieffenbachia, philodendron	Swollen tongue and throat, difficulty breathing	DO NOT induce vomiting; keep airway open; give CPR if necessary; offer milk or water to wash out mouth
Crown of thorns, English ivy	Thirst, vomiting, diarrhea, stomach pain, death in 1 to 2 days	Induce vomiting
Daffodil, tulip, wisteria bulbs	Depression, violent vomiting	Induce vomiting unless pet is already vomiting; give water and/or milk to dilute poison and coat stomach
Foxglove, larkspur, lily of the valley, monkshood, oleander	Depression, bloody diarrhea, fast or slow heartbeat, severe stomach pain, coma, death	Induce vomiting
Holly	Stomach pain, vomiting, diarrhea	Induce vomiting
Jerusalem cherry, potato (green parts and eyes), nightshade	Vomiting, bloody diarrhea, trembling, weakness	DO NOT induce vomiting; *antidote available from vet*
Lily	Kidney failure, with excess urination and drinking	Induce vomiting
Mother-in-law's tongue (snake plant)	Vomiting, salivation, diarrhea, staggering, collapse, mouth irritation	DO NOT induce vomiting; offer milk or water to wash out mouth
Rhubarb	Vomiting, salivation, stomach pain, convulsions, kidney damage	Induce vomiting
Seeds and pits of apple, apricot, cherry, peach, and hydrangea	Cyanide poisoning: bright red gums, involuntary urination and defecation, labored breathing, seizures, frothing at the mouth, coma	Induce vomiting; *antidote available from vet*
Walnuts (hulls)	Vomiting, diarrhea, convulsions	Induce vomiting
Yew	Muscle weakness, difficulty breathing, dilated pupils, sudden death without signs	Induce vomiting; keep airway open; give CPR if necessary

motor oil are easily drawn into the lungs if vomited. Never induce vomiting if you suspect that your pet has swallowed one of these types of poisons. Instead, soak a piece of bread in 2 tablespoons of mineral oil or vegetable oil and feed it to your pet. The oil helps coat the lining of the stomach and intestines to protect them, and it slows absorption of the poison. Pets can accidentally inhale oil when it's given by syringe, so eating it with bread helps avoid that problem.

Pets never swallow caustic material willingly—at most, they might suffer mouth burns from tasting it. If you suspect that your pet has tasted something caustic, encourage him to drink as much water as possible to dilute the poison and wash out his mouth. Milk also helps coat the stomach, and some pets may prefer it to water. You can use a clean spray bottle filled with water or milk to cool off the burn until you get to the vet's office. Spritz your pet's mouth for at least 15 minutes on the way.

For poison on the coat or skin: Any time a dog or cat has a toxic reaction to something on his skin, the best first aid is to give him a bath. Most flea products (even the once-a-month spot-on treatments) are oil-based, and using these products inappropriately may cause poisoning from absorption through the skin. You can use a degreasing shampoo or dishwashing detergent like Dawn to cut through topical poisons. Be sure to rinse your pet very thoroughly to get rid of the detergent, though, because soap not designed for pets can dry out the skin. Then wrap your pet in a towel and get him to the animal hospital.

For paint, tar, or motor oil on the skin: These substances won't wash away with soap and water, and you must never use paint thinner or mineral spirits to dissolve them, because they are just as toxic. Instead, put on rubber gloves and rub in lots of mineral oil or vegetable oil before the material hardens on the fur or skin. Let it soak until it loosens. Then use cornmeal, cornstarch, or flour to dust over the contaminated areas—the powder absorbs the toxin efficiently, and it can then be washed away with dishwashing liquid. You may need to lather up and rinse your pet repeatedly. Be sure to cover his face with a cloth or towel before applying the powdery substances to minimize the amount of powder that gets into his nose and eyes. (For more information about fur contamination, see page 221.)

If your pet has a seizure: Poisoning can cause seizures in pets: They fall over, whine and cry, paddle with their feet, and urinate or defecate. Almost all seizures stop within 3 minutes, and then you can wrap your pet in a towel. Covering his eyes with a dark cloth may help bring him out of the fit. (For more information about seizures, see page 330.)

FOLLOW-UP CARE

■ Many kinds of poison disrupt the digestive tract, so a bland diet will often help your pet recover more quickly. There are therapeutic diets available by prescription from your veterinarian that help heal damage to the kidneys or liver. You can also make an acceptable bland diet at home. Boil skinless chicken or turkey breast or brown and drain ground beef, then mix the meat 50/50 with cooked white rice.

■ Introduce food again very slowly. If your pet was throwing up for 3 days, just rest his tummy for 24 hours and offer only water to drink. Then give tiny amounts of the bland diet several times a day—1 teaspoon for each 10 pounds of body weight. Once his tummy has settled, feed the bland diet by itself for 2 to 3 days, then mix it 50/50 with the old diet for a couple of days before returning to regular food.

■ With poisons that cause bleeding disorders, vitamin K therapy is needed for 3 weeks or even longer. The amount depends on the size of your pet and the kind of poison he ingested. Vitamin K is usually given as an oral medication when your pet is well enough to be at home. Your vet will give you dosage instructions. Watch for any signs of a bloody nose, blood in the stool, or problems breathing for up to 6 weeks after the poisoning. If any of these signs appear, call the vet immediately.

THE BEST APPROACH

Activated Charcoal

Activated charcoal works well as an antidote to many kinds of poison, but the tablet form isn't concentrated enough to do much good. You can buy liquid suspensions or tubes of commercial paste that veterinarians use, and they're both much more effective. You don't need a prescription for them, but pharmacies probably don't carry them routinely, so you'd have to order them in advance just to have them on hand. The most convenient activated charcoal preparation is ToxiBan made by Vet-a-Mix.

Activated charcoal tastes absolutely awful, so it can be a trick to get your pet to take it willingly. It can also stain carpeting and upholstery as well as your skin and clothing. Veterinarians either force-feed the solution or use a stomach tube to get it down the pet, and if you are near a clinic, it's best to let a vet handle the treatment. But in an emergency, when a vet isn't available, something like ToxiBan could save your pet's life.

Advisors

■ Shane Bateman, D.V.M., D.V.Sc., is board certified in the American College of Emergency and Critical Care Medicine and assistant professor of emergency and critical care medicine at Ohio State University College of Veterinary Medicine in Columbus.

■ Patricia Hague, D.V.M., is a veterinarian at the Cat Hospital of Las Colinas in Irving, Texas.

■ Janie Hodges, D.V.M., is a veterinarian at Valley View Pet Health Center in Farmers Branch, Texas.

■ Chris Johnson, D.V.M., is a veterinarian at Westside Animal Emergency Clinic in Atlanta.

■ Barry N. Kellogg, V.M.D., is a veterinarian at the Center for Veterinary Care in Great Barrington, Massachusetts, and the head of VMAT 1 (Veterinary Medical Assistance Team), the national disaster team for veterinary medicine.

■ Mike McFarland, D.V.M., is a veterinarian at the Emergency Animal Clinic in Dallas.

Porcupine Quills

CALL YOUR VET: **IF NEEDED**

At about 18 inches tall, 3 feet long (counting the tail), and up to 40 pounds, the "thorn pig," more commonly called the porcupine, is the bane of curious dogs and, rarely, cats. This vegetarian rodent is native throughout the Pacific Northwest and most of North America and is known for its unique fur coat. A porcupine typically sports 30,000 quills—hardened, modified hairs—scattered over its tail, back, and sides, and each one is under direct muscular control.

Porcupines don't "throw" their quills, but the spines are held only loosely in the skin and drop out when ejected by agitated skin or a lashing tail. If a curious dog happens to be on the receiving end of that tail, she'll get a face full of quills, ranging in size from ½ inch to more than 4 inches long. Each quill has backward-projecting scales near the tip that are designed to work their way deeper into the victim's flesh by his own muscle action. Left in place, a quill could enter a dog's nose and come out at her shoulders, causing excruciating pain all along the way.

If your dog ends up with a face that looks like a pincushion or with quills stuck inside her mouth, she'll need medical help to remove them all. Pulling out the quills takes care of the problem, though, and if there are only a couple, first aid may be all that's needed.

DO THIS NOW

Give her an antihistamine. Any foreign material stuck into the skin can prompt an allergic response, with swelling and pain. An over-the-counter antihistamine like Benadryl not only reduces the skin reaction and swelling but also tends to make pets a bit drowsy, so it can calm them down. The liquid form of Benadryl usually comes in a dose of 12.5 milligrams per teaspoon; pills are usually 25 milligrams each. Pets will need 1 milligram per pound of body weight every 6 to 8 hours. That means a 10-pound cat or dog should get about ¾ teaspoon of liquid or half a pill. Use a needleless syringe or turkey baster to squirt the liquid to the back of your pet's tongue. Most of the time, the quills will be in or around your pet's mouth, so it may be hard to get a pill down. Try hiding the medicine in an irresistible treat, which may also help distract your pet from her discomfort. If you manage to get the Benadryl down, give it about 30 minutes to take effect, but be aware that it won't make a very frightened pet who is also in pain all that sleepy.

Keep your pet still. It's best to have someone help you restrain your pet, but you can manage alone if necessary. Position a large dog in a corner of a room. Have her sit, then you should stand with one leg on either side of her to stabilize her chest with your knees. Use gloved hands to firmly hold your dog's head and muzzle. If you're restraining a cat or small dog, wear a heavy coat and wrap one arm around your pet's body, pressing firmly on the underside of her chest. Your pet should face toward the right if you are right-handed. Firmly grasp your pet's muzzle with your other hand.

Wear heavy gloves to remove quills. It's an old wives' tale that cutting off a quill makes it easier to remove—the opposite is true, and you won't have as much to grab. To remove a quill, put on a pair of heavy work or garden gloves and, using a hemostat (a long, thin clamp available from pet-supply catalogs) or a pair of pliers, grasp the quill close to where it enters the skin.

Removing porcupine quills really hurts, so make sure that you or someone else can restrain your pet before you start, and wear heavy gloves to protect yourself.

Use slow, even pressure to pull it straight out. Don't yank, or you could break off the quill, which will then need to be surgically removed. Don't be surprised if your pet yelps—it's very painful. And if she protests or struggles too much, it's more humane to let your veterinarian remove all the quills after giving your pet a sedative or short-term general anesthetic.

Look for hidden quills. If your pet has short fur and has been stuck in the face, you'll easily see most of the quills. But longer-haired pets may have quills hidden beneath their fur, and they can fester if not removed. To find them, carefully feel all over your pet's body several times. Go over the skin slowly in several directions. You'll be looking for the blunt end of the quill because the sharp end is still in your pet. If you can't feel the quills, remove your gloves and very carefully check again.

Wash the affected areas. Once the quills are removed, wash the wounds with warm water and antiseptic liquid soap like Betadine Skin Cleanser, and rinse well. This will also help ease the pain of the punctures. Do this two or three times a day for 2 to 3 days. As long as all of the quill is removed, pets rarely develop infections from the quills because the spines are coated with a fatty acid that protects even the porcupine from infection from accidental jabs.

 ## FOLLOW-UP CARE

■ If your dog still has pain, you may give buffered aspirin like Bufferin. The usual dose is 10 to 25 milligrams per 2.2 pounds of body weight two or three times a day. Do not give aspirin to cats.

■ Tiny quills or pieces of quills left in the skin may develop little abscesses as the body tries to eject them. As long as they're small (pinpoint size), you can pop them like pimples and dab antiseptic solution like Betadine Solution on the wounds. (Dilute it with distilled water to the color of weak tea.) You can use it two or three times a day for 2 to 3 days. If the sores haven't cleared up in that time, take your pet to the vet.

■ Watch the wounds for several days after you've removed the quills. If there's any swelling, redness, or discharge, your pet will need antibiotics from the vet.

■ Porcupine quills can break off and remain undetected. They will travel through the body to places such as the eyes, brain, and spine. Continue to watch your pet for several months after the injury for anything unusual. If anything happens, be sure to tell your vet that your pet had quills; they may be related to her current problem.

THE BEST APPROACH

Hemostats

Needle-nose or regular pliers will work for pulling out porcupine quills, but hemostats are really the best choice. You can get them from a pet-supply catalog. They're easy to use because their scissors grip locks onto the quill so that you can concentrate on removing it. You'll find hemostats handy for all kinds of pet care—like removing foreign objects—even if your pet never meets a porcupine.

Advisors

■ Janie Hodges, D.V.M., is a veterinarian at Valley View Pet Health Center in Farmers Branch, Texas.
■ Karen Hoffman, V.M.D., is a veterinarian at Delaware Valley Animal Hospital in Fairless Hills, Pennsylvania.
■ Dennis L. Wilcox, D.V.M., is a veterinarian at Angeles Clinic for Animals in Port Angeles, Washington.

Puppy Strangles

CALL YOUR VET: **SAME DAY**

Puppy strangles have all kinds of fancy technical names, including juvenile cellulitis and puppy pyoderma. Fortunately, the condition isn't very common. The skin, primarily on the face, becomes infected with deep sores that can reach into the lymph nodes of the neck. Puppy strangles are caused by a malfunction of the immune system. Puppies less than 12 weeks old are affected most often, and Labrador retrievers, golden retrievers, dachshunds, Brittany spaniels, and springer spaniels tend to be at highest risk.

Puppies with strangles run a fever, stop eating, and act lethargic. They develop pustules and painful swelling of the lips, eyelids, face, and often, the groin area. Once puppy strangles reach the lymph nodes, big, swollen knots develop on the neck under the jaw. They look as if they might strangle the puppy, hence the name. The lymph nodes often abscess, break open, and drain. Puppy strangles aren't usually life-threatening, but they do need prompt medical attention, and first aid can help.

DO THIS NOW

Apply a hot pack. Soak a washcloth in water as hot as you can stand, wring it out, and apply it to the swollen area on the puppy's throat. This will bring blood circulation to the area and help clean out the poisons and heal the wound more quickly. Hold the moist hot pack against the area—5 minutes on, 5 minutes off—until it cools, then rewet and reapply it. Do this two to five times a day.

Clean the sores. Sores on the face and lips typically burst, then dry and develop a crust. Clean these places once a day by first soaking them with warm water. The soaking will soften the crusts, and you may wipe them away gently with a clean, wet washcloth. After removing the softened crusts, gently cleanse the areas with a full-strength 2.5% benzoyl peroxide shampoo like Oxy 5, then rinse.

FIRST ALERT

Mange

The draining sores on the face and skin folds of young puppies need to be carefully diagnosed because pyoderma-infected skin can have a number of causes. While puppy strangles is often caused by a malfunction of the immune system that can often be cured with antibiotics and steroids, juvenile demodectic mange can cause very similar signs. And steroids can actually make the mange worse.

Demodectic mange is caused by microscopic cigar-shaped mites that burrow and live under the skin and cause the sores and infection. In fact, these tiny creatures are normal inhabitants of most dogs' skin and cause no problems. But puppies often don't have fully developed immune systems, which makes them susceptible to the mite. Most juvenile demodectic mange goes away as pups mature, but some dogs develop severe disease as adults that covers the whole body. They need aggressive medical treatment that includes antibiotic therapy and medicated dips to kill the mites.

Keep abscesses clean. If the swelling in the lymph nodes has burst, keep the abscess clean with warm water applied with a clean, soft cloth three or four times a day for 5 to 10 minutes at a time. Be gentle, not only because the area is very sore but also because vigorous cleaning could make the area scar permanently.

FOLLOW-UP CARE

■ Until the abscess has healed, continue to use moist hot packs or compresses on the swollen area as described on page 322. This will help bring the abscess to a head so that it opens on its own. Once it's open and draining, continue to apply moist hot packs to keep it open.

■ Your veterinarian may lance the abscessed lymph node if it doesn't open by itself. And often, you will need to flush the deep wound with an antiseptic solution like Betadine Solution. Purchase this solution from the vet or pet-supply store in a strength of 0.01 to 0.1%. If you purchase higher-strength Betadine, dilute it with distilled water until it's the color of weak tea. (If you're not sure about dilution, call your pharmacist or veterinarian for complete instructions.) You can use a needleless syringe or turkey baster to squirt the solution into the wound to rinse out the debris so that it heals from the inside out. Your vet will show you how and tell you how often to do it.

■ After flushing the wound, you can keep it clean with Betadine Solution (diluted as described above) or warm Burow's Solution, an astringent solution available in drugstores. Moisten a clean cloth or gauze pad with the solution and wipe away the discharge as needed.

■ For the crusty areas of skin on the lips and face, bathing your pet with a warm antiseptic liquid soap like Betadine Skin Cleanser, or 2.5% benzoyl peroxide shampoo, several times a day will help with healing and make your puppy more comfortable by soaking away the crusts. If accidentally ingested in small quantities, the Betadine and benzoyl peroxide solutions aren't harmful, but the benzoyl peroxide may make your puppy salivate excessively or vomit. Don't be alarmed—it's a normal reaction to the peroxide's bad taste.

■ Just keeping the skin clean won't cure the problem. You'll usually have to give your pup antibiotics for up to 3 weeks to prevent secondary bacterial infections from occurring in the open and draining wounds. Many times, steroids are also prescribed to fight the inflammation. Puppies may get liquid medicine. To give it, tip the pup's head back, insert a needleless syringe or eyedropper into the pouch of his cheek, squirt in the medicine, and hold his mouth closed until he swallows. (This technique is illustrated on page 30.)

THE BEST APPROACH

Catheter-Tipped Syringe

Flushing deep wounds like abscesses can be tricky without special tools to get the medicine where it needs to go. Usually, the veterinarian will give you a special syringe with a long, flexible tip and show you how to use it. First, fill the syringe with the prescribed flushing solution, insert the catheter tip into the sore, and push the plunger. You will see the wound fill with fluid, and debris will wash out. This will help the wound heal from the inside out.

Advisors
■ Kevin Doughty, D.V.M., is a veterinarian at Mauer Animal Clinic in Las Vegas.
■ Grady Hester, D.V.M., is a veterinarian at All Creatures Animal Clinic in Rolesville, North Carolina.
■ Jeff Nichol, D.V.M., is the hospital director and a veterinarian at Adobe Animal Medical Center in Albuquerque.
■ George White, D.V.M., is a veterinarian at I-20 Animal Medical Center in Arlington, Texas.

Rectal Prolapse

CALL YOUR VET: **IMMEDIATELY**

It's common for young cats and dogs—especially puppies—to have rectal prolapse from straining with diarrhea. (For more information about diarrhea, see page 150.) Basically, the inside of the tract turns inside out, like a sock rolled down over your foot. You'll see pink to gray tissue bulging under the tail—it might be mistaken for hemorrhoids, but pets don't get those. Usually, just a small amount protrudes, but in severe cases, several inches can be exposed. The longer the tissue stays outside the body, the more it dries out and swells, and the more unlikely it is to return to normal. That feeling makes the pet strain even more.

The tissue is extremely tender and easily damaged, and prolapse always needs immediate medical attention. But first aid can help prevent or reduce the damage until you can get help.

DO THIS NOW

Clean the area thoroughly. Use a gentle touch—this area is very tender. A saline wash is perfect. Plain water would be absorbed into the tissue and make the swelling worse, but saline more closely matches the body's natural composition. Sterile saline contact lens solution in a squirt bottle works fine. If you don't have that, make saline solution by dissolving 1¼ teaspoons of table salt in a pint of lukewarm water and put the solution in a clean squirt bottle.

Keep the tissue moist. In most cases, the tissue won't return to normal with first aid. But you can keep the tissue from being further damaged by keeping it moist. Squirt the saline solution over the area. Then, wearing disposable medical gloves (available in drugstores), apply liberal amounts of lubricant like K-Y Jelly to the exposed tissue and wrap the area in a small, saline-moistened towel until you can get to the veterinarian's office.

Use a collar restraint. One of the biggest dangers of rectal prolapse is damage to the tissue. When the rectum is outside the body, the pressure can cut off the blood supply and pinch the nerves. That odd, numb feeling almost always prompts your pet to want to lick or chew on it, which can result in self-mutilation that takes surgery to correct. Protect the tissue by fitting your pet with a collar restraint that keeps her from reaching the area. If you don't have a collar restraint, you may need to temporarily muzzle your pet or try fitting a pair of boxer shorts on her to offer some protection. In any case, you'll need to watch your pet closely until you get her to the vet to prevent her from causing further damage.

 FOLLOW-UP CARE

■ Very often, a dog or cat needs worm medicine to get rid of the cause of the straining and prolapse. Look for signs of worms and take a stool sample to your vet. The type of medicine that your vet recommends will depend on the kind of worms that are diagnosed. (For more information about worms, see page 413).

■ Most pets won't have relapses as long as the cause of the straining has been corrected. In some older pets, the muscles may be flabby, so

a "purse-string suture" may be temporarily placed around the anus to tighten the opening while the injury heals. You'll need to watch your pet to be sure that she doesn't lick or bite at the area until it's completely healed. A collar restraint may be necessary. If you use an Elizabethan collar, your pet won't be able to eat while wearing it, so be sure to remove it during feedings.

THE BEST APPROACH

Pet-Friendly Collar Restraint

Cone-shaped collar restraints called Elizabethan collars have been the standard for years to prevent dogs and cats from damaging themselves by chewing or licking wounds. But these collars are often unwieldy or uncomfortable for pets because they can't see anything on either side and may not be able to eat while wearing the collar. A newer alternative called a Bite-Not Collar is much more comfortable and readily accepted by dogs and cats. It's similar to the stiff cervical collars that people wear after neck injuries. The collar still prevents the pet from turning around and reaching a forbidden area, but it doesn't interfere with her vision or eating. Bite-Not Collars and similarly designed restraints are available from pet-supply stores and catalogs.

Advisors
■ Michael G. Abdella, D.V.M., is a veterinarian at Alisa Viejo Animal Hospital in Alisa Viejo, California.
■ Lorrie Bartloff, D.V.M., is a veterinarian at Three Point Veterinary Clinic in Elkhart, Indiana.
■ Doug McConkey, D.V.M., is a veterinarian at Canyon Creek Pet Hospital in Sherman, Texas.

Scorpion Stings

CALL YOUR VET: **IMMEDIATELY**

There are more than 1,050 species of scorpions, and at least 30 are found in the southwestern United States. Although all scorpion stings hurt like crazy, most aren't any more dangerous than a beesting. The exception is the sting of the bark scorpion, one of the smallest species. Bark scorpions are only 1½ inches long, yellow to brown in color, with two black stripes on their backs. You can tell the bark scorpion from its nonpoisonous cousins by its more slender pincers and tail segments. The bark scorpion can be deadly. It's found in Arizona, western New Mexico, northern Mexico, and the west bank of the Colorado River in California.

All scorpions carry hypodermic-like stingers on the ends of their tails, and they can regulate the amount of venom that's injected. The nontoxic stings cause intense, fiery pain that lasts up to an hour. This then gives way to numbness and tingling, which fades after about 24 hours. Pets may yelp and hold up the stung leg or lick and bite at the sting. Some stings aren't visible, while

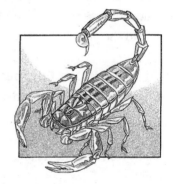

Bark scorpions are small but deadly. They are found in the Southwest, and they tend to hide under pieces of wood and rocks.

others cause massive swelling within 15 to 30 minutes of the sting. A bark scorpion sting hurts just as much, but it also causes drooling, paralysis, breathing problems, and ultimately, collapse and death in as little as 15 minutes. The best treatment for a scorpion sting is rapid transportation to the animal hospital, but first aid can help ensure that your pet gets there in time.

🔋 DO THIS NOW

Apply a cold pack. It's important to make sure that the toxin doesn't spread. First, place a cold, wet washcloth on the sting. Then put a cold pack, a plastic bag filled with ice, or a bag of frozen peas or corn on top of the cloth. Apply the cold pack for 10 to 30 minutes several times a day. This will constrict the blood vessels and slow circulation in that area. The cold also helps numb the pain.

Restrict movement. Put your stung pet in a carrier or box. Prevent him from walking or jumping around, and try to keep him calm. Too much activity will speed up his circulation and spread the poison.

Fit him with an Elizabethan collar. Even when the scorpion isn't a dangerous kind, a dog who is stung will chew at the sore, which can make the reaction worse. Fit your pet with a collar restraint like a cone-shaped Elizabethan collar.

Apply a soothing baking soda poultice. For most scorpion stings, a poultice of baking soda will help take the pain away just as it does for beestings. That can be messy on furry areas of the body, but it works well on sparsely furred regions like the tummy. Try to get the paste directly on the skin by separating the fur around the sting. Make a poultice by mixing 1 tablespoon of baking soda with enough water to create a thick paste and dab it on the swelling.

Give an antihistamine. Scorpion venom contains histamine, which causes the pain and inflammation in the wound. So if you have an antihistamine like Benadryl, it may help reduce your pet's discomfort. Benadryl can also make him sleepy, which may help keep him calm and quiet until you can get medical attention. The liquid form of Benadryl usually comes in a dose of 12.5 milligrams per teaspoon; pills are usually 25 milligrams each. Pets will need 1 milligram per pound of body weight every 6 to 8 hours. That means a 10-pound cat or dog should get about ¾ teaspoon of liquid or half a pill.

🥫 SPECIAL SITUATIONS

If your pet stops breathing: If your pet isn't breathing, you'll need to start artificial respiration right away. Close your pet's mouth with your hand and seal his lips, then blow into his nose with two quick breaths, watching to see if his chest rises Then let the air escape back out. Give 15 to 20 breaths a minute until he starts breathing again on his own or you reach medical help. (This technique is illustrated on page 20.)

For stings on the tail or leg: If veterinary help is more than 2 hours away and the sting is on a leg or the tail, apply a snug bandage between the bite and the heart. Wrap a small towel around the limb, then cover it with an elastic bandage like an Ace bandage. This will be more effective and safer than a tourniquet in slowing the spread of the poison.

🩹 FOLLOW-UP CARE

■ Most of the time, veterinarians prescribe antibiotics for pets who have been stung by scorpions. This helps prevent a secondary infection from the toxin in the venom. To give a pill to a dog, circle the top of his snout with your hand, pressing both sides of the jaw along the gum line, just behind the large, pointed canine teeth. Use your other hand to push the pill over the hill of his tongue, close his mouth, and gently stroke his throat until he swallows. (This technique is illustrated on page 30.) For a cat, put him on a tabletop, grasp the scruff of his neck, and gently arch his neck backward—his mouth will automatically fall open a bit. Use your other hand to pull down his chin until you can see the V-shaped indentation in the center of his tongue. Drop the pill on the V, close the cat's mouth, and usually, he'll swallow it right down. Offer a treat immediately so he is more interested in swallowing that than in spitting out the medicine.

■ Scorpion stings that become infected can develop areas of dying skin, which need to be cleaned out. You may need to flush out the wound twice a day with an antiseptic solution like Betadine Solution. Purchase this solution from the vet or pet-supply store in a strength of 0.01 to 0.1%. If you purchase higher-strength Betadine, dilute it with distilled water until it's the color of weak tea. (If you're not sure about dilution, call your pharmacist or veterinarian for complete instructions.)

THE BEST APPROACH

Professional Pest Control

Scorpions feed on insects like crickets and grasshoppers, but they can survive for weeks without food. (They may resort to cannibalism when food becomes scarce.) They like to lie in wait for prey in trees, rock piles, old buildings, swimming pools, and other dark, cool places. You'll know you have a scorpion problem if you see insect body parts piled neatly in remote corners. The safest way to control these creatures is to contact a certified pest-control operator.

Pesticides aren't very effective; the best way to control the scorpions is to get rid of their food source and have a pest-control operator remove them one by one. Scorpions are most active at night, and they glow in the dark, fluorescing green when they are hit with a black light. Pest-control operators may wear gloves to safely collect them in a bag, then dispose of them.

Advisors

■ E. Murl Bailey Jr., D.V.M., is professor of toxicology at Texas A&M University College of Veterinary Medicine in College Station.

■ Kevin Doughty, D.V.M., is a veterinarian at Mauer Animal Clinic in Las Vegas.

■ Alvin C. Dufour, D.V.M., is a veterinarian at Dufour Animal Hospital in Elkhart, Indiana.

■ Doug McConkey, D.V.M., is a veterinarian at Canyon Creek Pet Hospital in Sherman, Texas.

■ Scott Stockwell, Ph.D., is a combat entomologist at the Academy of Health Sciences Department of Preventive Health Services Medical Zoology Branch in Fort Sam Houston, Texas.

Seizures

CALL YOUR VET: **SAME DAY**

MEDICINE CHEST

Towels
Sheet
Karo syrup or honey
Pet carrier or other
    rigid object
Ice packs
Rubbing alcohol
3% hydrogen peroxide
Needleless syringe,
    eyedropper, or
    turkey baster

Seizures are much more common in dogs than in cats, and they can happen at any age. Injury to the brain short-circuits the normal electrical activity of the nerves, so the pet loses control of his body. Brain injury can happen from a thump on the head from a car accident or fall, from low blood sugar or low blood calcium, from some poisons, or from kidney or liver problems. Seizures that happen for the first time in a pet older than 6 are usually due to a brain tumor.

Most of the time, nobody knows why a pet develops recurrent seizures, and that's called idiopathic epilepsy. Pets are born with the condition, which can be inherited, and they can start having seizures by the time they're 6 months old. Pets having seizures may fall over, cry out, paddle with their legs uncontrollably, lose consciousness, and urinate and defecate involuntarily.

Seizures look scary, but they usually last only seconds to minutes and aren't dangerous unless they go on for too long (longer than 5 minutes). First aid can help pets recover faster and prevent injury, but for a first-time seizure, you'll want your veterinarian to examine your pet the same day, if possible. If your pet has more than one seizure in a 24-hour period, or if he has one seizure or a series of seizures that lasts longer than 5 minutes, take him to the veterinarian immediately. When the cause of seizures can be treated, they'll usually go away, and medication is available that helps control seizures so that pets can live comfortably with epilepsy.

DO THIS NOW

Move your pet to a safe place. Pets cannot swallow their tongues, so don't try to put anything in your pet's mouth, or you could be bitten. He can be injured during a seizure, however, if he falls or bangs himself against an object. Use towels to pick him up and move him off a high place, away from stairways, and away from objects that he could bump into.

⊕ FIRST ALERT

Poisoning

A wide range of poisons can cause seizures in pets. In most cases, the poison is swallowed, but some-times it can be absorbed through the skin. If you suspect that your pet's seizure is caused by poison, take the container or plant with you to the vet's office, or take a sample of the vomit, if there is any. Some poisons have specific antidotes, and prompt treatment will stop the seizure and cure your pet.

In most cases, poisons absorbed through the skin should be washed off with plain water for 15 to 20 minutes. Make your pet vomit swallowed poisons by giving him 1 to 2 teaspoons of 3% hydrogen peroxide for every 10 pounds he weighs. Use an eyedropper, needleless syringe, or turkey baster to squirt it toward the back of his throat. The exceptions are acid and alkaline poisons and ingested petroleum products; with these poisons, vomiting can make the problem worse. (For more information about poisoning, see page 311.)

Seizures commonly can be caused by:

■ Flea treatments absorbed through the skin
■ Petroleum products ingested or absorbed, like turpentine, gas, or kerosene
■ Pest baits that contain strychnine, bromethalin, or cholecalciferol
■ Plant materials like apple seeds, peach pits, jimsonweed, or azalea
■ Household products like ingested match heads (phosphorus), antifreeze, or chocolate

Keep him cool. A seizure burns a huge number of calories and can quickly overheat your pet. Turn on the air conditioner or a fan to keep the surroundings cool.

Reduce stimulation. Outside noises or sights can prolong a seizure or prompt a new one. Don't touch or talk to your pet during the seizure except to move him to safety. Turn off any music and dim the lights. Cover your pet with a sheet to shut out outside stimulation, then wait for him to come out of the seizure. Most seizures last from 10 seconds to 3 minutes.

Give him Karo syrup or honey. Very young puppies and kittens or young toy-breed dogs like affenpinschers could have seizures from hypoglycemia (low blood sugar) if they don't eat enough at the right times. Hypoglycemia can also affect older pets who have diabetes or have been sick for a long time. You really can't tell if the seizure is caused by low blood sugar levels, but trying to raise the levels may be helpful.

Dribble Karo syrup or honey onto your pet's gums, where it will be absorbed through the membranes. Use 1 teaspoon for pets under 50 pounds. Large dogs (50 to 80 pounds) can have

2 teaspoons, and extra-large dogs (over 80 pounds) get 2½ teaspoons. Giant breeds (over 120 pounds) can have 3 teaspoons. It's important to do this during the seizure because if it is caused by low blood sugar, the seizure won't stop until the sugar level gets high enough again. (For more on low blood sugar, see page 281.)

SPECIAL SITUATIONS

For a seizure caused by a head injury: A blow to the head often causes a seizure, and if you suspect a head injury, move your pet as little as possible. Put a small dog or cat in a carrier or box and a larger dog on a flat surface like a wide board or even an ironing board to transport him to the clinc. (For more information about head injuries, see page 232. For an illustration of how to safely move your pet, see page 29.)

For seizures that last longer than 5 minutes: Status epilepticus means that a seizure lasts longer than 10 continuous minutes or that one seizure follows another without the pet regaining consciousness. This is a medical emergency because the body temperature will continue to climb, prompting more seizures—a vicious cycle that can cause permanent brain damage or even death. Place a small pet in a carrier or box, wrap a large dog in a light sheet, and go to the animal hospital immediately. Take ice packs along, and

some rubbing alcohol if you have time to quickly grab it. Put the ice packs on your pet's groin and armpits and the back of his neck to try to keep him cool. Apply the alcohol to his footpads and the lower parts of all four of his legs.

FOLLOW-UP CARE

■ If the seizure was short and it was your pet's first, your veterinarian may not prescribe drug therapy. Pets who have occasional seizures probably won't need medication, but those who have violent seizures every month or more need oral medicine to reduce the frequency or severity. It can take up to 30 days for the medicine (usually phenobarbital) to take effect. Potassium bromide is also given to epileptic dogs. The dosage is different for each dog, but once medication starts, you have to be faithful about giving the pills; while missing one dose probably won't bring on a seizure, suddenly stopping the medication or not following the dosage directions probably will.

■ Watch for the "aura" phase of the seizure—a period just before your pet loses consciousness and during which he may vocalize, become agitated, or stare off into space. This can alert you so you're prepared to keep him safe and comfortable during the seizure. Some pets do not have auras or give any signs before losing consciousness. They simply fall over and start paddling.

Advisors
■ Bernadine Cruz, D.V.M., is a veterinarian at Laguna Hills Animal Hospital in California.
■ Melissa A. Gates, D.V.M., is a veterinarian at Cordova Veterinary Hospital in Rancho Cordova, California.
■ James M. Harris, D.V.M., is a veterinarian at Montclair Veterinary Hospital in Oakland, California.
■ Carin A. Smith, D.V.M., is a veterinarian in Leavenworth, Washington, and author of *101 Training Tips for Your Cat.*

Shock

CALL YOUR VET: **IMMEDIATELY**

Shock is a life-threatening condition that occurs when the body doesn't get enough oxygen. There are many causes of shock, including heart failure, blood infection (sepsis), and serious trauma, in which the body is flooded with adrenaline. (Adrenaline is a hormone that constricts blood vessels and reduces the flow of blood and oxygen.) The most common type of shock is hypovolemic shock, which results from blood loss.

Pets who are going into shock will be woozy and weak. They'll have difficulty standing and may be unaware of their surroundings. In addition, their gums will first turn dark pink or red, then become pale in 5 to 10 minutes as oxygen levels fall. A cat's gums are normally paler than a dog's, and they will look gray, white, or very pale when the cat is in shock.

Pets who are treated quickly will recover from shock within a few hours. But because shock is so serious and acts so quickly—pets can die within minutes—fast first aid and veterinary attention are essential.

DO THIS NOW

If your pet is bleeding, apply direct pressure to the wound. You can use gauze, a clean soft cloth, a sanitary napkin, or even your hand to stop the bleeding. This won't stop shock, but it will slow the effects while you get your pet to the veterinarian. Don't remove the cloth or pad if it soaks through; just put another pad on top and continue the pressure. (See page 95 for information about bleeding.)

If your pet has been in an accident, stabilize her body. A pet who has been in an accident may have spinal damage or internal injuries that may get worse when you move her. Carefully putting her on a board or some other rigid surface will protect the spine. A towel or blanket makes a good temporary stretcher if you don't have a rigid object. But don't let the search for a suitable carrier delay your trip to the vet.

FIRST ALERT

Blood Loss

About 7 percent of a dog's weight comes from blood; in cats, it's about 5 percent. Pets can start developing shock when they lose 10 to 15 percent of this precious fluid. You'll see serious signs of shock with blood loss of 20 to 30 percent, and rapid losses of 40 percent of blood volume are often fatal. For an 11-pound dog or cat, a blood loss of 10 to 15 percent is as little as about 1 to 2 ounces of blood—the amount of liquid in similarly sized bottles of McCormick's vanilla extract. If a pet loses about 10 to 12 percent of her blood, her gums will start to look white or pale and they will take longer than 2 seconds to refill with blood after you press on them with your finger. If you see these signs, take your pet to the emergency clinic right away. The symptoms will get worse with further blood loss and shock.

(See page 117 for information about car accidents.)

Place a towel or blanket on your pet.
Cover your pet with a towel or blanket to keep her warm. The disrupted circulation that causes shock can also cause hypothermia, a plunge in body temperature, which makes shock worse.

Rub her gums with Karo syrup or honey.
Pets who have gone into shock may have very low blood sugar levels. Raising blood sugar may be helpful in these cases. If you have time to find some, the quickest way to raise blood sugar is to rub a drop or two of Karo syrup or honey on the gums. It will be absorbed through the tissues almost instantly.

 SPECIAL SITUATIONS

If you suspect a stopped heart: This can happen as shock approaches the final stage. Be prepared to give artificial respiration and CPR. First, determine if your pet's heart has stopped by taking her pulse. Press your fingertips into the crease where the inside of the thigh meets the body and feel for the pulse in the femoral artery, which is very big and near the surface. (This technique is illustrated on page 13.) If you can't feel it, try listening or feeling for the heartbeat. Put your ear or hand flat against your pet's left side directly behind the elbow.

If your pet's heart is beating but she's not breathing: Start artificial respiration. First, make sure that your pet's airway is clear. Then, wrap your hands around her mouth and muzzle to seal her lips closed and put your mouth over her nose. Give two quick breaths, watching to see her chest expand, then pull your mouth away to let the air escape back out. Give 15 to 20 breaths per minute until your pet starts breathing on her own or you reach the veterinarian. (This technique is illustrated on page 20.) Watch for her reactions because if she regains consciousness, she may bite you out of fear.

If your pet's heart has stopped and she is not breathing: You'll need to give artificial respiration and chest compressions—CPR. If you are by yourself, give 5 chest compressions alternating with 1 breath. The goal is 80 to 100 compressions and 15 to 20 breaths per minute until your pet revives or you reach medical help. If you have someone there to help, one person gives 5 compressions, then pauses for the other to give a breath.

To give CPR, you'll need to compress the chest of any size pet in a sharp thrusting action, about one pump per second. Don't go any faster, or the heart won't have time to fill with blood between compressions. Put your pet on a flat, firm surface like a table or linoleum floor.

For a cat or small dog, cup your hand over the point of the chest just behind the elbows and squeeze firmly between your fingers and thumb, pressing in about ½ inch, about 80 to 100 times a minute.

A larger dog should be placed on one side. Put both hands flat on top of each other against the chest to do compressions. Compress the chest by 25 to 50% each time, and each minute, stop CPR to check for a pulse or breathing. If the heart starts again, stop the compressions but continue artificial respiration until she breathes on her own or you reach help. Keep doing this in the car until you get to the vet. (This technique is illustrated on page 21.)

FOLLOW-UP CARE

■ After your pet's shock has been treated by the veterinarian, follow-up care is usually not needed. If the shock was caused by a car accident, she may be sore and slower after her visit to the hospital. Be patient and follow your vet's instructions for care of bandages and incisions, medications, and feeding when she comes home.

Advisors

■ Shane Bateman, D.V.M., D.V.Sc., is a veterinarian board certified in the American College of Emergency and Critical Care Medicine and assistant professor of emergency and critical care medicine at Ohio State University College of Veterinary Medicine in Columbus.

■ John Rush, D.V.M., is a veterinarian board certified in the American College of Emergency and Critical Care Medicine and section head of emergency and critical care service at Tufts University School of Veterinary Medicine in North Grafton, Massachusetts.

■ David Wirth-Schneider, D.V.M., is a veterinarian at the Emergency Clinic for Animals in Madison, Wisconsin.

Skin Infections

CALL YOUR VET: **IF NEEDED**

The skin is the body's first line of defense, and it often takes a beating from bacteria, fungi, and parasites. Both cats and dogs can develop skin infections, but dogs are more commonly affected.

Infected skin typically becomes red and itchy, or oily and flaky with or without itching and hair loss. It can be infected in isolated patches or the whole body may be covered with oozing sores that turn scabby and crusty and smell bad. It's not life-threatening except in very severe cases, but it is always irritating for your pet. Although medical treatment often is necessary to cure the skin problem, first aid is a great first step.

DO THIS NOW

Muzzle your pet. To treat her skin, use a muzzle so she won't bite if you touch a sore spot. For a dog, use a length of fabric like a necktie and loop it around her nose. Knot it on top of her muzzle, then bring the ends under her chin and knot them. Finally, draw the ends behind her ears and tie them. (This technique is illustrated on page 17.) You can place a pillowcase over the head of a short-nosed pet like a cat or a pug.

Clip the fur. If the infection is in a small area, trim the fur close to make it easier to apply med-icine. Blunt scissors are okay, but electric clippers work best—even an electric mustache trimmer or shaver will work. Be sure to trim beyond the margins of the affected area. If the whole body is involved, it's best to have the veterinarian shave your pet if necessary.

Wash the infected area. Clean the parts of the skin that are affected. (When the whole body is affected, put your pet in the sink or tub and bathe her.) Be sure to use cool water, which soothes inflammation. Warm or hot water

⊕ FIRST ALERT

Hormone Imbalance

Hormones help regulate all kinds of body functions, and when there is too much or not enough of them, your pet can develop an endocrine disorder. Very often, the signs include skin changes like infections and hair loss that are difficult to treat and cure with regular therapy.

One of the most common imbalances in dogs is hyperthyroidism, in which the thyroid gland generates too much of the hormones that affect body growth, organ function, and metabolism. Hair loss and skin changes are the earliest signs of a thyroid malfunction. The skin turns thick, rough, and dark, sometimes oily and scaly, but not itchy, and fur falls out, especially on the trunk. If you suspect your pet has hyperthyroidism, call your vet. Readjusting the hormone balance cures the problem in most cases.

makes itching worse. A 2.5% benzoyl peroxide shampoo like Oxy 5 works best, but you can use antibacterial soap like Dial if necessary. Be sure to thoroughly rinse off the soap, or when it dries, it could make the skin infection worse. Also be sure to dry your pet thoroughly.

Give your pet an antihistamine. If you aren't able to bathe your pet, an over-the-counter antihistamine like Benadryl may help reduce the inflammation until you can get treatment. The liquid form of Benadryl usually comes in a dose of 12.5 milligrams per teaspoon; pills are usually 25 milligrams each. Pets will need 1 milligram per pound of body weight every 6 to 8 hours. That means a 10-pound cat or dog should get about ¾ teaspoon of liquid or half a pill.

✎ FOLLOW-UP CARE

■ Hair mats and skin debris make perfect breeding grounds for bacteria and fungi. Brush your pet once or twice a day to remove any crust, scale, or dead fur that accumulates. This not only helps the skin infection heal more quickly but also can prevent a recurrence.

■ Antibiotics or antifungal medications like griseofulvin (Grifulvin V) for ringworm will be necessary in most cases—a topical ointment often isn't effective. Usually, the pills are necessary for a minimum of 7 days, and sometimes for 2 weeks or longer. With dogs, you can hide the pills in treats, and they'll often take the medicine willingly. Cats take a bit more persuasion. To pill a cat, place her on a tabletop, grasp the scruff of her neck, and gently arch her neck backward. The cat's mouth will open a little bit. Use your other hand to gently pull down her chin until you can see the V-shaped indentation in the center of her tongue. Drop the pill on the V and close her mouth; usually, a cat will swallow the pill right away. Quickly offer her a tasty treat so she will forget to spit out the pill.

Common Causes of Skin Infections

There is a huge range of causes for skin infections, and each needs a specific treatment. You can't always tell without medical tests, but some of the more common types have fairly distinctive symptoms. Here are some to watch for.

Bacterial infections: red bumps or pimples, bull's-eye sores, scabs, redness, flaky skin, patchy moth-eaten coat

Demodex (mange): circular or patchy hair loss with bald patches showing red to gray skin, usually around the eyes and muzzle, which aren't painful or itchy; may spread over the whole body with bumps and crusts and swelling of feet

Ringworm (fungus): crusty circular area of hair loss, usually first on the face and front legs

Scabies (skin mites): itching, scaling, hair loss, crusty skin, rancid odor

Seborrhea: thick dandruff or a greasy, smelly coat

Yeast: itchy skin, redness, dandruff, thickening of skin, greasy coat, rancid odor

■ When skin infection is caused by excessive scratching, you can help soothe the itch with cool-water soaks for 10 to 20 minutes every couple of days. Oatmeal can soothe inflammation and itching, and a product like Aveeno or an oatmeal-based pet shampoo is always a good choice.

■ Medicated shampoos are an important treatment for most skin infections, and the kind of shampoo depends on the type of infection. For instance, a tar shampoo helps strip away the oil and dandruff flakes of seborrhea, while a sulfu-rated lime dip may be prescribed for ringworm or mange. No matter the kind, though, you'll use it the same way: Soak your pet and let the shampoo or dip set on the skin and fur for at least 10 minutes before you rinse it off. (Some dips are supposed to dry on the skin and not be rinsed off.) It can be hard for a pet to stand patiently in the tub for that long, so tether her to the faucet with a leash. This will also keep your hands free. Don't leave your pet unattended while she is tethered.

Advisors

■ Lowell Ackerman, D.V.M., is a veterinarian at Mesa Veterinary Hospital in Scottsdale, Arizona, and author of *Skin and Coat Care for Your Dog* and *Skin and Coat Care for Your Cat.*

■ Clint Chastain, D.V.M., is a veterinarian at Preston Road Animal Hospital in Dallas.

■ Steven A. Melman, V.M.D., is a veterinarian and dermatological consultant at Derma Pet, a pet skin-care products company in Potomac, Maryland.

■ Jeffrey Werber, D.V.M., is a veterinarian at Century Veterinary Group in Los Angeles.

Skin Pulled Away

CALL YOUR VET: **IMMEDIATELY**

MEDICINE CHEST

Sterile saline contact
   lens solution
Clean cloths
Towel or sheet
Plastic wrap (Saran
   Wrap)
Warm water
Gauze pads
Plastic bag
Elizabethan collar

Skin contains structures called elastins that look kind of like broken rubber bands. These fibers give skin the ability to recoil after stretching. But skin has its limits, and when enough force impacts the body, a degloving injury results. Degloving, in which the skin rips or peels away—like removing a glove from your hand—most often results from fan belt injuries, car accidents that scrape skin off by dragging the pet against pavement, or the blunt impact of a car against the body. Pets need medical attention within 30 to 60 minutes of the injury to have the best chance to heal.

DO THIS NOW

Flush the wound with saline solution. Many times, dirt and gravel are ground into the tissue and needs to be picked out when your pet is sedated at the animal hospital. But if you wash out the injury and keep it moist, it can help preserve the tissues so that they heal better.

Water isn't the best choice for washing raw tissue because the flesh will absorb the liquid into the cells and swell. Saline solution matches the body's liquid content more closely and won't cause swelling. If you don't have sterile saline contact lens solution, you can make saline by mixing 1¼ teaspoons of table salt with a pint of water. Use the saline solution to flush out the wound and keep it moist. If you have nothing else, use a stream of lukewarm water to flush out as much dirt as you can.

Keep the wound moist. Soak clean cloths with the saline solution and cover the wound with them so that it doesn't dry out. This will also protect the exposed flesh from further contamination.

SPECIAL SITUATION

For larger wounds: The wound may look awful, but it isn't as dangerous by itself as the long-term problems that can develop from bacteria and dirt. For a degloving injury, the best thing you can do is protect the wound with saline-soaked cloths until you get medical attention.

For a big laceration that peels back the hide, it's best if you can close it back up. Gently lay the skin flap back into place. Then cover the area with a towel or sheet moistened with sterile saline contact lens solution and hold the whole works in place with plastic wrap like Saran Wrap.

 ## FOLLOW-UP CARE

■ When the skin of a degloving injury is promptly returned to its original position, similar to pulling on your socks, it generally heals pretty well as long as there's no open wound. Whether the injury is located on a leg, the tail, or the body, the vet's stitches will secure the skin back in place. After your pet is stitched, you'll need to keep the area clean. Wipe away any drainage with a bit of warm water on a gauze pad.

■ Sometimes, part of the skin is damaged so severely that it dies and leaves open, gaping wounds. These injuries need frequent bandage changes that may go on for several weeks. It's important to keep the bandages clean and dry, so if your pet has injured his leg, slip a plastic bag over it before he goes outside. Be sure to take it off when he comes back inside.

■ Skin can often heal and cover the missing areas, but it takes time. Usually, the healing begins at the margins of the skin and moves inward. When recommended by your veterinarian, water therapy can help speed the healing process, and it also helps keep the area clean. Rinse the area two or three times a day for 10 to 15 minutes with a stream of pressurized lukewarm water from the hose or a handheld showerhead.

■ You may need to fit your pet with a collar restraint to keep him from licking the wound or bothering the bandage. Cone-shaped Elizabethan collars are available from veterinarians and pet-supply stores. Dogs and cats frequently have trouble eating while wearing these, though, so remove the restraint long enough for supervised meals.

Advisors

■ Ann Buchanan, D.V.M., is a veterinarian at Glenwood Animal Hospital in Tyler, Texas.

■ Kenneth J. Drobatz, D.V.M., is a veterinarian and associate professor of critical care emergency service at the Veterinary Hospital of the University of Pennsylvania in Philadelphia.

■ Barry N. Kellogg, V.M.D., is a veterinarian at the Center for Veterinary Care in Great Barrington, Massachusetts, and the head of VMAT 1 (Veterinary Medical Assistance Team), the national disaster team for veterinary medicine.

■ Kevin Wallace, D.V.M., is an instructor in the department of clinical sciences at Cornell University College of Veterinary Medicine in Ithaca, New York.

■ Dennis L. Wilcox, D.V.M., is a veterinarian at Angeles Clinic for Animals in Port Angeles, Washington.

Skin Swelling

CALL YOUR VET: **IF NEEDED**

MEDICINE CHEST

Hot pack or compress
Cold, wet washcloth
Cold pack or compress
Antihistamine (Ben-
  adryl)
Warm water
Epsom salts
Antiseptic liquid soap
  (Betadine Skin
  Cleanser)
Gauze pad
3% hydrogen peroxide
Vicks VapoRub
Elizabethan collar
Bitter Apple

Skin swelling can be caused by a serious condition like a fracture or edema. Pets refuse to put any weight on a broken leg, or they flinch from your touch and refuse to move the affected part of the body. They may act lethargic and lose their appetites with heart or liver disease, which makes the legs or body swell with edema. You'll know it's edema if you push on the swelling and it leaves a dent in the skin. These conditions need medical attention as soon as possible.

Pets with itchy ears who scratch themselves or shake and flap their ears from discomfort can bruise the earflaps so that they swell up like balloons with blood and fluid. And dogs, as they age, often develop skin tumors—soft little lumps that move around when they're massaged. The only way to know if a skin tumor is benign or malignant is to have a veterinarian perform a needle biopsy or surgically remove the lump. Earflap swelling needs surgery to correct, but the skin tumors are usually harmless and just need to be monitored. If you feel a growth on or underneath your pet's skin, have a vet check it right away.

Skin swelling caused by a beesting, a bruise, or an allergic reaction can be treated with first aid. The most common causes of skin swelling, though, are infections from bite wounds, an abscessed tooth, or even a splinter. Pets often develop deep pockets of pus, called abscesses, from bite wounds or being jabbed with a sharp stick. Abscesses need medical attention, but first aid can help speed up the recovery and keep pets more comfortable until you can get help.

🩹 DO THIS NOW

Apply a hot compress. When the swelling is from an infection, cellulitis (tissue inflammation), or an abscess, it will feel hot to the touch, and your pet may have a fever. The best first aid for swelling in these cases is a hot, wet compress. The compress helps pull the blood circulation to

FIRST ALERT

Tumors

Most types of skin swelling are soft to the touch because the skin is filled with excess fluid from edema or inflammation. But a swelling that's solid or one that doesn't go away but continues to grow is likely to be a tumor.

The growth can be either harmless (benign) or malignant (cancerous), but there's no way to tell without a veterinary exam and laboratory tests. Skin swelling caused by a tumor is usually surgically removed. If cancer is diagnosed, a variety of treatments, from radiation to chemotherapy, may be recommended in addition to the surgery.

You'll need to be sure that the area stays clean and your pet doesn't pull out the stitches. You can wipe around the incision line as needed with a bit of 3% hydrogen peroxide on a gauze pad. To keep your pet from licking at the area, apply a thin coat of Vicks VapoRub around—but not directly on—the incision line. Or fit him with a cone-shaped collar restraint called an Elizabethan collar.

the area and bring the infection to a head so that it heals more quickly. Soak a washcloth in water as hot as you can stand and wring it out. Alternate the hot pack 5 minutes on, then 5 minutes off until the cloth cools. Repeat the treatment two to five times a day.

Ice the area. Skin swelling that is caused by blunt trauma—perhaps your dog ran his shoulder into a tree, or your cat bruised her chin when she fell—are best treated with a cold pack. It helps numb the pain and also constricts the blood vessels in the area so that the swelling and inflammation go away. You can use a commercial cold pack, or put a wet washcloth in the freezer for a few minutes. You can also use a plastic bag filled with ice or a bag of frozen peas or corn that conforms to your pet's body shape. First, lay a cold, wet washcloth on the swollen area, then put the cold pack on top of the cloth. Leave it in place for 10

to 30 minutes several times a day, until the swelling goes away.

Give an antihistamine. Skin swelling from an allergic reaction can cause hives—lumps all over the body—or a single swollen area. A bug bite or sting or even a contact allergy reaction may cause the skin to swell. To help give some immediate relief, you can give your pet an over-the-counter antihistamine like Benadryl. The liquid form of Benadryl usually comes in a dose of 12.5 milligrams per teaspoon; pills are usually 25 milligrams each. Pets will need 1 milligram per pound of body weight every 6 to 8 hours. That means a 10-pound cat or dog should get about ¾ teaspoon of liquid or half a pill.

Soak the area in warm water and Epsom salts. Pets who have a swollen paw, leg, or tail often benefit from a warm-water soak. When the

Warbles

Outdoor pets, especially cats who hunt and come in contact with rabbit and mouse habitats, are at risk for cuterebra parasite, or warbles. The parasite is more prevalent in the southern United States but is found as far north as Canada. The larvae of the botfly usually target rodents, but will make do with pets. The tiny worms attach themselves to the pet's skin and enter the body through the mouth or nose as the pet licks himself. Then a worm migrates to a location just beneath the skin, usually on the neck or chest. The area swells, getting bigger and bigger as the worm grows.

At first, the swelling feels firm; then it fills with fluid and becomes soft. It often looks like an abscess. There will be a "breathing hole" in the skin in the center of the swelling that leaks blood-tinged fluid. The larva inside may grow to more than an inch long and ½ inch in diameter. It is brownish and covered with small, prickly projections. The worm stays in the skin for about a month before it comes out on its own. Usually, the warble doesn't bother the cat or dog, but the cyst may become infected.

Don't try to squeeze out the worm yourself, because crushing it can cause a life-threatening anaphylactic (allergic) reaction. The warble must be surgically removed by the veterinarian, who will enlarge the breathing hole enough to pull the worm out. Once the parasite is removed, you'll need to keep the wound clean by swabbing it with an antiseptic liquid soap like Betadine Skin Cleanser once or twice a day as needed.

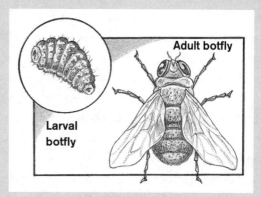

Warbles are caused by the larva of the botfly when it burrows into your pet's skin.

If your pet has been infested, it's easy to recognize the problem. Look for an abscesslike swelling on her neck or chest. Then see if there is a breathing hole in the center of the swelling that's leaking blood-tinged fluid. Don't try to crush the larva. Instead, take your pet to the vet.

swelling is caused by a splinter or thorn, the warm water helps the body eject the foreign material and can prevent the wound from becoming infected. Mix 1 cup of Epsom salts in 2 gallons of water and have your pet stand in the liquid, or dunk his tail, for 10 minutes at a time.

Fit him with an Elizabethan collar. Male pets who scratch or chafe the scrotal sac often can't stop licking themselves to soothe the sore, and that makes the scrotum swell to gigantic proportions. This can also happen after neutering surgery. In these cases, if you can prevent your pet from licking himself, the swelling will go away. Fit him with a cone-shaped Elizabethan collar to keep him from reaching the area until the swelling starts to subside. (For more information about scrotal swelling, see page 377.) For dogs who still try to lick or chew at the area, try dabbing on some Bitter Apple or a bit of Variton ointment, which is available from veterinarians.

✎ FOLLOW-UP CARE

■ Swelling that's caused by cellulitis or an abscess usually requires antibiotics for several days or even a couple of weeks to help the infection go away. You can hide the pills in tasty treats for dogs. For cats, you can crush the pill to a powder with the bowl of a spoon and mix it into strong-flavored food like tuna.

■ If your veterinarian recommends it, continue applying the hot, wet compresses—5 minutes on, then 5 minutes off—two to five times a day. More often is better. This helps speed up the healing if there's an infection.

■ Once the swelling ruptures and begins to drain, or when the sore is lanced by your vet and a drain tube is inserted in the wound, keep the area clean by wiping away the pus with an antiseptic liquid soap like Betadine Skin Cleanser. Dampen a clean cloth or gauze pad with the solution and wipe material away as needed.

■ Earflap swelling (technically called an aural hematoma) requires minor surgery to clean out the pocket of fluid. Often, a bandage is needed to help reshape the ear tissue, and you'll need to be sure to keep the bandage clean. An Elizabethan collar will keep your pet from pawing and scratching at the bandage. (See page 161 for more information about aural hematomas.)

Once the hematoma has been repaired, you'll probably need to apply ear medication to treat the irritation that caused the trauma in the first place. Tip your pet's head so that the affected ear points upward, then drip in several drops of the medication. Massage the base of the ear to spread the medication. (This technique is illustrated on page 32.)

Advisors

■ Peter Davis, D.V.M., is a veterinarian at Pine Tree Veterinary Hospital in Augusta, Maine.

■ Anna Worth, V.M.D., is a veterinarian at West Mountain Animal Hospital in Shaftsbury, Vermont.

■ Sophia Yin, D.V.M., is a veterinarian in Davis, California, and author of *Small Animal Veterinary Nerdbook*.

Skunk Spray

CALL YOUR VET: **IF NEEDED**

Skunk spray is not a medical emergency, but it is aggravating for you and potentially painful for your pet. A direct hit in the face can irritate the eyes and even cause temporary blindness. You may be able to smell your skunked pet up to a mile away, but he must deal with the odor at ground zero—and a dog's sense of smell is hundreds of thousands of times more sensitive than yours.

Hunting dogs are the most common victims because they're more likely to meet skunks during rambles through the woods. But skunks also invade urban settings, and they love to swipe cat food. Often, they'll even use a pet door into the kitchen! A pet doesn't have to get up close and personal to become a target. Musk glands on each side of the skunk's anus have retractable ducts that are able to spray the stink 10 to 15 feet to reach and repel an inquisitive pet. But first aid is all you need to de-skunk your smelly pet.

DO THIS NOW

Keep your pet out of the house. If at all possible, keep your pet outside to clean him, or you'll need to deodorize your entire house as well. Be sure to wear gloves and old clothes, or you'll end up getting the smell on you, too. Before doing anything else, check your pet's eyes. If they're watering or red, chances are he took a direct hit. Use a stream of sterile saline contact lens solution to wash them out. If you don't have saline, gently running water from the hose will

also work to rinse the eyes and reduce the sting. Five to 10 minutes is a good rule of thumb.

Comb the fur. A simple bath won't be enough—and before you get him wet, be sure to comb out the fur. Once water hits any snarls, the fur turns to cement, and you'll have to cut out the mats.

Keep him still. You'll need both hands to effectively scrub up your odoriferous pet, so it's a good

345

idea to tether him by the outdoor faucet or in the tub. For dogs, just attach the leash to his collar and loop the leash around a stationary object like a clothesline post if you're outside or the bathtub faucet if you're inside. For cats, it's best to use a harness so that they don't choke trying to escape. Don't leave your pet unattended while he is tied.

Use skunk odor cleaners. In most cases, regular pet shampoo won't get rid of the odor as effectively as commercial cleaners like Skunk Kleen or Skunk Odor Eliminator. Both are available at pet-supply stores.

Try Massengill brand douche. Professional groomers say it works wonders to get rid of skunk odor. Mix about 2 ounces of Massengill with a gallon of water for small to medium-size pets, or double the recipe for larger dogs. Pour the mix over your pet and make sure that it soaks into the fur thoroughly. Wait 15 minutes, then rinse with plain water. Follow with a bath using his regular shampoo.

 **FOLLOW-UP CARE**

■ Once you've "de-skunked" your pet, there's no need to follow up.

THE BEST APPROACH

Homemade Chemistry Cure

Skunk musk is made up of chemical compounds called thiols. Chemist Paul Krebaum found the answer to skunk odor by figuring out how to change the thiols into other compounds that don't smell with a homemade solution.

Here's how to make his formula: Mix 1 quart of 3% hydrogen peroxide with ¼ cup of sodium bicarbonate (baking soda) and 1 teaspoon of liquid soap—pet shampoo will work. Wet your pet's coat down, apply the solution to his wet coat while the mixture bubbles, and leave it on for 3 to 4 minutes. Then rinse thoroughly. This mixture works better than anything on the market, and you can't buy it Krebaum never patented the formula because it can't be bottled for resale. It will pop the lid off any container because of the gas that's generated, so mix up only as much of the solution as you can use at one time. Don't let your pet ingest any of this mixture, and before soaping, put a thick protective eye ointment like Neosporin Ophthalmic Ointment into his eyes to protect them.

Advisors

■ Doug McConkey, D.V.M., is a veterinarian at Canyon Creek Pet Hospital in Sherman, Texas.

■ Laura Solien, D.V.M., is a veterinarian at Maplecrest Animal Hospital in Goshen, Indiana.

■ Dennis L. Wilcox, D.V.M., is a veterinarian at Angeles Clinic for Animals in Port Angeles, Washington.

Smoke Inhalation

CALL YOUR VET: **IMMEDIATELY**

Fire produces gas, which suspends carbon particles in the air, creating smoke. Five common components of smoke make pets—and people—sick when they're inhaled. The ash or soot irritates or clogs the lungs, but it's the invisible gases that often kill. These include acrolein, benzene, formaldehyde, and carbon monoxide. In fact, most fire deaths are caused by smoke inhalation rather than burns.

Pets who breathe smoke gasp or cough, and they often faint from lack of oxygen. Their gums can change color, turning pale or blue (cyanotic) from lack of oxygen.

Smoke inhalation is a major medical emergency and needs veterinary attention immediately, even if your pet seems to recover. Smoke can be insidious and kill hours to days after it's inhaled. And pets who stop breathing need artificial respiration (and CPR, if the heart stops beating) to survive.

 DO THIS NOW

Get your pet out of the smoke. Most cases of smoke inhalation involve large, severe fires where the pet is unable to escape from the smoke. Do not go into a dangerous situation to rescue your pet unless you have professional training. Wait until a firefighter or someone with the proper equipment for entering a burning building brings her out. Once she's outside, if possible, move your pet away from the smoke and into fresh air. With mild cases of smoke inhalation, this may be all that's needed to revive your cat or dog. But even if your pet acts like she feels okay, restrict her activity until your veterinarian gives her a clean bill of health.

Transport her carefully. On the ride to the veterinary clinic, don't hold your pet in your arms. Instead of comforting a pet, holding her may increase her stress levels. If that happens, she'll breathe faster and need more oxygen, and

⊕ FIRST ALERT

Carbon Monoxide Poisoning

Carbon monoxide is the deadliest component of smoke, and victims of fire most often succumb to this poison. It kills with chemical suffocation by replacing and crowding out any oxygen in the bloodstream. Even after the smoke is gone, the carbon monoxide remains trapped in the system and blocks oxygen from getting into the body, even though the pet breathes clean air.

Along with the common signs of smoke inhalation, the gums of a pet poisoned with carbon monoxide will be a distinctive cherry-red color. She may act depressed or drunk. The signs of severe poisoning are apparent very quickly. Dogs and cats can collapse, fall into a coma, and die immediately. The poisoning could also injure major organs by gradually displacing oxygen so that the organs receive an inadequate supply. The symptoms of this secondary injury depend on which organs are involved, but they include malaise, vomiting, difficulty breathing, and increase or decrease in urination or diarrhea. These signs may not show up until hours later.

The only way to get rid of the carbon monoxide is to breathe it out. When a pet inhales a small amount of the poison, she will recover in a few days on her own, but it's hard to tell the degree of poisoning by yourself. And when the blood saturation level reaches 10 percent or higher, pets need oxygen therapy to speed up the process, or they'll die before they can breathe enough out. If you suspect carbon monoxide poisoning, get your pet to the vet immediately. (For more information about carbon monoxide poisoning, see page 122.)

because she's already oxygen-deprived, it could tip her over the edge into a heart attack or respiratory failure. Put a small pet in a dark box or carrier and a large dog on the backseat. If you have a small, uninjured dog or cat, however, and she seems more comfortable and less stressed if you hold her, then do so. Turn on the air conditioner because cool air is easier to breathe.

🗑 SPECIAL SITUATIONS

If your pet stops breathing: Give artificial respiration. Wrap your hands around her mouth and muzzle to hold it closed and put your mouth over her nose (with a small dog or a cat, your mouth will be over both the nose and mouth). Give two quick breaths, watching to see her chest expand.

Once her chest begins to rise, pull your mouth away so that the air will flow out. Give 15 to 20 breaths a minute until your pet starts breathing on her own or you reach medical help. (This technique is illustrated on page 20.) Be very careful and alert to your pet's reactions, because if she regains consciousness, she may bite you out of fear.

If there's no breathing or heartbeat: Do CPR. Feel or listen for the heartbeat with your ear or your palm against your pet's left side, right behind the elbow. If you can't find a heartbeat, you must begin CPR.

For cats and small dogs, cup a hand over the point of the chest just behind the elbows and squeeze firmly between your fingers and thumb, pressing in about ½ inch, about 80 to 100 times a minute. Continue to give 15 to 20 breaths per minute, and alternate five compressions for every breath.

Put a medium or large dog on her side and place both hands, one on top of the other, on the highest part of her chest. You should compress the chest 25 to 50% and give the same number of compressions and breaths as for small pets. (This technique is illustrated on page 21.)

Continue CPR and artificial respiration while someone drives you to the animal hospital. Every minute, stop CPR to check for a pulse or breathing. If the heart starts again, stop the compressions, but continue artificial respiration until your pet breathes on her own or you reach medical help.

 FOLLOW-UP CARE

■ Breathing smoke irritates your pet's lungs and throat. She may continue to cough or sound hoarse for several days. A humidifier can help speed recovery. Moist, cool air soothes the respiratory passages and reduces coughing, which can make the irritation worse. Place the humidifier in the room where your pet sleeps and run it for 2 to 3 days after the event.

■ Make plenty of cool water available to your pet. Add a couple of ice cubes to her water dish because cold water will help soothe the irritation and rehydrate tissues that were damaged by the smoke.

Advisors
■ Grace F. Bransford, D.V.M., is a veterinarian in Corte Madera, California.
■ Kevin Wallace, D.V.M., is an instructor in the department of clinical sciences at Cornell University College of Veterinary Medicine in Ithaca, New York.
■ H. Ellen Whiteley, D.V.M., is a veterinarian in Guadalupita, New Mexico, and author of *Understanding and Training Your Cat or Kitten* and *Understanding and Training Your Dog or Puppy*.

Snakebites

CALL YOUR VET: **IMMEDIATELY**

Snakebites are common in pets, especially dogs, because dogs are often curious and try to play with moving critters. In fact, about 15,000 dogs and cats are bitten by poisonous snakes each year in the United States alone. Nonpoisonous snakebites cause pain and infection, but venomous snakes can kill a dog or cat within only an hour or two. In fact, dogs are much more sensitive to snake venom than cats, and fatal snakebites are more common in dogs than in any other domestic animal. Every state but Maine, Alaska, and Hawaii has at least one of the 20 poisonous snake species native to the United States. Your pet is most at risk for a poisonous snakebite if you live in Alabama, Arizona, Florida, Georgia, South Carolina, or Texas.

Most pets are bitten on or near the face and neck when they try to catch snakes, but bites to the body typically are more dangerous. The severity of the bite depends on the size of the snake compared with the size of the pet, the number of bites, and the amount of venom that's injected. Some types of venom attack the central nervous system, in which case the pet may act drunk, have seizures, or stop breathing suddenly. But the most common snakebite sign when venom has been injected is sudden, severe swelling that often hides any fang marks, so the wound looks like an insect sting or spider bite.

The venom from pit vipers like copperheads actually digests the flesh, so the area around the bite becomes discolored within minutes. It can also cause bleeding disorders (bruising or bloody nose) that look like rat poisoning. Quick medical attention is important because even if the bite isn't life-threatening, irreversible damage from the venom begins immediately.

Because it's often difficult to tell the difference between harmless and deadly bites, rush your pet to the vet if you think that she has been bitten. First aid can help your pet while you're on the way.

🐾 DO THIS NOW

Check for signs of shock. Any poisonous snakebite can cause shock, which may lead to stopped breathing. (For more on shock, see page 333.) Coral snake venom and some rattlesnake venom can paralyze the respiratory system. Bites to the face can cause the nostrils or windpipe to swell and make it hard to breathe, too. Be prepared to perform artificial respiration if your pet stops breathing. Wrap your hand around your pet's muzzle to seal her lips and blow into her nose with two quick breaths, watching to see her chest rise. Give 15 to 20 breaths per minute until she starts to breathe again on her own or you reach medical help. (This technique is illustrated on page 20.)

Keep your pet still. Keep your pet as calm as possible and do not let her move at all. Get her to the vet by transporting her in a pet carrier or restrained on a board. (This technique is illustrated on page 29.) Movement speeds up the blood circulation so the poison travels more quickly, and you want to prevent the venom from spreading from the bite to the rest of her body.

Take off her collar. Remove your pet's collar or harness so that it won't constrict the body as the bite swells the tissue.

Turn up the air-conditioning in the car. This can help slow down the blood circulation.

Rinse the wound. If the bite is visible, don't cut the wound, because that increases the blood supply to the area and makes the condition worse.

Dead but Deadly

Even after a poisonous snake is killed—even if it's decapitated—it is still dangerous. Dead snakes retain a reflexive action for up to an hour after death and can still bite and poison a victim. So don't grab a "dead" snake, and don't allow your children or pets to go near it.

Instead, rinse the surface off quickly with water to wash away any surface venom. Do this in the car while another person drives you to the vet's office.

Vacuum the venom. Vacuum pump devices that come with commercial snakebite kits have been shown to remove up to 30% of venom without an incision when used within 3 minutes of the bite. If someone is going with you and you have a pump, you can do this en route to the vet.

Put a cold pack on the bite. Ice will not only reduce the pain and help bring down the swelling, it will also slow the blood circulation and can help prevent the poison from spreading. Many times, the bite is too painful for your pet to tolerate a hard chunk of ice, so use a package of frozen peas or corn wrapped in a cold, wet washcloth. If you can, have someone go with you to the clinic so that one person can apply the cold treatment while the other drives. Apply the cold pack for 10 to 30 minutes at a time.

Keep the bite below the level of the heart. Lower the bitten area so that it's not as easy for circulation to spread the venom throughout the rest of the body.

Identifying Poisonous Snakes

Try to get a good look at the snake that bit your pet so that you can describe it, but don't risk trying to kill or capture it. The pit vipers include rattlesnakes, copperheads, and water moccasins. These snakes have triangular heads, and they strike and retreat, using long, hollow, hinged fangs to inject venom when they bite. Their venom is toxic to blood cells and tissue and typically kills the skin and muscle that surround the bite. You'll see discolored flesh and terrible swelling at the bite site.

Coral snakes have short fangs that are not hinged, so instead of injecting their venom, these snakes tend to hang on and "chew" the venom into the victim. Their venom is a neurotoxin that paralyzes the respiratory system, so the victim suffocates. There may not be much swelling, and the bite will look like two small cuts. Signs may not appear for up to 7 hours.

A rattlesnake is usually a clearly patterned, brown or reddish snake, but its most distinctive trait is the rattle on the end of its tail. It gets larger as the snake gets older. A rattler will warn you of its presence by shaking the rattle, but only if it senses you coming.

You may encounter a water moccasin in a swamp or near a stream. These pit vipers are 4 to 6 feet long and dark brown to black. When one opens its mouth, the white interior makes a striking contrast to its dark coloring and gives this snake its other name, cottonmouth.

The copperhead is one of our most beautiful venomous snakes, with red-brown coloring and hourglass markings. Copperheads are usually between 2½ and 4 feet long. Because it blends in so well, be especially careful around woodpiles and leaf litter—two of its favorite hiding places.

You can tell the venomous coral snake from its harmless look-alike, the king snake, by the way the colors are lined up: In coral snakes, the yellow bands are next to the red bands, while in king snakes, the black bands are beside the red. Just remember the rhyme: "Red next to yellow kills a fellow."

Antivenin Treatment

Antivenin is made from antibodies created by a horse's body that has been exposed to venom, and it is designed to neutralize the effects of the poison. It's most effective when given within 4 to 8 hours of the bite, but in severe cases, it may still be helpful up to 24 hours later. It's typically injected into the tissue around the fang marks as well as given intravenously. Most veterinary clinics don't have antivenin on hand, though, because it's quite expensive and can be hard to find. Human hospitals located in "snake country," however, often keep supplies. Your veterinarian may be able to supply you with an emergency dose if, for instance, your hunting dogs or other pets are at potential risk during a camping trip.

Bandage the limb. If veterinary help is more than 1 hour away and the bite is on a leg or the tail, apply a snug bandage between the bite and the heart. Wrap a small towel around the limb, then cover it with an elastic bandage like an Ace bandage. This will be more effective and safer than a tourniquet in slowing the spread of the poison.

 FOLLOW-UP CARE

■ Most pets who die from snakebite succumb within 1 to 2 hours of the encounter, and pets who survive beyond that point usually recover. But they won't be out of the woods for up to 10 days after the bite. Any snakebite, whether poisonous or not, needs antibiotics to fight possible infection from bacteria that are found in snakes' mouths. Usually, the veterinarian will give tetanus and antibiotic injections. You may also need to give oral antibiotics or anti-inflammatory medication like steroids—possibly for several weeks—to help protect against tissue damage until the sore has healed.

■ If your pet's wounds are tender, check with your vet about pain medications. Or you can ease the pain with cold compresses two or three times a day.

THE BEST APPROACH

Water Therapy

Many kinds of venom eat away the flesh at the site of a snakebite, and about 4 to 5 days after the bite, tissue starts to rot away. These wounds are slow to heal and can spread without the right follow-up treatment. Water therapy is the best way to speed healing, and it also keeps the area clean. Use a high-pressure stream of water from a handheld sink sprayer or showerhead to flood the wound for 5 to 10 minutes at a time two or three times each day.

Advisors

■ Ann Buchanan, D.V.M., is a veterinarian at Glenwood Animal Hospital in Tyler, Texas.

■ Charles DeVinne, D.V.M., is a veterinarian at Animal Care Clinic in Peterborough, New Hampshire.

■ Larry Edwards, D.V.M., is a veterinarian at the Canyon Creek Pet Hospital in Sherman, Texas.

■ Ken Lawrence, D.V.M., is a veterinarian at the Texoma Veterinary Hospital in Sherman, Texas.

Spider Bites

CALL YOUR VET: **IMMEDIATELY**

Spiders would rather avoid pets altogether, but they will bite cats and dogs if they feel threatened. Most spider bites are more uncomfortable than dangerous and can be treated in the same manner as bee or wasp stings to relieve the pain and reduce the swelling. (For more information about bee and wasp stings, see page 79.)

Almost all spiders are venomous, but only a few can actually penetrate the skin with their bites and also have enough venom (and venom that's potent enough) to cause serious illness. Bites on pets are usually hidden by fur, and often, the spider will be gone by the time symptoms appear. Signs of distress can develop as soon as 30 minutes after the bite, but some venomous bites won't cause problems until up to 6 hours after the encounter. Your pet may shiver uncontrollably or run a high fever (over 104°F). As the poison spreads throughout her body, she can go into shock or even develop paralysis. First aid helps control the spread of the venom, but your pet will need immediate medical attention. If your pet has a nonpoisonous spider bite, first aid is usually all that's necessary.

DO THIS NOW

For Poisonous Bites

Restrict your pet's movement until you get to the vet. Running around or even walking will increase her circulation and make the venom in her system travel more quickly. The reaction can go from bad to worse if the venom reaches her heart or brain.

Keep the bitten area below heart level. This also slows the spread of the venom.

Wash the bite wound. Use cold water and soap to get rid of bacteria on the skin surface. This reduces the chance of secondary infection.

Identifying Poisonous Spiders

It can be hard to know if your pet has been bitten unless you actually see the spider. But it's helpful to know if deadly spiders live in your part of the country, and if so, how to identify dangerous spiders by the way they look and where they live.

Widow spiders: The widow spiders may be the most common and deadly type of venomous spiders in the United States. They are about the size of a blueberry and have bright red hourglass designs on their undersides, although this shape varies according to species and individual. Widows bite only when accidental contact is made with the skin. Three species of widow spiders are shiny and black: the southern widow, the western widow, and the northern widow. The southern widow is most commonly found in southeastern states, west to central Texas and Oklahoma, and north to New York State. It builds its web in cool, dark places, such as under woodpiles and well covers and beneath trash. The southern widow's hourglass marking is shaped more like an anvil.

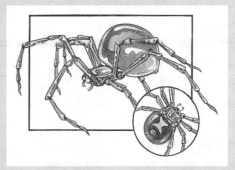

The western black widow likes to inhabit abandoned rodent holes, but like the other widows, it can be found in any urban or suburban setting, even in downtown areas. This spider is the common

The characteristic red hourglass is on a black widow's underside. You're more likely to see her shiny black back.

black widow of the western United States. Although its distinctive marking is usually a perfect hourglass shape, it can be divided into two separate parts in some individual spiders of this type.

The third black widow, the northern widow, prefers to live in wooded areas. Stone walls and tree stumps are other favorite habitats of this species. It usually has an hourglass marking that is divided into two long, separate markings. The northern widow is found in extreme southeastern Canada, throughout New England, and south to northern Florida.

There are other species of widow spiders in the United States that are not black. The brown widow is most commonly found in southern states. It can vary in color but is usually brown to gray, and its marking is a complete hourglass. Brown widows can be found in almost any kind of building. The red widow, which can also be orange in color, is typically found only in central and southern Florida and possibly Louisiana. Its hourglass is usually a single elongated marking. This spider lives in sandy, scrub-pine areas.

(continued)

Identifying Poisonous Spiders (cont.)

Widow spider venom is a neurotoxin and causes severe, painful cramps in all the large muscles. It can also sometimes cause paralysis.

Brown spiders: There are at least 10 species of brown spiders, but the brown recluse spider is the most common, followed by the Missouri brown spider. Most brown spiders have violin-shaped markings on their thoraxes, so they're often referred to as fiddle-back spiders. They are found all over the United States. Brown spider bites usually kill the surrounding tissue, and without prompt treatment, a tiny bite can develop into a massive ulcer that can take months to heal. The venom can also cause severe blood disorders that won't appear until 3 to 4 days after the bite.

Tarantulas: The largest and hairiest North American spiders are found in the southern and southwestern states, including the dry and warmer parts of southern California, and they can have a leg span of 4 inches or more. Most tarantulas are shy and avoid contact with pets and people. The bite is not considered terribly toxic, but some pets can develop an anaphylactic reaction to tarantula bites. (For more information about anaphylactic shock, see page 79.)

Brown recluse spiders, as their name implies, like to hide in and under things, such as linens in closets. They have six eyes rather than the eight that are common to most spiders.

Most of us are familiar with tarantulas from pet stores and horror movies. These brown, hairy spiders can have a 4-inch leg span.

Apply cold packs to the bite. This will help numb the pain and reduce swelling. Cold also helps decrease bloodflow in the area, slows the spread of venom, and can prevent some tissue death. Place a cold, wet washcloth against the injury first, then apply the cold pack as you travel to the vet.

For Nonpoisonous Bites

Err on the side of caution. If you have seen a spider bite your pet, and it doesn't fit any of the descriptions in "Identifying Poisonous Spiders" (beginning on page 355), it is probably not poisonous. But if you're not sure, call your vet right away.

Keep him from moving. Restrict your pet's movement for 2 to 4 hours.

Wash the wound. Use cold water and soap to get rid of bacteria on the skin surface and reduce the chance of secondary infection.

Ice it. Hold a cold, wet washcloth to the wound, then apply a cold pack for 10 to 30 minutes several times a day.

Watch for infection. Monitor your pet closely for signs of infection, which include fever, discharge of pus, and a red, swollen area that is hot to the touch and painful. If you see any of these signs or if your pet is acting strangely in any way, go to your veterinarian immediately.

🥫 SPECIAL SITUATION

For allergic reactions: Your pet may have an allergic reaction to spider venom. If you see any of the following symptoms, take her to the vet right away: breathing difficulty, diarrhea, skin swelling, weakness, or collapse.

🩹 FOLLOW-UP CARE

■ Pets bitten by widow spiders often will remain weak or have partial paralysis for several days.

You may need to carry your pet to the yard or litter box until she regains her strength. Keep food and water within easy reach.

■ Pets may receive intravenous pain medication like morphine at the hospital after a black widow bite. Depending on how severe the muscle contractions are, you may need to give oral muscle relaxants or seizure-control medicine at home.

■ Bites from brown spiders often develop into massive sores that can spread, and you'll need to give antibiotics prescribed by your veterinarian for up to several weeks to fight secondary infection. A drug called avlosulfon (Dapsone), which is used in humans to treat leprosy, may also be prescribed for up to 25 days.

■ When the spider bite causes tissue necrosis, in which the skin dies and sloughs away, water therapy can help heal the wound. Flood the area with water that's under pressure—from a hand-held showerhead or a hose nozzle—two or three times a day. This will clean away dying flesh, massage the tissue, and increase blood circulation to the area, which promotes healing. Your veterinarian will show you the best way to do this.

Advisors

■ Ann Buchanan, D.V.M., is a veterinarian at Glenwood Animal Hospital in Tyler, Texas.

■ Dale C. Butler, D.V.M., is a veterinarian at Best Friends Animal Hospital in Denison, Texas.

■ Ken Lawrence, D.V.M., is a veterinarian at the Texoma Veterinary Hospital in Sherman, Texas.

■ Julie Moews, D.V.M., is a veterinarian at Bolton Veterinary Hospital in Connecticut.

Splinters

CALL YOUR VET: **IF NEEDED**

Dogs and cats don't get splinters very often because their skin is protected pretty well by fur. But on the less hairy areas, such between the toes or on the lower legs, they can get thorns or splinters stuck into their skin. These are not particularly dangerous, but they can be very painful and can often cause infection unless treated with antibiotics.

Hunting dogs are especially prone to splinters. Because they run through woods and fields or swim in ponds and lakes, they can get jumbo-size splinters that look more like pieces of sticks. Dogs and sometimes cats can run into bushes and get sticks jammed into their chests, and hunting dogs often ram into underwater trees or fence posts while swimming.

It can be hard to tell from the outside how deeply a large splinter intrudes into the body, and some injuries can be life-threatening. Any time a dog or cat has a large splinter or stick fragment stuck deep in the chest or trunk, he needs medical attention as soon as possible. Small splinters in the feet and legs can usually be removed with first aid.

DO THIS NOW

Trim the fur. If your pet is very furry, you may need to clip the fur to get a clear view of the splinter. Electric clippers are safest for doing this, or use an electric razor or mustache trimmer so that you don't risk cutting the skin with scissors. While you are clipping, be careful not to cut off the end of the splinter or push it in deeper.

Wash the area. Wash the area with soap and water to get rid of any bacteria on the wound. You can use a mild antiseptic liquid soap like Betadine Skin Cleanser or plain hand soap. Be sure to rinse off the suds thoroughly.

Clean your tweezers. Clean blunt-tipped metal tweezers by wiping them with rubbing alcohol, then placing them under running water. Wipe them dry with a gauze pad before you use them.

Remove the splinter. Grab the end of the splinter firmly with the tweezers and pull it out in the direction that it entered the skin. You may need to carefully tease open the skin around the splinter first with a clean needle before trying to remove it.

Encourage the wound to bleed. Splinters are incredibly dirty and can carry infectious debris into the skin. So if the wound bleeds a bit, that's good because it can flush debris out of the wound. You can gently press on both sides of the wound to prompt it to bleed a small amount.

Wash the wound again. Once the splinter has been removed, wash the sore area again.

SPECIAL SITUATIONS

For especially hard-to-get splinters: If the end of the splinter isn't easy to grab or a small piece breaks off, don't try to pick it out—you could just make the wound more painful. Instead, apply a hot, wet compress. This will prompt the body to slowly eject the splinter by itself. Soak a washcloth in water as hot as you can comfortably stand against your skin for a few seconds, then hold it against the sore—5 minutes on, 5 minutes off until the cloth cools—three times a day. If a large piece of the splinter breaks off, see your vet to have the rest removed.

For splinters in the chest or trunk that look like pieces of sticks: These are dangerous to remove at home. Your pet needs immediate emergency care, just as if he'd been shot by an arrow. It's hard to tell how deep a splinter may go, and wiggling or pulling at it could cut an artery or damage a nerve or organ deep inside.

Keep your pet as quiet as possible by putting him on a blanket or towel to use as a stretcher. Carry him to the car and get medical help right away. (For more information about arrow wounds, see page 69.)

 ## FOLLOW-UP CARE

■ If the splinter was in the foot or lower leg, it's a good idea to use warm water and Epsom salts to soak the area. Add 1 cup of the salts to 2 gallons of water and soak the affected area for 10 minutes at a time twice a day for 3 days. This will help the body eject any leftover debris and bacteria that may have been left behind in the wound.

■ For wounds that aren't easy to soak with a foot bath, continue to use the hot, wet compresses for 2 days after the splinter is gone. The warmth increases blood circulation to the area to help speed healing.

■ Even when you're able to remove the splinter successfully at home, antibiotics are important to prevent infection from developing. An injection of penicillin at the vet's office may be followed by a week's worth of pills, depending on the severity of the wound. Usually, you can hide pills in treats like a hunk of cheese, and a dog will swallow it right down. For cats, try crushing the pill and mixing the powder in a tablespoon of strong-smelling canned food.

■ Stick-size splinters that have been removed can leave large wounds that you'll need to keep clean. Wash the area as needed with mild antiseptic liquid soap to help speed the healing and prevent infection from developing.

■ With severe injuries, the vet will place a drain in the deep tissues to help the wound get rid of foreign material. You may need to flush the wound every day with an antiseptic solution like Betadine Solution. Purchase this solution from the vet or pet-supply store in a strength of 0.01 to 0.1%. If you purchase higher-strength Betadine, dilute it with distilled water until it's the color of weak tea. (If you're not sure about dilution, call your pharmacist or veterinarian for complete instructions.) Your vet can give you a special syringe with a long, catheter-shaped tip and instructions on how to use it to squirt medicated solutions deep into the wound.

Advisors

■ Nina Beyer, V.M.D., is a veterinarian at Greenfield Veterinary Associates in Mantua, New Jersey.

■ Peter Davis, D.V.M., is a veterinarian at Pine Tree Veterinary Hospital in Augusta, Maine.

Sties

CALL YOUR VET: **IF NEEDED**

Cats almost never develop sties, but dogs do because they commonly suffer from blepharitis—an inflammation of the eyelid margin. The inflamed tissue is hairless, itchy, red, or scaly. A sty can develop as a result of blepharitis, or a sty can cause the condition to begin with.

Sties are not dangerous by themselves, but they are so uncomfortable that dogs may scratch and injure their eyes when they paw at the area. Sties are easy to treat at home with first aid. But more serious conditions can masquerade as sties, so get some medical attention if home treatment doesn't resolve the problem within 2 to 3 days.

DO THIS NOW

Fit your pet with an Elizabethan collar. Keep your pet from rubbing or pawing at the sore place on his eye. He could scratch his eye and injure it severely as he tires to relieve the itch. Fit him with a cone-shaped collar restraint called an Elizabethan collar so that he can't rub his face against the furniture or floor and can't reach to paw the sty.

Apply a hot, wet compress to the affected eye. A hot, wet compress not only helps relieve the pain and itch but also increases the blood circulation to the area in cases of infection. The bloodflow helps the sore heal. It can also bring the sty to a head so that it ruptures and the in-

fection drains. A sty that comes to a head and pops looks ugly, but it means that the healing has begun. Wet a washcloth with water as hot as you can stand, wring it out, and lay it against the affected eye—5 minutes on, 5 minutes off until the cloth cools—three or four times a day, until the sty begins to drain.

FOLLOW-UP CARE

■ Continue to use hot, wet compresses several times a day, and the sty should open up, drain, and go away within 2 to 3 days. If it doesn't, it may not be a sty and could need medical attention.

FIRST ALERT

Eyelid Tumors

Along the edges of a dog's eyelids, in the spaces between the lashes, are meibomian glands that produce an oily secretion, which keeps the skin lubricated. They are prone to growing benign (noncancerous) tumors, and when the growth is small, it looks exactly like a sty. In fact, 9 times out of 10, what seems to be a sty in a dog's eye turns out to be one of these tumors.

These tumors can usually be easily removed with surgery when they're small. But the larger they grow, the more chance there is that they'll leave defects or notches in the eyelid rim when they're removed. So make sure that you take your dog to the vet if you see a suspicious growth that doesn't respond to treatment after 2 to 3 days.

■ It's a good idea to apply over-the-counter antibiotic drops or ointments made specifically for the eyes to reduce the chance of infection. To apply eye medication, tilt your pet's head up,

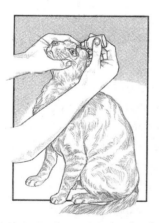

It's easy to give your pet eye medication. Tilt her head up, pull down her lower eyelid to form a cup, and drip the medication into the cupped tissue.

gently pull down the lower eyelid, and drip the medicine into the cupped tissue. Your pet's blinking will spread the medicine naturally.

■ Usually, a sty won't need any treatment but hot compresses, but some adult dogs develop a chronic sty condition that's hard to clear up. In addition to oral antibiotics and hot compresses, your veterinarian may prescribe cortisone. You can hide the antibiotics and cortisone medication in tasty treats when you give them to your dog.

■ In stubborn sty cases, your veterinarian may need to lance and open the infected gland with a sterile needle after sedating your pet. You'll need to keep the area clean. Usually, all that's required is wiping away any discharge with a gauze pad dampened with sterile saline contact lens solution.

Advisors
■ Nina Beyer, V.M.D., is a veterinarian at Greenfield Veterinary Associates in Mantua, New Jersey.
■ Sophia Yin, D.V.M., is a veterinarian in Davis, California, and author of *The Small Animal Veterinary Nerdbook*.

Strangulation

CALL YOUR VET: **IF NEEDED**

Strangulation happens most often to dogs because they're leashed or tied more often than cats. Tethered dogs wrap themselves around and around a pole or tree, and when they become entangled, they struggle to get loose and strangle themselves in the process. Dogs may also be tied incorrectly inside a vehicle and may hang themselves when they leap out a window or off the back of a pickup truck. Pets can catch their collars on something and end up strangling themselves. Cats especially are prone to getting tangled in draperies or the cords of venetian blinds. Strangulation tends to affect younger pets most often, perhaps because older animals have learned to avoid dangerous situations.

It takes only a few minutes for strangulation to kill your pet, so you must discover the situation very quickly. First aid is the only thing that can help, and you must act immediately to save your pet. Take him to the vet right away if he has lost consciousness or is still having trouble breathing. On the way there, perform artificial respiration or CPR if necessary.

DO THIS NOW

Free the neck. Lack of oxygen for only 3 to 4 minutes can cause brain damage and death, but pets will lose consciousness before that. The most important step is to remove the constriction around the neck as soon as possible. Don't waste time trying to unwrap the leash or unbuckle the collar—cut it off. Use sharp household scissors or, for thick collars, pruning shears. Take care not to cut your pet's skin, if possible.

Slip one blade of the scissors between the skin and collar, over the back of the neck where the muscle is thick and protects the deeper-lying veins. The collar may be so tight that even the dull side of the scissors scrapes or cuts the skin, but don't let that stop you. A cut will heal

363

⊕ FIRST ALERT

Neurogenic Pulmonary Edema

Cats and dogs who have been without oxygen for a time can develop breathing or heart problems even after they've been resuscitated. Fluid can accumulate in the lungs (pulmonary edema), causing shortness of breath, tiring easily, or coughing. These symptoms mean that your pet needs medical attention immediately.

Signs of problems can develop minutes to hours following a strangulation injury, so watch your pet closely for at least 12 hours before you consider him fully recovered. Treatment can be complicated if symptoms develop. Your pet may require medication to get rid of the water in his lungs, antibiotics to fight pneumonia, or even oxygen therapy to help him breathe.

in time, and protecting the skin isn't as important as cutting off the noose.

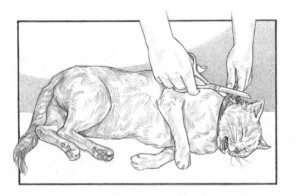

If your pet's collar is choking him, cut it off.

Open his airway. Removing the constriction may be enough to allow your pet to start breathing again on his own. You can open his airway to make it easier by gently extending his neck. If he's unconscious and still doesn't breathe, grasp his tongue near the tip and pull it forward; otherwise, it may fall to the back of the throat and block the airway. The wet tongue can be slippery, so it helps to use a piece of gauze or clean cloth to get a good grip.

Give artificial respiration if needed. Watch for his chest to rise and fall, and if it does not, you'll need to breathe for him. Close his mouth with your hand, put your lips over his nose, and give two quick breaths, watching to see if his chest rises. Breathe gently, particularly with cats and small dogs because blowing too hard can rupture their lungs. Think of blowing up a paper bag and stop as soon as you see the chest expand, allowing the air to escape back out. Repeat the process, giving 15 to 20 breaths a minute until your pet starts breathing again or until you reach the animal hospital. (This technique is illustrated on page 20.)

Be ready to give CPR. If your cat or dog stopped breathing for several minutes, chances are that his heart stopped, too. Feel or listen for the heartbeat by putting your palm or ear against the left side of his chest, right behind the elbow. If you can't find a pulse or heartbeat, you must give CPR, alternating five chest compressions for each breath. You should give 80 to 100 compressions and 15 to 20 breaths per minute.

To give heart compressions to cats or small dogs, cup your hand over the point of the chest just behind the elbows. Squeeze firmly in a "coughlike" manner, pressing in about ½ inch, with your thumb on one side and your fingers on the other.

Lay a larger pet on his side on a firm, flat surface. Place one hand on his chest behind the elbow, then put your other hand on top of the first. Use both hands to thrust downward, compressing the chest by 25 to 50%. (This technique is illustrated on page 21.)

 ## FOLLOW-UP CARE

■ Dogs and cats who have been strangled will have sore throats from the constriction on their necks. It can hurt to swallow until the bruising and swelling have healed. Soften your pet's regular diet for 3 to 5 days to make it easier for him to swallow. You can add some warm, low-fat, no-salt chicken broth to the food to soften it, or run it through the blender with warm water to make it a puddinglike consistency.

Advisors

■ Kenneth J. Drobatz, D.V.M., is a veterinarian and associate professor of critical care emergency service at the Veterinary Hospital of the University of Pennsylvania in Philadelphia.

■ Jean C. Hofve, D.V.M., is a veterinarian and Companion Animal Program coordinator for the Animal Protection Institute in Sacramento.

■ Barry N. Kellogg, V.M.D., is a veterinarian at the Center for Veterinary Care in Great Barrington, Massachusetts, and the head of VMAT 1 (Veterinary Medical Assistance Team), the national disaster team for veterinary medicine.

Suffocation

CALL YOUR VET: **SAME DAY**

Suffocation, also called asphyxiation, happens when air can't get into the lungs. Cats especially like to play with plastic bags from the grocery store or dry cleaner, and if they aren't able to claw their way out, they can quickly suffocate. Cats also get their collars caught or become tangled in venetian blind cords until they strangle, while dogs tend to get tangled in leashes. A pet can suffocate if exposed to toxic fumes like smoke or carbon monoxide, if she gets a foreign body stuck in her throat, or if she suffers an open chest injury.

During suffocation, a pet gasps for breath, usually with her neck extended. She'll quickly lose consciousness and stop breathing, and her gums and tongue will turn blue from oxygen starvation. She'll die within minutes without oxygen. Immediate first aid is the only thing that can save your pet's life. Then you must get to the veterinarian for further treatment.

DO THIS NOW

Get her some fresh air. For smoke or carbon monoxide inhalation, the best treatment is to get your pet into clean, fresh air. Unlike with other kinds of suffocation, your pet's gums and tongue will turn bright cherry red with carbon monoxide toxicity. (For more information about carbon monoxide poisoning, see page 122.)

Free her from smothering material. If your pet has been smothered in plastic, tear or cut the material from around her face before removing it from the rest of her body. Often, that's all you'll need to do for your pet to resume breathing on her own. If she doesn't start breathing on her own, see page 367 for instructions on how to perform artificial respiration and CPR.

Remove constrictions. Use scissors or pruning shears to cut a constricting collar, leash, or other material away from your pet's throat. Cut the material at the back of your pet's neck;

avoid the throat area because a slip of a sharp tool there could injure your pet even more. (For an illustration of this technique, see page 364.)

Clear the airway. Dogs often get objects caught in their throats and choke, and your pet can pass out and die if the object isn't quickly removed. If you can't pull the object out with your fingers or pliers, a modified Heimlich maneuver may pop it out of the airway. Hold a small pet with her back against your stomach, with her head up and feet down. Put your fist in the hollow area directly under her rib cage and pull in and up toward your chin with a strong thrusting movement. For a bigger dog, kneel behind her as she lies on one side. Put your knees against her backbone, bend over her, fit your fist into the hollow under the ribs, and push sharply up and in toward her head. (This technique is illustrated on page 22.) Repeat the maneuver two or three times in a row, then check to see if the object has come loose in her mouth. If it hasn't, you can continue the maneuver in the car on your way to the veterinarian. (For more information about choking, see page 131.)

Extend her neck. If your pet doesn't spontaneously begin breathing, extend her neck so her throat isn't bent, grasp her tongue, and gently pull it forward to get it out of the back of her throat, where it may block breathing. You can use gauze or cloth to get a grip on the wet tongue.

Check for stopped breathing. You must begin rescue breathing if your pet doesn't start breathing on her own. Close her mouth with one hand, put your lips over her nose, and blow with two quick breaths. Watch for her chest to expand and wait for the air to escape back out. Give 15 to 20 breaths a minute until your pet starts breathing again on her own or you reach medical help. (This technique is illustrated on page 20.)

Check for a stopped heart. Feel or listen for the heartbeat with your palm or ear on the left side of her chest, right behind the elbow. If the heart has stopped, give CPR, alternating five chest compressions for each breath.

Put your pet on a flat, firm surface like a tabletop or linolcum floor. For cats and small dogs, cup your hand over the point of the chest just behind the elbows and squeeze firmly between your fingers and thumb, pressing in about ½ inch, about 80 to 100 times a minute.

For larger dogs, put both hands on top of each other against the chest and compress by 25 to 50%. Give a breath into the nose after every fifth compression until your pet revives or until you reach medical help. (This technique is illustrated on page 21.) It's best to have someone drive you and your pet to the animal hospital while you're performing CPR.

🥫 SPECIAL SITUATION

For sucking chest wounds: Pets who have been hit by cars or shot or who have suffered other traumatic injuries can have "sucking" chest wounds. Air leaks into the chest cavity from an open wound and collapses the lungs, so the pet can't breathe and suffocates. Seal the hole in the chest by pinching the skin together over the wound. You can use plastic wrap like Saran Wrap to seal the opening until you can get your pet medical help. (For more information about chest injuries, see page 128.)

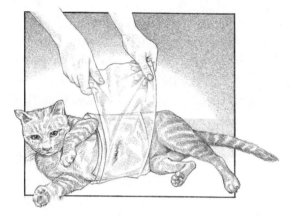

Wrap an open chest wound with plastic wrap to protect the wound until you can get to the vet.

 ## FOLLOW-UP CARE

■ A pet who has breathed caustic fumes or been strangled will have a sore throat from irritation or the constriction on her neck. A soft diet makes it easier for her to swallow. Mix her regular food in the blender with warm water or low-fat, no-salt chicken broth to make a gruel, and feed it for 3 to 5 days. Gradually return her to a regular diet by mixing the gruel with her regular food.

■ When your pet feels herself suffocating, she'll do nearly anything to get air—even claw the constriction around her throat and tear up her own flesh. Wash any lacerations with plain soap and water, and apply an antibiotic ointment like Neosporin to fight infection. Use the ointment two or three times a day until the wounds have scabbed and begun to heal.

Advisors

■ Kenneth J. Drobatz, D.V.M., is a veterinarian and associate professor of critical care emergency service at the Veterinary Hospital of the University of Pennsylvania in Philadelphia.

■ Barry N. Kellogg, V.M.D., is a veterinarian at the Center for Veterinary Care in Great Barrington, Massachusetts, and the head of VMAT 1 (Veterinary Medical Assistance Team), the national disaster team for veterinary medicine.

■ Kate Lindley, D.V.M., is veterinarian and owner of Kitty Klinic in Lacey, Washington.

■ Kevin Wallace, D.V.M., is an instructor in the department of clinical sciences at Cornell University College of Veterinary Medicine in Ithaca, New York.

Suture Problems

CALL YOUR VET: **IF NEEDED**

Nearly every pet will have stitches at some time during her life, if only for a spay surgery. Sutures are used to repair cuts in the body and pull them together; veterinarians may use metal staples, wire stitches, absorbable sutures that don't need to be removed, or threadlike material that does need to come out once the incision has healed. Occasionally, the body has a reaction to the material, and the tissue becomes red, swollen, and inflamed. At other times, a stitch comes loose or is removed by the pet, and the incision gapes open.

The irritation from an infected suture makes it nearly impossible for a pet to resist the urge to lick and nibble at it, and without first aid to relieve the itching, dogs especially are likely to lick their incisions.

A little inflammation is easy to treat at home. Although a gaping hole in the incision needs immediate veterinary attention, first aid is still vital to keep your pet from doing further damage to herself.

DO THIS NOW

Apply a hot compress. A small amount of swelling directly around the stitches, staples, or incision line is normal. But if the area looks very red or feels hot in an area beyond the incision line, or if the tissue seems to have a discharge of pus, take your pet to the vet. She may have an infection. In the meantime, apply a hot, wet compress to help speed the healing and clean out any drainage. Run water from the tap as hot as you can stand, soak a cloth, wring it out, and place it on the incision line two or three times a day, 5 minutes on, 5 minutes off until the cloth cools.

Keep the incision line clean. Use a bit of water or sterile saline contact lens solution on a gauze pad or clean cloth. When there's a small gap in the incision where your pet has removed a stitch or a staple, clean the area the same way and blot it dry with a paper towel or dry gauze pad. If medical care isn't available, you may be able to close the wound yourself with one or more butterfly bandages, which are available in drugstores. Then call your vet, who may want to check the incision.

Cover large openings with plastic wrap. If a gaping wound is visible into the abdomen, cover the area with a clean gauze pad or cloth soaked in water or sterile saline contact lens solution. Wrap plastic wrap like Saran Wrap all the way around the body to hold the wound together, then seek immediate medical attention.

Keep your pet from bothering the wound. If there is only a little inflammation and the sutures are intact, but your pet keeps bothering them, apply a thin coat of Vicks VapoRub on each side of the incision with a cotton swab. For 90% of pets, one whiff of the strong-smelling stuff will make them leave the incision alone until you can get medical help. It tastes nasty, too, so even determined dogs won't go beyond one lick. Or ask your vet for a product called Variton, which has a bad taste that pets dislike. Bitter Apple or hot sauce like Tabasco works with about 40% of pets. Many, though, actually like the flavor, and it won't deter them from licking.

Try an Elizabethan collar. A cone-shaped collar restraint called an Elizabethan collar works well to keep pets from reaching most incisions. You can get these at most pet-supply stores or the vet's office.

Make a body stocking. If your pet is small, you can cut the top off a tube sock or heavy-duty tights and make a sort of girdle or body stocking. The tube of material fits snugly over the entire body, leaving the legs and tail free, and covers the incision to protect it from licking or chewing. If he's bigger, you can make a body wrap with a sheet and some safety pins. (This is illustrated on page 27.)

Put him in a T-shirt. With a larger pet, you can put a T-shirt on him and wrap it with tape or an elastic bandage like an Ace bandage to keep it in place. This not only offers a barrier to the teeth but also gives your dog something to work on other than himself.

 FOLLOW-UP CARE

■ Once the incision has healed and the sutures have dissolved or been removed, no follow-up care is needed.

Advisors

■ Lyndon Conrad, D.V.M., is a veterinarian at Noah's Landing Pet Care Clinic in Elkhart, Indiana.

■ Kevin Doughty, D.V.M., is a veterinarian at Mauer Animal Clinic in Las Vegas.

■ Grady Hester, D.V.M., is a veterinarian at All Creatures Animal Clinic in Rolesville, North Carolina.

■ Chris Johnson, D.V.M., is a veterinarian at Westside Animal Emergency Clinic in Atlanta.

■ Doug McConkey, D.V.M., is a veterinarian at Canyon Creek Pet Hospital in Sherman, Texas.

Tail Infections

CALL YOUR VET: **IF NEEDED**

Tail infections are common in cats who fight and get caught by teeth or claws as they run away. Dogs can also develop tail infections from bite wounds or from trauma if their tails are banged, caught in fences, or lacerated by thorns.

Pets also have specialized "preening glands" in their tails that contain oil and scent, which are used to mark objects and keep the skin and coat healthy as they groom. Occasionally, that gland kicks into overdrive, and a waxy or oily secretion clogs the tail fur and can lead to infection. Called stud tail, the condition is most common in intact male cats, but dogs can have a similar problem.

An infected tail is swollen and sore. It may drain pus and make the fur look nasty. Your pet may hold his tail in an odd way to keep it from being touched. Infections usually need prescription antibiotics, but first aid can keep the infection from getting worse and help speed healing. If your pet has a fever, is not eating, has what appears to be an abscess (a fluid-filled, soft swelling), or you think that he may have stud tail, see your vet right away.

DO THIS NOW

Trim the fur. Clip off the fur surrounding the infected area. Fur collects infectious material and can recontaminate the sore. Removing the fur also makes the infection easier to treat. Electric clippers are the best choice, but even an electric razor or mustache trimmer will work. If you don't have these, slip your index and second fingers through the fur and hold them against the skin. Use blunt scissors to cut the fur level with your fingers. (This technique is illustrated on page 114.)

Wash the area. Clean up the wound with an antiseptic liquid soap like Betadine Skin

371

⊕ FIRST ALERT

Tail-Wag Trauma

Very large dogs like Labrador retrievers and Irish wolfhounds have such long tails that they often injure themselves just by wagging and banging them into objects. Usually, it's just the tip of the tail that's injured. Typically, it bleeds, the dog licks at it, and even once it heals, the cycle repeats, and the tail is injured over and over again. When the injury isn't treated promptly or the tail is repeatedly injured, it can become infected. Some dogs end up losing the damaged part when it must be amputated.

Most of the time, minor tail-wag trauma can be treated at home. An antihistamine like Benadryl can reduce the swelling. The liquid form of Benadryl usually comes in a dose of 12.5 milligrams per teaspoon; pills are usually 25 milligrams each. Pets will need 1 milligram per pound of body weight every 6 to 8 hours. That means a 10-pound dog should get about ¾ teaspoon of liquid or half a pill. Then, something as simple as moving furniture out of the way can keep the sore from becoming worse and prevent reinjury. If it doesn't heal in a week, however, or it happens again, take your dog to the vet.

Cleanser, unless there's an oily or waxy residue clogging the skin that caused the infection. Dawn and Sunlight dishwashing liquids are about the only things that will cut this buildup. You don't need to bathe the entire body—just dip the tail in a pan of warm water, lather up the affected area, rinse well to get off the soap, and blot dry with a towel.

Gently press out pus. If the wound is already open, press out any pus that you can. Put an absorbent sanitary napkin or other material on top of the wound and gently press on each side to clean out infectious matter—the pad will absorb and capture the debris. Again, do this only if the wound is already open and draining pus. If the wound is not open, do not attempt to drain it.

Apply a hot compress. Heat dilates the blood vessels and brings in blood, antibodies, and white blood cells to the wound to fight infection and promote healing. Soak a washcloth in water as hot as you can stand, wring it out, and hold the compress against the wound—5 minutes on, 5 minutes off until the cloth cools—two to five times a day. The warm moisture will also help soften and remove the scab, which can act like a cork in a bottle to hold in infection and prompt an abscess to form.

Keep your pet confined. If the tail is very messy, it's best to confine a cat or small dog to a carrier. Otherwise, he may swish his tail around, spray or smear infectious fluid everywhere, and potentially cause more damage to the tail. If your dog is too large or you don't have a carrier, keep him confined to a small room that's easy to clean, like a bathroom or laundry room.

Fit your pet with an Elizabethan collar. Pets usually want to lick at the tail infection. Prevent your pet from bothering the wound by fitting him with a collar restraint like a cone-shaped Elizabethan collar. Pets have trouble eating while wearing the collar, though, so be sure to remove it at feeding time.

FOLLOW-UP CARE

■ Continue to apply hot compresses to the infection as described on page 372. The moist heat will speed up the healing and keep scabs from forming so that the wound drains out infectious material.

■ Give oral antibiotics as prescribed, usually for 7 to 10 days. Dogs take pills readily if you hide them in tasty treats. Cats can be tricky to pill, but most medicines can be crushed with the bowl of a spoon and mixed into strong-smelling canned cat food so that your cat will eat it willingly.

■ A prescription ointment like Panalog Ointment or Otomax helps control the inflammation and relieves the pain. Use it according to your veterinarian's instructions.

■ Some tail infections need to be bandaged. Cats hate having their tails bandaged, but it can help keep dogs from doing further damage to the area. First wrap gauze around the tail. Start from the tip and work toward the body, keeping the wrap firm but not tight. Then tear strips of tape and wrap each one individually over the gauze (this will help keep you from taping the bandage too tight and cutting off the circulation). Be sure that the tape extends beyond the gauze and sticks directly to the fur so that your dog can't pull it off. (This technique is illustrated on page 25.)

■ For dogs who try to lick or chew at the bandage, try dabbing on Bitter Apple or Variton ointment, which is available from your veterinarian.

Advisors
■ John Brakebill, D.V.M., is a veterinarian at Brakebill Veterinary Hospital in Sherman, Texas.
■ Jeff Nichol, D.V.M., is the hospital director and a veterinarian at Adobe Animal Medical Center in Albuquerque.
■ Raymond Russo, D.V.M., is a veterinarian at Kingston Animal Hospital in Massachusetts.
■ Drew Weigner, D.V.M., is a veterinarian at The Cat Doctor in Atlanta.

Tail Swelling

CALL YOUR VET: **IF NEEDED**

A swollen tail isn't a life-threatening medical emergency, but it can be painful. Tails can be bruised when they're stepped on or fractured when they're shut in doors or caught under rocking chairs. Car accidents can also result in tail injuries.

More commonly, tails that are bitten by other animals can swell and become infected. A bee or wasp sting may also make your pet's tail swell. (For more information about insect stings, see page 79; for tail infections, see page 371.)

Because pets' tails are usually covered with thick fur, it can be hard to see when they're swollen. If your pet is licking, biting, or grooming her tail or holding it in an odd position, feel it gently to see if swelling is the reason. If you can provide first aid in time, you can often prevent a swollen tail from becoming infected.

DO THIS NOW

Restrain your pet. When her tail is painful, you'll need to restrain your pet before you can even examine the swollen area to see what's wrong. Small dogs and cats do well on a tabletop. Grasp the loose skin at the back of your pet's neck—the scruff—with one hand and capture both hind paws with the other. Stretch your pet on her side while another person treats the tail.

For a big dog, kneel on the floor beside her with one arm under and around her chest and the other underneath her neck, and hug her close to your chest. It helps to talk soothingly to her while another person examines the swollen tail. (Both of these techniques are illustrated on page 18.)

Look for the cause. You may need to clip away the fur from the swelling to see exactly what has caused the problem. Electric clippers are the safest for trimming fur, but you can use blunt scissors as long as you protect the skin. Slip your index and second fingers through the fur and hold them against the skin. Use the scissors to cut the fur level with your fingers.

Check for thorns. Carefully examine the swollen area for a foreign body, like a thorn or splinter. If you can grasp it readily, use blunt-tipped tweezers to remove it. (For more information about splinters, see page 358.)

Wash the cut. If there's an abrasion, cut, or puncture, wash the area with water and antiseptic liquid soap like Betadine Skin Cleanser. For pets who dislike baths, you can use a plant sprayer to soak the tail, then lather the area, and finally, spray off the soap. If your pet still objects, you can wet a gauze pad with sterile saline contact lens solution and sponge off the area.

Apply soothing ointment. To reduce the pain and inflammation of minor abrasions or irritations, spread on a small amount of antibiotic ointment like Neosporin. Distract your pet with a treat so that the ointment is absorbed before she tries to lick it off. Do not use this if the skin is broken.

SPECIAL SITUATIONS

If there's string wrapped around the tail: Check above the swelling to be sure that there's nothing constricting the tail. Sometimes a playful cat gets string wrapped around her tail, or a child slips a rubber band on a pet's tail and the constriction becomes hidden in the fur. If you can do so without injuring your pet, carefully cut the string or rubber band with blunt scissors or a seam ripper. If you're unable to do this, take your pet to the vet.

If the swelling is the result of a bruise or insect sting: Apply cold compresses for 10 to 30 minutes several times a day. This will help reduce the swelling and relieve the pain. You can hold an ice cube covered with a wet towel directly on the swollen area or drape a bag of frozen peas or corn wrapped in a cold, wet washcloth across the tail.

If the tail itches from an insect bite: Insect bites or stings on the tail can be helped with a dose of antihistamine like Benadryl. The liquid form of Benadryl usually comes in a dose of 12.5 milligrams per teaspoon; pills are usually 25 milligrams each. Pets will need 1 milligram per pound of body weight every 6 to 8 hours. That means a 10-pound cat or dog should get about ¾ teaspoon of liquid or half a pill. This will help reduce the swelling, and it also tends to make pets sleepy so that they stop banging their tails around.

You can also make a paste of Ac'cent Flavor Enhancer by mixing it with water, then apply it to the sting. This product contains mono-sodium glutamate, which helps neutralize the sting by pulling out the venom. If the fur isn't trimmed, though, the paste will make a mess.

If the tail is broken: A badly bruised tail may be a sign of a broken bone. There's no good way to splint a tail—the best you can do is put your dog or cat in a carrier to protect her during the ride to the animal hospital. (For more information about fractures, see page 212.)

 FOLLOW-UP CARE

■ If cellulitis (tissue inflammation) is diagnosed, your pet may get an injection of an antibiotic, like penicillin, at the vet's office. She may also need to take antibiotics for a week or longer at home. This can often prevent the tail swelling from developing into an infection or abscess. At other times, your vet may prescribe an anti-in-flammatory medication to help reduce the bruising.

To give your dog a pill, put your hand around her muzzle and gently press your thumb and middle finger against the gum line behind the large canine teeth to prompt her to open wide. Then drop the pill on the back of her tongue, close her mouth, and stroke her throat until she swallows. (This technique is illustrated on page 30.) For a cat, you'll need to grasp her scruff and gently tilt her head up. Then, pull down on her chin until you can see the V-shaped indentation in the center of her tongue. Drop the pill on the V and close her mouth. Immediately follow the medicine with a tasty treat that your pet can't resist so that she swallows it along with the pill and forgets to spit out the medicine.

■ If recommended by your veterinarian, a prescription cortisone-type ointment like Panalog can be helpful to soothe the inflammation. Use it two or three times a day directly on the swelling.

■ You can continue to reduce the pain of bruises with cold packs. Apply them for 10 to 30 minutes at a time several times a day until the swelling goes down.

■ When the swelling is on the verge of infection, apply hot compresses to the area to bring it to a head so that it can heal. Soak a washcloth in water as hot as you can stand, wring it out, and hold the moist heat against the swollen tail—5 minutes on, 5 minutes off until the cloth cools—two to five times a day. This promotes blood circulation to the area, which helps clean out infectious agents and heal the sore.

Advisors

■ John Brakebill, D.V.M., is a veterinarian at Brakebill Veterinary Hospital in Sherman, Texas.

■ Jeff Nichol, D.V.M., is the hospital director and a veterinarian at Adobe Animal Medical Center in Albuquerque.

■ Raymond Russo, D.V.M., is a veterinarian at Kingston Animal Hospital in Massachusetts.

■ Drew Weigner, D.V.M., is a veterinarian at The Cat Doctor in Atlanta.

■ George White, D.V.M., is a veterinarian at I-20 Animal Medical Center in Arlington, Texas.

■ Anna E. Worth, V.M.D., is a veterinarian at West Mountain Animal Hospital in Shaftsbury, Vermont.

Testicular or Scrotal Swelling

CALL YOUR VET: **IF NEEDED**

A pet's testicles may become inflamed and swell from trauma like a bite or scratch wound or a bruise from a fall. More often, the scrotum–the sac of tissue that contains the testicles–swells from an injury. The problem is more common in dogs because they can suffer burns, frostbite, cuts, or scrapes simply by sleeping on a hot, cold, or abrasive surface. Dogs who regularly go to a groomer may be nicked or burned with clippers.

Orchitis–testicular inflammation, in which one or both testicles become hard and swollen–always needs immediate medical attention. But most of the time, scrotal swelling happens after castration surgery. The discomfort of the surgery prompts the pet to lick, and that bruises the tissue, which makes the inflammation worse. As a result, the scrotum swells up, sometimes to enormous proportions. The poor dog may walk straddle-legged with his belly tucked up, or he may sit a lot on cool surfaces to relieve the pain. Most of the time, first aid is all that's needed to bring relief.

DO THIS NOW

Muzzle your pet. Your pet won't want you handling this area of the body, and when it's swollen and sore, he will readily snap or bite if you hurt him when you try to treat the area. To muzzle a long-nosed dog, use a necktie or panty hose. Loop it around his nose and tie it on the bridge of the nose, then bring the ends down and around and tie them beneath the jaw. Finally, bring both ends of the fabric back behind your pet's ears and tie them in a knot or bow. (This technique is illustrated on page 17.)

For a short-faced dog like a pug, you can put a pillowcase over his head. Restrain your cat with one hand on the scruff—the loose fur at the back of the neck—and your other hand grasping both rear legs. Gently hold him on his side on a tabletop while a second person exam-

FIRST ALERT

Testicular Cancer

Cancer of the testicles is quite common in dogs. It usually develops in middle-aged dogs (10 years old or older), and a common sign is enlargement of the affected testicle. The tissue can be soft or hard, but it usually isn't painful.

Other signs may include bloody urine, difficulty urinating, or constipation when the tumor interferes with elimination. Some dogs show signs of feminization when these tumors produce estrogen, the female sex hormone. Their breasts may enlarge, for example, and they may squat to urinate like female dogs or become attractive to other intact male dogs. If you see any of these signs or if you can feel a mass in your pet's testicles, take him to your veterinarian by the following day.

Diagnosis requires laboratory examination of the affected tissue. The tumor is usually removed, and if the cancer has spread beyond the testicles, chemotherapy or radiation therapy is performed. Testicular cancer can be prevented by neutering (castrating) your dog—the earlier the better.

---

ines and treats the swollen area. (This technique is illustrated on page 18.)

Wash scratches. When there is a scratch or abrasion of the tissue, wash off the area with sterile saline contact lens solution or plain water. The best way to do this is with a sink sprayer or a plant sprayer. That way, your hands never touch the tender area, and the cool liquid is also soothing to your pet.

Apply antibiotic ointment. For minor scrapes or abrasions on the scrotum, apply an antibiotic ointment like Neosporin to the area. This helps prevent infection.

Wrap an ice pack. Usually, an ice pack would bring down the swelling and also relieve the pain by numbing the tissues. But testiclular swelling can be so sensitive that the pressure of an ice pack against the area may make the pain worse. Instead of using an ice pack, gently place a gauze pad over the area, then use a spray bottle filled with ice water to keep the pad soaked and cold. Put a towel under your pet to catch the dripping water. Apply it for 10 to 30 minutes several times a day.

Ask about aspirin. You may be able to give your dog buffered aspirin like Bufferin to relieve the pain on a temporary basis. If there is bleeding into the scrotum, though, aspirin may make it worse, so ask your veterinarian about giving it. The usual dose is 10 to 25 milligrams per 2.2 pounds of body weight two or three times a day. Do not give aspirin to cats.

Use a collar restraint. Because you can't watch your pet constantly to be sure that he's not licking the irritated area, use a collar restraint like a cone-shaped Elizabethan collar. You may need to remove it at mealtime, because it can be hard for pets to eat with the collar on.

 FOLLOW-UP CARE

■ Swelling from excessive licking usually goes away when your pet is prevented from bothering the area. So keep the Elizabethan collar on until the swelling goes down and the area heals.

■ Apply an antibiotic ointment like Neosporin, which also helps reduce inflammation, a couple of times a day.

■ Your vet may prescribe pain medication or an anti-inflammatory to help relieve the discomfort until the inflammation goes away. For dogs, you can usually hide the pills in a tasty treat. For cats, you can try crushing the pill with the back of a spoon and mixing it into strong-smelling cat food.

■ In cases where swelling is caused by infection, you'll need to give antibiotics for up to 2 weeks as prescribed by your veterinarian after diagnosis. Signs of infection include fever, discharge of pus, loss of appetite, lethargy or hiding behavior, and constant licking of the area. The area may be red or discolored and painful to the touch. If you suspect that the infection has turned into an abscess, and there is an open wound with a red discharge of pus, have the vet check your pet again.

■ In rare cases, the swelling after neutering becomes so severe that it leads to damage of the scrotum. In these cases, a repeat of the surgery or the insertion of a drain may be needed. Clean the incision and drain area as needed with sterile saline contact lens solution on a gauze pad.

Advisors
■ Denise Petryk, D.V.M., is a veterinarian at Puget Sound Veterinary Medical Referral Center in Tacoma, Washington.
■ Anna E.Worth, V.M.D., is a veterinarian at West Mountain Animal Hospital in Shaftsbury, Vermont.
■ Sophia Yin, D.V.M., is a veterinarian in Davis, California, and author of *The Small Animal Veterinary Nerdbook.*

Ticks

CALL YOUR VET: **IF NEEDED**

Ticks affect dogs much more often than cats because cats tend to groom them away, unless they just can't reach them. Ticks bury their heads beneath the pet's skin and stay there for days as they suck blood. You'll see a BB- to lima bean–size leathery pest that balloons as it becomes full.

The sparsely furred and hard-to-reach regions of a pet's body, like the ears, armpits, and between the toes, are prime tick targets, but ticks can be found anywhere on your pet. Most of the time, your pet won't even feel the bite. Tick wounds almost never get infected or sore.

Two types of ticks, the black-legged tick (formerly known as the deer tick) and the American dog tick, are known to transmit infections to humans. The black-legged tick, in its nymphal (most infectious) stage, is about the size of a pinhead or sesame seed. It has eight legs and is translucent, with a slight tinge of gray. The American dog tick is most infectious as an adult. The adult female has gray markings in a shield shape on her back, and her body is reddish brown. The male has gray markings over his entire back, and the rest of his body is reddish brown. Nonfeeding adult dog ticks are about ¼ inch long. Ticks carry their own tiny parasite hitchhikers, and those microscopic bugs can make pets—and people—very sick once they get into the bloodstream. That's why it's so important to remove ticks from your pet as soon as possible. It's easy to remove ticks at home, however, and it's seldom necessary to see your veterinarian unless you suspect that a tick has given your pet a disease.

🩹 DO THIS NOW

Remove the tick. Do not use your fingers to remove the tick; use blunt-tipped tweezers or a hemostat (a long, thin clamp available from pet-supply catalogs). Wear disposable medical gloves (available in drugstores) and be very careful not to crush the tick's body as you remove it. (Often, your fingers have tiny cuts or abrasions that you can't even see, and if you crush the tick's body, some of the infected tick parts could transmit diseases to you.)

Grasp the body very close to the pet's skin and the tick's mouthparts and pull it straight out, slowly and gently, in the opposite direction from the mouth end. That will allow the mouthparts to slide back out most easily instead of dragging the buried head through your pet's flesh.

The tick will almost always come away with a tiny pinch of skin. Don't worry if the head comes off and stays buried in the flesh—

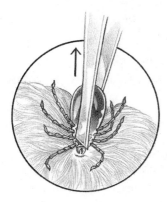

To remove a tick, grasp it near the head with tweezers and pull it straight out.

that almost never happens, but if it does, it won't cause problems for most pets. The pet's body will either absorb the material or eject it in a few days.

Dispose of the tick carefully. Either drop the tick into a container of rubbing alcohol or flea spray or flush it down the toilet. Washing it down the sink isn't the best choice because ticks can often cling to sink drains and climb back out. If you live in an area where Lyme disease is prevalent, you may want to save the tick, since examining it may be the only way to know if it is carrying Lyme disease. Use a moistened cotton swab to place it in a plastic bag or a glass or plastic bottle. Take the tick to your veterinarian so that he can send it to a lab that specializes in the identification and analysis of Lyme disease bacteria.

🩹 FOLLOW-UP CARE

■ It's a good idea to wash the tick bite with an antiseptic liquid soap like Betadine Skin Cleanser or swab it with some 3% hydrogen peroxide to remove any residual tick parts.

■ Dab on an antibiotic ointment like Neosporin. Usually, once will be enough.

■ When you remove a tick, it's normal for a small, pimple-size bump to be left behind. That should go away in 1 to 2 days. But if it doesn't go away or grows bigger than pea size, have your veterinarian take a look. The vet will prob-

FIRST ALERT

Tickborne Diseases

Many diseases are spread by ticks because their saliva transmits microscopic organisms when they bite. Usually, though, a tick must be feeding on a pet for at least 12 hours for the pet to become infected, so prompt removal can prevent most diseases. Dogs and people can be infected by some of the same diseases, but ticks don't hop off the dog and onto another host, so it's nearly impossible to catch something from your pet. Handling ticks with your bare hands can expose you, though. Here are some of the more serious diseases that dogs (and sometimes people) can get from ticks. The veterinarian has to diagnose the problem, but disease-specific medications will usually take care of the illness.

Babesiosis causes severe anemia that can damage the liver, kidneys, and spleen, and the first symptom is a fever as high as 107°F. Urine will turn dark due to blood leakage. Sometimes, the disease causes neurological symptoms, such as tooth grinding or drunken behavior, and dogs can die within 4 days. Antiprotozoal drugs are used to treat babesiosis.

Ehrlichiosis causes a wide range of symptoms, from a bloody nose and fever up to 105°F to a suppressed immune system. Antibiotics like tetracycline are the treatment of choice.

Lyme disease is the best-known and most common tick disease. It takes 12 to 24 hours of sucking for the tick to transmit the disease. Dogs with Lyme disease usually limp, act depressed, and have high fevers. Rarely, they'll also have a bull's-eye rash pattern on the skin, but fur makes this hard to see. The treatment is antibiotics.

Rocky Mountain spotted fever causes high fever, stiffness, labored breathing, vomiting, diarrhea, leg and face swelling, and eventually, bleeding from the nose and in the urine and feces. Antibiotics like doxycycline reverse the symptoms within 1 to 2 days.

Tick paralysis is believed to be caused by a neurotoxin in the tick saliva that slowly paralyzes the dog over a 48- to 72-hour period. If you remove all the ticks, the paralysis will usually go away within a day or so.

ably give your pet an antibiotic like tetracycline to take care of any infection that might have caused the problem.

■ In areas that have high occurrences of Lyme disease, watch your pet very closely for 14 days. If you see any limping, take your pet to the vet immediately. He will probably prescribe a course of antibiotics to stop Lyme disease before it gets worse. Left to develop, Lyme disease can cause major health problems such as intense joint pain, fever, and loss

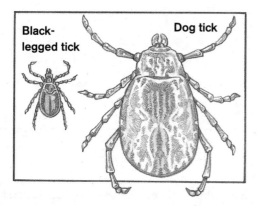

Black-legged tick

Dog tick

Black-legged (deer) ticks are so tiny that they're hard to see unless they're moving. Fortunately, you can often spot them crawling across the short hair on top of your dog's head.

Dog ticks attach themselves, then become bloated as they feed, so they're easy to feel. Check for ticks when you bring your dog inside after warm-weather walks. And if you see your dog scratching around his neck, check for a tick.

of appetite. A bite from any type of tick can cause tick paralysis, usually striking the pet's hind legs first. If your pet suddenly begins dragging his back legs or is having trouble moving, take him to the vet right away. Most cases of tick paralysis will disappear within a short time (up to a day or so) after the tick is removed. Some veterinarians believe that a toxin secreted in the tick's saliva causes the paralysis, so when you remove the source of the toxin (the tick), the symptoms go away.

■ To keep ticks from infesting your pet, apply a topical tick treatment like Frontline. Just a drop between the shoulder blades once a month should keep your pet tick-free. You don't have to apply treatment during the winter months as long as the temperature stays below freezing.

Advisors

■ Clint Chastain, D.V.M., is a veterinarian at Preston Road Animal Hospital in Dallas.

■ Karen Hoffman, V.M.D., is a veterinarian at Delaware Valley Animal Hospital in Fairless Hills, Pennsylvania.

■ Laura Solien, D.V.M., is a veterinarian at Maplecrest Animal Hospital in Goshen, Indiana.

Toad Poisoning

CALL YOUR VET: **IMMEDIATELY**

Young dogs—those less than 18 months old, in particular—seem fascinated by toads, and they often try to pick them up. All toads secrete mucus through the skin that's noxious and causes strings of saliva to spill from a dog's mouth, but the Colorado River toad and the marine toad can kill. Catching any toad in his mouth can cause a pet to salivate and paw his mouth. But poisonous toads produce many substances that are absorbed through the mouth tissues and affect the heart and nervous system. A poisoned pet develops seizures, collapses, and can die within 30 minutes. See the veterinarian immediately if you live in or travel to places where there are poisonous toads and your pet licks or mouths a toad

🧰 DO THIS NOW

Rinse his mouth with water. When you see your dog mouth a toad, don't wait for him to start to drool. Immediately rinse his mouth out to get rid of the nasty taste of nonpoisonous toads and reduce the toxicity of deadly ones. Use the garden hose or sprayer from the sink and run water into his mouth for at least 3 to 5 minutes. A squirt gun or plant sprayer also works, but you'll need to continue for longer.

Get your dog to the vet. Toad poisoning is a medical emergency. Don't fool around—once you've rinsed your pet's mouth, get him to the veterinarian immediately.

Watch for signs of shock. Keep in mind that a dog poisoned by a toad can very quickly go into shock. His eyes become glazed, his gums turn pale, and he may collapse. Rub a bit of Karo syrup or honey on your pet's gums on the way to the vet. It's absorbed through the skin and can help stabilize his blood sugar levels and slow down the process of shock. (For more information about shock, see page 333.) Wrap him in a towel or blanket to transport him in the car.

Raise his head. Keep your dog's head elevated. This will help him breathe more easily and prevent him from choking if he vomits.

FIRST ALERT

Seizures

Nearly any kind of poison can cause seizures by affecting the brain, and toad poisoning is no exception. Sometimes, an affected pet may just seem disoriented and stare into space. More often, he will yelp, fall to the floor, paddle his legs, and jerk his body. He may urinate or defecate involuntarily. Seizures that last only a minute or so are more frightening than they are dangerous. But in cases of toad poisoning or any kind of intoxication that causes seizures, the seizure can go on so long without pause that the body temperature becomes dangerously elevated. (For more information about seizures, see page 330.)

 SPECIAL SITUATION

If there's no breathing and/or heartbeat: Be prepared to perform artificial respiration or CPR if your pet collapses. Toad poisoning can stop the heart and respiration very quickly.

If your dog stops breathing, you'll need to breathe for him. Put on disposable medical gloves (available at drugstores), then form one hand into a cylinder and place the pinky end over his nostrils. Put your mouth over the opposite end of that hand, then seal his lips with the other hand so air doesn't leak out. Blow two quick breaths into his nostrils, watching to see his chest rise (blow just hard enough to expand the chest). Let the air escape back out through his nose, then give another breath. Continue rescue breathing, giving 15 to 20 breaths per minute, until he starts breathing on his own or you reach medical help. If you don't have gloves, you should administer artificial respiration only through a barrier like a piece of plastic wrap

(Saran Wrap) so you don't come in contact with the poison yourself. Cut a small hole in the material and place it over the dog's nostrils before beginning rescue breathing.

Check to see if his heart has stopped by taking his pulse. You won't be able to feel a pulse in the carotid artery in the neck as you can with people. Instead, press your fingertips into the crease where the inside of the thigh meets the body and feel for the pulse in the femoral artery, which is very big and near the surface. (This technique is illustrated on page 13.) If you can't feel it, try listening or feeling for the heartbeat. Put your ear or hand against your pet's left side directly behind the elbow.

If you can't feel a beat, begin chest compressions. For a small dog, cup your hand over the point of the chest just behind the elbows and squeeze firmly between your fingers and thumb, pressing in about ½ inch, about 80 to 100 times a minute. Give one breath for every five compressions. Put a larger dog on his side

Identifying Poisonous Toads

Most toads are harmless; in fact, they're garden heroes, eating insect pests and slugs by the bucketful. But two species of toads may harm your pet if you live in an area where they flourish. If you live near the habitat of either the Colorado River or marine toad, make sure that you know what they look like. If you find any in an area that your pet goes into, try to protect him by restricting unsupervised free time. It may save his life.

Colorado River toads are found from the Pecos River west into southern California in the southwestern United States. They are about 7½ inches long, have small red spots on their backs, and are most often found in the desert after it rains.

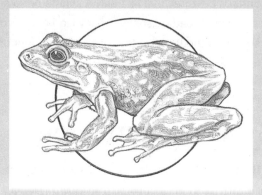

Marine toads are found in Hawaii as well as from Corpus Christi, Texas, east along the Gulf Coast, down into Florida, and back up the Atlantic Coast. They can grow up to 9½ inches, have cream spots on their brown skin, and flatter heads and bodies than most toads. They are typically found near water sources.

on a firm, flat surface and place both hands on top of each other against the chest. Press firmly, compressing the chest by 25 to 50%, about 80 to 100 times a minute. Alternate breaths and compressions as for small dogs.

 FOLLOW-UP CARE

■ After you bring your pet home from the vet, there is usually no follow-up care required. Your veterinarian will advise you if any is needed.

Advisors

■ E. Murl Bailey Jr., D.V.M., Ph.D., is a professor of toxicology at Texas A&M University College of Veterinary Medicine in College Station.

■ Tam Garland, D.V.M., Ph.D., is a veterinarian at Texas A&M University College of Veterinary Medicine in College Station.

■ Grady Hester, D.V.M., is a veterinarian at All Creatures Animal Clinic in Rolesville, North Carolina.

Toe Cysts

CALL YOUR VET: **IF NEEDED**

MEDICINE CHEST

Blunt-tipped tweezers
Epsom salts or anti-
    septic solution (Be-
    tadine Solution)
Elizabethan collar or
    cotton sock
Antihistamine (Ben-
    adryl)

Interdigital furuncles—toe cysts—develop on the webs of a dog's feet between his toes. The painful, knotty sores are inflamed tissue that's almost always caused by a deep bacterial infection. Cats don't develop toe cysts, but they're quite common in dogs, especially breeds like shar-peis, Labrador retrievers, and bulldogs. That's because these dogs have either webbed feet or very short, bristly fur on their feet that easily becomes ingrown and causes infection. Another cause is a foreign body like a foxtail seed that implants itself in the webbing. And occasionally, a microscopic skin mite that causes demodicosis—a kind of mange—may prompt toe cysts.

Toe cysts almost always need treatment with oral antibiotics, and they sometimes require surgery to remove a foreign body. And demodectic mange requires specific medical diagnosis and treatment to cure. But first aid usually relieves the dog's discomfort and helps speed his recovery.

DO THIS NOW

Remove any foreign object. Before doing anything else, examine your dog's foot for a foreign body like a grass awn or splinter. If you can see and reach the material, use blunt-tipped tweezers to grasp and pull it out. This will be painful for your dog, so expect him to flinch and jerk his foot away. You may need a second pair of hands to steady or restrain him.

Soak the paws. Soak your dog's feet for 10 minutes in a solution made with 1 cup of Epsom salts dissolved in 2 gallons of warm water, or an antiseptic solution like Betadine Solution in a strength of 0.01 to 0.1%. If you purchase higher-strength Betadine, dilute it with distilled water until it's the color of weak tea. (If you're not sure about dilution, call a pharmacist or veterinarian for complete instructions.) This not only washes

FIRST ALERT

Allergies

People with hay fever often sneeze a lot and develop itchy, red, watery eyes. But dogs with hay fever—more correctly called atopy—instead develop itchy skin, especially on their feet.

When toe cysts develop and won't heal, or they keep coming back, it's probable that your dog is allergic to something that he's breathing. It could be pollen, dust, molds, or just about anything that also affects people.

If you can figure out what's triggering the reaction and get rid of it, your dog's itchiness will go away. Unfortunately, that's rarely easy to do. There are a number of skin tests that your veterinarian can perform to help identify the culprits. (For more information about allergies, see page 63.)

off fungi and bacteria that could cause infection, it's also soothing to the sore, itchy feet and can help bring a foreign body or ingrown hair to the surface. You can fill the tub so that your dog can stand in the water and soak all four feet at once. Be sure to rinse and dry his feet after he soaks, because moisture makes the pads more attractive to infection. Also, Epsom salts are laxative if swallowed, so you don't want your dog to lick off too much or to lap up any of the water that he's standing in.

 SPECIAL SITUATIONS

If the sores are infected: With infection, you'll see a discharge of pus. It's best to clean and soak the feet in antiseptic solution as described on page 387. When only one or two feet are affected, you can use a small pan and treat one foot at a time. Remember to rinse and dry your dog's feet afterward because antiseptic solutions shouldn't be swallowed.

If surgery is required: If the sores fail to heal despite your efforts, surgery may be necessary to try to clean out any ingrown hair, sharp seeds, or infection. Keep the incision site clean by wiping away any drainage from around the wound with a gauze pad dampened with sterile saline contact lens solution.

After foot surgery, the vet may tape a bandage to your dog's foot. Keep the bandage clean and dry by slipping a plastic bag over the foot whenever your dog goes outside.

You'll need to change the bandage every 2 to 3 days. Watch for swelling above or below the bandage or a sudden interest in licking—that could mean trouble beneath the covering that needs veterinary attention.

 FOLLOW-UP CARE

■ Many dogs may start licking a paw from an itch, but then the licking becomes a habit and eventually, sores develop. And the more they lick, the more the sore itches, so they continue to lick. The most important thing you can do at home is to stop this cycle by physically restraining your dog from licking or chewing his feet. The easiest way is to fit him with a cone-shaped Elizabethan collar restraint so that he can't reach his paw with his tongue. (For more information on lick sores, see page 276.)

Or you can put a sock on him to protect the foot—something made of cotton that breathes is better than a tight bandage. That's because dogs have sweat glands in the pads of their feet, and bandaging the feet can create a dark, moist environment that bacteria and yeast love.

Use a clean athletic sock and tape the cuff directly to your dog's fur at his wrist. Even if your pet decides to chew on the sock, it will keep his teeth and tongue busy and away from doing more damage to his toes.

■ An antihistamine like Benadryl can help relieve the itching while the sores heal. The liquid form of Benadryl usually comes in a dose of 12.5 milligrams per teaspoon; pills are usually 25 milligrams each. Pets will need 1 milligram per pound of body weight every 6 to 8 hours. That means a 10-pound dog should get about ¾ teaspoon of liquid or half a pill. Your veterinarian may prescribe stronger antihistamines.

Keep your dog from compulsively licking or chewing his toes by using a sock bandage. Place a clean cotton athletic sock over his foot and tape the top to the fur of his leg.

■ Soak the foot two or three times every day in warm water with an antiseptic or antibacterial solution. Diluted Betadine Solution (see page 387) or a 5% benzoyl peroxide solution works well.

■ Toe cysts almost always require long-term prescription antibiotics like penicillin (Oxacillin) or cephalexin (Keflex), which you can get from your veterinarian. Your dog may have to take the medicine for up to 8 weeks before the sores heal.

Advisors
■ Gerald Brown, D.V.M., is a veterinarian at City Cat Doctor in Chicago.
■ Bernadine Cruz, D.V.M., is a veterinarian at Laguna Hills Hospital in California.
■ Jeffrey Werber, D.V.M., is a veterinarian at Century Veterinary Group in Los Angeles.

Tongue Swelling

CALL YOUR VET: **IMMEDIATELY**

A swollen tongue is most often caused by an allergic reaction. Beestings, injections, drug reactions, or food allergies can all cause a dog or cat to have trouble breathing, drool, and refuse to eat when his tongue swells.

If a small, sharp plant seed like a grass awn or a nettle, burr, or thorn gets caught in your pet's coat, he may try to remove it by licking—and the irritant may embed in his tongue and cause swelling. If the cause is not removed, the sore can ulcerate and become infected. At other times, curious pets lick something caustic, hot, or poisonous, which burns the tongue and prompts swelling. Less commonly, thread or a rubber band—even the string from salami—gets wrapped around the tongue and cuts off the circulation so that it swells.

Tongue swelling can be very serious because it may point to other problems, such as a mouth burn from electrocution, for instance. Medical treatment is important, and your cat or dog should be seen immediately after you notice the problem. In the meantime, though, first aid can reduce the trauma and may even save your pet's life.

DO THIS NOW

Offer ice or ice water. When the tongue is dramatically swollen, the best and most effective treatment is to offer your pet ice water to drink, ice cubes to lick, or crushed ice to eat. Ice works wonders to bring down swelling by restricting bloodflow to the area. It also numbs the pain. Encourage your pet to take the cold water or ice, but don't force anything into his mouth, or you risk making him choke.

Check for a foreign body in the mouth. Your dog or cat may not like your messing with his sore mouth, though, and he may need to be sedated by your vet before the object can be removed. If he'll let you, open his mouth and shine a flashlight over the surface of the tongue. The underside often hides a grass awn, and strings can wrap around the very back part of the tongue.

Don't remove string-type material. You could severely injure a squirmy pet with scissors by trying to cut string free from the tongue. Worse, if even part of the thread has been swallowed, it could be anchored deep inside to a needle or fishhook, so it requires medical attention for removal. But when a grass seed or thorn can be reached easily, you can grasp it with blunt-tipped tweezers and pull it out, just as you would a splinter. (For more information about splinters, see page 358.)

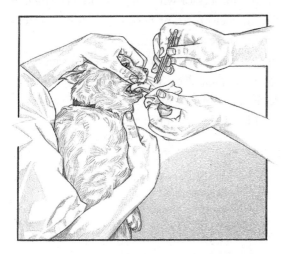

To get a good grip on your pet's tongue, hold it with a piece of cloth or gauze as you pull it. With your other hand, remove the embedded object from the tongue with blunt tweezers. Remember that your pet won't stand for this unless a second person holds her securely.

You'll need two people to gently try to remove something stuck into your pet's tongue. Have one person hold him securely and grasp the top of his muzzle. Then you can gently grasp your pet's tongue, using gauze or a dry cloth to get a better grip. Gently hold the tongue, and don't pull too hard. Use the tweezers with your other hand. (For more information about foreign objects in the mouth, see page 199.) If your pet resists or becomes agitated, you'll need to take him to the vet.

SPECIAL SITUATIONS

If the swelling is from contact with a caustic or toxic substance: It's important to dilute the effects of these substances. It's dangerous to try to pour water into your pet's mouth because you could drown him if he inhales and it goes down the wrong way. Instead, use a squirt bottle with plain water or sterile saline contact lens solution so that you can control the direction of the flow all around his mouth. Be careful not to direct the spray toward the throat so that you don't choke him. Flush the sore tongue for at least 10 minutes, or as long as your pet will allow.

If the swelling is from an allergic reaction: If your pet is having an allergic reaction to something like a beesting, you can give him an antihistamine like Benadryl to help reduce the swelling. The liquid form of Benadryl usually comes in a dose of 12.5 milligrams per teaspoon; pills are usually 25 milligrams each. Pets will need 1 milligram per pound of body weight every 6 to 8 hours. That means a 10-pound cat or dog should get about ¾ teaspoon of liquid or half a pill. A swollen tongue can make giving a pill much more difficult, though, so you might try crushing the pill, mixing it in a little water, and squirting it into his cheek with a needleless syringe. (This technique is illustrated on page 30.)

FOLLOW-UP CARE

■ When the swelling is caused by an infection, you must give antibiotics to help heal the wound and get rid of the problem. A liquid medicine usually is prescribed when the mouth is painful. You can tip your pet's head up, squirt the medicine into his cheek with an eyedropper or needleless syringe, and watch to be sure that he swallows. You may need to give antibiotics for a couple of weeks.

■ Any sore left behind by a foreign object may need to be flushed with an antiseptic solution like Chlorhexidine, which can help prevent infection. Purchase the solution from the vet. The flushing not only helps heal the wound and prevent infection, but the antiseptic has some numbing properties that can help relieve pain. You can put the solution in a squirt bottle or even a squirt gun to give you some directional control. Treat only the affected areas.

■ Continue to offer ice for your pet to lick. Ice is soothing to inflamed tissues, and it helps ensure that your dog or cat gets enough fluid. A pet with a swollen tongue is often reluctant to eat or drink and can become dehydrated very easily. (For more information about dehydration, see page 148.)

■ Soften food by running it through the blender or food processor with low-fat, no-salt chicken broth, beef broth, or bouillon to turn it into a gruel. These add a strong flavor to the food that makes it more appealing. Feed a soft diet for at least the first 2 to 3 days, or until your pet's tongue has lost its tenderness and he can easily eat his regular diet once again.

Advisors

■ Margaret J. Rucker, D.V.M., is a veterinarian at Southwest Virginia Veterinary Services in Lebanon, Virginia.

■ Raymond Russo, D.V.M., is a veterinarian at Kingston Animal Hospital in Massachusetts.

■ George White, D.V.M., is a veterinarian at I-20 Animal Medical Center in Arlington, Texas.

Tooth Damage

CALL YOUR VET: **IF NEEDED**

Dogs and cats commonly experience tooth damage, but pets are so stoic that they rarely show extreme discomfort, and you may not realize that there's a problem until it has gone on for some time. By the age of 3, 80 percent of dogs and 70 percent of cats have dental problems.

Tooth damage most often happens when the teeth decay and break, or they loosen and fall out from gum disease. At other times, traumas like falling from a tree or being hit by a car may break or knock teeth loose. And dogs who chew hard objects like rocks, bones, wire fences, and hard toys may grind down the teeth or break them off.

Pets with broken, split, or worn teeth probably won't need first aid unless the roots become exposed. An abscessed tooth or exposed root is painful, and can make pets drool a lot or refuse to eat. They'll need medical attention, but first aid can offer some temporary relief and may even save a tooth.

DO THIS NOW

Save knocked-out teeth. If a tooth has been knocked out by blunt trauma, as long as the root hasn't been damaged and the tooth is healthy, it can be reimplanted in your pet's mouth. Preserve the tooth by dropping it in a glass with a small amount of milk to keep the tooth moist and protect the tissues until you can get to the vet.

Offer your pet ice water. Or rinse her mouth out with cold water from a hose. The cold helps ease pain and constrict the blood vessels to control any bleeding. Don't offer ice cubes, because chewing on them could cause more tooth chipping. Shaved ice like the kind used for snow cones is fine.

Try Anbesol. Tooth damage can be so painful that your pet will refuse to let you handle her mouth. But if she will allow it, an over-the-counter medicine can help numb the pain until

FIRST ALERT

Broken Jaw

A pet who drools, refuses to eat, and has broken or damaged teeth may also have a broken jaw if blunt trauma has caused the injury. Often, a pet who has been hit by a car may suffer a broken jaw and teeth. Most often, though, cats who fall from high places end up cracking their chins on the ground and splitting the jawbone in two.

A broken jaw requires medical attention, and sometimes, it will be wired back together to help stabilize it while the bone heals. You'll need to feed your pet soft or liquid foods for up to several weeks. (For more information about fractures, see page 212.)

you can reach medical help. Anbesol, a human product for mouth pain, is safe and effective to use for a day or two on dogs. Apply some on a cotton swab and dab it on the sore spot. Follow the package directions for how often to use it. *Don't use Anbesol for cats more than one time*—it could be toxic.

Give your dog a painkiller. You can give dogs buffered aspirin like Bufferin for 1 to 2 days, but only if your veterinarian recommends it. Aspirin can be dangerous for cats, as well as for dogs who have kidney or liver disease or are dehydrated. It could also cause upset stomach in dogs if used for too long. The usual dose is 10 to 25 milligrams per 2.2 pounds of body weight two or three times a day. If your dog's mouth is very sore, you can crush the medicine and mix the powder in a bit of milk for your dog to lap up.

Offer only soft foods. They should be easy for your pet to eat. Meat baby foods are fine for a day or two.

 FOLLOW-UP CARE

■ A mouth rinse that contains the antiseptic chlorhexidine, like Nolvadent, works well to help prevent infection. You can get Nolvadent from pet-supply stores or catalogs, or from your veterinarian. Use a needleless syringe, a squirt gun, or a turkey baster to provide directional flow to rinse the area.

■ If your pet has a draining abscess, just removing the tooth won't be enough. It's probable that the vet will prescribe antibiotics to help cure the infection. When a pet's mouth is very sore, a liquid medicine is usually prescribed. Tip your pet's head up, squirt the medicine into her cheek with a needleless syringe or an eyedropper, and watch until she swallows. (This technique is illustrated on page 30.)

■ Until your pet's mouth has healed, a soft or liquid diet is best. Use a food processor and add water or low-fat, no-salt chicken broth to commercial foods to create a gruel that's easy for your pet to eat.

THE BEST APPROACH

Dental-Care Products for Pets

More effectively than anything else, brushing your pet's teeth will stop degenerative tooth damage or prevent it from happening in the first place. But toothpaste for humans won't work for a couple of reasons. Pets hate the foaming action as well as the taste. And the fluoride in human dental products can damage a pet's liver when it's swallowed (pets can't spit it out the way people do). So veterinarians recommend toothpaste designed specifically for cats or dogs. These pastes contain enzymes that help kill the bacteria that damage teeth, and they're safe when swallowed. In fact, they come in flavors that pets relish like treats. Petrodex comes in poultry and beef flavors for dogs and poultry and malt flavors for cats.

A child-size toothbrush or one designed for

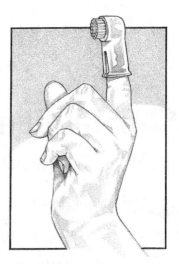

Your pet will be more willing to let you stick your finger in her mouth than a toothbrush. Try using a finger toothbrush to brush her teeth.

cats and dogs works best. There are also toothbrushes with tiny bristles, designed to slip over your finger, that pets seem to accept easily.

Once a week, brush your pet's teeth by slipping the brush loaded with paste into her cheek and rubbing the outside of the tooth surfaces.

Advisors

■ Terry Kaeser, D.V.M., is a veterinarian at Goshen Animal Clinic in Goshen, Indiana.
■ Emily King, D.V.M., is a veterinarian at Kryder Veterinary Clinic in Granger, Indiana.
■ Margaret J. Rucker, D.V.M., is a veterinarian at Southwest Virginia Veterinary Services in Lebanon, Virginia.
■ Drew Weigner, D.V.M., is a veterinarian at The Cat Doctor in Atlanta.

Unconsciousness

CALL YOUR VET: **IMMEDIATELY**

MEDICINE CHEST

Dry cloth
Towels
Pet carrier or other
    rigid object
Rubber gloves
Pliers or tongs
Blanket
Karo syrup or honey
Rubbing alcohol
Wet washcloths
Ice
Hot-water bottle or
    plastic soda bottles

Anything that affects the bloodflow to the brain or disrupts the normal actions of the central nervous system can cause a pet to lose consciousness. Low blood sugar, especially in puppies and toy dog breeds, is a common cause. (For more information about low blood sugar, see page 281.)

Trauma—like being hit by a car or falling from a tree—is the most common cause of unconsciousness. But extremes of body temperature, poisoning, drowning, choking, or metabolic diseases like diabetes and kidney failure can also leave a pet unconscious.

An unconscious pet is always a medical emergency, but first aid can keep her alive until you reach emergency help.

DO THIS NOW

Remove your pet's collar. A collar can sometimes interfere with breathing, so it's a good idea to take it off your pet right away.

Check for breathing and a heartbeat. Open your pet's mouth and gently pull her tongue forward to be sure there's an open airway. You may need to use a dry cloth to get a good grip on her wet tongue. Determine if your pet's heart has stopped by taking her pulse. Press your fingertips into the crease where the inside of the thigh meets the body and feel for the pulse in the femoral artery, which is very big and near the surface. If you can't feel it , try listening or feeling for the heartbeat. Put your ear or hand flat against your pet's left side directly behind the elbow. If you can't find a pulse or heartbeat, you will have to perform CPR. (For instructions, see page 398.)

Elevate your pet's head. Keep her head slightly elevated as long as she's unconscious. Keeping her head up on a folded towel with her

FIRST ALERT

Fainting

Fainting occurs when the brain doesn't receive enough oxygen or sugar. As with people, a pet will suddenly lose consciousness and fall over. A number of conditions can cause your dog or cat to faint, including heart failure, low blood sugar, coughing fits, asthma, or hyperventilation.

The affected pet typically acts weak or uncoordinated, walks with a drunken gait, and then falls over. When associated with heart disease, a fainting spell may happen after exertion like running up the stairs or romping in the yard. Pets who faint usually regain consciousness within a few minutes of passing out, because the fainting mechanism promotes blood and oxygen flow to the brain by forcing pets to lie down.

Recovery from fainting is so quick that no first aid is required. But because the causes can be debilitating or even life-threatening, medical attention to diagnose the underlying problem is important. Diet manipulation can help regulate blood sugar, drugs may stabilize a failing heart, and medication can calm coughing fits.

neck extended helps with breathing and bloodflow. Don't let her head dangle off the car seat.

Watch for vomiting. An unconscious dog or cat won't be able to stop herself from inhaling material if she vomits. That can be deadly, so watch to be sure that she doesn't vomit. If she does, position her head and neck at a downward angle so that the material flows away from the airway.

Keep movement to a minimum. Move your pet as little as possible when transporting her to the animal hospital. Often, a pet found unconscious may have internal injuries or even trauma to the neck or back that could be aggravated by movement. You can use a blanket or large bath towel as a makeshift stretcher.

One person should grasp your pet's shoulders and head while the other person handles the hips, then quickly slide her onto the blanket. A board also works, or an ironing board. (This technique is illustrated on page 29.) This will keep your pet from being jarred when she's carried. With small pets, you can use a pet carrier, cookie sheet, or even the lid of a trash can.

SPECIAL SITUATIONS

If you suspect electrical shock: If you think that your pet is unconscious from chewing an electrical cord, disconnect the source of electricity before you touch her. The safest way to cut the power is through the main circuit breaker. If you are not sure where it is or you can't get to it quickly, you'll have to pull the plug. If you can find rubber gloves quickly, put them on first. Be very careful not to get too close to your pet—if you touch her, you'll be shocked, too. (For more on electrical shock, see page 165.)

For smoke inhalation or carbon monoxide poisoning: When smoke or other air contaminants like carbon monoxide are affecting your pet, move her into fresh air. This may be all that's needed for her to wake up. (For more information on carbon monoxide poisoning, see page 122; for smoke inhalation, see page 347.)

If your pet may have drowned: Unconscious pets found in or near water may be victims of drowning.

Hold your pet upside down—grasp small pets by the hind legs and larger ones around the hips—and swing her or shake her for 10 seconds or so to get rid of any water in the lungs. If another person is available, have him thump sharply on both sides of your pet's chest while she's upside down. (For more information about drowning, see page 153.)

If there's something stuck in your pet's throat: Look inside your pet's mouth to see if the unconsciousness is caused by choking. Often, a stick or toy lodges in the back of the throat and interferes with breathing so much that the pet passes out. If you see an object and it's within reach, use your fingers, pliers, or tongs to pull it out. (For more information, see page 209.)

If you can't reach or get a grip on the object, a modified Heimlich maneuver can pop the obstruction out of your pet's throat. This can also help empty water from the lungs of drowned dogs who are too big to hold upside down.

Hold a small pet with her back against your stomach, her head up, and her feet hanging down. Put your fist into the hollow place directly under her ribs and pull in and up toward your chin with a sudden thrusting action. Put a larger dog on her side and kneel behind her with your knees against her back. Lean over to fit your fist into the hollow beneath the ribs and push sharply up and in toward the dog's head and your knees. Quickly repeat the Heimlich maneuver two or three times, then see if the object has come loose. (This technique is illustrated on page 22; for more information about choking, see page 131.) If there is still a blockage, you can continue the maneuver in the car while someone drives you to the veterinarian.

If your pet's heart is beating but she's not breathing: Pets who have stopped breathing will need artificial respiration to keep them alive until you can get medical attention.

If your pet's heart is beating but she's not breathing, start artificial respiration. Make sure that her airway is clear—rescue breathing won't help if it is not. Then wrap your hands around your pet's muzzle to seal her lips closed and put your mouth over her nose. Blow with two quick breaths, watching to see her chest expand, then pull your mouth away to let the air escape back out. Give 15 to 20 breaths per minute until your

Collapsing Trachea

The little dog breeds, like the toy poodle, Maltese, Pomeranian, Chihuahua, Italian greyhound, and Yorkshire terrier, often have an inherited tendency to develop collapsing tracheas—usually after the age of 5, but it could happen sooner. Signs include shortness of breath, fatigue, and loud, honking coughing fits that can lead to fainting spells.

The trachea is a sturdy tube of cartilage through which the dog breathes. But when the cartilage weakens, as in this condition, the trachea can collapse in on itself while the dog is breathing. The harder the dog coughs to clear the obstruction, the worse it becomes. Have your pet checked by the veterinarian if she develops a cough that continues to worsen or persists longer than 24 hours. Dogs with collapsing tracheas often cough loudly just after eating or drinking.

During a coughing fit, you can help soothe your pet's distress by cupping your dog's muzzle—this acts like putting a paper bag over her head, as people do to counteract hyperventilation. Stroke her throat and talk gently to her to calm her.

Once the vet diagnoses a collapsing trachea, there are drugs available that may help manage and dilate the airways to suppress the cough. Strict diet and exercise restrictions also can help. Dogs who suffer from collapsing tracheas are easily affected by secondhand smoke from cigarettes because the smoke usually settles near the ground where they breathe, so it's helpful to have a smoke-free zone for tiny dogs. They must also never wear collars, since this could cause further damage to the trachea. Use a harness instead.

pet starts breathing on her own or you reach the veterinarian. (This technique is illustrated on page 20.) Watch for her reactions because if she regains consciousness, she may bite you out of fear.

If your pet's heart has stopped and she's not breathing: You must give artificial respiration and perform chest compressions, or CPR. It's best to have someone drive you and your pet to the vet while you're performing CPR.

For cats and small dogs, cup your hand over the point of the chest just behind the elbows and squeeze firmly between your fingers and thumb, pressing in about ½ inch, about 80 to 100 times a minute. Give a breath into the nose after every fifth compression until your pet revives or until you reach medical help.

For a larger dog, put her on her side on a firm, flat surface. Put both hands on top of each other against the chest and compress by 25 to 50%. Alternate breaths and compressions as for small pets. (This technique is illustrated on page 21.)

Every minute, stop CPR to check for a pulse or breathing. If the heart starts again, stop the compressions, but continue artificial respiration until she breathes on her own or you reach help.

Continue CPR in the car on the way to the emergency clinic.

If you suspect shock: Pets often become unconscious from shock, which can develop from any traumatic injury. If your pet is going into shock, she'll be woozy and weak. She will have difficulty standing and may not be aware of her surroundings. In addition, her gums will first turn dark pink or red, then become pale in 5 to 10 minutes as oxygen levels fall. A cat's gums are normally paler than a dog's and will look gray, white, or very pale if she is in shock. Shock can kill a pet in as little as 10 to 20 minutes, and she'll need *immediate* veterinary care to survive. Wrap her in a blanket to keep her warm—this can slow down the shock process—then drive her to the clinic. You can also put a drop or two of Karo syrup or honey on your pet's gums to help keep her conscious. (For more information about shock, see page 333.)

If your pet has had seizures: Prolonged seizures can also cause unconsciousness. Seizures burn an enormous store of calories, which can cause your pet's body temperature to rise. Turn on the air conditioner in the car on the way to the clinic and wrap your pet in cold, damp towels to transport her. (For more information about seizures, see page 330.)

If your pet has been exposed to extreme heat: Anything that overheats your pet could cause unconsciousness. A pet who is exposed to extremely hot weather or becomes trapped in a clothes dryer, for instance, can suffer heatstroke.

If your pet is unconscious, call the veterinary clinic to tell them that you're on your way, and let them know how high your pet's temperature is—that will tell your veterinarian exactly what type of emergency treatment your pet will need. (For information about taking your pet's temperature, see page 9.) Then rush her off to the animal hospital.

Make sure that your car is cool for the trip, and try to grab a bottle of rubbing alcohol and some ice and a couple of wet washcloths on your way out the door. Position your pet in front of the air vent to achieve as much evaporation as possible. Try to cool her on the way by applying ice and alcohol to her armpits and groin. Before putting ice on the skin, place a wet washcloth on the area, then put the ice on top of the cloth. It's safest to do this with another person to help, either by driving or by taking care of your pet while you drive. (For more information about heatstroke, see page 237.)

If your pet has been exposed to extreme cold: A cold body temperature can also lead to unconsciousness when pets have hypothermia. A pet who has a temperature of 90°F or less for more than 30 minutes—severe hypothermia—needs immediate medical attention. Make sure that your pet is dry, then wrap her in a blanket and go to the veterinarian as soon as possible. Monitor her breathing and heartbeat on the way and administer artificial respiration and CPR if necessary.

If your pet's temperature has been 90°F or below for less than 30 minutes or your vet is more than 30 minutes away, you need to try to warm her before leaving the house. Use hot-water bottles or fill empty plastic soda bottles with hot water. Wrap each bottle in a thick towel so that it won't burn your pet, then put them on the armpits and groin, where large arteries lie near the skin. This helps rewarm the blood, which then circulates to rewarm the whole body. (For more information about hypothermia, see page 248.)

 ## FOLLOW-UP CARE

■ For choking victims, you'll need to feed a soft diet for a day or two until the sore throat heals. Soften your pet's regular food with water or low-fat, no-salt chicken broth and run it through the blender.

■ Metabolic problems like kidney failure or diabetes may require special diets or medications. Injuries from car accidents, drowning, or electrocution often require that pets be hospitalized for tests and supportive care until they're out of danger. The specific follow-up care depends on what caused the unconsciousness. For instance, dogs diagnosed with epilepsy may require daily pills to control seizures, while pets with diabetes often need insulin injections. For dogs, you can hide pills in treats; for cats, you can crush the pill with the bowl of a spoon and add it to strong-smelling cat food. Your veterinarian will give you specific instructions on how to give injections if that's required.

Advisors
■ Dawn Crandell, D.V.M., is a veterinarian at the Veterinary Emergency Clinic of York Region in Aurora, Ontario, Canada.
■ Grady Hester, D.V.M., is a veterinarian at All Creatures Animal Clinic in Rolesville, North Carolina.
■ Denise Petryk, D.V.M., is a veterinarian at Puget Sound Veterinary Medical Referral Center in Tacoma, Washington.
■ George White, D.V.M., is a veterinarian at I-20 Animal Medical Center in Arlington, Texas.

Urinary Blockage

CALL YOUR VET: **IMMEDIATELY**

Imagine that you've finished a giant soft drink while driving on the interstate, then notice that the next rest stop is 50 miles away. Multiply your discomfort by 10, and you'll understand how a blocked dog or cat feels.

Depending on the food he eats and his individual metabolism, your pet's urine contains a range of mineral components that can develop into microscopic to sand-size crystals, mucus, or even large stones that can plug the urethral opening like a cork in a bottle. This is excruciating to your pet, and it can be deadly because toxins that can't be voided begin to build up in the bloodstream, and the kidneys shut down. Even if the bladder doesn't rupture, a complete blockage can kill a pet within 12 to 72 hours.

The female urethra leads directly from the bladder to the outside of the body and is pretty wide the whole way, so female pets almost never get blocked. But the urethra narrows by half in male cats as it enters the penis, and a male dog's urethra must pass through a tiny V-shaped opening in the bone called the os penis before reaching the outside. These anatomical differences mean that male dogs and cats most commonly experience urinary blockage.

Cats and dogs who are blocked spend lots of time in the litter box or yard, straining and crying as they try to pass urine but can't. Cats typically squat right in front of you or try to go in the sink as a way to express their distress. Dogs may adopt an awkward straddle-legged posture, and the urine stream many dribble, start and stop, or be nonexistent. Pets may lick themselves, and any urine they manage to squeeze out may be bloody.

Without prompt medical attention, the pet acts depressed, stops eating, begins to vomit, and can fall into a coma and die. Urinary blockage is a life-threatening emergency, and although first aid can offer temporary relief to some cats, partial or complete urinary blockage requires immediate medical help.

🧰 DO THIS NOW

For Cats Only

Restrain your cat. Cats with urinary blockage are very tender and sore and won't take kindly to having their nether regions examined. You must protect yourself by restraining your cat before you can help him, and you'll need someone to help you. Firmly grasp the loose skin at the back of his neck with one hand, capture both rear feet with the other, and gently stretch him out on his side on a table. Or you can use a pillowcase and put him in headfirst, with just his tail exposed. If your cat struggles excessively or becomes too upset, don't waste time at home—just get him to the veterinarian.

To examine or treat a small pet, hold the scruff of his neck with one hand and his back feet with the other, then stretch him out. You can wear a thick glove on the hand that holds the feet.

Prepare the area. Make sure that your cat is on a towel or positioned with his tail toward some sort of container or a sink to catch any urine. Be aware that it can be so bloody that it looks like port wine, and it can stain clothing. Avoid putting pressure on your cat's abdomen to express the bladder, or you may accidentally pop it like a balloon. If you are successful in dislodging the blockage, the cat will spontaneously urinate without any encouragement.

Give a gentle massage. Some cats with blockage have only a small bit of debris stuck at the end of the urethra, right where the urine exits. In these cases, gentle massage of the tissue at the end of the penis may be enough to loosen the debris and unblock your cat, but you still should have him examined afterward.

An obstructed male cat often protrudes his penis. If he doesn't, you can express the organ by gently pressing the tissue directly above the urethral opening. If there is crystallized or mucous debris stuck to the end of the penis, soak a soft cloth or gauze pad in warm water, place it on the tip, and gently soak the debris away.

Even if the plug isn't visible on the outside, it may be stuck near the opening on the inside. If you have them, put on disposable medical

If your male cat seems unable to urinate, the tip of his penis may be blocked with mucus or urine crystals. You can often clear the blockage by rolling his penis gently between your thumb and index finger.

FIRST ALERT

Cystitis and Bladder Infection

Dogs and cats with bladder irritation (cystitis) or infection probably feel just the same as people with the condition do. The signs are similar to those of blockage, but as long as urine is produced, the pet is not blocked.

Often, both the bladder and urethra become irritated, and the pet thinks she has to go to the bathroom when it's just the irritation that she feels. She'll strain and get out a few drops, but that's all there is. Classic signs are frequent urination but in only tiny amounts, or accidents in the house. Cats often squat outside the litter box, while dogs may urinate on the bedspread.

Although annoying, cystitis usually isn't dangerous, but it needs to be diagnosed to see how it should be treated. If you notice any of these signs, have the vet examine your pet the same day, if possible. Veterinarians usually take a sample of urine and culture it, then prescribe a specific antibiotic to get rid of any bacteria. You'll usually have to give your pet the antibiotic for about 3 weeks.

In more than half of feline cystitis cases, there is no sign of infection. Researchers believe that these cats suffer from a condition similar to interstitial cystitis in women, which is thought to be brought on by stress.

---

gloves (available in drugstores) and gently roll the penis between your finger and thumb to crush the debris and open the passageway so that the material can be expelled.

FOLLOW-UP CARE

■ Dogs often require surgery to remove the stones that caused the blockage. Keep the incision clean and wipe away any drainage as needed with a sterile gauze pad dipped in warm water.

■ Blockage from urinary tract infections happens especially in dogs, and they may develop what are called infection stones. Acidifying the urine can prevent the most common kind of crystals that cause blockages in cats. Cranberries help prevent bacteria from sticking to the lining of the bladder and also help acidify the urine, so they can be a helpful part of follow-up care for both dogs and cats.

Most pets don't care for the taste of cranberry juice, however, and it would take lots of juice to help prevent the problem. Instead, give a cranberry supplement like CranActin. It's available in most health food stores. Give one capsule of CranActin for every 20 pounds your pet weighs.

■ Sometimes, in order to flush out all the debris that created the blockage, the pet is anesthetized so that a soft catheter can be placed

Surgical Correction

Most of the time, changing your pet's diet can prevent recurrence of urinary blockage. But if the diet isn't adjusted, repeated treatment using a catheter to unblock the pet can cause scar tissue in the urethra. Scar tissue narrows the passageway even more, which makes blockage even more likely.

Chronic problems in cats sometimes benefit from surgery called a perineal urethrostomy, which essentially redesigns the urethra so that a male cat can urinate like a female cat. The narrowest part of the urethra is the opening of the penis, so to widen the conduit, the end of the penis is removed, and the urethra is split and opened. This enlarges the exit for the urine and lowers the chance that crystals or mucus plugs will cause a blockage.

into the urethra, and it may be temporarily sutured in place to keep the urine flow moving. Usually, the pet remains in the hospital during this time, but if he comes home with the catheter still in place, you'll need to monitor it and be sure that your dog or cat doesn't pull it out. A cone-shaped collar restraint called an Elizabethan collar will keep him from bothering it.

■ More than 50 percent of cats who have urinary tract problems relapse one or more times. Pets often have chronic problems with the condition, and without specific preventive home treatment, the blockage will recur. One of the best preventives is to get your pet to drink more. A large amount of water dilutes the urine, which helps flush the minerals and mucous substances out of the bladder and urethra before they can develop into stones and plugs.

Here's how you can make water more attractive: Put a tablespoon of "juice" from water-packed salmon or tuna in the bowl to flavor it. Some cats and most dogs like icy water, so float ice cubes in the bowl or offer ice cubes as treats. Many cats prefer to sip running water and will drink more if allowed to lap from a dribbling faucet. Commercial feline water fountains like the Drinkwell Pet Fountain, available through pet-supply stores or catalogs, also may prompt cats to drink more. The fountains continually recycle and filter water from a 6-cup container.

■ Your veterinarian may recommend a specific therapeutic diet that helps dissolve stones and crystals that remain in the urinary tract. The most common kind of stones—struvite—won't form in acidic urine, and these diets help acidify the urine to prevent stone or crystal formation. Once the foreign material has been cleared, your pet may need to eat a preventive diet for the rest of his life. There are a number of commercial foods that work fine, but the kind of stones your pet has determines which diet works best, so check with the vet.

Remember that any sudden diet change can upset digestion and cause vomiting or diarrhea, so you need to make the change gradually over a period of 5 to 7 days. Begin by mixing 2 parts of the old food with 1 part of the new and feeding

Bladder Stones

Cats nearly always develop sand-size or smaller bladder stones, along with mucus that can plug up the urethra. But canine urinary tract stones can grow as big as Ping-Pong balls, which can block the flow of urine from the bladder. Large stones often require surgical removal. Not many dogs suffer from this problem, but stones are most common in small dogs and in Dalmatians, who have a genetic predisposition to this condition.

Most dogs develop struvite stones, a type that can be dissolved or prevented by feeding a diet that increases the acidity of the urine. The exception is the Dalmatian, a breed that isn't able to consistently process urea, so these dogs excrete a lot of uric acid. In Dalmatians, this acidic urine promotes the development of urate stones, so the dogs need a special diet and the drug allopurinol (Zyloprim) to control stone formation.

it for 2 days. Then, mix them half-and-half for a couple of days, followed by 2 parts new to 1 part old food. Finally, you can offer the new therapeutic diet exclusively.

THE BEST APPROACH

Diagnostic Cat Litter

Cats who have suffered a bout of urinary blockage often have recurring problems, but one kind of litter offers an early warning system for detecting problems before they turn deadly. Total Concentrated Cat Litter not only works like conventional cat box fillers, it also changes color—to pink or red—if the cat's urine is abnormal.

Most urinary tract crystals and mucus plugs won't develop when the urine pH remains acidic. The litter acts like an at-home laboratory test that literally raises a red flag if the urine pH becomes unbalanced, which can indicate a possible infection or show that conditions are ripe for a blockage to develop.

Total Concentrated Cat Litter can be ordered through specialty pet stores and veterinary offices, or you can order it directly from the manufacturer at their Web site, www.petecology.com.

Advisors

■ Shane Bateman, D.V.M., D.V.Sc., is a veterinarian board certified in the American College of Emergency and Critical Care Medicine and assistant professor of emergency and critical care medicine at Ohio State University College of Veterinary Medicine in Columbus.

■ Patricia Hague, D.V.M., is a veterinarian at the Cat Hospital of Las Colinas in Irving, Texas.

■ Janie Hodges, D.V.M., is a veterinarian at Valley View Pet Health Center in Farmers Branch, Texas.

■ Chris Johnson, D.V.M., is a veterinarian at Westside Animal Emergency Clinic in Atlanta.

■ Barry N. Kellogg, V.M.D., is a veterinarian at the Center for Veterinary Care in Great Barrington, Massachusetts, and the head of VMAT 1 (Veterinary Medical Assistance Team), the national disaster team for veterinary medicine.

Vaginal Prolapse

CALL YOUR VET: **IMMEDIATELY**

Vaginal prolapse is nearly unknown in cats and very rare in dogs. It tends to happen right after a mother dog has given birth to puppies. The normal contractions of the uterus continue, and since no more puppies need to be born, the contractions turn the vagina inside out until it spills out of the opening.

There may be just a small amount of prolapse, or the entire organ can be pushed out. The tissue at first looks red and glistening, but it soon begins to dry out and can crack and become wrinkled. You cannot replace the organ with first aid, but you can help reduce the damage until you can get medical attention for your dog.

DO THIS NOW

Wrap and elevate the tissue. In most cases, the prolapse is only a fist-size wad of tissue protruding from beneath the tail. In rare cases, though, a long mass of tissue comes out and can hang halfway to the floor. If the uterine horns are involved, there is a Y-shaped mass at the end of the tissue. Soak a clean pillowcase in sterile saline contact lens solution and wrap the organ up for the drive to the vet. In order to prevent swelling and further damage, you should keep the tissue elevated. The safest way to do this is to have someone ride in the car with you and gently hold the organ level with your pet's body. Any time you handle the exposed tissue, be sure that your hands are clean, or wear disposable medical gloves (available in drugstores).

Keep the area moist, even when only a small amount of tissue is exposed. When the tissues dry out, the flesh can crack and become infected or even die. Sterile saline contact

⊕ FIRST ALERT

Vaginal Hyperplasia

Dogs don't have to be pregnant to suffer vaginal prolapse. A hormonal condition called vaginal hyperplasia is the most common cause of the condition, and it usually affects intact female dogs when they go into heat and are ready to accept a mate. Boxers and Saint Bernards seem to be affected most often.

Estrogen that prepares the dog for becoming pregnant stimulates the lining of the uterus, and in some cases, the lining of the floor of the uterus swells and spills out of the opening. The tissue at first looks smooth and glistening, but as it dries out, it looks similar to a rough tongue as fissures develop.

Vaginal hyperplasia should be treated the same way as other causes of vaginal prolapse: Keep the tissue clean and moist, apply a topical antibiotic ointment like Neosporin, and see your vet right away. Once the dog goes out of heat and hormone levels return to normal, the swelling will go down and the tissue will retract inside the body. Spaying your dog will prevent the condition from coming back every time she goes into season. Most dogs with this condition are reluctant to breed because the exposed tissue is painful, so usually spaying is the best choice.

lens solution is the best choice because it's very close to the fluid composition of the body. If you don't have saline solution, you can make some with 1¼ teaspoons of table salt in a pint of water. Dab it on with a gauze pad or put the liquid in a plant sprayer and spray the tissue to keep it moist. You'll need to keep spritzing the area every 5 to 10 minutes.

K-Y Jelly also works well as a lubricant and may keep the tissues moist for longer periods if you aren't able to spray the saline solution on a regular basis. You'll need to reapply the lubricant whenever the flesh looks dry. Use gentle pressure to avoid causing your pet any pain.

Prevent infection. When the tissue has been exposed and dried out for any length of time, it can develop sores and cracks. Apply antibacterial ointment like Neosporin to help protect the area from infection. Then get to the vet immediately.

Keep her from licking. Exposure to the air can damage the tissue, but that's not the greatest danger. The discomfort that a dog feels from the prolapsed vagina often prompts her to lick or even chew on the exposed organ and cause damage that requires surgery. A cone-shaped collar restraint called an Elizabethan collar will prevent her from reaching the area. You could

Vaginal Eversion

In rare cases, the first part of the dog's vagina everts—spills out—just before she begins to deliver her puppies. You'll see a gruesome red ball of tissue at the vaginal opening. Once it comes out, the tissue swells and may actually block the birth of the puppies.

This is a medical emergency. The dog will very likely need a cesarean section to deliver her babies. Delay may endanger not only the mother dog but also her unborn pups. (For more information about birthing problems, see page 83.)

also try fitting your dog with a loose pair of boxer shorts or muzzle her on the way to the vet.

To muzzle a long-nosed dog, use a necktie or panty hose. First, loop the fabric around your dog's nose and tie it on top. Next, bring the ends under her chin and tie them again. Finally, bring the ends up and tie them behind her ears. (This technique is illustrated on page 17.) For a short-nosed dog like a pug, slip a pillowcase over her head.

 FOLLOW-UP CARE

■ Once vaginal prolapse is treated, it won't happen again unless your dog gives birth again. Most of the time, your veterinarian will recommend that your dog be spayed to prevent this. If your dog has chewed on her vagina, spay surgery is the only treatment option. Watch your pet to be sure that she doesn't lick or bite at the sutures until they're completely healed. You can smear some Vicks VapoRub or Bitter Apple on each side of the incision line (but not the incision itself) to keep her from licking the stitches. Or your veterinarian may be able to recommend another ointment with an unpleasant taste that will do the trick.

Advisors
■ Michael G. Abdella, D.V.M., is a veterinarian at Aliso Viejo Animal Hospital in Aliso Viejo, California.
■ Lorrie Bartloff, D.V.M., is a veterinarian at Three Point Veterinary Clinic in Elkhart, Indiana.
■ Doug McConkey, D.V.M., is a veterinarian at Canyon Creek Pet Hospital in Sherman, Texas.

Vomiting

CALL YOUR VET: **IF NEEDED**

Some pets vomit at the drop of a hat—what goes down seems to come back up just as easily. A sudden change in diet or an emotional upset can prompt them to lose their lunch. Vomiting should never be considered normal, but it's probably not a cause for concern if it happens only once and the pet seems to feel fine.

Anytime a cat or dog vomits three or more times in a single day or two or more days in a row, there is cause for concern. Many illnesses can prompt repeated vomiting, which can leave pets dehydrated and dangerously ill. Cats who vomit intermittently for no apparent reason may have heartworms.

Continuous vomiting is an emergency that needs immediate medical attention. Even if it happens only once or twice a month, it's a good idea to find out why your pet vomits. First aid works very well to calm your pet's stomach until you can get help.

DO THIS NOW

Remove his feeding dish. Whether the vomiting is caused by an upset stomach or your pet's stomach becomes irritated from the vomiting, it's best to take away his food. Dogs especially tend to keep eating as long as food is available, and then they throw it all right back up. It's better to restrict food and give your pet's tummy a rest for at least 12 to 24 hours.

Give water sparingly. Vomiting will make your dog or cat feel very thirsty. But drinking a lot of water will only make the stomach more upset, and the water will come right back up. Instead, offer tiny amounts of water—maybe a tablespoon at a time—to your pet every 15 to 20 minutes.

Offer ice. Vomiting can cause rapid dehydration, so it's important to try to keep some liquid

✚ FIRST ALERT

Bloat

A dog who repeatedly tries to vomit but can't bring anything up—especially a large-breed dog like a Great Dane or mastiff—may be suffering from a twisted stomach. The common name for the condition is bloat, because gas and food become trapped in the stomach, causing it to swell. Bloat is excruciatingly painful, and it can kill dogs very quickly—it is a true veterinary emergency. Do not waste time using home remedies if you suspect bloat. Get your dog to the animal hospital immediately. (For more information about bloat, see page 100.)

down your pet. Try offering an ice cube for him to lick.

Give your dog some Pepto. Pepto-Bismol is an effective, safe, and reliable way to help manage vomiting in dogs. It coats the stomach wall to soothe the upset, and the ingredient bismuth absorbs the bacterial toxins that can prompt vomiting. The dose for dogs is ½ to 1 teaspoon per 5 pounds of body weight, to a maximum of 2 tablespoons up to three times a day. Draw up the liquid in an eyedropper, a needleless syringe, or even a turkey baster. Then tilt your dog's head up, insert the tip of the applicator in his cheek, squirt in the medicine, and hold his mouth closed until you see him swallow. (This technique is illustrated on page 30.) Do not give Pepto-Bismol to cats without a veterinarian's recommendation. It contains aspirin-like compounds that can be dangerous to them.

Try Pepcid AC. An alternative to Pepto-Bismol, this over-the-counter medication contains the active ingredient famotidine and may help vomiting cats and dogs as well. It decreases the secretion of stomach acid, so it can help calm the irritation. The dose is 5 milligrams per 10 pounds of body weight once or twice a day.

Give Kaopectate to cats. There aren't any really good over-the-counter products for cats who vomit. Kaopectate is the best choice. You can give ½ to 1 teaspoon for every 5 pounds your cat weighs, once every 6 hours, but don't use it for more than 1 day.

Treat hairballs. If your cat is throwing up hairballs, you'll see hair in the vomited material. In fact, sometimes all you see is a wet furball. Once he has the hairball out of his stomach, your cat won't act as if he feels bad.

Cats who vomit as a result of hairballs will benefit from an over-the-counter lubricant product such as Laxatone or Petromalt. You can buy these at pet-supply stores. Give the

Danger from Raw Salmon

Dogs who live in the Pacific Northwest states may be poisoned if they eat raw salmon. The fish carries a kind of worm called a fluke, and the fluke carries a rickettsial parasite as well. Dogs who eat the parts of the fish (usually the gills, head, and organs) that are infested with infected flukes get deathly ill and can die from salmon poisoning.

Salmon poisoning can be a problem throughout spawning season—summer through early January—because after spawning, the salmon die by the thousands and wash up on shore for dogs to find.

It takes 5 to 9 days after eating the salmon for a dog to get sick, and the illness usually lasts about 10 days if there's no treatment. Dogs typically run a fever of 104° to 106°F for a few days, and they vomit constantly and can't keep anything down. They also develop bloody diarrhea and may have swollen lymph nodes.

Take your dog to the vet as soon as possible if you suspect salmon poisoning. There is no first aid that can help. Dogs need intravenous fluids and supportive care to survive. Your vet will look for the fluke eggs in the feces to confirm the diagnosis. When the poisoning is caught in time, a 5- to 10-day course of antibiotics like tetracycline (Doolomyoin) or chloramphenicol (Chloromycetin) will get rid of the flukes and rickettsial organisms and cure the dog.

gel according the package directions. You may also want to talk to your vet about the new hairball-control cat foods and treats that are now available in pet-supply stores and supermarkets.

 FOLLOW-UP CARE

Once the vet has treated the cause of the vomiting, your pet should recover without follow-up treatment.

Advisors

■ John Brakebill, D.V.M., is a veterinarian at Brakebill Veterinary Hospital in Sherman, Texas.

■ Jeff Nichol, D.V.M., is the hospital director and a veterinarian at the Adobe Animal Medical Center in Albuquerque.

■ George White, D.V.M., is a veterinarian at I-20 Animal Medical Center in Arlington, Texas.

■ Dennis L. Wilcox, D.V.M., is a veterinarian at Angeles Clinic for Animals in Port Angeles, Washington.

Worms

CALL YOUR VET: **IF NEEDED**

Worms are so common that many puppies and kittens are born with them, or they become infected from their mother's milk shortly after they're born. Mother dogs or cats may have encysted worms in their bodies, which are held in a kind of suspended animation. These worms start to grow and infect the developing babies only when the hormones of pregnancy are produced.

Worms live in the intestinal tract and can cause diarrhea or sometimes vomiting. Heavy worm loads can lead to anemia, loss of appetite, and malnutrition as the parasites suck blood or live off the food in the pet's body. Roundworms look like long strings of spaghetti—you'll see them in the feces, or they may be vomited up. Fresh tapeworms look like tiny white square or oblong worms, but when they dry out, they look like grains of rice that stick to the fur near the tail. Hookworms, whipworms, and protozoans like coccidia and giardia are virtually invisible, though. You won't be able to see them, even if they're passed in the stool.

DO THIS NOW

Collect a sample. If your pet vomits or passes worms, or has diarrhea and you suspect worms that you can't see, collect a sample of the vomited material or stool to take to the veterinarian for identification and diagnosis. A different medicine is needed for each kind of worm, so it's important for the vet to know exactly what kind of parasite it is.

Forgo feeding for a day. When your pet has diarrhea, take away his food for 24 hours to help his stomach settle down.

Give dogs an antidiarrheal. You can give your dog an antidiarrheal like Pepto-Bismol to help control the diarrhea until you can get to the veterinarian. A safe dose is ½ to 1 teaspoon

FIRST ALERT

Fleas

Flea larvae eat tapeworm eggs that they find in the environment, and the baby tapeworms develop inside the developing flea. Cats typically groom away 50 percent or more of the fleas on their coats, but swallowing even one infected flea can give a dog or cat tapeworms.

Tapeworm medicine is very effective, but you must eliminate fleas, or your pet will be reinfected again and again.

for every 5 pounds the dog weighs, to a maximum of 2 tablespoons up to three times a day.

Give cats Kaopectate. Cats shouldn't take Pepto-Bismol without a veterinarian's recommendation because it contains aspirin-like compounds that can be dangerous to them. A better choice is Kaopectate at ½ to 1 teaspoon for every 5 pounds up to a maximum of 2 tablespoons up to three times in a day. Don't give your cat this medicine for more than 1 day. (For more information about diarrhea, see page 150.)

FOLLOW-UP CARE

■ Dogs and cats who have coccidiosis are given antibiotics, sometimes for 10 days or longer. Dogs may be given a drug called amprolium (Corid), which can be mixed in their food.

■ When pets are diagnosed with giardiasis, a prescription medicine called metronidazole (Flagyl) is usually given. It may take several weeks of treatment to get rid of the protozoan.

■ Pets with hookworms or roundworms are often given medicine like pyrantel pamoate (Nemex-2), which is available from your veterinarian and some pet-supply catalogs and stores. The dose is based on the weight of the pet and is generally given two or three times over a period of 2 to 3 weeks. Dewormers come in pill form or in liquid that can be squirted over your pet's food or into his mouth.

■ A prescription drug like fenbendazole (Panacur) is used to treat whipworms, which most often affect dogs. The medicine is usually given once a day for 3 days, then another dose in 3 weeks, and a final dose in 3 months.

■ Tapeworms are treated with praziquantel (Droncit), available from vets or pet-supply catalogs by prescription only. Usually, either one dose of pills or an injection takes care of the problem.

■ Dogs who take the monthly heartworm preventive milbemycin oxime (Interceptor) are also

Identifying Worms

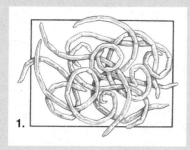

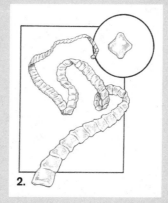

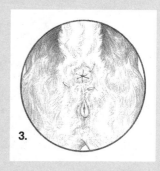

1. **Roundworms look like a mass of spaghetti when passed in the stool or vomited.**
2. **Tapeworms are segmented, flat worms that can be passed in a long chain of segments. Segments that break off look like small white square or oblong worms and can move independently of each other.**
3. **Once the segment dries, it resembles a grain of rice and may stick to the hair around the anus.**

protected against hookworms, roundworms, and whipworms.

▪ Dogs and cats may be reinfected with worms from the environment because an infected pet's bowel movements are chock-full of roundworm, hookworm, and/or whipworm eggs. When the feces are left in the yard to decompose, they can infect your pet all over again. Be sure to pick up the droppings every day or so to prevent reinfection and dispose of them in a sealed plastic bag. It is a good idea to wear disposable medical gloves to do this. Make sure that you keep children away from pet feces and cover your children's sandbox so that cats don't use it as a litter box.

Advisors
▪ Nina Beyer, V.M.D., is a veterinarian at Greenfield Veterinary Associates in Mantua, New Jersey.
▪ Grady Hester, D.V.M., is a veterinarian at All Creatures Animal Clinic in Rolesville, North Carolina.
▪ Janie Hodges, D.V.M., is a veterinarian at Valley View Pet Health Center in Farmers Branch, Texas.
▪ Emily King, D.V.M., is a veterinarian at Kryder Veterinary Clinic in Granger, Indiana.
▪ Peter Levin, V.M.D., is a veterinarian at Ludwig's Corner Veterinary Hospital in Chester Springs, Pennsylvania.

Index

Underscored page references indicate boxed text and tables. **Boldface** references indicate illustrations.

W

Walking, difficult, as symptom of
  back injuries, 75
  milk fever, <u>84</u>
Warbles, skin swelling from, **343**
Warfarin poisoning, bleeding from, <u>98</u>, 311
Wasp stings. *See* Bee and wasp stings
Water
  limiting, with incontinence, 257
  for preventing urinary blockage, 405
  for treating
    dehydration, 148
    diarrhea, 150–51
    heatstroke, 238, 240
    pad burns, 305, 306
    smoke inhalation, 349
    snakebites, 353
    spider bites, 357
Water dispensers, 241, 405
Water moccasin, identifying, **352**

Wax, removing from fur, 222
Weakness, as symptom of
  anaphylaxis, 79
  birthing problems, 83
  dehydration, 148
  kidney disease, <u>258</u>
  low blood sugar, 281
  shock, 333
Weight loss, with kidney disease, <u>258</u>
Wheezing, from anaphylaxis, 79
Whining, with constipation, 140
Whole-body symptoms, <u>50–51</u>
Witch hazel, for treating
  hot spots, 246
  inflammation, after clipping fur, <u>221</u>
Wobbler's syndrome, <u>76</u>
Wooziness, with shock, 333
Worms, 413. *See also* Parasites
  fleas and, <u>414</u>
  follow-up care for, 414–15
  identifying, **415**
  immediate care of, 413–14
  medicine chest for, <u>413</u>
  rectal prolapse from, 326

Wounds. *See also* Cuts and wounds; *specific types of wounds*
  bleeding from (*see* Bleeding)
  cleaning, 23–24
  after falls, 176, 177
  maggots in (*see* Maggots)
  protecting, after car accidents, 119
  sucking chest, sealing, 129, **129**, 130, 176–77, 226, 367–68

Y

Yeast infections
  in ear, 160, 161, 164
  on skin, <u>338</u>
Yesterday's News Cat Litter, for nail-bed infections, 297

Z

Zyloprim, for bladder stones, <u>406</u>